D1134715

BARON THUGUT

AND AUSTRIA'S RESPONSE TO

THE FRENCH REVOLUTION

Franz Maria, Baron von Thugut
(Courtesy Bildarchiv, Austrian National Library)

BARON THUGUT

AND AUSTRIA'S RESPONSE TO

THE FRENCH REVOLUTION

KARL A. ROIDER, JR.

PRINCETON

UNIVERSITY

PRESS

Library of Congress Cataloging in Publication Data will be
found on the last printed page of this book

ISBN 0-691-05135-6

Publication of this book has been aided by a grant from the Whitney Darrow Fund of
Princeton University Press

This book has been composed in Linotron Granjon

i 000 610622

CONTENTS

ILLUSTRATIONS AND MAPS

ACKNOWLEDGMENTS

As is true of most scholars, I am grateful to many people for assisting me at important steps leading to the completion of the manuscript. I would like to thank particularly Stephen Bensman and Paul Wank of the Middleton Library at Louisiana State University for gathering the books and articles available in this country for my research. In Vienna I owe a special debt to the staffs of the Haus- Hof- und Staatsarchiv, the Austrian National Library, the Bildarchiv of the Library, and the Hofkammerarchiv, who not only brought to me the documents I requested but patiently answered the many questions that I posed. In London I appreciated the cooperation of the staff of the Public Record Office at Kew and in Paris the cooperation of the staff at the Archives du ministère des affaires étrangères. At the latter, Marie Gallup was especially helpful in providing the documents I needed to see. Those who offered special assistance at critical times included Professor Karl Vocelka of the University of Vienna, who gathered pieces of information that I had missed; Wayne Guillory, who selected most of the pictures for me; and Mary Lee Eggert of LSU's cartography section, who drew the maps.

For critiquing the manuscript, I wish to acknowledge Charles Ingrao of Purdue University, who is quick and sharp in finding numerous deficiencies in my arguments and evidence, and Gary Crump of LSU, whose knowledge of grammar and proper word usage far exceeds my own. For the financial aid that allowed me to study in Europe, I thank the National Endowment for the Humanities and the American Philosophical Society. At the end of the process, I appreciated very much the competence and consideration of Joanna Hitchcock and the fine staff at Princeton University Press.

Finally, I am most grateful to my wife. She assisted me in various ways in preparing the manuscript but provided the most help through her patience and encouragement. As to my children, I thank them most for their indulgence.

INTRODUCTION

WHEN I WOULD tell fellow historians at professional meetings that I was working on a political biography of Franz Maria Baron von Thugut, I usually encountered two reactions. Those who had not studied Habsburg foreign affairs wrinkled their noses and asked, "Who's he?" Those who had smiled knowingly and said, "You certainly aren't going to try to rehabilitate him, are you?" For the first group I always tried to describe briefly who Thugut was: first graduate of the Oriental Academy in Vienna; Austrian minister to the Ottoman Empire, Poland, and Naples in the 1770s and 1780s; and from 1793 to 1800 foreign minister of the Habsburg Monarchy and leader of its vigorous struggle against revolutionary France. To the second group I replied, as befits a cautious historian, that I was not seeking to "rehabilitate" Thugut but to "understand" him, knowing full well that seeking an understanding of a historical personage can sometimes become a form of rehabilitation. I must admit that, like many biographers, I found myself often in sympathy with my subject.

My decision to write a biography of Thugut came about in a somewhat unusual way. I first encountered him in my research not in his post as foreign minister, but in the lesser position of Austrian envoy to the Ottoman Empire in the early 1770s. In reading the reports and recommendations that he sent from Constantinople to Vienna during those years, I found him to be not only a perceptive and practical person, as one would expect a diplomat to be, but also a man concerned with ethical matters in foreign affairs, one even troubled when his superiors advised a course of action that he considered dishonorable or disreputable. I found such qualities in an eighteenth-century diplomat rather unusual and also attractive, since in my research I, like most other diplomatic historians, had found ethics rarely entering into discussions of foreign policy except when necessary to justify one's own actions or to condemn someone else's. Having said that, let me hasten to assure the reader that what follows is not a morality tale in which Thugut the Right and Honorable struggles against the forces of evil and darkness. I merely intended to explain how I became interested in studying the man. Ethical questions did not dominate his personality or his foreign policy—as we shall see.

From that beginning, I pursued my study of Thugut and his time. He had been examined widely before. In fact, he was the subject of a significant and at times bitter historical controversy that began in the middle of the nineteenth century and continued with varying intensity into the first years of the twentieth. As with many historical controversies, the issue at stake involved far more than simply an academic assessment of the goals and achievements of his foreign policy. It concerned the major question facing the German political world in the nineteenth century: was Austria or Prussia, Habsburg or Hohenzollern, the worthier leader of Germany and the German people? The issue arose with the publication of Heinrich von Sybel's *Geschichte der Revolutionszeit*, the first edition of which appeared in 1853 to be followed by many more as Sybel incorporated new findings and new interpretations into his work. Based on materials found largely in the archives of Prussia and Saxony, his study from the beginning reflected a Prussian bias that became particularly pronounced in the 1860s during the rivalry leading to the Austro-Prussian War of 1866. Partly to justify Prussia's victory in that war in the long view of history, Sybel argued that Austria had not lost its influence in Germany because of the battles of 1866; it had forfeited its leadership in the 1790s when, under Thugut's guidance, the Habsburg dynasty surrendered Germany to the mercy of revolutionary France while it searched indiscriminately for territory to add to its patrimony. In fact, Sybel contended, even as Austria was formally engaged in war against France, it was primarily intent upon thwarting Prussia; moreover, by its abandonment of Belgium in 1794 and its policies toward Poland between 1792 and 1795, Austria threatened Prussia to such a degree that Berlin was compelled to halt its own struggle against France in order to protect the Hohenzollern lands from Habsburg malice and greed.

Blistering at Sybel's charges, Austrian historians rose to the defense of Thugut in particular and their monarchy in general. At their head was Alfred von Vivenot, a former officer in the Austrian army who had fought against the Prussians with considerable distinction in 1866, even leading a group of raiders behind enemy lines with such success that the Prussians had put a price on his head. Vivenot passionately disputed Sybel's interpretation of Thugut. He described Thugut as "a strong, clear spirit, a pure character, a statesman of premier genius," who possessed alone "the united spirit of a Pitt and a Carnot."[1] He was not crafty and sinister as Sybel would have it, but a "tragic hero in the Greek sense, struggling against his fate."[2] When scolded by other historians for defending Thugut with too much emotion, Vivenot explained his passion as the only honorable response of a loyal Austrian who, like Thugut, had experienced a *Drangperiode* in Austria's history.[3] Beginning in 1869 Vivenot published a flood of works defending Thugut and Habsburg policy in the 1790s. Fortunately for historians, these works were almost all editions of documents; they included among others the single-volume *Thugut, Clerfayt und Wurmser* (Vienna, 1869); the five-volume *Quellen zur Geschichte der deutschen Kaiser-politik Oesterreichs während der französischen Revolutionskriege* (Vienna, 1873–1890), co-edited with Heinrich von Zeissberg; and—especially valuable for the study of Thugut—the two-volume *Vertrauliche Briefe des*

[1] Alfred von Vivenot, ed., *Vertrauliche Briefe des Freiherrn von Thugut* (Vienna, 1872), 1: xvii–xviii.
[2] Alfred von Vivenot, ed., *Thugut, Clerfayt und Wurmser* (Vienna, 1869), xxix.
[3] Ibid., iv.

Freiherrn von Thugut (Vienna, 1871). Vivenot died at the age of thirty-seven in 1874, before he could publish promised additional volumes and before he could pen a biography. Vivenot's death did not end the controversy. Taking up the cudgels on Thugut's behalf were Hermann Hüffer and Zeissberg, who both pursued Vivenot's earlier theses but with considerably more restraint. They also published additional volumes of source materials, notably Hüffer's collections on the period from 1797 to 1800.[4] Sybel too was not without supporters, notably Heinrich von Treitschke and Dimitrii Miliutin, but after the restoration of Austro-German friendship in the 1870s, the controversy subsided, helped along by the work of Hüffer and Zeissberg and especially by the balanced scholarship of K. T. Heigel in his *Deutsche Geschichte vom Tode Friedrich des Grossen bis zur Auflösung des alten Reiches* (Stuttgart, 1899–1911).[5]

Notwithstanding this scholarly activity, no biography of Thugut appeared and thus no effort to examine seriously the man's policies and decisions in light of his own past or his own character. Moreover, despite the published materials of Vivenot and Hüffer, the scholarly impression of Thugut continued to be largely that first offered by Sybel, namely, that Thugut cared most of all about the undoing of Prussia and the pursuit of territorial gain for Austria. In his study of the Second Partition of Poland that appeared in 1915, Robert Lord wrote that Thugut "believed that territorial aggrandizement was the Alpha and Omega of statecraft, and that all means were hallowed by that end."[6] In 1960 Max Braubach described Thugut as willing to exploit the revolutionary wars not to de-

[4] Hermann Hüffer, ed., *Quellen zur Geschichte des Krieges von 1799* (Leipzig, 1900); *Quellen zur Geschichte des Krieges von 1800* (Leipzig, 1901); *Der rastatter Congress und die zweite Coalition*, 2 vols. (Bonn, 1878–1879).

[5] Heinrich von Treitschke, *Deutsche Geschichte im neunzehnten Jahrhundert*, vol. 1 (Leipzig, 1879); Dimitrii Miliutin and Alexander Mikhailovskii-Danilevsky, *Geschichte des Krieges Russlands mit Frankreich unter der Regierung Kaiser Paul's I im Jahr 1799*, 5 vols. (Munich, 1856–1858).

[6] Robert Howard Lord, *The Second Partition of Poland* (Cambridge, Mass., 1915), 406.

feat France but "to build the domination of Austria on the demise of the hated Prussia."[7] In 1983 Derek McKay and H. M. Scott assessed Thugut's policy thus: "The notion of total victory was no part of Habsburg thinking. . . . They assumed that military successes could be turned to immediate account in the shape of territorial acquisitions."[8] And in 1984 Piers Mackesy wrote, "indifferent to the counter-revolutionary crusade against the French republic, the Austrians saw their national interests in terms of expansion in South Germany and Italy. The Chancellor Thugut was not planning to march on Paris, but looked forward to consolidating the Habsburg lands in Italy by further acquisitions."[9]

One can in part account for the persistence of these views because they are based not on Thugut's own writings but rather on the writings of contemporaries about him. In the correspondence of many Russians, Englishmen, Prussians, Frenchmen, and even Austrians, one frequently encounters harsh words describing Thugut's intentions and character. Historians have accepted such assessments at face value without studying seriously Thugut's own explanations and justifications for his decisions and acts or by seeking reasons for the hostile expressions of the time.

Underlying these historical judgments is the assumption that Thugut's actions represented little more than an extension of the eighteenth-century international politics pursued by his predecessor and instructor, the great Habsburg chancellor, Wenzel Anton von Kaunitz-Rietberg. Throughout his long tenure, Kaunitz was concerned in foreign affairs very much with territorial aggrandizement and the defeat of Prussia, all clothed in the appropriate garb of maintaining the balance of power among the great states of Europe. Since Thugut

[7] Bruno Gebhardt, ed., *Handbuch der deutschen Geschichte*, 8th ed. (Stuttgart, 1960), 3: 14.
[8] Derek McKay and H. M. Scott, *The Rise of the Great Powers, 1648–1815* (London, 1983), 216.
[9] Piers Mackesy, *War Without Victory: The Downfall of Pitt, 1799–1802* (Oxford, 1984), 4–5.

rose in the foreign ministry from junior translator to foreign minister under the auspices of Kaunitz, many have assumed that his views of foreign policy and its goals reflected those of his mentor. As Kaunitz was the great practitioner of eighteenth-century diplomacy, so Thugut must have followed his principles right through the 1790s even though the social, intellectual, and political upheavals brought on by the French Revolution had made those principles not only obsolete but also dangerous for the monarchy to pursue. Thugut was facing a new world of international politics with outmoded precepts. Therefore, it was inevitable that he and Austria should suffer defeat.

Just as scholars have argued that the legacy of his predecessor blinded Thugut to the changes around him, so too have they at times unfavorably compared him to his later successor, the great Clemens von Metternich, who assumed the reins of Habsburg foreign policy nine years after Thugut's fall. While Kaunitz was the master of diplomacy in the eighteenth century, Metternich was the master in the nineteenth. Metternich recognized that the French Revolution had added new and complicated forces to the making of foreign policy and understood that, to preserve the Habsburg Monarchy in a changed world required a greater vision of the present and future Europe. Balance of power became in itself a goal worth pursuing and no longer merely a stated principle under which European powers pushed and shoved one another for advantage. Peace and order also became objectives to be actively sought; they were no longer conditions looked upon as existing naturally in the absence of war. Thugut, many have suggested, never understood that the revolution had changed Europe; consequently, he sought only to grab land here or insult Prussia there, and in doing so he missed the significance of the French Revolution for Austria and for the entire continent.

The problem with these time-honored interpretations of Thugut and his goals is that they do not accord with the policies that he actually pursued in the 1790s. Had territorial gain dominated his intentions, he would have made peace with revolutionary France and divided with it parts of Germany or Italy. It is true that such a course might not have made the monarchy more secure because France was then both a dynamic and unsettled power not always willing or able to keep its agreements. Nevertheless, during Thugut's tenure as foreign minister, various French revolutionary governments did offer Austria inducements to make a separate peace, but Thugut rejected such offers—and even refused to discuss them—except when French armies were at Vienna's doorstep. If territorial aggrandizement was his principal goal, this stance makes no sense.

Likewise, the view that Thugut was more eager to hurt Prussia than to defeat France seems difficult to accept in the light of the path he followed. All the governments of revolutionary France sought peace more ardently with Austria than with Prussia. Indeed, even after Berlin concluded its own peace with Paris in 1795, French statesmen looked upon Prussia with considerable disdain and continued peace probes to Vienna. Thugut had repeated opportunities to reach a settlement with France and to direct Austria's hostility toward the north; he even had opportunities to enlist French assistance against Prussia. Had Prussia's ruin been Thugut's chief objective, he would not have spurned these opportunities so consistently as he did.

To achieve the goals usually attributed to him, the most obvious step for Thugut was to seek peace with revolutionary France. Yet he steadfastly resisted such a step, and at the end of his career he was removed because he had come to symbolize everywhere, but especially in Vienna, the irreconcilable pursuit of war against France. His steadfast determination to continue the fight, especially in the wake of serious and at times devastating reversals, make the traditional explanations of Thugut's policies seem inadequate.

Thugut was in fact by no means bound by Prussophobia and a lust for territorial gain; rather, he was dedicated to the defeat of revolutionary France, a state he understood to be truly a danger to the established social and political system of the Europe that he valued. And he assumed that such a defeat could be achieved only with the cooperation of the other traditional great powers of Europe: Britain, Russia, and Prussia; in other words, he sought an allied victory much like that achieved by Metternich in 1814. However, it was in the forming and maintaining of the coalitions that the heritage of eighteenth-century diplomacy hamstrung his efforts. The statesmen of the allied powers wasted much time and effort squabbling about territorial gain, imagining insidious purposes on the part of others, and doubting their allies' intentions to fulfill their promises. Thugut's greatest undertaking was convincing the traditional powers that the defeat of France must be paramount for all of them; as we shall see, he failed to do so for many reasons, not least of which was others' perceptions of his character and his goals.

The purpose, then, of this book is to probe more deeply into Austrian policy toward revolutionary France during the 1790s by examining the man responsible for making that policy, Thugut himself. The book will examine the influences upon him from his early years onward, what he believed to be important for himself and the state that he served, and how he dealt with the persons and ideas surrounding him. Its primary aim is to reach a better understanding of Thugut and through him a better understanding of Austrian statesmanship and politics during a tumultuous time in the history of the Habsburg Monarchy.

BARON THUGUT

AND AUSTRIA'S RESPONSE TO

THE FRENCH REVOLUTION

CHAPTER I

YOUTH, 1736–1769

ON A BRIGHT SPRING DAY, amidst a spectacle of blossoming fruit trees, colorful songbirds, and greening fields that natives and visitors love so much, Maria Theresa and her imperial entourage approached the right bank of the Danube River near the village of Pöchlarn in Lower Austria. Her purpose was to visit the elegant, baroque pilgrimage church at Maria Taferl, on the other side of the river. As she reached the water's edge, she found the local ferry and its master waiting to carry her and her company across. Descending from their carriages, the queen and her closest courtiers boarded the craft, settled as comfortably as possible into the available seats, and signaled the ferryman to begin the crossing. As the boat set out, she noticed a small ragamuffin sitting near the helmsman and surveying the distinguished passengers with a bright, inquisitive gaze. To the ferryman she asked, "Who is this boy with such intelligent eyes?" The man replied, "Your Majesty, he has no name; he is a foundling; he is a *Thunichtgut*, a good-for-nothing." "He is no *Thunichtgut*," remarked the queen. "Not this boy. He is instead a *Thugut*, one who will do well." Then she turned to one of her courtiers and told him that the boy would come under her care and that she would see to his upbringing and education. As the years passed, this Thugut rose from Maria Theresa's favorite foundling to court secretary, personal envoy to the empress-queen, ambassador, and finally foreign minister of the Habsburg Monarchy. He did well indeed.

As much as one would like to believe this story of the humblest origins and grand success, it is, alas, apocryphal. Thugut was indeed a commoner who rose to foreign minister largely by virtue of his own talent, but he was not an orphan or the offspring of a ferryman. He was born the son of a minor bureaucrat and was blessed not only with innate gifts but also with a good education, which in large part launched him on his career. Before proceeding to the facts of his origin and his family, however, we should examine this legend further, because it does have a bearing on the understanding of Thugut and what others thought of him. The story told above is not without variations from other sources. One has him born the son of a ferryman in the city of Linz, where his schooling and not his bright eyes brought him to Maria Theresa's attention. Another relates that the *Thunichtgut* name was a play on his real name of Tunicotti, which makes him not of German but of Italian origin, perhaps the son of a Venetian gondolier. A third tells of Maria Theresa's finding Thugut not in the back of a boat but as an abandoned infant in a corner of the main staircase of the Hofburg, the Habsburg winter palace in Vienna. Sweeping him into her arms, she reportedly announced, "Thugut will be the name of this poor little creature."[1]

These legends are notable for many reasons, not least of which is that Thugut was a man important enough to have legends told about him. Indeed, these stories were not later creations, but were current when Thugut was actively involved in affairs. The diarist Karl von Zinzendorf wrote that part of the entertainment at a dinner party he attended in 1796 was listening to "satires about Thugut, whose father had been a ferryman."[2] The primary source for the introduction of the

[1] These stories can be found in various places, but they are neatly summarized in the old *Allgemeine Deutsche Biographie* (Leipzig, 1891), 38: 138. The *Allgemeine Deutsche Biographie* and the *Biographisches Lexikon des Kaisertums Österreich* by Constant von Wurzbach (Vienna, 1882), 45: 1, both explain Thugut's true origins and the falseness of these various stories. Nonetheless, the legends appeared in historical literature for some time afterward.

[2] Hans Wagner, ed., *Wien von Maria Theresia bis zur Franzosenzeit: Aus den Tagebüchern des Grafen Karl von Zinzendorf* (Vienna, 1972), 72.

ferryman legend into historical scholarship is *Lebensbilder aus dem Befreiungskriege* by Josef Hormayr zu Hortenburg, contemporary of Thugut, participant in the Tyrolean rising of 1809, and later official historian of the House of Habsburg. As his authority for the ferryman story, Hormayr cited Emperor Joseph II, who, he said, learned it from another Danubian ferryman during one of his own crossings of the river.[3]

As is well known, legends often persist long after they are shown to be nothing more than fanciful stories because they serve some purpose: to illustrate a quality of human character, to explain what appears inexplicable, or to teach a lesson. Such interpretations can also apply to the legends of Thugut's origin. In the positive sense, these tales show Thugut as the example of the self-made man, one who seized an opportunity and made the most of it. The only born commoner in the history of the Habsburg Monarchy to rise to the rank of foreign minister, he did so not by virtue of family connections or aristocratic origin but by his own talent. One could argue that, while he loathed the French Revolution and its principles, he represented one of its most cherished precepts: that ability and not social or family background should be the primary criterion for promotion or advancement in any occupation.

Just as it praises Thugut for his rise to prominence, so too the legend reflects credit on the Habsburg Monarchy for allowing him to do so. It endorses the view that, although its society was structured in the feudal manner found throughout Europe at the time, the monarchy was always looking for talented officials regardless of their nationality, religion, or social origin. Indeed, positive interpretations of the legend usually served not to commend Thugut's rise from modesty to greatness, but to illustrate the beneficence, compassion, and good judgment of Maria Theresa. The hero in the story is not the child but the great queen.

But many dismissed the positive implications of the legend

[3] Josef Hormayr zu Hortenburg, *Lebensbilder aus dem Befreiungskriege* (Jena, 1841), 1: 459. The story is told in English in E. Vehse, *Memoirs of the Court, Aristocracy, and Diplomacy of Austria* (London, 1856), 2: 381. Vehse's discussions of Thugut are copied literally from Hormayr.

as it dealt with Thugut himself. They saw it instead as further evidence that Thugut was a parvenu, an interloper, a self-serving and ungracious manipulator who used all possible wiles and stratagems to hoodwink a youthful and naive emperor and his inept advisers in order to place himself ahead of the honorable and selfless noblemen who truly deserved to hold the distinguished position Thugut had usurped. For some of his aristocratic detractors, even being an ordinary orphan or the son of a ferryman was not degrading enough. In 1794 the socially active Zinzendorf recorded that at a party the wife of Prince Georg Adam Starhemberg "went so far as to say that Thugut was purchased from a convent."[4] The legend, in other words, served both to praise and to condemn Thugut, depending upon one's view of the man and his deeds.

Yet, if Thugut was not found on a boat, discovered in a staircase, or purchased from a convent, then where did he come from? He was born Johannes Amadeus Franciscus de Paula to Philipp Joseph and Maria Eva Thueguett in the city of Linz in the province of Upper Austria on March 31, 1736.[5] His father was an administrator (*Verwalter*) of the Bancalitäts-Militär-Zahlamt, a somewhat low-paying post in the provincial bureaucracy of the Habsburg government that administered the military payroll and acquisition of supplies in the Linz area.[6] Thugut's mother was the daughter of a master miller and town councilman in the village of Gundramsdorf bei Wien, where the couple married in 1716. She gave birth to five children, including three daughters, named Maria Anna, Sophia, and Josepha, and another son, born Thomas Johannes.[7]

[4] Zinzendorf's diary entry, July 14, 1794, in Wagner, ed., *Tagebüchern*, 75.

[5] My special thanks to Heinrich Berger and Peter Gradauer of the Bischöfliches Ordinariat Linz for sending photocopies of the baptismal records of Thugut and his brother from the *Liber baptizatorum Parochiae Linciensis coeptus, 1731–1756.*

[6] This is the official title for Philipp Joseph Thugut listed in the *Hofschematismus* (later *Hof- und Staats-Schematismus*), the yearly publication listing the Habsburg administrative offices and personnel in them. My thanks to the staff of the Hofkammerarchiv in Vienna for directing me to it.

[7] B. Pillwein, *Linz: Einst und Jetzt* (Linz, 1846), 2:34.

The Thugut ancestry traced itself to southern Bohemia near Budweis (Budejovice). Curiously, the original name was indeed Thunichtgut, or Thuenitgut, a holdover from the peasant wars of the sixteenth century when many men were branded with names that labeled them as criminals or at least hostile in some way to conventional society.[8] Thugut's great-grandfather Andreas Thunichtgut was a schoolmaster in a village in southern Bohemia, and it was he who changed the name to Thugut. Andreas had two wives, the first of whom bore a number of "cobblers, farmers, and linen weavers"; the second gave birth in 1673 to Urban Thugut, Philipp Joseph's father and our Thugut's grandfather.[9]

Just as there is a bit of confusion about Thugut's last name, so too there is some about his first. Although christened Johannes Amadeus Franciscus de Paula, Thugut as an adult used the name Franz Maria when exchanging correspondence or signing documents, and it is these names that are listed in the *Hof- und Staats-Schematismus*, the official Habsburg listing of offices and their holders. When he began to use the name Franz Maria is unclear, but he had already dropped Johannes Amadeus by the time he entered the Oriental Academy at the age of eighteen in 1753.[10] The addition of Maria as a middle name may have been in honor of Maria Theresa, whom he greatly admired, but it also may have been in honor of his mother.[11] His brother also altered his name. Christened Thomas Johannes at his birth on March 8, 1739, he is listed in the *Hof- und Staats-Schematismus* of the 1790s (when he served as ordinary court secretary—*wirklicher Hof-secretär*—in the principal administrative office of the monarchy) as Johann de Deo Thugut. When he changed his name is also unclear, but the use of the name Johann at one time or another by both

---

[8] Other such names common in the same area were Bauernfeind and Bauernschelm.

[9] Vivenot, ed., *Vertrauliche Briefe*, 1: 391.

[10] Joseph Franz to Maria Theresa, October 22, 1753, Vienna, Haus- Hof- und Staatsarchiv, Staatskanzlei, *Interiora*, 55. (Hereafter cited as Vienna, HHSA, SK.)

[11] The *Allgemeine Deutsche Biographie*, 38:138, suggests the former.

brothers has caused some minor confusion among historians ever since.[12]

The early years of Thugut's life are for the most part unknown. He never wrote about his childhood and rarely mentioned his family, even when he and his brother worked together in different government offices in Vienna. He attended the Jesuit Gymnasium in Linz, where, according to the necrology that appeared in the *Österreichischer Beobachter* upon his death in 1818, his teachers "even at that time forecast a brilliant career and recognized as one of the dominant qualities in his character that perseverance and determination that were so obvious throughout his life."[13] While this description smacks of hindsight, he was apparently a promising youth, for in 1753 as part of his explanation for admitting Thugut as one of the first students of the Oriental Academy, the headmaster wrote, "He can speak Italian, French, Spanish, and read Greek and was through all schools far and away the first."[14] Promising scholastic achievement was well and good, but, as this passage indicates, his linguistic skills were what propelled him forward in the formative stages of his career. He could learn foreign languages easily and quickly, and in the world of Austrian foreign affairs that was always a gift highly valued by the powers that be. Facility in languages won for Thugut his openings; hard work, intelligence, and dedication brought advancement.

Thugut apparently did not go directly from Linz to the Oriental Academy but spent a brief interval at the University of Vienna. In a biography of her father, Johann Georg Obermayr, written in 1858 for her family, Emilie Weckbecker cast

---

[12] The *Allgemeine Deutsche Biographie* lists Thugut's birthday as the correct one (p. 138); Wurzbach's *Biographisches Lexikon* lists the brother's birthday, March 8, 1739, as the one for our Thugut but admits that it might be incorrect (p. 1).

[13] *Österreichischer Beobachter*, September 5, 1818, p. 1305.

[14] Josef Franz to Maria Theresa, October 22, 1753, Vienna, HHSA, SK, *Interiora*, 55. As foreign minister he complained that his Italian was not good enough for him to write official documents in that language. Thugut to Colloredo, June 8, 1793, in Vivenot, ed., *Vertrauliche Briefe*, 1:18–19.

some light on Thugut's university days when she described her own father's entry into that institution in 1751 or 1752. Obermayr entered as a *Bettelstudent*, a mendicant student, an official status that provided certain prerogatives including a free bed if one was available; the right to be first in line at some cloisters that fed the poor; free university attire (although without the dagger permitted to regular students); and the right on weekends and holidays to sing spiritual songs or to read scriptural passages in the courtyards and streets in exchange for coins from passersby. According to Weckbecker, her father reached Vienna too late for ordinary admission, but, since he and two other late arrivals showed such promise, all three were admitted as *Bettelstudenten*. The other two were "Franz Thugut of Linz" and "Bernard Jenisch of Carinthia."[15] The three became good friends, sharing rather primitive accommodations and meals together. Within a short time Obermayr, the most outgoing and sociable of the three, secured a post as tutor to children of a well-to-do Spanish family in Vienna. The other two, in order to continue their studies, applied for openings in the newly created Oriental Academy.

One wonders if Emilie Weckbecker's tale of these university days is true. Some of her facts are wrong—for example, Jenisch was Viennese, not Carinthian—and Thugut, just sixteen years old in 1752, never formally matriculated at the university. However, neither his youth nor his failure to matriculate means that he was excluded from classes. Sixteen-year-olds were a common sight at European universities, and the academic promise that he had already shown could have inspired his teachers to send him to the university at an early age. Besides, the *Österreichischer Beobachter* of 1818 notes that he studied law and mathematics there before he entered the Oriental Academy.[16] He also may have been a *Bettelstudent*. His father's post was a low-paying one, and he probably could not afford to give his son much money. Moreover, Thugut

[15] Wilhelm Weckbecker, *Die Weckbeckers: Karriere einer Familie* (Graz, 1966), 19.

[16] *Österreichischer Beobachter*, September 5, 1818, p. 1305.

throughout his life remained a frugal man, requiring little money on which to live, spending virtually none on frivolities, but investing as carefully as he could either in economic ventures that he believed promised a good return (but rarely brought one, as we shall see) or in individuals from whom he expected to derive favors and influence. Such traits he may have first acquired as a son in a family of limited means and then reinforced as a mendicant student in Vienna.

Without doubt, however, the opportunity that launched Thugut on his career in diplomacy and statecraft was his admission to the Oriental Academy. The Oriental Academy was a school created to train boys in the Ottoman language and in Ottoman customs, so that they could be employed as translators for Austrian officials serving in the Ottoman Empire, along the Habsburg-Ottoman borders, or in parts of the Austrian interior visited by Ottoman envoys or businessmen. Of all the states with which Austria had diplomatic relations in the early modern period, the Ottoman Empire posed the most difficulties in the day-to-day conduct of affairs. And the greatest difficulty was the Ottoman language itself. Whereas an Austrian diplomat assigned to a court in the rest of Europe would assuredly find his hosts speaking one or more of the common upper-class languages—French, German, or Italian—he would just as assuredly find almost no one among the Turks who could converse in any of those tongues. Not only was knowledge of Ottoman a rarity in Christian Europe, but the language was also difficult to learn, being a blend of Turkish, Persian, and Arabic words written in Arabic characters. In the sixteenth and early seventeenth centuries, Habsburg envoys to the Turkish Empire had relied largely on translators they could find at hand, usually Greeks or Italians living in Ottoman territory. Frequently, however, these persons proved unreliable, and in the 1630s the Austrian embassy in Constantinople established a school for what were called *Sprachknaben*, young Austrian boys who would be trained in the language, history, customs, and political dealings of the Ottoman Empire and then serve as translators, messengers, and secretaries.

The school proved quite successful, and by the late seventeenth century the official Habsburg representatives to the Ottoman state were almost all chosen from its alumni.

The school in Constantinople continued until 1753 when, upon Kaunitz's recommendation that the boys could be trained better and more cheaply in Vienna, Maria Theresa replaced it with the Oriental Academy.[17] To head the new school, Maria Theresa appointed Josef Franz. Franz was a Jesuit, a tutor of the future Joseph II, a specialist in the natural sciences, an assistant to Gerhard van Swieten in his reform of the University of Vienna, and a master of the Ottoman language. It was he who selected the first class of the academy, and for the places in that class he chose "*Landeskinder*, who have had an honorable education and come from such parents who have been true to the imperial-royal service for long years or were associated with it earlier, their extraction or estate honorable, and who have been blessed by God with many children."[18] Undoubtedly these criteria reflected the wishes of Maria Theresa, who always held loyal service to her house and the blessing of many children to be two of the greatest virtues possible both for herself and for her subjects.

Second on the list of the eight boys accepted was Franz de Paula Thugut, praised for his excellent linguistic skills and also for his father's devotion to the imperial family. "His father," wrote Franz, "is administrator of the imperial-royal war chest in Linz and in the last war risked his life to bring the military and cameral treasures to Vienna."[19] Franz was referring to a deed of some distinction on Philipp Thugut's part; when the Franco-Bavarian forces approached Linz in the early months of the War of the Austrian Succession, he packed up the funds for which he was responsible and fled with them, so that they would not fall into enemy hands. It was an act of

[17] Karl A. Roider, Jr., "The Oriental Academy in the *Theresienzeit*," *Topic: A Journal of the Liberal Arts* 34 (1980): 21.

[18] Josef Franz to Maria Theresa, October 22, 1753, Vienna, HHSA, SK, *Interiora*, 55.

[19] Ibid.

loyalty appreciated by Maria Theresa, who, after Philipp's death in 1766, granted his family a pension, half of which went to his widow and half to his three daughters. Upon the wife's death in 1772, her half of the pension was supposed to revert to the state, but, because of Thugut's own valuable service by this time, Maria Theresa added the wife's portion to that of the daughters.[20]

In late 1753 at the age of eighteen, Thugut entered the Oriental Academy. Of the eight classmates, he was the third oldest, two being nineteen and the other five ranging from fourteen to seventeen. All were living in Vienna at the time of their acceptance, lending credence to Emilie Weckbecker's contention that Thugut was attending classes at the university when he was chosen. The academy's facilities were even located in one of the university's buildings. Thugut's friend Bernhard Jenisch was also in that first class. The courses the students took were not confined to Ottoman studies, but were designed to provide training generally in languages and liberal arts. In a report of January 1, 1754, Franz listed the subjects as Ottoman, Latin, French, Italian, Greek, German, geography, and history.[21]

Thugut remained in the Oriental Academy for less than two years, and his departure in September 1755 marked the end of his school days. It is rather difficult to assess the impact of his formal education upon his personal life in later years. In his writings he never credited his school in Linz, the University of Vienna, the Oriental Academy, or any of his instructors with any particular influence upon him. One may assume that these schools provided him with an education from which he could develop his general talents in later life, and there is no doubt that they gave him the language training that proved to

---

[20] Pillwein, *Linz*, 2: 34; *Österreichischer Beobachter*, September 5, 1818, p. 1306; Wurzbach, *Biographisches Lexikon*, 45: 1.

[21] Josef Franz to Maria Theresa, January 1, 1754, Vienna, HHSA, SK, *Interiora*, 55. Later in the eighteenth century the curriculum would include, among other studies, mathematics, natural sciences, philosophy, calligraphy, dancing, and riding.

be the key to unlock doors of early opportunity. But what else did he learn?

Although he was wholly educated by Jesuits, he later expressed no strong opinions of their order or the Church in general. Hormayr, his great detractor, wrote of him, "He was about as pious as the writer of the book *De Tribus Impostoribus* [a somewhat notorious book of unknown authorship and date praising atheism by arguing that Moses, Jesus, and Mohammed were charletans]. Always treading in the track of Voltairian philosophy, he loved the clergy and the oligarchy in that way which is formulated in Diderot's well-known saying about what should be done with kings and priests ['Let us strangle the last king with the bowels of the last priest']. He would not even hear of the priesthood as an energetic tool of passive obedience or of obscurantism."[22] As an assessment of Thugut's formal opinion of Church and aristocracy, Hormayr's view seems exaggerated, although it may reflect Thugut's mutterings when he was particularly annoyed about some matter or other. Nonetheless, one doubts that he believed much that the Church taught, and if he attended services at all, they made no impression upon him. He was too cynical a man to accept either the spiritual or moral precepts offered by the eighteenth-century Church, preferring instead a kind of natural value system in keeping with the Enlightenment. He rejected outright the notion that the Church should have any say about what he was allowed to read.

One often assumes that in the eighteenth century the Church and the Enlightenment were bitter enemies, each side condemning the other as a curse upon mankind. That was certainly true in polemical writings, but both groups agreed on one matter: the great books they advised young men to read. The Jesuits who guided Thugut's formal education taught him the classical literature that the Enlightenment valued and that he himself loved for the remainder of his life. Hormayr wrote that Thugut never forgot the writings that he learned as

[22] Vehse, *Memoirs*, 384.

13

a student: "The Roman classics he knew well and even in his seventies he quoted many important passages from memory."[23] His love of the classics led to an appreciation of modern literature, and he read extensively from writers of the Enlightenment, particularly from great French figures such as Voltaire, Diderot, and Montesquieu. Following his dismissal as foreign minister in 1801, his correspondence with his former colleagues from his exile in Pressburg (Bratislava) often included lists of books for them to send to him. While most items requested were commentaries, memoirs, and histories of the French Revolution, others included travel literature, commercial studies, commentaries on ancient writings, and some popular scientific works—in other words, what one would expect of an eighteenth-century man of enlightened tastes.[24]

Although familiar with many of the writers of the Enlightenment, Thugut never hinted that any of them had a profound impact upon his ideas, nor did he write essays or letters discussing any philosophical conjectures that he read. Moreover, like most of the Viennese literati, he revealed no interest in the contemporary achievements in German literature. In the late 1780s, when he was ambassador to Naples, his secretary may have invited him to join a literary circle to which Goethe belonged, but no evidence suggests that he did so.[25] He read widely, but more to gather information and to keep informed than to reflect deeply on the great ideas of the time or to stimulate his own insights into the human condition. He knew that he was not an imaginative thinker and devoted no time to pretending that he was one.

Thugut's credentials as a man of the Viennese Enlightenment would be considerably enhanced if he had belonged to a lodge of the Freemasons or Illuminati, the standard-bearers of enlightened thought in the Habsburg Monarchy. From the founding of the first lodge in Vienna in 1742 to the 1780s,

[23] Hormayr, *Lebensbilder*, 1: 319.
[24] Thugut to various correspondents, 1802–1810, Vienna, HHSA, SK, *Grosse Korrespondenz*, 447.
[25] *Allgemeine Deutsche Biographie*, 38: 143.

Freemasonry expanded to such an extent that a number of prominent men in governmental and intellectual circles belonged to it.[26] Many of the men Thugut later knew and worked with were members of lodges, including his chief agent in Germany, Count Konrad Ludwig Lehrbach, and his most trusted negotiator, Count Louis Cobenzl. Moreover, in the late 1780s Thugut served as ambassador to the court of Naples whose queen, Maria Carolina, was one of Freemasonry's most enthusiastic proponents. Nevertheless, there as yet is no explicit evidence that Thugut was a member. In a recent study, Helmut Reinalter identifies Thugut as a Freemason, based on a document listing a Thugut among the Illuminati in Vienna.[27] However, the name on that document is "Johann Thugut," and it is clear from other evidence in the manuscript that it refers not to our Thugut but to his brother.[28] After Thugut's death in 1818, the officer dispatched by Metternich to inspect Thugut's papers discovered a bundle of letters "under a Freemasonry seal" but gave no other indication that he belonged to a lodge.[29] One can safely say that Thugut was closely associated with men who were Freemasons and perhaps with the movement itself, but, without better documentation, one cannot prove that he was a member.

A trait of Thugut not commonly shared by other men of the Enlightenment was his fondness for Ottoman literature. Like many of the graduates of the Oriental Academy, he was fascinated by Turkish and Arabic writings and acquired over time a collection of Ottoman books and manuscripts. He liked

[26] For recent studies of Freemasonry in Austria see Helmut Reinalter, *Aufgeklärter Absolutismus und Revolution: Zur Geschichte des Jakobinertums und der frühdemokratischen Bestrebungen in der Habsburger Monarchie* (Vienna/Cologne, 1980); Helmut Reinalter, ed., *Der Jakobinismus in Mitteleuropa* (Innsbruck, 1977); and Leslie Bodi, *Tauwetter in Wien: Zur Prosa der österreichischen Aufklärung, 1781–1795* (Frankfurt, 1977).

[27] Helmut Reinalter, "Aufklärung, Freimaurerei, und Jakobinertum in der Habsburger-Monarchie," in Reinalter, ed., *Jakobinismus*, 259.

[28] Vienna, HHSA, SK, *Vertrauliche Akten*, 38, folio 61.

[29] Brettfeld to Metternich, June 1, 1818, ibid., SK, *Grosse Korrespondenz*, 447.

to quote Ottoman aphorisms and sayings, especially to his life-long friend Jenisch, to whom he could write them in the original Arabic characters. A good friend in his later days was a young man who would become the father of Middle Eastern studies in the Western world, Joseph von Hammer-Purgstall. Himself a graduate of the Oriental Academy and an officer attached to the Austrian embassy in Constantinople, Hammer not only corresponded with Thugut on matters of Ottoman literature and history but also purchased Ottoman books and manuscripts for him. But Hammer was apparently not particularly familiar with what material Thugut possessed. A few months after Thugut's death he noted, "In the night I realized that I had missed the auction of Thugut's oriental manuscripts; I did not know their value at all."[30] Upon his death Thugut's collection of Ottomania reverted to the state; the court library absorbed what it could use into its collection and sold the remainder.

Thugut's formal education with its emphasis on literature undoubtedly trained him in the important art of speaking and writing clearly and logically. His mother tongue may have been German, but, like so many eighteenth-century figures, he preferred to use French. Of his expression Hormayr wrote, "His manner of speaking was precise but not unpleasant, the oral as well as written language academically correct, consistent, clear, exact." His intellect was "surprisingly learned, never frivolous, never petty or inspired by arrogance; pure and complete reasoning, as prudent as it was thorough, without decoration; the words he used, however, were full of caustic wit and not without teasing."[31] When telling a friend what should be included in memoranda and dispatches, Metternich noted, "There is in writing a certain confusion, I feel, that cannot be fully clear to the reader. So I follow the advice of an old, experienced practitioner, Baron Thugut, who once taught me that in such situations I should not try to find new and differ-

[30] Joseph von Hammer-Purgstall, *Erinnerungen aus meinem Leben, 1774–1852* (Vienna/Leipzig, 1940), 249.
[31] Hormayr, *Lebensbilder*, 1: 319.

16

ent ways to present my ideas or to argue from a new direction, but instead to concentrate solely on doing away with what is superfluous and address the rest to the topic squarely and surely. And so I do it."[32] Thugut's letters and instructions are generally direct and concise, and his wit is certainly caustic. His handwriting is tiny and, while not the clearest, easy to read.

His formal schooling over, in September 1755 Thugut left the Oriental Academy for his first official assignment as "border translator" (*Grenzdolmetsch*) at the fortress of Esseg (Osijek) on the Drava (Drau) River in Slavonia. Esseg was the post near the Habsburg-Ottoman border that monitored affairs in northern Bosnia. As *Grenzdolmetsch* Thugut translated for the Austrian military officers, customs officials, and plague watchers who had to deal with border incidents, commercial traffic, and travelers in the area. Unfortunately, we have no writings of Thugut from this period and can only wonder how he viewed leaving the vibrant capital city for a remote border outpost. Whatever his thoughts, he did become familiar with an area and people unlike any he had seen before, and he got the opportunity to practice the profession for which he had been trained.

His tour in Esseg lasted until December 1757, when his old headmaster at the Oriental Academy recommended that he be sent to Constantinople because he was "the best in the first class."[33] Granted a salary of a thousand gulden, he set out for the Ottoman capital, the first graduate of the academy assigned there. By 1758, the Ottoman Empire had passed the zenith of its power. Since the catastrophic defeat of its armies at the gates of Vienna in 1683, Turkey had been in a state of certain, if spasmodic, decline. At the time of Thugut's arrival, that decline had slowed somewhat, in part because the Seven Years' War in western Europe had temporarily relieved the

[32] K. A. Varnhagen von Ense, *Denkwürdigkeiten und vermischte Schriften* (Leipzig, 1859), 8: 112.

[33] Josef Franz to Maria Theresa, December 1, 1757, Vienna, HHSA, SK, *Interiora*, 55.

17

pressure on the Ottoman Empire from the outside. Moreover, in 1758 the Ottomans were enjoying the administration of one of the few grand viziers of the eighteenth century who truly understood the growing weakness of the empire and who tried to remedy it. He was Koca Mehmet Ragip Pasha, a scholarly and able man who believed that Turkey could be revived only by staying out of the bloody wars that engulfed western Europe and by introducing internal reforms that would promote the welfare, loyalty, and prosperity of the entire population. To that end his government introduced revised codes of justice, restricted the powers of landlords to exploit their peasants, tried to balance the budget, and began the construction of libraries and mosques. After his death in 1763, these reforms, like many earlier and later ones, were abandoned, and the Ottoman Empire resumed its decline. But at least Thugut was there to observe a brief attempt at Ottoman recovery.

And observe he did, for that was his principal assignment during his first stay in Constantinople. Thugut was not thrust into a translator's role immediately, for he was considered too inexperienced for any task of consequence. Instead, he continued his study of Ottoman language, literature, and history, now augmented by journeys through the city during which he was to absorb as much of the civilization of the streets as he could. A mark of distinction first among the *Sprachknaben* and later among graduates of the Oriental Academy in Constantinople was the wearing of Turkish dress (the long robes of a scholar) within the Austrian embassy in the suburb of Pera as well as in the streets of the Moslem city. The distinction was not bestowed, however, until the young man was regarded as fluent in the Ottoman language.[34] It is likely but not certain that Thugut enjoyed this honor during his first tour of duty.

Thugut remained in Constantinople only briefly on this first assignment, but in 1762, following a stint as translator in Transylvania, he returned to the Ottoman capital, this time in the company of one of the truly skillful Austrian envoys to the

[34] Hammer, *Erinnerungen*, 38.

Ottoman Empire, Heinrich Christoph Penkler. In 1762 Penkler was the old Turkish hand of the Habsburg foreign service. A *Sprachknabe* in his youth, he had held a number of posts as translator and adviser until 1741, when he became "resident"—the common eighteenth-century title of the official Austrian representative at the Sublime Porte, the Ottoman governmental establishment—in Constantinople. Penkler possessed not only a superb knowledge of the Ottoman language and of Ottoman practices, but also the rare ability to become close friends with Turkish officials. He had used these talents to influence the Porte to remain neutral during the long War of the Austrian Succession (1740–1748) and to maintain friendly relations between Constantinople and Vienna until his retirement in 1755.

In 1762 Penkler was pressed back into service by Maria Theresa and Kaunitz, who perceived serious trouble arising between Austria and the Ottoman Empire. Since the outbreak of the Seven Years' War in 1756, Frederick the Great of Prussia had been soliciting Ottoman aid in his struggle against the Habsburg Monarchy. Although Penkler's able successor, Josef Peter von Schwachheim, had repeatedly assured Vienna that Ragip Pasha had no intention of joining the war against Austria, the resident had never completely convinced his superiors. In 1762 a combination of circumstances eroded what confidence Vienna still retained. In 1760 and 1761 Prussian military fortunes had sunk to a low ebb, and Frederick had intensified his efforts to convince Turkey to enter the war on Prussia's side. Lured by bribes of all kinds (including Nürnberg dolls for the women of the harems of the sultan and his important officials), the Porte finally consented to a treaty of friendship and commerce with Berlin in April 1761. But Frederick wanted more; in March 1762 his envoy proposed a full treaty of alliance to the grand vizier. Such offers had been made before, but Vienna found this one by far the most threatening. In January 1762 Austria's stalwart ally, Empress Elizabeth of Russia, had died, leaving the throne to her notoriously Prussophile nephew, Peter III. The possibility that Russia would abandon Austria and ally with Prussia was alarming; if the Ottomans also joined the alliance, it would place the Habsburgs in a dangerous, if not hopeless, position. Kaunitz and Maria Theresa wanted desperately to reassess the likelihood of Prussian success in Constantinople.[35]

In answer to the growing concerns expressed by Vienna, Schwachheim insisted that there was not the slightest evidence of Turkish preparations for war against Austria or anyone else. No supply depots had been established, no ships built, no unusual recruitment taking place. The Porte could not make war at this time even if it wanted to.[36] But Kaunitz was unconvinced. Hence he dispatched to the Turkish capital the veteran Penkler and, as *wirklicher dritter Dolmetsch*—ordinary third translator—Franz Maria Thugut, now on his second trip to Constantinople.

Penkler's job was to find out if Schwachheim's confidence was justified. Upon his arrival, he set out to check all of the known sources in order to make the most accurate judgment possible of Turkish intentions. After completing the investigation, Penkler notified Kaunitz that Schwachheim had been exactly right. To underscore his point, Penkler informed the chancellor that he had not even used the large sums of bribe money provided him to obtain his information because his sources all believed it to be common knowledge. Kaunitz could be assured, Penkler concluded, that Turkey would not enter the war.[37] He was correct, and within a year Austria and Prussia themselves negotiated peace, as much because of mutual exhaustion as any other factor.

On this second trip to the Ottoman capital, Thugut was no longer a novice. Instead of simply receiving more training, he served this time in the traditional capacity of translators: running messages to and from the Austrian embassy, providing oral translating services for lesser Habsburg officers or civil-

[35] Kaunitz to Schwachheim, April 6, 1762, Vienna, HHSA, SK, *Türkei*, 2: 40.
[36] Schwachheim to Kaunitz, May 1, 1762, ibid., 38.
[37] Penkler to Kaunitz, September 15, 1762, ibid., 39.

Wenzel Anton von Kaunitz-Rietberg
(Courtesy Bildarchiv, Austrian National Library)

ians, purchasing supplies and goods for the embassy, and, most important of all, copying and translating documents. This last job was the most time-consuming, especially for a *wirklicher dritter Dolmetsch*. And it benefitted Thugut the most, for as he did his work he was improving and refining his language skills and slowly but surely learning the trade of the diplomat, a trade he would practice most of his life.

Shortly after Penkler's mission ended, Thugut was recalled to Vienna, this time to work at the very center of Austrian might, the chancellery, where the great Kaunitz himself held sway. He was appointed assistant to the official translator of the Ottoman language, Anton Seleskowitz, but in an administrative reform of the foreign affairs section of the chancellery in 1766 he was also assigned the post of court secretary. The purpose of the joint appointment was to give the translators more to do. Their tasks had been to translate documents to and from the Ottoman Empire or the Habsburg-Ottoman borders and to serve as guides and translators whenever Ottoman officials were received in Vienna. When no such services were required, the translators remained largely idle. By assigning secretarial status to both the official translator and his assistant, Kaunitz could employ them in routine office tasks during slack periods.[38] But Thugut's appointment was not simply an accidental result of the reform alone. Kaunitz selected Thugut specifically because he possessed "not only various languages but good knowledge and talent."[39]

Just as his assignments in Constantinople had given him insight into the duties and practices of a diplomat at a foreign court, so too his appointment as court secretary gave him ex-

[38] Johann Josef Khevenhüller-Metsch, *Aus der Zeit Maria Theresias* (Vienna, 1917), 6: 450–57.

[39] Quoted in Alfred von Arneth, *Geschichte Maria Theresia's* (Vienna, 1876), 7: 316. The promotion of Thugut the commoner to the office of court secretary offers evidence for Grete Klingenstein's argument that Kaunitz tried to make the chancellery a professional service. See Grete Klingenstein, "Institutionelle Aspekte der österreichischen Aussenpolitik im 18. Jahrhundert," in Erich Zöllner, ed., *Diplomatie und Aussenpolitik Österreichs* (Vienna, 1977), 74–93.

perience in the day-to-day operations of the Ministry of Foreign Affairs. Moreover, he was able to observe the great Kaunitz in action and to meet some of the men with whom he would be closely associated later on.[40] In the long run, however, his most important experience was to break from the confines of Ottoman affairs and to learn more about Habsburg relations with the rest of the world. He now summarized, transcribed, and edited documents relating to the greater and lesser powers of Europe. Still an Ottoman specialist, he nonetheless was gaining a deeper awareness of the overall concerns of Habsburg foreign policy.

In 1768 his area of specialty leaped again to the forefront of Vienna's concerns. The trouble this time had begun farther north, in Poland. The death of King Augustus III in 1763 had led to the election as king of that country Stanislaus Poniatowski, member of the powerful Czartoryski family but, of greater importance, lover and protégé of Catherine II of Russia. One assumed that, with Russia as its master, Poland would now become a peaceful if not necessarily contented place. The opposite occurred. A crisis within Poland between the Roman Catholic majority and the Protestant and Orthodox minorities led in 1767 to armed intervention by the Russians on behalf of the minorities and in 1768 to an uprising among the Poles against that intervention. Within a short time, practically all of Poland was beset by conflict.

Habsburg policy in the face of this situation was to remain uninvolved. Kaunitz was not enthusiastic about Russian domination of Poland, but he certainly had no intention of actively opposing it. His chief concern was that Turkey might do so. Since the 1740s, the Sublime Porte had viewed Russia as its most dangerous foe and had looked upon the growth of Russian influence in Poland as particularly threatening to the Ottoman Empire. Polish resistance seemed to many of the sultan's advisers an opportunity to drive the Russians out of

---

[40] A fellow young secretary at the time was Anton Spielmann, whose policies Thugut would first criticize and then overturn in 1793.

Poland and to put an end to their encroachment toward the Black Sea. To others at the Sublime Porte, however, the whole affair was simply too problematical to risk any involvement. Relying on Polish insurgents for help seemed an especially chancy business. For Kaunitz, Ottoman involvement would only spread uncertainty along another of Austria's borders, an uninviting prospect indeed.

In mid-July 1768 occurred an incident everyone had anticipated might happen and Kaunitz and the sultan's peace party had hoped would not. A zealous Russian commander, chasing some Polish insurgents, crossed the Polish-Turkish border and razed the Ottoman town of Balta, massacring many local inhabitants. The outrage in Constantinople was predictable. On October 6 the sultan declared war on Russia.

With the outbreak of Russo-Turkish hostilities, Kaunitz's policy was still to remain neutral. He believed that Russia and Turkey were evenly matched and hoped that they would fight each other to mutual exhaustion. The result would then be no change in the scales of power between the two empires but the substantial weakening of both relative to Austria. That in turn would render them unable to cause trouble for each other or for any of their neighbors for some time.

It was not long, however, before Kaunitz had to reassess his policy. On September 17, 1769, the Russian and Ottoman field armies fought a major battle on the Dniester (Dnestr) River near the Ottoman fortress of Khotin. For a long time the battle swayed back and forth until the famous janissary corps, the traditional keystone of the Ottoman army, suffered heavy casualties. Seeing their proudest troops badly pummeled, the rest of the Ottoman army wavered, then broke and ran. The garrison at nearby Khotin, although well provisioned and well armed in anticipation of a long siege, fled also. No one could rally the soldiers to make a stand. The Russians occupied the city of Iasi (Jassy) in Moldavia in early October, then Bucharest in Walachia in November, and finally reached the Danube River. Ottoman resistance had vanished.

Kaunitz was profoundly disturbed by these events. His immediate task, as he saw it, was to get more information. How badly had Turkey been damaged in terms of material strength? How badly was Ottoman morale affected? Could the army be restored quickly? And behind each of these lay the most important question of all: was the Ottoman Empire at last on the brink of its long-predicted extinction? The man to provide the information needed to shed light on these issues was the Habsburg resident in Constantinople, but at this critical juncture that official, Franz Anton Brognard, had unexpectedly died. Kaunitz had to find a new man, one with sufficient skill, talent, and facility to reach Constantinople quickly and gather the intelligence he required so urgently. For this important task he turned to a ready officer, his assistant translator and court secretary Franz Maria Thugut. The Eastern adventure had begun.

CHAPTER II

THE EAST, 1769–1775

THUGUT'S FIRST ASSIGNMENT in a truly responsible post had an inauspicious beginning. During the trip down the Danube to Belgrade and then overland to Constantinople he became ill. By the time he reached his destination he was quite sick. In his first report to Kaunitz, he described his illness, apologized for not providing the chancellor with the information he so eagerly awaited, but assured him that a change of diet would improve his health in a short time.[1] Thugut's incapacity was an unwelcome development to Kaunitz, who by November 1769 was really fretting. He pleaded with Thugut to send him news, especially since various reports indicated that the Turkish army was fleeing everywhere and that the janissary corps was "almost totally destroyed."[2]

Thugut did recover and soon began to send the intelligence Kaunitz needed. The Turkish army was indeed a shambles; after six months of campaigning it had reportedly fallen tenfold in strength, from two hundred thousand to twenty or thirty thousand men. The catastrophe was so great, Thugut reported, that the Porte had delayed his formal reception until mid-November because it feared that any audience with an Austrian envoy would be interpreted by the religious leaders and people of the city as an occasion to request mediation in

[1] Thugut to Kaunitz, October 3, 1769, Vienna, HHSA, SK, *Türkei*, 2: 55.
[2] Kaunitz to Thugut, November 4, 1769, ibid.

preparing to surrender to the Russians.[3] As to morale, Thugut was uncertain. It seemed that the public and most officials in the capital wanted peace but that the sultan and the grand vizier opposed it because they did not wish to humiliate themselves before the Russians and before their own subjects.[4] In any case, Thugut concluded, the Ottoman Empire was in pitiable condition.

Based on reports of Thugut and others from around Europe, Kaunitz, Maria Theresa, and Emperor Joseph II formulated a policy to deal with the situation in the East. The problem, as Kaunitz observed, was Russia. Russia was becoming a dangerous power. Already dominant in Poland and influential in Denmark and Sweden, it was by virtue of its military victories threatening to become the preeminent power in southeastern Europe as well. "If the Turks are compelled to conclude a disadvantageous peace," Kaunitz wrote to Thugut, "the Russian court could win so many advantages through its conquests that it would have little or nothing to fear from the Turks for a long time and would have totally free hands in this area." Such a situation would tip the balance of power in all of eastern Europe in favor of St. Petersburg, and that could only damage Habsburg interests. Given these circumstances, Vienna should try, Kaunitz explained, to stop the Russo-Turkish war and restore conditions to what they had been before it began. To that end, Kaunitz ordered Thugut to inform the Porte that Vienna was genuinely concerned about Russian expansion and that it would do all it could "not only to establish all affairs between the two warring powers as they were before but to reestablish the former independence of the Republic of Poland from Russia." To show that Austria was sincerely concerned about Turkey's future, two infantry and two cavalry regiments would reinforce the Austrian troops in Transylvania, indicating Habsburg dissatisfaction with the Russian march to the Danube. In the meantime, Thugut should recommend that the Porte request Austrian

[3] Thugut to Kaunitz, November 18, 1769, ibid.
[4] Thugut to Kaunitz, October 18, 1769, ibid.

27

mediation in any peace negotiations with Russia so that Austria could aid Turkey diplomatically in limiting Russian expansion.[5]

As this instruction reveals, Thugut, in his first major role as an Austrian diplomat, was taking part in a profound change in traditional Habsburg foreign policy. For the previous three centuries, the monarchy had confronted two certain enemies: France and Turkey. France contended with the Habsburgs for predominance in the West, and Turkey contended with them for predominance in the East. But the rivalry between Austria and Turkey was different from the one between Austria and France. It was a struggle not only for men's property but for their hearts and souls. Moslem Turkey was the infidel, the threat to Christianity, the menace to all of European civilization. Habsburg struggles with the Ottoman Empire had always been accompanied by daily prayers, bell-ringings, hymn-singing, and invocations to saints to spare Austria from the unbeliever. But by the time Thugut reached Constantinople, the Ottoman state no longer appeared a danger to Christian Europe. For Kaunitz and men like him, it was now simply another player in the great European diplomatic game. At this moment Russia was the threat, so traditional ideologies and viewpoints had to be set aside. Catholic Austria and Moslem Turkey must cooperate to put Orthodox Russia in its place. It was a policy of Realpolitik, and it was the first in which Thugut actively participated.

The offer of mediation delivered by Thugut was not immediately accepted by the Porte, however. The Ottomans wished to engage in another military campaign in 1770 to see if it would bring better results. It brought disaster—worse than in 1769. During the night of July 6 the entire Turkish fleet was destroyed at Çeşme by Russian cannon and fire ships, and three weeks later the regrouped Ottoman army was destroyed at Kartal on the Danube, with one third killed in action and another third drowned in the river while fleeing the battlefield.

[5] Kaunitz to Thugut, January 5, 1770, ibid.

In the wake of these defeats, the Porte requested joint Austro-Prussian mediation to end the war. The two powers agreed to the Porte's appeal and, as part of their duties, asked Catherine to set forth her conditions for peace. She submitted the following: Russian acquisition of the fortress of Azov on the Sea of Azov, freedom for all navigation in the Black Sea, an independent Crimea, and the Russian occupation of Moldavia and Walachia for twenty-five years.[6]

Kaunitz was flabbergasted. In his eyes the realization of Catherine's demands would utterly overturn the balance in the East. It would place thousands of square miles of territory and millions of people if not inside Russian borders at least under Russian domination. Moreover, should Russia retain its influence in Poland and add to it predominance in Moldavia and Walachia, the Habsburg Monarchy would have Russians along its eastern border from Austrian Silesia around Transylvania to the Banat of Temesvar (Timişoara). Since the first decade of the eighteenth century, a tenet of Viennese policy had been to allow no contiguous border with Russia. Now Vienna faced the prospect of having practically no other immediate neighbor to the east except Russia. Such demands could not be accepted. Even the old Austrian foe Frederick the Great called them "exorbitant and intolerable."[7]

After extensive debates in Vienna about responses to the Russian demands, the empress, emperor, and chancellor formed a policy that Kaunitz dispatched to his envoy in Constantinople. The time had come, he explained, to notify both the Turks and the Russians that Austria would not allow Russia to overrun the Ottoman Empire. Austria would warn Catherine not to send a single Russian soldier across the Danube and would impress upon her the seriousness of the warning by mobilizing one hundred thousand men in Transylvania. In the meantime, the Porte should apprise the Russian army commanders in the field that it wished only

[6] Adolf Beer, *Die erste Theilung Polens* (Vienna, 1873), 2: 13.
[7] Quoted in Saul K. Padover, "Prince Kaunitz and the First Partition of Poland" (Ph.D. diss., University of Chicago, 1932), 59.

peace, that it was willing to open peace talks with or without mediators, but that it would fight on rather than permit the Russians to establish themselves on the Black Sea, from which they could threaten Turkey's very heart.

To assure that Vienna and Constantinople coordinated efforts and policies in the affair, the emperor and the sultan must conclude a secret agreement. It must not be an alliance—that would appear too friendly and entail too many obligations—but a "concert." Since its basic purpose would be to save the Ottoman Empire, Austria would receive some compensation for its efforts, notably a substantial cash payment (Kaunitz suggested thirty-four million gulden), the provinces of Little Walachia (the area between the Danube and Aluta [Olt] rivers east of Orsova), the fortress-cities of Belgrade and Vidin, most-favored-nation status in commerce, and a guarantee of Austrian treaties with the Barbary pirates loosely under the suzerainty of the sultan.[8] Orders to present these proposals to the Porte were dispatched to Thugut.

Thugut was thus charged with negotiating the first Austrian accord with the Ottoman Empire. Even in this time of Realpolitik it was a remarkable incident in Habsburg diplomatic history. One historian has called it "an event without precedent, a true rejoinder to the reversal of alliances [between France and Austria] in 1756, or, more exactly, the logical outcome of that reversal."[9] Even Kaunitz realized that his proposal was an astonishing step. "To save our archenemy is rather extraordinary," he wrote to Thugut, "and such decisions can be justified only under extreme pressure, such as in maintaining our own self-preservation."[10]

---

[8] Kaunitz to Thugut, January 21, 1771, Vienna, HHSA, SK, *Türkei*, 2: 58. Kaunitz was uncertain if these proposals for compensation were realistic and asked Thugut for his advice on the matter.

[9] Gaston Zeller, *Les temps modernes. De Louis XIV à 1789* (Paris, 1955), 259.

[10] Kaunitz to Thugut, January 27, 1771, Vienna, HHSA, SK, *Türkei*, 2: 58.

The task of negotiating this concert with the Turks was Thugut's first difficult assignment as a senior diplomat, and he fulfilled it with distinction. Since Kaunitz's orders specified that the talks be kept secret, they took place late at night in the villa of the Ottoman foreign minister (*reis effendi*) on the Asiatic side of the Bosphorus. The issues in contention were how much the Turks would pay for Austrian services and exactly what those services would entail. Thugut was authorized to promise virtually any form of diplomatic and political support needed to help the Turks but to avoid any commitment to military cooperation. The Turks quite naturally welcomed the assurances of diplomatic and political help, but they sought most of all a firm Austrian promise of armed intervention should peaceful efforts yield no results. As to payment, Thugut presented Kaunitz's demands; in response the Turks offered much less: one-third of the amount of money that Kaunitz wished, only Little Walachia in territory, and some limited commercial advantages. The talks opened on the last night in February 1771 and continued with increasing intensity into the early summer.

The high point came in mid-June when the Turks began to show reluctance about concluding any agreement at all. Vienna had gone ahead (as it planned to do anyway) with the reinforcing of its army in Hungary and Transylvania, and the Russians, fearful about Austrian intentions (precisely the reaction Kaunitz had hoped for), undertook no operations near the Danube but focused upon the Crimean Peninsula instead. Since the Russian threat now seemed less immediate, the Turks informed Thugut that they had no compelling need for an accord with Austria, especially one that did not guarantee military cooperation. By this time Thugut had been instructed to press for agreement because Vienna needed the money to pay for its military posturing; he argued vigorously that Turkey was still in great danger and required Austrian assistance as much as ever. The "verbal battles," Thugut reported, "became at times so intense that I . . . often believed the moment to have arrived when the negotiation of the whole thing would collapse."[11]

On July 6, 1771, after one last night of hard bargaining, the agreement was concluded. As Austrian compensation, Thugut procured an Ottoman promise of 20,000 *Beutel* of gold (11,250,000 gulden, far less than the 34,000,000 Kaunitz had originally proposed and approximately what the Turks had wanted to pay), Little Walachia, and most-favored-nation status for Austrian commerce. In exchange for all of this, Austria pledged "to deliver, by way of negotiations or of arms . . . the fortresses, provinces, and territories which were possessions of the Sublime Porte and which have been invaded by the Russians since the commencement of the war." Also, Austria promised to restore the freedom of Poland and the pre-1769 Russo-Turkish borders "or, according to time and circumstances, to establish peace on those conditions which accord with the dignity of and are agreed to freely by the Sublime Porte."[12]

Kaunitz recognized the treaty as a fine piece of work. In exchange for concrete rewards—gold, territory, and commercial advantages—Austria had made no commitment that would necessarily require material sacrifices. Every important Austrian promise was qualified by an "or." Austria could employ negotiations "or" arms, but was not pledged to use the latter if the former proved unsuccessful. Austria would restore to Turkey all of its former territory "or" reach a settlement that the Porte would freely accept. The Porte would surely "freely" accept whatever Vienna insisted that it should. The Turks might assume that the agreement provided for Austrian military aid, but it certainly did not say so specifically. For such a success Kaunitz believed Thugut deserved recognition and reward; thus the chancellor recommended to Maria Theresa that Thugut be promoted from resident to the rank of internuntius in honor of his service. The empress agreed but expressed some

[11] Thugut to Kaunitz, June 17, 1771, ibid.
[12] The concert is published in Joseph von Hammer-Purgstall, *Geschichte des Osmanischen Reiches* (Pest, 1832), 8: 567-70.

misgivings about concluding a somewhat disreputable treaty with infidels. "I do not like to take money from these people," she told Kaunitz. "God grant us peace this winter."[13]

If Thugut believed that the conclusion of the Austro-Turkish treaty would make his diplomatic chores easier, he was sadly mistaken. In the autumn and winter of 1771–1772 the decision makers in Vienna revised Austrian policy toward the Ottoman Empire. The cause of the revision rested in the proposal of Frederick of Prussia that the differences among Austria, Prussia, and Russia could all be resolved by each power taking a slice of Poland. One must always be aware that the term "balance of power" in eighteenth-century foreign affairs did not mean the maintenance of the status quo and certainly had nothing to do with respecting the rights of all nations great and small. Rather, it represented a framework within which the European great powers seized as much territory as they could while at least paying lip service to the maintenance of a general equilibrium. However, that equilibrium was not necessarily a matter of fact but one of perception. Any of the great powers might perceive that the balance was tilting against it (whether it was or not) and thus embark on a diplomatic or even military campaign to rectify it. Likewise, any state might detect an opportunity to gain advantage over another and then seize that opportunity, again by diplomatic or military means. Balance of power in the eighteenth century meant competition among the powers, not the preservation of an acknowledged concert among them. Therefore, the partition of Poland was an acceptable exercise of balance-of-power diplomacy providing that the states involved could agree on the shares.

By late February 1772, Austria's leaders concluded that the monarchy would participate in what would become the First Partition of Poland. They did so, however, on the condition that Russia withdraw from Moldavia and Walachia and return both provinces to the Ottoman Empire. When Russia ac-

[13] Beer, *Theilung*, 2:98.

cepted the condition, Austria had all that it wished. Poland would still exist (although somewhat smaller) as a buffer between Austria and Russia in the northeast, and Moldavia and Walachia would continue as a buffer between Austria and Russia in the southeast. There would be no Austro-Russian border, and the Ottoman Empire would remain in existence. It was true that the Russo-Turkish war would continue and that the Russians might ultimately wrest from Turkey some land along the northern coast of the Black Sea, but that did not concern Vienna. In fact, with the Russian promise to evacuate Moldavia and Walachia, the Austro-Turkish concert had now become an embarrassment since in it Austria had promised to do its best to restore the entire territorial status quo ante bellum. Accordingly, on April 8, 1772, Kaunitz ordered Thugut to advise the Turks that the concert was abrogated. Excuses were easy to find: Vienna had never formally ratified the treaty; the Ottomans had not paid the money that they owed on time; the Turkish army was in such a poor state that it could not help Austria against Russia in any meaningful way; Prussia was now an ally of Russia and the treaty of July 6 did not pledge Austria to resist Russia and Prussia together.[14] Any or all would do, Kaunitz noted, but in any case the concert was at an end.

It was easier for Kaunitz to write these words in Vienna than it was for Thugut to present them face-to-face to the Ottoman officials with whom he had negotiated. To be sure, both Thugut and these officials had known that something was amiss for some time. In the autumn of 1771 Thugut had transmitted request after request for payment of the subsidy owed by the Turks but could offer only lame excuses when asked why Vienna was delaying formal ratification of the treaty and making no preparations for war. Indeed, in late January 1772 the *reis effendi* had called Thugut to an audience in which he read to the internuntius a formal statement "in the most forceful manner possible" that Vienna must negotiate a general

---

[14] Kaunitz to Thugut, April 8, 1772, Vienna, HHSA, SK, *Türkei*, 2: 60.

peace by spring or be prepared to join with the Ottoman Empire in its war against Russia.[15]

Given the Porte's suspicions and distrust, Thugut was reluctant to present Kaunitz's formal renunciation of the treaty when it arrived in May. He knew that he would have to do so eventually, but he also knew that the Turks were conducting armistice talks directly with the Russians in the field. If these talks brought an end to the fighting, the Porte might accept Austria's rejection of the treaty with less ill will than it would otherwise.[16] When no armistice was concluded, however, Thugut decided that he had to tell the Turks anyway. Their first reaction was one of resignation, then came anger, and then insistence that Thugut help draft a statement explaining Austria's action in a way that would placate the religious legalists and popular opinion of Constantinople so that the Ottoman ministers who had concluded the treaty could keep their heads.[17] During the night of June 6, 1772, Thugut and the Ottoman officials composed a document declaring that Austria, while unable actually to declare war on Russia, would do everything possible in future negotiations to insure that the Ottoman Empire kept Moldavia, Walachia, and the Crimea. In other words, Austria would fulfill its obligations under the treaty of July 6, short of war.[18] The pronouncement was a successful one: Kaunitz thought it fine, and the Ottoman ministers escaped decapitation. At the same time news of the long-awaited Russo-Turkish armistice and the scheduling of peace talks made it even more palatable to all concerned.

Yet Thugut's tasks were not immediately eased. Whatever the intent of the above statement, it still obligated Austria to assist the Porte in its negotiations with Russia. That meant that Thugut himself would have to accompany the Ottoman delegation to the town of Fokşani in southern Moldavia, where the peace talks would take place. When Thugut ar-

---

[15] Thugut to Kaunitz, January 26, 1772, ibid., 58.
[16] Thugut to Kaunitz, May 4, 1772, ibid., 59.
[17] Thugut to Kaunitz, May 4, May 21, and June 8, 1772, ibid.
[18] Thugut to Kaunitz, June 8, 1772, ibid.

rived, however, he was forbidden to attend the talks in any capacity because the Russians barred all participants except the Russian and Ottoman delegates. Thugut issued some appropriate objections, but Kaunitz was actually pleased at his envoy's exclusion. With Thugut left out, the Turks could not fault Austria for any of the results, and the Russians could not accuse Austria of being excessively pro-Turkish. "If the congress is exploded or does not reach a successful peace before the end of the campaign," Kaunitz wrote to Thugut, "no blame or partisanship can be attributed to us."[19]

It seemed that Thugut could at last relax. The problems with the treaty of July 6, 1771, were essentially at an end, and the two warring powers had rejected Austrian mediation. His tasks would now presumably be reduced to gathering information about the progress of the Russo-Turkish talks and evaluating Ottoman preparations for a campaign in 1773 if no agreement were reached. But Vienna soon presented him with new challenges. The First Partition of Poland, formalized by treaties in August 1772, and the ongoing Russo-Turkish conflict whetted rather than satisfied Kaunitz's appetite for territorial gain. His mind turned to Little Walachia, which had been promised to Austria in the treaty of July 6 but not ceded because of Vienna's failure to ratify the pact. After exchanging memoranda with Maria Theresa about the matter, Kaunitz instructed Thugut to offer to the Turks a "few million gulden" for the territory. The Russians were demanding substantial reparations as the price for peace, and Kaunitz assumed that the Turks could use the money either to pay the indemnity or, if they decided to fight on, to invest in their army.[20]

Thugut barely had time to point out the difficulties in presenting such a request to the Porte when he received new instructions. After Kaunitz had dispatched his initial proposal, Emperor Joseph II visited certain border areas to assess personally what lands would be most valuable for Austria to ac-

[19] Kaunitz to Thugut, August 4, 1772, ibid., 60.
[20] Kaunitz to Thugut, February 20, 1773, ibid., 62.

quire. He concluded that Little Walachia represented "more a liability to the state than an advantage," but that the monarchy would truly benefit from possessing the Turkish fortified city of Old Orsova on the Danube and the Bukovina, a land connecting Transylvania and Galicia, the newly acquired Austrian portion of Poland.[21] The Bukovina, Joseph wrote, "would facilitate our communications and our commerce as well as win for us the passageways for our troops in case of war."[22] Instructions were duly sent to Thugut to replace the request for Little Walachia with demands for Old Orsova and the Bukovina. Because some excuse had to be found to justify the demands, Kaunitz suggested that Thugut search through the Austro-Turkish Treaty of Belgrade of 1739 to discover some "Turkish chicanery" for which Austria could claim reparation. If no excuse could be found, then Thugut could ask for the territories as a token of Ottoman appreciation for the treaty of July 6, 1771.[23]

From his arrival (or at least after his initial illness passed) at his post in Constantinople, Thugut had performed his duties skillfully and well. But one wonders what he in fact thought of Austrian policy at this time. He was, after all, participating in diplomacy at its most cynical. Vienna had manipulated, deluded, betrayed, and finally sought to dispossess a power that it had vowed to protect, and Thugut had been its agent in these actions. To many observers then and to some historians since, diplomacy at its most cynical was Thugut's métier. After visiting Thugut in 1798, the American Gouverneur Morris remarked, "All those who know M. de Thugut intimately agree that he is cunning, indolent, and false in the extreme."[24] Later on Metternich wrote of him, "Subtle and dexterous, he owed the success of his career to these qualities, which, when supported by deep dissimulation and a love of intrigue, pass only

[21] Joseph to Maria Theresa, n.d., June 1773, ibid., *Vorträge*, 112.
[22] Joseph to Maria Theresa, June 19, 1773, in Arneth, *Geschichte Maria Theresia's*, 8: 613.
[23] Kaunitz to Thugut, June 23 and July 6, 1773, Vienna, HHSA, SK, *Türkei*, 2: 62.
[24] Gouverneur Morris, *Diary and Letters* (New York, 1888), 2: 348.

too easily for real talents."[25] The words "cunning," "sordid," "unprincipled," "immoral," "false," "intriguing," and "dissembling" are commonly used to describe Thugut in both contemporary accounts and later histories. No one denied that in foreign affairs Kaunitz possessed many of the same characteristics, but observers detected in him and not in Thugut a quality of statesmanship that overrode them. "From his master," wrote one scholar, "Thugut had learned the small and underhanded methods of diplomacy, but he lacked the patience and confidence that the great man so often displayed."[26]

Whether or not this description of Thugut was accurate, in his days as envoy to the Porte he made it known that he did not wholly endorse Kaunitz's policies precisely because he found them not only contrary to Habsburg interests but fundamentally dishonest. Thugut had not objected openly to any of his instructions concerning the concert of July 6, nor did he raise much complaint about asking for Little Walachia. But when he received orders to demand Old Orsova and the Bukovina, he began to resist. In response to the orders, Thugut sent to Kaunitz a long, rambling letter objecting for many reasons to this latest Austrian request, but his major point was that Austria was simply not dealing with the Ottoman Empire in an honorable way. To ask the sultan for territorial concessions, especially in appreciation for the treaty of July 6, was hypocritical, wrote Thugut, because in light of its cancellation the Porte did not consider the treaty a sign of "good will" as Kaunitz seemed to think. Rather the Turks viewed it as treachery. Now the Porte did not regard Austrian neutrality as something to be purchased but as a point of Habsburg honor.

When the letter reached Vienna, Kaunitz was on vacation at his estates in Moravia. An official in the chancellery read it and was sufficiently impressed to recommend to Maria The-

---

[25] Clemens von Metternich, *Memoirs* (New York, 1881), 2: 19.

[26] Karl and Mathilde Uhlirz, *Handbuch der Geschichte Österreichs und seiner Nachbarländer Böhmen und Ungarn* (Graz/Vienna/Leipzig, 1927), 1: 436.

resa that a clarification of Austrian policy be sent to Thugut. The empress decided instead to wait for the return of Kaunitz, who mildly admonished Thugut for overstepping his bounds and reassured him that Vienna was doing what was best for Habsburg interests. In the meantime, Thugut was to calm himself, follow orders, and send information when instructed to do so.[27]

Whether it had roots in his childhood, his familiarity with classical literature, his enlightened credo, or even his sympathy for the Turks, Thugut's sense that there should be some honor in relations among states remained with him throughout his career. He especially felt this sense of honor when it came to treaties. In the great struggles of the French Revolution, his bitter hostility toward Prussia resulted not only from his exaggerated perception of a Prussian threat but also from his loathing for the Prussian failure to honor solemn obligations set forth in treaties with Austria and Britain. By the same token, when factions opposed to the revolutionary wars brought pressure on Thugut to abandon the alliance with Britain, he argued vigorously that Austria must stand by its treaty commitments. Many historians have dismissed such arguments as simply convenient excuses for continuing the war with France, but his expressions of respect for treaties dating from the 1770s and his apparently sincere regret at having to conclude a separate peace with France in 1797 indicate that, for him, treaties and promises in international affairs were not made to be broken. After he succeeded in acquiring the Bukovina in 1775 (which will be discussed shortly) and received praise and recognition for doing so, Thugut confided to a friend that the affair in fact represented a stain on Habsburg honor for violating sacred agreements. The whole business "has renewed the ancient reproaches regarding our failure to observe all of our conventions," he wrote. "It is a great evil, but what can one do about it?"[28]

[27] Kaunitz to Thugut, October 6, 1773, Vienna, HHSA, SK, *Türkei*, 2: 62.
[28] Thugut to unknown correspondent (probably Jenisch), December 15, 1775, ibid., *Grosse Korrespondenz*, 447.

Perhaps Thugut did have a sense of honor sometimes at variance with that of Kaunitz and of some of his diplomatic contemporaries, but one series of incidents during his tenure in Constantinople (incidents that would emerge to haunt him later) suggests that his ethical standards were not overly high. At that time Thugut was a spy for the French. In 1766 a Viennese agent of King Louis XV made Thugut's acquaintance and, after a time, offered to pay him for information that he could procure as secretary in the chancellery. The following year Thugut accepted the offer and, in exchange for thirteen thousand livres annually and the promise of a lieutenant colonelcy in the French guards should he seek asylum, began to provide intelligence to the French king. His posting to Constantinople did not alter his secret mission, for while there he regularly delivered reports and assessments regarding Austrian policy, Ottoman policy, and various other matters to the French ambassador, Count François Emmanuel Saint-Priest.

This episode in Thugut's life is certainly a curious one. In the archives of the French Foreign Ministry, volume 158 of the *Turquie* collection carries the title *Correspondance secrète entre Saint-Priest, la cour et divers, 1772–1775* and contains the secret information and advice that Thugut passed on to Versailles. It also confirms that Thugut was keeping the French abreast of his negotiations with the Turks (but only after the signing of the concert of July 6, 1771) and of any news that he uncovered regarding Turkish policy toward Russia.[29] Of particular significance was Thugut's informing Saint-Priest in February 1772 of the forthcoming partition of Poland and advising him that, since Kaunitz still had some doubts as to its value, Versailles might persuade Vienna yet to back out of it.[30] This was the first firm news France received of the coming partition, and in 1774, when Saint-Priest was trying to persuade the newly appointed foreign minister, Count Charles Gravier

---

[29] Paris, Archives du ministère des affaires étrangères, *Turquie*, 158.

[30] Saint-Priest to Choiseul, March 27, 1772, ibid. Saint-Priest first reported the coming partition on February 8, 1772.

Vergennes, to retain Thugut's services, he cited the news of the partition of Poland as evidence of the Austrian's value.[31]

But aside from this piece of intelligence (and even it may have been planted by Kaunitz to elicit a French protest that he might later use in some manner), one wonders if Thugut passed on any information of real significance. Some Frenchmen clearly thought so. In 1771 Count Victor François Broglie wrote to Louis XV, "This Thugut appears to be a fine fellow and renders us a great service in divulging the secrets of the court of Vienna, at least relative to the pacification of Turkey; with a little application, one can exploit to a great degree the infidelity of this Austrian minister."[32] Two years later Broglie had lost none of his enthusiasm for Thugut's services, remarking that he continued to serve France "with zeal" and recommending that "we generously recompense his services in a manner proportionate to their importance."[33]

Saint-Priest was equally fervent. He often expressed concern that Vienna would discover Thugut's activities and took elaborate precautions to disguise them. He alone wrote the reports relaying Thugut's words; he allowed no secretary to know about them; and he insisted that Thugut be referred to as "friend," so that his identity would be unknown should letters fall into the wrong hands.[34] A few times Saint-Priest expressed fear that his secret correspondence had been discovered.[35] In 1774, when Louis XVI became king and Ver-

[31] Saint-Priest to Vergennes, January 20, 1775, ibid.

[32] Broglie to Louis XV, September 14, 1771, in Didier Ozanam and Michel Antoine, eds., *Correspondance secrète du Comte du Broglie avec Louis XV* (Paris, 1961), 2: 310. Broglie's enthusiasm for Thugut is suspect since he borrowed substantial sums from the baron. This borrowing probably occurred, however, in the 1780s.

[33] Broglie to Louis XV, June 12, 1773, ibid., 407.

[34] Saint-Priest to Choiseul, October 10, 1772, Paris, Archives, *Turquie*, 158. In June 1773, Saint-Priest advised Choiseul that whenever he used the expression "man of law" he meant Thugut. That expression does not appear, however, in later correspondence. Saint-Priest to Choiseul, n.d. June 1773, ibid.

[35] Saint-Priest to Choiseul, January 9 and March 3, 1773; Saint-Priest to Vergennes, July 18, 1774, ibid.

gennes became foreign minister, Saint-Priest sent a lengthy letter to the new leaders underscoring Thugut's importance as a source of information and pleading with them to protect his anonymity and to continue his services.[36] Vergennes wrote in reply, "I assure you that I have the greatest concern regarding the security of your friend. It will remain only between me and Mr. Gerard, and it will be managed with all the care required." As to Thugut's continued employment, "The promises made to your friend are sacred, and they will be carried out with punctuality. I know the value of his devotion and services."[37]

Two decades later, other Frenchmen believed Thugut's work to be of considerable value. Following the proclamation of the First Republic in September 1792, the new rulers of revolutionary France discovered Saint-Priest's correspondence in a secret cabinet in the Tuileries palace. They recognized Thugut's activity as treason and as a means by which he could be blackmailed into doing what they wished in his capacity as Habsburg foreign minister. In the autumn of 1795 they appointed an agent to deal with Thugut, a "Marquis" de Poteratz, a former acquaintance of Thugut and one of the truly unsavory characters of the revolutionary period. The Directory, the French executive body at the time, sent Poteratz to Vienna to persuade Thugut to give serious thought to a treaty to end the Austro-French war that had begun in April 1792.[38] As an additional arguing point, Poteratz proposed and the Directory approved using Saint-Priest's secret correspondence "to render Baron Thugut more tractable in this matter, . . .

---

[36] Saint-Priest to Vergennes, August 24, 1774, ibid.

[37] Vergennes to Saint-Priest, September 12, 1774, ibid. Saint-Priest remained good friends with Thugut for a long time after. In 1795 Thugut recommended that he become the principal adviser of Louis XVIII, since all of the king's "current advisers were incompetent." Thugut to L. Cobenzl, September 6, 1795, in Vivenot and Zeissberg, eds., *Quellen*, 5: 347–49.

[38] The story of Poteratz is told in Albert Sorel, "Le mission de Poterat à Vienne," *Revue historique*, 29 (1885): 280–315; and very well in Sydney Seymour Biro, *The German Policy of Revolutionary France: A Study in French Diplomacy during the War of the First Coalition, 1792–1797* (Cambridge, Mass., 1957), 1: 459–62, 2: 515–19, 969–73.

and to compromise him personally and to deprive him of the confidence and favor of his sovereign."[39] In his initial effort Poteratz was coy, dropping hints that the Directory had the means to place considerable pressure on Thugut personally to come to an agreement. Thugut pretended not to understand these hints and kept the talks focused strictly on the reasons why Austria could not agree to the Directory's terms.[40] Since the negotiations led nowhere, Poteratz left Vienna with no results. In March 1796, however, he wrote to propose another meeting and this time held back nothing. If Thugut did not cooperate, Poteratz would expose him as a traitor—although he pretended that he did not want to. "I say to you frankly and advise you to profit from the opportunity to make peace with me: fear the wicked; remember the day, during my first trip to Vienna, that I told you a certain person had formed a project to accuse you of serious transgressions at your court. . . . I dared not tell you then, but here it is: This person knows of the secret correspondence of M. de Saint-Priest when he was ambassador of France at Constantinople during 1772 and 1773. . . . I have read it entirely, and it compromises you seriously." If Thugut listened to reason, Poteratz assured him, the compromising letters would never see the light of day. If he did not, they might.[41]

To Poteratz's surprise (and to the surprise of scholars since), Thugut did not seem particularly disturbed by these threats. He referred to Poteratz as "a shrewd fellow, dangerous . . . against whom one must be ever on guard," and later as an "odious intriguer," "archknave," and "scoundrel," but he never expressed much concern about the effort to blackmail him.[42] When he received Poteratz's ultimatum, Thugut

[39] Instructions to Poteratz, November 28, 1795, in Sorel, "Poterat," 292.

[40] Biro, German Policy, 2: 518.

[41] Poteratz (in Basel) to Thugut, March 8, 1796, in Hermann Hüffer and Friedrich Luckwaldt, eds., Der Frieden von Campoformio (Innsbruck, 1907), 33.

[42] Thugut to Degelmann, January 10, 1796, in ibid., 21; Thugut to Colloredo, May 29 and July 15, 1796, in Vivenot, ed., Vertrauliche Briefe, 1: 302 and 317.

seemed anxious only that rumors and leaks spread by French agents might make Britain suspect Vienna of seeking a separate peace. As to Poteratz himself, Thugut refused to answer any of his letters or to grant him a passport to return to Vienna.[43]

Thugut's lack of concern about the exposure of his French ties suggests that he never really was a French agent or that he was perhaps a double agent for Austria. When approached in 1766, he may well have informed Kaunitz of the French offer. Kaunitz could then have advised him to accept the money and to pass to the French information that Kaunitz wanted them to have or that was judged to be of no special significance. At the same time, Thugut would have been able to gain intelligence about French intentions from his contacts and to transmit it to his superiors.[44] There is no explicit proof for this interpretation, but the secret correspondence itself does provide circumstantial evidence; aside from the early news of the Polish Partition (and, as mentioned earlier, even that might have been planted), it contains little of value. Perhaps even the leaders of revolutionary France suspected a double role, for they never published the correspondence despite their threats. That Thugut's superiors seemed aware of his activity provides the best explanation of his apparent indifference to Poteratz's pressures.

Before dropping this affair, however, we should consider how important the money Thugut received was to him and if he ever seriously considered the offer of asylum in France and perhaps a post in the French government. During his lifetime, many people considered Thugut to be a venal man. Because he accepted money while on duty in Constantinople, the French

[43] Thugut to Degelmann, April 20, 1796, in Hüffer and Luckwaldt, eds., *Frieden*, 40–42.

[44] Biro seems convinced that this is true. Biro, *German Policy*, 2:520–21. Sorel writes, "He [Thugut] won his way into the secrets of Louis XV, but he was far from admitting that too-credulous libertine into the secrets of the court of Vienna." Albert Sorel, *The Eastern Question in the Eighteenth Century* (1898; reprint, New York, 1969), 151.

assumed that he would do anything for a sufficient sum. In fact, the revolutionary leaders always expressed a certain bewilderment whenever he ignored their offers to bribe him. A few of his enemies in Vienna also expressed the conviction that he was in the pay of some foreign power—especially when he pursued policies they did not like—and the nineteenth-century historians who criticized Thugut relied upon those expressions to prove his greed. But some of his severest contemporary opponents admitted that money carried no weight with him. The Prince de Ligne noted that on one occasion he turned down a gift of two hundred thousand gulden which the emperor offered him, while two successive Prussian ambassadors in Vienna reluctantly expressed their admiration for his incorruptibility.[45] One of Thugut's harshest scholarly critics, Oskar Criste, wrote somewhat grudgingly in 1908 that Thugut's unselfishness "can no longer be in doubt."[46]

But Thugut's lack of interest in money as foreign minister does not necessarily mean that he had no use for it earlier. Indeed, he may have needed it in the 1770s because evidence suggests that he then wished to leave Habsburg service either to take up a post in France or to retire altogether. Several of Saint-Priest's letters to Versailles state that Thugut was considering retiring and emigrating to France. Although one might dismiss these comments as a part of Thugut's efforts to gain the confidence of the French, letters from an English merchant in the Levant named Peter Tooke indicate that retirement was certainly on Thugut's mind. Tooke and another Englishman named George Baldwin headed a company involved in the purchase of Indian goods at Suez and their shipment to England for sale. Thugut invested in their efforts and became a particularly good friend of Tooke. Apparently both

---

[45] Joseph Alexander Helfert, *Der Rastadter Gesandtenmord* (Vienna, 1874), 246; Hermann Hüffer, *Östreich und Preussen gegenüber der französischen Revolution bis zum Abschluss des Friedens von Campo Formio* (Bonn, 1868), 183–84.

[46] Oskar Criste, "Thugut und die Kriegführung, 1793–1801," *Streffleurs militärische Zeitschrift*, 49 (1908): 385.

hoped that the business would return a considerable profit and enable them to retire together to a pastoral existence in Italy. Tooke wrote to Thugut in early 1780, "I hope the end of all these enterprises and the success of some other schemes I have in view will lead me to a quiet life, and, you may be persuaded, my happiness will be greatly increased if our plan of settling together in Italy takes place." He admitted that his investment might not pay off for some time, but "we are young enough still to put off our retirement for five or six years to come; if it takes place sooner, so much the better."[47] A year later Tooke was still looking forward to retirement with Thugut but now in England rather than in Italy. "Indeed, Sir," he wrote from London, "we must change our plan and instead of living amongst a poor-spirited, priest-ridden people, we must retire to this Country."[48]

One factor that may have prompted Thugut to consider early retirement was that, during this period, he expressed increasing disgust with the Ottoman Empire and Constantinople. He may have believed that, as a Turkish specialist and a born commoner, he would be permanently assigned to Ottoman affairs if he remained in Habsburg service. Indeed, by 1774 he was openly contemptuous of the whole Ottoman system, and by then it seemed worthy of his contempt. In January 1774 Sultan Mustapha III died and was succeeded by Abdul Hamid I, a product of the unwise Ottoman custom of keeping all males of the ruling family hidden away in the palace until called upon to serve as sultan. Thugut described him as "in prison for forty-three years with no knowledge of world affairs," and a man who "considers the details of business as unworthy of him, allows the ministers no hearing and no audience except on matters of etiquette, and condemns his dead brother for having made himself contemptible by caring for the ways of the Porte and for his ministers."[49]

---

[47] Tooke to Thugut, April 4, 1780, Vienna, HHSA, SK, *Grosse Korrespondenz*, 447.

[48] Tooke to Thugut, August 31, 1781, ibid.

[49] Thugut to Kaunitz, January 3 and February 3, 1774, ibid., *Türkei*, 2:62. Actually Abdul Hamid I later became one of the reforming sultans.

The growing incompetence of the Ottoman government reached its climax, Thugut believed, in the Treaty of Kuchuk-Kainarji (Kücük Kaynarca), which was concluded by Russia and Turkey on July 21, 1774, finally ending the war that had begun in 1769. The treaty was indeed a milestone in the history of southeastern Europe. In his book *The Eastern Question*, M. S. Anderson has dated the origin of that diplomatic problem from this point; he argues that the treaty first made Europe aware that the Ottoman Empire was collapsing and that, without a general European effort, Russia would replace Turkey as the dominant power in eastern Europe and in the eastern Mediterranean.[50] The treaty's most important provisions gave Russia a foothold on the Black Sea, proclaimed the Crimean Peninsula independent of the Ottoman Empire (and thus open to Russian influence), and granted Russia vague rights to protect the Orthodox faith in the sultan's territories. Thugut clearly judged the treaty to mark the end of the Ottoman Empire. "From now on," he wrote to Kaunitz, "it [Turkey] falls into the position of being a form of Russian province, from which the Petersburg court can get people, money, etc. as it wishes. . . . After a few years, Russia will tire of this arrangement and decide to annex it formally for good."[51] What made it all worse, he added, was that the Ottoman ministers did not even know what was happening to them. "Unbelievable foolishness" pervaded the administration, and the state might collapse upon itself before the Russians pushed it over. In any case, "Never was a nation at its destruction less worthy of condolences than this one."[52]

Shortly before the treaty was signed, Thugut asked to be relieved of his duties. The reason he gave was health. He needed "a long period of rest and a good Christian doctor."[53] Given his despair at the state of Ottoman affairs, his health may have

[50] M. S. Anderson, *The Eastern Question, 1774–1923* (London, 1966).
[51] Thugut to Kaunitz, September 3, 1774, in Hammer, *Geschichte des Osmanischen Reiches*, 8: 582.
[52] Thugut to Kaunitz, August 17, 1774, Vienna, HHSA, SK, *Türkei*, 2: 63.
[53] Thugut to Kaunitz, June 3, 1774, ibid.

been only an excuse. Two years earlier Saint-Priest had reported that Thugut was already thinking of asking to be recalled under the pretext of illness.[54] Yet his health may have suffered; for some time after his departure from Constantinople, he was on vacation ostensibly to restore it, and both Kaunitz and the Austrian ambassador to France, Count Florimund Mercy d'Argenteau, expressed concern that he be given sufficient time to recover.[55] Perhaps sick both in body and in spirit, Thugut was simply eager to leave the Ottoman Empire.

There remained, however, a piece of unfinished business: Austria's acquisition of the Bukovina. As part of his request to be recalled, Thugut had expressed his willingness to remain at his post until that matter was resolved, and Kaunitz was eager for him to do so. To encourage him to carry on in Constantinople for a short time longer but also to thank him for a job already well done and to recognize his skill as a diplomat, Kaunitz recommended at this time that Maria Theresa award Thugut the title of baron (*Freiherr*) and thus promotion to noble status. On September 20, 1774, Kaunitz dispatched to Thugut the notification of the empress's approval of the new title.[56] By his ennoblement, not at all common for a man of his position, the son of a lowly bureaucrat from Linz had achieved significant recognition for his service to the Habsburg Monarchy.

With the new title, Kaunitz also sent further advice on how Thugut should proceed with the Bukovina affair. Basically, he urged him to continue to search for a way to convince the Porte to turn over the Bukovina to Austria at practically no cost. Thugut tried various stratagems, but the one that finally worked was a simple combination of force and intimidation. The Austrian army occupied the Bukovina in late 1774, and in

[54] Saint-Priest to Choiseul, May 11, 1772, Paris, Archives, *Turquie*, 158.

[55] Kaunitz to Mercy, May 23, 1777, and Mercy to Kaunitz, September 12, 1777, Vienna, HHSA, SK, *Frankreich*, 157.

[56] Kaunitz to Thugut, September 20, 1774, ibid., *Türkei*, 2:64. Maria Theresa granted him the title as a mark of the "highest personal appreciation" for his service.

early 1775 Thugut presented to the Porte a statement full of implied threats of what might happen should the Turks fail to cede formally that province to Austria. The Turks were suitably impressed; negotiations began, and on May 7, 1775, Thugut signed the agreement granting Austria possession of the Bukovina. Kaunitz was delighted. Upon his recommendation Maria Theresa added to Thugut's title of baron the knight's cross and then the commander's cross of the Order of St. Stephen, the Habsburg order created for meritorious service in civilian affairs.[57]

For Thugut, acquisition of the Bukovina was his last major accomplishment during his tenure as Habsburg envoy to the Sublime Porte. With the region secured and the Russians and the Turks at peace, Thugut's responsibilities were at an end. He could now return to Vienna.

Before turning to his subsequent career, however, we must note another event in his life that occurred in Constantinople: he fathered his one and only known offspring. The role of romance in Thugut's life is rather difficult to assess. He was a lifelong bachelor, never seemed to take delight in the company of women, and apparently had none in whom he confided. Many of his contemporaries assumed that he had no sexual appetite, some even calling him a Jesuit to make sport of his denial of the flesh. Hormayr wrote, "The pleasures of the table had no charm for him; comfort he did not value; and voluptuousness did not sway him. In [his view of] love affairs he was a downright cynic. An Italian lady, distinguished as a beauty and as a singer, had her interviews given her in the more than Corregian darkness of a hallway between Thugut's office and the room of the Messenger of the Chancelleries."[58]

Thugut was also no prude when it came to sexual matters. One of his secretaries when he was foreign minister was the famous historian Johannes von Müller, who did not hide his homosexuality even in the rather straightlaced Habsburg court at the time. After Thugut's retirement, Müller com-

---

[57] Wurzbach, *Biographisches Lexikon*, 2.   [58] Vehse, *Memoirs*, 2: 385.

plained to him of his successor's reluctance to renew Müller's appointment "because of matters of religion." Müller continued, "Finally I understood that the obstacle was the opinion that I was Greek in matters of love. I told them that I thought the matter at hand did not concern how to make love but how to save the state." He then praised Thugut for understanding the difference between making love and saving the state when he was in office.[59] Clearly Thugut, though not homosexual himself, was quite tolerant toward those who were. As a man of the Enlightenment, he did not care at all about his subordinates' sexual proclivities as long as they did not interfere with work.

Thugut may have had little interest in romance by the time he was foreign minister in the 1790s, but during his days in Constantinople he had an affair that left a daughter who became, according to Hammer-Purgstall, the toast of the European community there. Her mother was Thugut's washerwoman, "who had been let go when she struck him on the ear."[60] The daughter inherited from Thugut his outstanding physical feature: his chin. "Her face would have been beautiful had it not been for the great, protruding chin that was a legacy of her father, Baron Thugut." But she overcame that deficiency, wrote Hammer, by the "courage, decisiveness, spirit, and intelligence she inherited from both her parents." When Thugut left Constantinople, his daughter remained behind, presumably in the care of her mother. It appears that she enjoyed her father's support and the Austrian embassy's concern that she be introduced to the appropriate society of Pera, for at the age of fourteen she married the Neapolitan legation secretary named Marini "whose own age can be determined because he had been legation secretary in Lisbon before the great earthquake more than fifty years earlier."[61] She also be-

---

[59] Müller to Thugut, February 2, 1802, Vienna, HHSA, SK, *Grosse Korrespondenz*, 447.

[60] Hammer gives no further information about this woman, although it seems likely that she was of European rather than of Turkish origin. Hammer, *Erinnerungen*, 144–45.

[61] Hammer's dates are incorrect. The Lisbon earthquake occurred in

came the mistress of Count Viktor Pavlovich Kochubei, Russian ambassador and later head of the Russian College of Foreign Affairs, and by him she had a daughter and two sons who were raised in Russia. According to Hammer, in her mature years Madame Marini held a form of court of her own at her husband's dairy farm on the shores of the Black Sea north of Constantinople. He recounted that in 1803, as a young officer in the Austrian embassy, he and a companion would regularly visit her there. "We spent so many evenings with her in spirited and intelligent conversation and so many mornings on rides to her farm that she named us her suitors in common."[62] After Marini's death of old age she moved to London, where she spent the rest of her life. Like the other members of his family, this daughter never appeared in Thugut's correspondence and, since he left no will, was not named his heiress.

Whether or not the affair with the washerwoman represented his last serious entanglement with the opposite sex is difficult to say. One remaining bit of evidence suggests that it was not. Following Thugut's death in 1818, Metternich ordered an assistant to go immediately to his house in Pressburg to conduct an inventory of his private papers in preparation for bringing them to Vienna. Among those papers the official found "a whole correspondence with the fair sex that could cloud the memory of his earlier position and service in the eyes of the world."[63] Regrettably, this author could not find that tantalizing correspondence.

In early 1776 Thugut turned over the responsibilities of his office at the Sublime Porte to an interim envoy, Emanuel Isidore von Tassara, and shortly after set out for Vienna. Constantinople may have been the site of his first great achievements, but he would never visit it again.

1755, forty-eight years before Hammer described these events in 1803. Still, the marriage of the secretary and Thugut's daughter would have happened around 1788, which would have made the husband substantially older than his bride.

[62] Hammer, *Erinnerungen*, 144–45.

[63] Brettfeld to Metternich, June 1, 1818, Vienna, HHSA, SK, *Grosse Korrespondenz*, 447.

51

CHAPTER III

SEEING EUROPE,

1776–1790

WHEN THUGUT left Constantinople, he did not return by the traditional overland route to Vienna. Instead, he set out on a journey through the Aegean and Ionian islands, landing eventually at Trieste and then proceeding to Vienna via the famous road over the Semmering Pass. The trip was a relaxing one and reflected a fondness for travel, which he indulged often until he settled into the job of Habsburg foreign minister in 1793. When he reached Vienna, he intended to continue his vacation for some time in order to restore his health, but in early 1777 Kaunitz found another task for him. The problem was the same—the fate of the Ottoman Empire—but the direction in which he had to go was different: west instead of east, to Paris instead of Constantinople.

A provision of the Treaty of Kuchuk-Kainarji provided for the independence of the Crimean Peninsula under the governorship of the Girey family, the traditional rulers of the Tartars who lived there. Shortly after independence, however, the Girey family split into pro-Russian and pro-Ottoman factions that contested with one another for domination of the peninsula. In late 1776 the squabble within the family became sufficiently serious to warrant Catherine's dispatching Russian troops to reinforce her protégé and his supporters, an act answered by an Ottoman promise to send troops to aid its faction as well. It appeared that the situation could lead to a clash between Russian and Turkish regulars and to another Russo-Turkish war.

If war erupted again, Vienna believed that the Russians might destroy the Ottoman Empire once and for all, so a policy was needed to try to preserve the Ottoman Empire as it was. To prepare a course of action, however, the Habsburg statesmen had first to obtain the opinions of their friends and allies in Europe. Austria still dared not challenge Russia by itself; any effort to aid Turkey would require cooperation by two or more great powers acting together. Among Austria's allies, none was more likely to help at this time than the traditional friend and trading partner of the Ottoman Empire, France. Kaunitz believed that France was the only great power of Europe with sufficient political and commercial interests in Turkey to join Austria in trying to save it. But France, despite its interests and traditions, had taken no active role in the Eastern troubles of 1769–1774, and Kaunitz feared that French concern for the fate of the Turks was declining. Accordingly, the chancellor decided that he would send a special emissary to Versailles to bring the French court up to date on conditions within the Ottoman Empire, describe the threats to its existence, and, with "information and enlightenment," convey the disastrous results for all of Europe that the dismemberment of the Ottoman state would entail. No man could better carry out this mission in Kaunitz's mind than Thugut.[1]

In late June 1777, Thugut set out on his new assignment. It was his first trip to France, and it would not be his last. Although he left no record describing his impressions at the time,

---

[1] Kaunitz to Mercy, May 23, 1777, Vienna, HHSA, SK, *Frankreich*, 157. Kaunitz wrote, "Because he knows completely the internal Turkish constitution and the character of the Porte, its resources, and its weaknesses, because he is such a good friend of the French ambassador to Constantinople who is now in Paris, Saint-Priest, so can he serve Your Excellency as a very useful instrument."

it is evident that he found France in general and Paris in particular delightful places to be. When his mission ended, he requested permission to remain "for a few months longer,"
ostensibly to aid the Austrian ambassador there and to continue recovering his health, but more likely because he enjoyed
the country so much. In 1783, following his term as ambassador to Poland, Thugut would return to France, where he
would spend most of the following four years, again on leave.
Then would come revolution and another visit to a very different France in 1791, a France that would repel and depress
him.

Upon his arrival in Paris in July 1777 he was greeted by the
man he was assigned to help, Count Florimund Mercy d'Argenteau, Austrian ambassador to the French court. Born a bas-
tard in the Low Countries, Mercy was a dramatist's vision of
the ideal diplomat. Handsome, elegant, tactful, reserved, intelligent, adroit, and clever, he had served at Versailles since
1766 and would continue to do so until the French monarchy
became engulfed in revolution. A skilled diplomatist under
normal circumstances, he revealed his exceptional ability after
1770 when he became the confidant of the daughter of Maria
Theresa and wife of Louis XVI, the difficult Marie Antoinette.
He served as adviser to the young queen, informer for her
mother, and trusted correspondent of Kaunitz, all with remarkable sensitivity and understanding.

Like almost everyone else who became acquainted with
Mercy, Thugut grew fond of him, and the feeling was reciprocated. Both were bachelors, both enjoyed the same cultural
interests, and both would later share the same views of the
French Revolution. Of the two, Mercy was undoubtedly the
more perceptive, able to judge events within a broader context
than Thugut could visualize. Mercy's ability to foresee the
consequences of events and trends was a talent that Thugut
greatly admired but did not possess to the same degree. Nor
could Thugut articulate his ideas and assessments with the
skill of Mercy—or of Kaunitz—and to some extent this failing
made it difficult for him to convince others to support the pol-

54

Florimund Mercy d'Argenteau

icies he believed essential to the survival of the Habsburg Monarchy. Although Mercy excelled Thugut in vision and insight, he also lacked two qualities that Thugut enjoyed: ambition and an elemental strength of will. Mercy, while having strong and perceptive views on the nature of foreign policy, its role, its purpose, and the course that it should take, had no desire to direct foreign policy himself. Delicate in constitution, he repeatedly complained that human events and natural phenomena conspired to make him suffer physically. The thought of being at the center of policy making in Vienna made him ill. "Every storm threatened to topple this man, who was no fighter and did not wish to be."[2] Thugut also complained much about his health, but he possessed a stubbornness and toughness of mind that never let his illnesses interfere with his work. In the midst of the worst adversity, Thugut always mustered an internal strength to try to overcome it—and he always believed that other persons, and the monarchy as a whole, could do the same. For states and for individuals, failure in Thugut's mind often reflected a simple lack of determination.

Upon his arrival in Paris, Thugut was first briefed by Mercy on the ins and outs of the French court; then he opened discussions on the future of the Ottoman Empire with various French officials. To his surprise, they hardly listened to him. Wrote Mercy, "He [Thugut] found so little interest among these ministers that only with Vergennes was he able to speak seriously twice, and the second time for over an hour. In the discussion Vergennes told Thugut what he told me: he knew Turkey was in danger, that it would fall to the Russians unless someone did something, and that we were closer to Turkey so we should do something." But Thugut could get no more out of Vergennes, which led him to conclude that France had "no formal project or policy" toward the Ottoman Empire.[3] In

[2] Georg Küntzel, *Fürst Kaunitz-Rittberg als Staatsmann* (Frankfurt, 1923), 157.

[3] Mercy to Kaunitz, August 15, 1777, Vienna, HHSA, SK, *Frankreich*, 157.

truth, France was becoming absorbed in Britain's troubles in North America, and the East seemed unimportant for the time being. His mission may have accomplished little, but Thugut remained for an interval in the Paris he was growing fond of; then he journeyed to Florence and Naples to discuss Eastern affairs with the courts there; and in early 1778 he returned to the Austrian capital, just in time to play a role in the third Austro-Prussian struggle in the eighteenth century, the War of the Bavarian Succession.

This war had its origins in the ongoing search of Joseph II and Kaunitz for territorial gain. The two had arranged with the elector Palatine, Charles Theodore of the House of Wittelsbach and legal heir to his family's possessions in Bavaria, that upon the death of the childless elector of Bavaria, Maximilian Joseph, Austria would take possession of the Wittelsbach lands of Lower Bavaria and the Upper Palatinate in exchange for Belgium or a motley collection of small Habsburg territories in western Germany. This rather elaborate agreement was still being worked out in December 1777 when Maximilian Joseph died. To insure that all would be well until the final arrangements were concluded, Emperor Joseph ordered his army to occupy Bavaria. This act caused a storm of protest in Germany. It loosed an outpouring of pamphlets, books, and newspapers arguing about the rights, privileges, and traditions of the smaller states of the Holy Roman Empire. But far more important, it inspired Frederick of Prussia to take steps to prevent the Habsburg annexation of Bavaria. Frederick had no intention of seeing his archrival increase its wealth and population to such an extent in Germany. After a flurry of diplomatic activity produced no results, on July 5, 1778, Frederick sent Prussian military forces into Austrian territory.

From the beginning, Maria Theresa had opposed the Bavarian annexation if it meant war. Since it now did so, she summoned Kaunitz to discuss measures to end the hostilities quickly. The two agreed that she should compose a personal letter to Frederick expressing her wishes for peace and proposing some terms to get talks started. Carrying such a message to the Prussian king could not be entrusted to a simple courier; it would require a messenger of standing. Kaunitz recommended Thugut, a man whom he described as possessing "all the necessary characteristics, skills, discretion, loyalty, and devotion."[4]

In the early morning of July 13, Thugut left Vienna for Frederick's military headquarters at Welsdorf in northern Bohemia. He carried with him Maria Theresa's letter to the king, a set of instructions regarding his own presentations, and a passport in the name of a Russian legation secretary named Rossdorf, which was the alias he was to use until he reached the Prussian camp. He arrived during the night of July 16, and the following morning he was ushered into the presence of the by now legendary Frederick the Great.

In 1778 Frederick was sixty-six years old with the appearance represented in prints and portraits done in his later years. By this time his legs were enfeebled by gout and disease, his back hunched, his body thin, and his eyes weak enough to require a lorgnette even when he was on horseback. His dress consisted only of a plain undecorated uniform of common woolen cloth, soldier's boots, the famous tricornered hat, and a simple sword. An observer at the time wrote, "Either economy, or carelessness, or both, induce him to wear his cloaths [sic] as long as decency will permit; indeed, sometime longer. He is accustomed to order his breeches to be mended, and his coat to be pieced under the arms. . . . To complete the negligence of his appearance, he takes a great deal of snuff, and lets no small portion of it slip through his thumb and fingers, upon his cloaths. It must be owned that this custom gives him sometimes a disgusting appearance."[5] Lest superficial appearances deceive, this same contemporary detected in Frederick's eye "a fire and intelligence, which widely distinguishes him from

[4] Arneth, *Geschichte Maria Theresia's*, 10: 450.

[5] Nathaniel William Wraxall, *Memoirs of the Courts of Berlin, Dresden, Warsaw, and Vienna, in the Years 1777, 1778, and 1779* (London, 1800), 1: 110.

common men."[6] Thugut found this clever old warrior a more than worthy antagonist.

Maria Theresa's appeal for peace surprised Frederick somewhat, but he was not unhappy to receive it. He no longer possessed the enthusiasm for war that he had enjoyed in his younger years, and he had no objections to ending this one without a test of strength, providing he could get what he wanted. He and Thugut spent the whole of July 17 expressing sincere desires for peace and exchanging proposals concerning the conditions under which peace could be made. The sides were far apart. In her note Maria Theresa had offered to give up most of Bavaria if she could keep a part that would provide her with an annual income of one million gulden and if Frederick would allow her to negotiate for another part that would yield an additional million. In response, Frederick insisted that the empress abandon all claims to Bavaria (except for the town of Burghausen and a small part of the Upper Palatinate, which he would allow her); make a few concessions to his friends, the elector of Saxony and the duke of Mecklenburg; and not contest Prussian claims to the margraviates of Ansbach and Bayreuth (apparently on Kaunitz's oral instructions, Thugut had challenged these claims as one of the Austrian conditions). To show his willingness to reach a settlement, however, Frederick assured Thugut that for the time being he would honor Maria Theresa's request to cease all military operations.[7]

Thugut's assignment was not to negotiate these terms with Frederick but to take them back to Vienna. On July 18 he left the Prussian camp and three days later arrived in the Austrian capital, where he reported all that had taken place to the em-

<hr/>

[6] Ibid., 109.

[7] These points are explained in detail in a number of places, including Paul P. Bernard, *Joseph II and Bavaria* (The Hague, 1965), 112–23; Arneth, *Geschichte Maria Theresia's*, 10: 462–70; and Adolf Beer, "Die Sendung Thuguts in das preussische Hauptquartier und der Friede zu Teschen," *Historische Zeitschrift*, 38 (1877): 403–76.

press and the chancellor.[8] He discovered that in his absence a dispute had broken out among the Austrian policy-makers; Emperor Joseph was angry because Maria Theresa had sent peace overtures to Frederick without his knowledge or consent. After suffering initial anxiety at the beginning of the war, Joseph was now eager to test his military mettle against that of Frederick and so objected mightily to any settlement at this time. Over his protests, Kaunitz and Maria Theresa decided to persist in their efforts to restore peace and to keep using Thugut as their agent to do it. On August 6, armed with new proposals and the authority to negotiate, Thugut set out again for Welsdorf, where he arrived on the morning of August 10.

His talks with Frederick began at 11:00 A.M. that day, after the king had returned from a short inspection tour of part of his army. The exchanges were polite but stiff. Thugut seemed anxious about the great differences in status, reputation, and experience between himself and Frederick, and, as a result, he was noticeably ruffled by a few of Frederick's barbs. At the outset, Thugut proposed to the king that Vienna would abandon its claim to Bavaria, as Frederick wished, on condition that he abandon his claim to the margraviates of Ansbach and Bayreuth. Frederick steadfastly refused on the grounds that the rights of his house to the two lands were not recently concocted as were Austria's claims to Bavaria but were firmly rooted in time-honored dynastic laws. Beginning with this exchange, the two then sparred over other suggestions, each searching for acceptable terms while trying to gain psychological advantages over the other.

Toward the end of the day, as the talks seemed to stagnate, Thugut announced that the intent of his orders was to conclude peace by whatever means he could; thus, he proposed a scheme by which Prussia could keep its claims to Ansbach and Bayreuth or trade those claims to Saxony for a part of Saxon Lusatia. Then, as an equivalent, Austria would annex a strip

[8] Thugut's official report is printed in Frederick II, *Politische Correspondenz* (Leipzig, 1929), 41: 268–74.

of Bavarian territory to round off its borders. If Thugut expected the Prussian king to find such an offer attractive, he was bitterly disappointed; indeed, Frederick's reply was not simply a rejection but an affront. "You play the supplicant not badly," Frederick sneered at Thugut, "as you try to persuade me to turn over the Palatine house [Wittelsbach] to the imperial court so that it can plunder it at will." Stung by Frederick's remark, Thugut insisted that equal advantages must be the basis for an agreement and moved on to other suggestions. As night approached, the king tired of the exchanges, which he now believed would lead nowhere, and suggested that Thugut take his proposals to the Prussian ministers in charge of foreign policy, who were staying not far away in the town of Reichenbach. Thugut knew that such a move would merely delay a settlement because the ministers would have to ask the king for orders regarding any terms proposed. To avoid interposing unnecessary middlemen, Thugut asked the king to continue the talks there in Welsdorf, but Frederick had had enough. He told Thugut to meet the ministers if he wished, but direct negotiations were at an end.[9]

Frederick, however, had one last embarrassment to inflict upon Thugut. At one point in the day, the Austrian had unrolled some maps to show what the monarchy might consider as compensation in Bavaria and had put the casings for the maps aside. At the end of the talks, Thugut had rolled up the maps and was about to leave Frederick's tent, when he heard the king call him back. Believing that Frederick had decided to continue negotiating, Thugut returned eagerly to the king's presence. To Thugut's mortification, Frederick simply nodded at the casings that had been left behind and said, "Wait, Monsieur, these are yours; I do not like them either." Thugut absorbed the indignity, picked them up, and departed.[10]

Thugut's mission was not formally at an end, but it might as well have been. He met on August 13 with the Prussian

<hr />

[9] Bernard, *Joseph II and Bavaria*, 113–17; Arneth, *Geschichte Maria Theresia's*, 10: 486–92; Beer, "Sendung," 413–18.

[10] Wurzbach, *Biographisches Lexikon*, 1.

ministers Ewald Friedrich Herzberg and Karl Wilhelm Finkenstein, but no chance for an immediate settlement existed. As soon as Thugut had departed from the army camp, Frederick had made the negotiations public to show Austria's lack of concern for the traditions of the old German states, and Thugut found the Prussian ministers unwilling to agree to anything. On August 15 they presented a statement to Thugut "to end these fruitless negotiations," and the following day they left for Berlin.[11] Thugut had no choice but to return to Vienna. Dealing with Prussians, he had learned, was certainly different from dealing with Turks.

One can hardly blame Thugut for the failure of the negotiations at Welsdorf to reach a peace settlement. In fact, they served exactly the purpose Maria Theresa and Kaunitz intended: they opened the dialogue that would eventually lead to peace, a peace concluded at Teschen in 1779. What impact these talks with Frederick had upon Thugut personally is hard to say. One might argue that the embarrassment that he felt at some of Frederick's remarks and at his own inability to reach a satisfactory agreement planted the seed of the loathing he so often expressed for Prussia once he became foreign minister. But that is unlikely. He certainly had worked under the influence of Kaunitz's vigorous Prussophobia long before 1778, and besides, the later Prussian leaders would give him plenty of reason to despise them without our searching for a long period of gestating hatred.

Following his special mission to Frederick, Thugut enjoyed another short period of rest before his masters offered him another diplomatic assignment in 1779: a return to Constantinople, where there had been no senior Austrian diplomat since his departure in 1776. Maria Theresa particularly wanted him back in the Ottoman capital to improve the "system, alliance, and commerce" between Austria and Turkey. As an inducement, the empress suggested that his acceptance of the post

[11] Herzberg and Finkenstein to Frederick II, August 15, 1778, in Frederick II, *Politische Correspondenz*, 41: 364.

would lead to "other important positions or greater salaries," because she knew that he did not want to go.[12] One of Kaunitz's subordinates, after talking with Thugut about the appointment, told the chancellor that Thugut "desired never to return to Constantinople . . . for reasons well known to Your Excellency." He would, however, agree to a term of two years, "if Their Majesties absolutely insisted upon it."[13] Kaunitz recognized that it would serve little purpose to send someone who fervently hated the post, so he advised the empress to pass over Thugut and to appoint someone else. Maria Theresa accepted her chancellor's recommendation, and Thugut remained behind.[14]

Having no important work in the chancellery, Thugut returned again to western Europe, this time to visit Holland and the Austrian Netherlands. He was not gone long by eighteenth-century standards when he received the call to a new post in the East, that of Austrian ambassador to Poland. Poland at the time offered an atmosphere little better than Turkey. The eastern European wanderer Nathaniel Wraxall described the country: "In the midst of a soil naturally rich and fertile, they are in the want of common necessities." The only food of the people was a bread "so black, sour, and execrable" as not to be eaten.[15] Of Warsaw, Wraxall wrote, "This metropolis itself seems to me, like the Republic of which it is the head, to unite the extremes of civilization and of barbarism, of magnificence and wretchedness, of splendor and of misery; but, unlike all other great cities of Europe, these extremes are not softened, approximated, and blended by any intermediate gradations. . . . Even Constantinople is in this respect far less barbarous"—not a happy prospect for Thugut.[16]

[12] Maria Theresa's note on Kaunitz to Maria Theresa, May 9, 1779, in Arneth, *Geschichte Maria Theresia's*, 10: 548.

[13] Philipp Cobenzl to Kaunitz, May 28, 1779, in Hanns Schlitter, ed., *Kaunitz, Philipp Cobenzl und Spielmann: Briefwechsel (1779–1792)* (Vienna, 1899), 3–4.

[14] Arneth, *Geschichte Maria Theresia's*, 10: 648.

[15] Wraxall, *Memoirs*, 2: 1–2.   [16] Ibid., 3–4.

It took some time for Thugut to return from the Low Countries, arrange his affairs in Vienna, and make the trip to Warsaw. Even though he received his appointment in December 1779, he did not reach the Polish capital until the end of September 1780, just in time for the opening of the biennial Polish Diet on October 2. The Polish Diet was famous in its own time. An example of aristocratic republicanism gone mad, its most renowned tradition was the *liberum veto*, which demanded that every bill be passed unanimously. If the speaker of the Diet found any objection to a bill before the House, not only did that bill fail, but every bill that had passed in the same session failed as well. By the time Thugut arrived, the Poles were paying heavily for the retention of this and other silly practices, which they referred to collectively as their "sacred liberties." The First Partition of Poland had occurred, and to many observers it was clear that others would follow. Wraxall wrote during his visit in 1779, "I contemplate this country as the most instructive and awful of political lessons: I even esteem myself fortunate in being able to survey it, before Poland sinks and is erased from the list of nations, or is incorporated with the great surrounding monarchies; an event which, according to every appearance, cannot be very distant."[17] Thugut reached a companion opinion of the Diet within a week of his arrival. "Primarily," he informed Kaunitz, "my impression was that the whole Diet seems irrelevant, and, aside from normal business, approached no meaningful matter . . . probably because it would lead to great difficulties and confrontations."[18]

Thugut regarded his first audience with King Stanislaus Augustus as insignificant, telling Kaunitz that the reception followed "all those formalities and honors described by my predecessor."[19] According to others, however, the meeting was more eventful. When Thugut entered the formal audience chamber, he spied in the center of the room a man dressed in

[17] Ibid., 11.
[18] Thugut to Kaunitz, October 4, 1780, Vienna, HHSA, SK, *Polen*, 43.
[19] Ibid.

great finery and surrounded by what seemed to be great noblemen of the realm. Thinking this man to be the king, he approached him making the appropriate reverences and speaking the required words of presentation. The man let Thugut finish and then, with a bemused smile, confessed that he was not the king but the ambassador of Russia and pointed to the king standing in a corner of the chamber. Embarrassed by his mistake and annoyed that the Russian had compounded the embarrassment by letting him finish before revealing the error, Thugut then had to repeat the same introductions to the true king. That evening Thugut joined Stanislaus Augustus and the ambassadors of Russia and Prussia at cards; on two separate occasions during the game he played a jack as trump as if it were a king. The second time he was reproached by his partner for having made the same mistake twice, to which he replied, "Excuse me, I do not know what is happening to me; that is the third time today that I have mistaken a knave for a king." One source commented that Thugut "avenged himself [on the Russian ambassador] quite nicely."[20]

Thugut arrived in Poland during a period of notable national revival. Stung by the First Partition, elements in Polish society were experimenting with various changes in an effort to correct the weaknesses made so obvious in 1772. Included were the founding of new schools emphasizing modern subjects and enlightened views, the publication of books criticizing current political practices and calling for reform, and the beginnings of serious debate on how to improve the country's economy. Although considerable resistance to reform remained, the Diet did approve the creation of a permanent council which, while widely perceived and hated as an instrument of the pro-Russian faction in government, tried to enact a few progressive changes.

One would like to illustrate how Thugut perceived the stirrings of reform within Polish society and reported them to

---

[20] Louis Philippe Ségur, *Mémoires; ou souvenirs et anecdotes* (Paris, 1827), 3: 16; Vehse, *Memoirs*, 2: 303.

Kaunitz; unfortunately, he did not. Thugut never penetrated beneath the surface of Polish life or politics and, for the two years he served as ambassador, sent to Vienna mostly mundane and uninteresting reports.[21] The issues he confronted dealt largely with commercial affairs, notably the sale of Hungarian wine and the importation of salt from the Galician salt works that Austria had acquired as a result of the First Partition. In general Thugut was not happy at being accredited to another eastern European state that seemed on the verge of extinction, and in April 1782 he sent the customary letter to Kaunitz pleading for his recall because of ill health. "My health has greatly worsened since my arrival in Poland; I have suffered recently from serious attacks of dizziness that demand a long effort to get over and consequently prevent me from doing my work."[22] Kaunitz approved the request on condition that he remain through the session of the Diet that was to take place in the autumn. Only at the end of January 1783 did Thugut pay his final respects to Stanislaus Augustus and leave for Vienna. In later years, Thugut expressed no affection and no particular concern for Poland, and he did not hesitate to participate in its destruction as an independent state when he judged it in Austria's interest to do so.

For the next four years Thugut had no exact assignment and left little evidence about his activities. He spent much of the period in Paris, which he had loved so during his first trip there in 1777. He visited libraries, examined collections of art, and wandered through various parts of France, notably Brittany and Normandy, where he purchased some property. During this time he met a few of the men who would play roles in the forthcoming revolution—notably Mirabeau and Talleyrand—but the acquaintances did not apparently lead to friendship. He never mentioned having known any of the great figures of the revolution well, and he certainly did not hint later that he could call upon them in any personal way.

---

[21] Thugut early on even apologized for the low quality of his reports and promised to do better. Thugut to Kaunitz, December 2, 1780, Vienna, HHSA, SK, *Polen*, 43.

[22] Thugut to Kaunitz, April 17, 1782, ibid.

One aspect of Thugut's life during this period did provoke comment from both contemporaries and later historians: he invested money in France, even in French state bonds. Indeed, when Poteratz visited Thugut in early 1796, he hoped that, before resorting to blackmail, he could influence Thugut by promising in the name of the Directory to pay, with interest, the value of the state bonds that Thugut had purchased.[23] This offer did not sway Thugut any more than the threat of blackmail, but the incident shows that at least some of his investments were known.

It is not exactly certain how much or in what he invested. The archives contain an account of Thugut's investments in Paris dated July 31, 1791; the document is difficult to analyze, but it gives a total of 436,128 livres.[24] In October 1820 an official in the Finance Ministry, Simon Schreiber, explained Thugut's investments in France to a representative of the chancellery to aid him in determining how much of them the government as Thugut's heir should try to recover. According to Schreiber, the principal investment Thugut made was in the Paris branch of the English banking house of Boyd, Benfield and Company, called Boyd-Ker and Company. As of October 1793 the total invested was 78,145 francs; the interest earned from that time to March 1818 had reached 95,543.60 francs, making the total 173,689 francs, which, Schreiber added, the banking house was reluctant to pay to the Austrian government. Thugut also owned 38,410 livres in French bonds, which, Schreiber went on, would be redeemed at one-third of their value "as our treaty specified." Besides these formal investments, Thugut also possessed deeds to landed property in Normandy, and Broglie owed him outstanding personal debts.[25]

[23] Poteratz to Thugut, March 8, 1796, in Hüffer and Luckwaldt, eds., *Frieden*, 32–33. Biro, *German Policy*, 1: 461.

[24] Vienna, HHSA, SK, *Grosse Korrespondenz*, 447.

[25] Schreiber to Barbier, October 21, 1820, ibid. The correspondence within the Austrian government concerning Thugut's French investments went on until 1835, when the matter apparently was dropped rather than resolved.

In 1791, as will be seen later, Thugut went to Paris to try to salvage some of his fortune in the wake of the financial upheaval caused by the French Revolution. He had no luck then, and during his years as head of foreign affairs he devoted no time to his personal finances. After his retirement and the restoration of peace between Austria and France in 1801, Thugut turned again to the task of recovering his losses. He requested the secretary Kruthoffer, who had served earlier as a personal agent for him and for Mercy, to represent him in France and to recover his fortune, which he described in the autumn of 1802 as consisting of 40,000 francs owed to him by his tenants in Normandy, 30,000 owed to him by Broglie, and "at least" 160,000 owed to him by Boyd, Benfield.[26] Although he made no mention of state bonds, in another note of January 1802 he wrote, "For some time I have wanted to write to you to thank you for the attention that you have paid to the deplorable debris of my fortune in France, but, aside from my contemptible indolence in all that concerns my proper personal interests, I have found it difficult to quench my vigorous repugnance for those things that remind me of the injustice of those brigands who have overturned France in order to enrich themselves from the public wealth, namely the debts of the state."[27] Whatever the amount Thugut invested in France in the mid-1780s, the money, ironically, was probably the pay that he had received from the French government for his services as an informant. France got its revenge for Thugut's paltry information, but in a way that no one anticipated or wanted.

Thugut never explained why he invested so heavily in French persons, enterprises, and property. Undoubtedly he liked France, and perhaps he planned at this time to retire there on the returns from stocks and bonds and on the rents of his tenants in Normandy. The sums that he received as an informant may have been kept for him in France, and he may have wished to use them there in order to keep them secret

[26] Thugut to unnamed correspondent (probably Jenisch), July 31 and November 26, 1802, ibid.

[27] Thugut to unnamed correspondent, January 10, 1802, ibid.

from the Austrians. That is unlikely, however, because he later showed no hesitation about discussing his French investments among his colleagues in the chancellery. Finally, he may have simply judged investments in France to pay the highest returns at the least risk, certainly an understandable consideration following the repeated failure of Tooke's Levantine schemes. Little did Thugut anticipate that his investments in France would fail him as completely as those he offered to Tooke.

Thugut's sojourn in France came to an end in 1787, when he was appointed Austrian ambassador to the Kingdom of the Two Sicilies. Emperor Joseph wrote to his brother in Florence, "I have decided to write to Thugut, who is in Paris, to see if he will accept this post. . . . He will be quite proper and no one will make fun of him. He will also be able to give good advice to the queen if she will listen to it, for he has spirit and brains."[28] Thugut accepted the position, returned to Vienna for his instructions, and on November 24, 1787, arrived in Naples.

His two previous long-term diplomatic appointments had been to courts that were weak, somewhat pathetic, and seemingly bordering on extinction. Naples was bizarre. The court was partially a Habsburg one. The queen referred to in Joseph's letter was Maria Carolina, younger sister of Joseph and Leopold, tenth daughter and thirteenth child of Maria Theresa. Married to King Ferdinand IV at the age of fifteen, Maria Carolina resembled her mother in three ways: she looked more like her than any of the empress's other children; she had many children herself; and she became deeply involved in affairs of state. Unfortunately, she did not possess her mother's talent for government or her ability to foster the love and respect of her subjects. Her greatest weakness was a tendency to act on impulse rather than careful thought, which brought a confusion in both domestic and foreign affairs and

[28] Joseph to Leopold, March 8, 1787 in Alfred von Arneth, ed., *Joseph II und Leopold von Toscana: Ihr Briefwechsel von 1781 bis 1790* (Vienna, 1872), 2: 73.

which encouraged lethargy within the bureaucracy and intrigue at court.

But if Maria Carolina was inadequate as queen, her husband was hopeless as king. Wrote de Ligne, "The queen of Naples is imprudent, confounded, and compromised by her frequent changes of spirit; but what a king, good God, she has married, a nullity with the courage of a wild pig in flight."[29] Ferdinand vacillated between taking charge of affairs himself and allowing his wife to run everything while he hunted, fished, or exchanged practical jokes and conversation with the common folk in the streets of Naples. As early as 1768 an English observer noted, "His deficiency in delicacy and good sense is by many attributed to an organic defect approaching madness, but Lord Stormont assures me it proceeds totally from want of education."[30] With some luck, even a mercurial queen like Maria Carolina and an oafish king like Ferdinand IV might have found a minister who would serve them with compassion, care, and distinction, but such luck was not theirs. Their principal minister was John Francis Edward, Lord Acton, an English expatriate who dominated governmental affairs by playing the role of queen's favorite—except on those occasions when Ferdinand exerted his authority, at which times Acton deftly switched to playing the role of king's agent. In many ways Acton was as peculiar a personality as the couple he served, and Thugut had nothing but contempt for him. Within two weeks of his arrival Thugut sent to Kaunitz a highly critical analysis of the Neapolitan court "where one carries dissimulation to great lengths." Composing accurate assessments of matters here would be difficult, Thugut advised, not because of too little information but because of too much. The king, queen, and Acton seemed to compete with one another in their rush to tell him secrets. It appeared, nonetheless, that Acton was truly "at the head of all affairs, although the

[29] Quoted in Paul Morand, *Le prince de Ligne* (n.p., 1964), 20.
[30] Quoted in Constance H. D. Giglioli, *Naples in 1799: An Account of the Revolution of 1799 and the Rise and Fall of the Parthenopean Republic* (London, 1903), 2.

king pretends to refuse to make anyone prime minister. . . . But it is a fact that Acton enjoys the confidence of the queen with an assuredness that she will adopt his ideas and, since the queen is sure sooner or later to bend the king to her will, this minister even at this moment decides all the affairs of the realm arbitrarily."[31]

Notwithstanding Joseph's earlier letter to his brother, Thugut's immediate task was not primarily to advise the queen but to find out what Naples planned to do in an upcoming war between Austria and the Ottoman Empire. This conflict, the last of the Austro-Turkish wars, began not because of any serious Habsburg-Ottoman dispute, but because of Vienna's obligations toward Russia. One result of the War of the Bavarian Succession had been a revival of hatred for Prussia among Austrian policy-makers in general and in Kaunitz in particular. Kaunitz determined that, in order to embarrass and perhaps to defeat Prussia in any later confrontation, he must pry Russia away from its pro-Prussian policy and make it a loyal ally of Austria. That required convincing Catherine the Great that an alliance with Austria would be of greater benefit to her than an alliance with Prussia. To achieve this end, Austria must at least allow, if not actually help, the empress to realize her dreams of annexing more territory at the expense of the sultan. Diplomatic probes and exchanges finally led to a secret Austro-Russian alliance in 1781, a provision of which required each ally to offer unlimited support to the other in case either was attacked by the Ottoman Empire.[32]

This new compact was tested first in a crisis involving Russia, the Ottoman Empire, and the Crimea in 1783 and then in another Austro-Prussian confrontation over Bavaria in 1785. Neither difficulty led to war, but the incidents seemed to prove the value of the friendship for both powers. As an expression of this friendship, in the summer of 1787 Joseph joined Catherine in a tour through some newly won and newly improved

[31] Thugut to Kaunitz, December 8, 1797, Vienna, HHSA, SK, *Neapel*, 14.
[32] See Isabel de Madariaga, "The Secret Austro-Russian Treaty of 1781," *The Slavonic and East European Review*, 38 (1959–1960): 114–45.

provinces of southern Russia, a tour that, in the hands of Catherine's favorite minister and lover, Prince Gregor Potemkin, turned into a triumphal parade celebrating Russian strength and modernity. In Constantinople, this flaunting of comradeship by the two Christian rulers was interpreted as a direct threat of if not a first step toward war against the Ottoman Empire. To strike before his enemies were prepared, the sultan declared war on Russia in August 1787; he did not declare war on Austria because he believed the Habsburgs had no designs on Turkey and could be persuaded to remain neutral. Vienna was clearly unhappy about all these events. It regarded the Russian display as so much pretension and the Ottoman declaration of war as so much foolishness. But it had no real choice. The Ottoman Empire had formally declared war on Russia, and the Austro-Russian treaty explicitly stated that, in that event, Austria must aid Russia with all of its might. As Thugut arrived in Naples, the Austrian armed forces were making preparations to march against the Turks.

In earlier Habsburg wars against the Ottomans, Naples had often been an ally. After all, it was a Christian power, and it did have commercial and strategic interests in the Mediterranean, Adriatic, and Aegean seas. But the days of joining the emperor in crusades against the Turks had long since passed, and it was now Thugut's task to find out what policy the Neapolitan court would adopt regarding this new war. As to joining Austria in the fight, Thugut reported that possibility most unlikely. Naples would probably remain neutral, and, in Thugut's mind, that would be best because its armed forces could render Austria practically no assistance. "Generally, the army as well as the navy is still quite insignificant and quite distant from any sudden improvement." Moreover, neither the army nor navy would grow stronger in wartime. "Alone the disorganization and obvious confusion that rule everything here weaken the sources of strength, . . . and it is highly unlikely that anything meaningful can be expected from now on that might aid the interests of the two imperial powers." Better to leave Naples alone, advised Thugut, because its adherence to the Austro-Russian cause would be a liability rather than an asset.[33]

Naples's neutrality in the Austro-Turkish war did not mean that it could not be useful. Since the war had cut communication between Austria and the Ottoman Empire by the traditional overland routes, Naples could now serve as a principal source of information for Vienna about what was happening inside Turkey. This was particularly important not only to provide an avenue of communication in case the Porte wished to send peace probes, but also as a link with various semi-independent provincial governors within the Ottoman Empire who might be willing to promote insurgency behind Turkish lines if Vienna could offer sufficient incentive. Thugut's task then was to establish a rapid and reliable news and postal service from Constantinople and the southern Balkans through Naples to Vienna via Ancona and Trieste. Neither Kaunitz nor Thugut believed this task would be difficult, and both were surprised at the time and effort that it took. For Thugut, the cause of the difficulty lay in the nature of Naples. "I beg Your Highness's patience in that the long delays do not indicate a lack of application on my part. It is impossible to imagine any other place where the grip of chaos that clutches this administration tighter and tighter, where obstacles arise everywhere, and where local conditions are so confused that one could never believe one could find them in any other land."[34]

His primary task may have been to maintain Austrian communications during the war against the Turks, but his office as ambassador, especially Austrian ambassador, made it impossible for him to avoid being drawn into the intrigue that surrounded the Neapolitan court. As the envoy from the principal Habsburg power, he by necessity was closest to the queen. She found him sufficiently sympathetic to warrant some confidences, which in turn brought down upon him the

---

[33] Thugut to Kaunitz, February 3, 1788, Vienna, HHSA, SK, *Neapel*, 14.
[34] Thugut to Kaunitz, July 8, 1788, ibid., 15.

jealous wrath of the favorite, Acton, who "contradicted, sub-
verted, and sabotaged every effort of Baron Thugut to get
along."[35] The pettiness, envy, and rivalry that plagued the
court frustrated Thugut so much that in March 1788 he sent a
personal letter to Joseph bitterly complaining about the plots
and intrigues he had to face.[36] In reply he received from the
emperor a missive that displayed considerable understanding
and sympathy for Thugut's feelings and offered advice as to
how he should act in the future, advice that emphasized primarily patience and caution when dealing with the factions at
the Neapolitan court.[37] Thugut followed this advice as best he
could, but within a year he could stand no more. He submitted
his request for recall, and it was approved. On June 10, 1789,
he gladly left the court that had caused him such frustration
and resentment.[38]

Thugut would have considerable dealings with Naples during the revolutionary wars in his capacity as foreign minister,
and they would be colored greatly by the impressions of the
rulers, court, and people that he had acquired during his posting there. Several years after he had left, he called the court
"vile and ridiculous" and Acton "a most contemptible old
woman."[39] On one occasion in early 1797, when Naples was
encouraging the Papal States to join in concluding peace with
France, he wrote that the whole Neapolitan government was
"exactly like women: when one of them is compromised for
the first time, she works enthusiastically to see to it that all her
neighbors are seduced so that she will not be the only whore
on the block."[40] Of Maria Carolina he thought little better. In

---

[35] Leopold to Joseph, April 27, 1788 in Arneth, ed., *Joseph II und Leopold*, 2: 176.

[36] Thugut to Kaunitz, February 23 and March 27, 1788, Vienna, HHSA, SK, *Neapel*, 14.

[37] Joseph to Thugut, April 12, 1788, in Arneth, ed., *Joseph II und Leopold*, 2: 174–75.

[38] Hadrawa to Kaunitz, June 13, 1789, Vienna, HHSA, SK, *Neapel*, 15.

[39] Thugut to Colloredo, May 29, 1796, in Vivenot, ed., *Vertrauliche Briefe*, 1: 303.

[40] Thugut to Colloredo, January 2, 1797, ibid., 2: 1.

1795, when he heard that she was coming to Vienna to visit her daughter, the wife of Emperor Francis II, he warned, "Her Majesty is . . . the incarnation of curiosity and indiscretion, mixing in politics and affairs great and small. . . . From the highest peer to the chambermaids, no one will escape the most inquisitive examination and each will exaggerate the rumors which our august correspondent will spread to the four corners of the world."[41] Five years later when she again asked to visit, Thugut remarked that her presence "would be more harmful than the loss of a battle."[42]

Thugut clearly believed that his low opinion of Naples and its queen was fully reciprocated, and some historians agree, especially if they read Maria Carolina's correspondence in 1798 and view the Neapolitan court from the perspective of Admiral Horatio Nelson, the British ambassador Sir William Hamilton, and his far more famous wife Emma.[43] However, on a few occasions the queen expressed considerable respect for Thugut. When he received his appointment as foreign minister in 1793, Maria Carolina wrote to her envoy in Vienna, "Give my sincere compliments to Thugut and remind him that I prophesied his promotion, knowing his worthiness to occupy it."[44] After the final partition of Poland, she remarked, "Give my sincere congratulations to the honest and intelligent Thugut on the conclusion of the partition of Poland. He is the helm of the ship in the storm, indeed a steady helm."[45] Finally, on the day before Thugut left Vienna in disgrace following his dismissal in 1801, she lamented, "I swear my heart suffers. This man, in the midst of grave shortages, of insufficient means, was sincerely devoted to the monarchy and the glory of the emperor. We will miss him, and the emperor,

---

[41] Thugut to Colloredo, July 4, 1795, ibid., 1: 235.

[42] Thugut to Colloredo, May 17, 1800, ibid., 2: 218.

[43] Thugut to Colloredo, January 2, 1797, ibid., 2: 1. See Giglioli, *Naples in 1799*, 80.

[44] Maria Carolina to Gallo, April 13, 1793, in Maria Carolina, *Correspondance inédite de Marie-Caroline avec le Marquis de Gallo* (Paris, 1911), 1: 119.

[45] Maria Carolina to Gallo, December 1, 1795, ibid., 332.

tossed about, tormented by a cabal to make this sacrifice, I will pity."[46] In this woman, despite her faults, Thugut had a potential supporter and defender within the Habsburg family, but he felt nothing but scorn for her.

When Thugut returned to Vienna, he found another task awaiting him. The war with the Turks had begun badly for the Austrians, but after some adjustments the Austrians had begun to enjoy success. By the time Thugut reached the capital in the summer of 1789, a combined Austro-Russian army was inflicting serious defeats upon the Turks in Moldavia and Walachia, while another Austrian army was preparing for a siege of the mighty Ottoman fortress of Belgrade, the conquest of which would open the southern Balkans to Habsburg advances. While the military scene was showing promise, however, trouble had appeared on the foreign and domestic fronts. Austria's old nemesis Prussia was showing considerable interest in the war and was hinting that it might organize a coalition with the Ottoman Empire and Britain to force a settlement of its own making upon the warring powers. Should Prussia enter the conflict on the Turkish side, Austria would be hard-pressed to defend itself on two fronts. Besides this danger from abroad, upheaval was threatening at home. In the autumn of 1789, open rebellion erupted in the Austrian Netherlands, and stirrings of revolt were spreading throughout Hungary and Galicia. In the face of these troubles, peace with the Turks was becoming absolutely necessary. When Thugut reported to the chancellery, he was ordered to be ready at any time to open talks.[47]

Negotiations of a sort had already begun while Thugut was in Naples. Vienna had retained official contact with the Turks through the French ambassador at the Porte and had granted to the Austrian commander in Walachia, Field Marshal Josiah

[46] Maria Carolina to Gallo, March 30, 1801, ibid., 2: 225.
[47] See Joseph II to P. Cobenzl, July 21, 1789, in Sébastien Brunner, ed., *Correspondances intimes de l'empereur Joseph II avec son ami le comte de [Philipp] Cobenzl et son premier ministre le prince de Kaunitz* (Mainz/Paris/Brussels, 1871), 89–90.

von Saxe-Coburg, the authority to meet with his Ottoman counterpart and to arrange peace in the field. But by the autumn of 1789, no progress toward a settlement had been made. Moreover, rumors were spreading that the Russians had opened separate talks already with the Turks, and the Austrians feared that their ally might conclude a surprise treaty and leave them to fight alone. To get Austro-Turkish talks underway, Vienna decided to send a special delegation to Saxe-Coburg's camp to take over the peacemaking process. The men Vienna appointed to lead it were Thugut and the recent Austrian ambassador to the Porte, Peter Herbert-Rathkael. But Herbert was in Belgium at the time, and Vienna was eager to get talks started; thus, Thugut was ordered to set out on his own, which he did on December 19, 1789. Since Saxe-Coburg still held the formal peacemaking authority, Thugut needed a title to give him significant official status. The one chosen was commissioner of "the interim government of the districts in Moldavia and those in Walachia occupied by the army of Saxe-Coburg."[48] A bit clumsy, but Thugut was told not to be concerned about administration; peace was his object.[49]

For the first time in thirteen years, Thugut was heading east to do business with the Turks. And he hated it. To his old friend Jenisch he complained of the bad roads, bad weather, bad air, and expressed his own lack of enthusiasm. His hope was to reach Bucharest, where Saxe-Coburg had his headquarters, do his job, and go home, all in as short a time as possible.[50] When Thugut arrived, this hope was quickly disappointed. The Russians, he discovered, were neither actively engaged in peace talks, nor eagerly preparing for another campaign, nor willing to join the Austrians in opening negotiations, nor interested in an armistice.[51] He learned that

[48] Official appointment dated December 10, 1789, Vienna, HHSA, SK, *Türkei*, 5: 24.
[49] Instructions dated December 19, 1789, ibid.
[50] Thugut to Jenisch, January 3, 1790, ibid., *Grosse Korrespondenz*, 447.
[51] Robert Golda, "Der Friede von Sistov" (Ph.D. diss., University of Vienna, 1941), 45.

a representative of Saxe-Coburg was at Ottoman headquarters with instructions to arrange a truce but that the Turks seemed indifferent. Within a month of his arrival, Thugut advised Vienna that peace talks were utterly stalled, and no one seemed to care about seriously starting them. He recommended that other avenues of negotiation be sought, especially through the French ambassador in Constantinople. In reply, Vienna ordered him to stay where he was and to keep trying.[52]

Throughout the spring of 1790 no progress was made toward peace in Walachia, but combat picked up again, and rather unexpectedly Thugut found himself in the middle of an engagement. In early April the eighty-year-old Turkish grand vizier died—a man Thugut believed was delaying the talks—and, to show the new one that Austria still meant business, Saxe-Coburg besieged a Turkish bridgehead at Georgiu. The Turks protested the move but seemed willing to engage in talks if the siege were raised. To encourage such sentiments, Coburg ended the siege and ordered his soldiers to observe a fourteen-day cease-fire. To the Austrians' surprise, as they were evacuating the siege works the Turkish defenders poured from their positions and attacked the now exposed Habsburg troops. Among them was Thugut. Panic set in, and the Austrians began to flee. According to official and unofficial sources, Thugut drew his ceremonial dagger and, under considerable Turkish gunfire, rallied a few men to his side. He managed to hold off an assault, enabled additional Austrians to escape, and was nearly captured himself.[53] It was a courageous act for the only civilian in the trenches.

Some of Thugut's critics have argued that his experience in the siegeworks of Georgiu convinced him that he possessed exceptional military ability and gave him the arrogance to give advice and orders to senior military commanders during the wars of the revolution. If he was proud of his deed at Georgiu, however, he never mentioned it in his writings. Nor did he

[52] Ibid., 45–50.
[53] Dietrichstein to the Duc d'Angoulême, n.d. but circa September 1790, Vienna, HHSA, SK, *Grosse Korrespondenz*, 443.

ever suggest that he had unusual military talents. Then and later he was content to leave warfare to the specialists, if they performed satisfactorily. As with most of his deeds, he shrugged off his act of courage as being in the line of duty.

In his main task—finding an end to the Austro-Turkish war—Thugut was making no progress, but he did find some comfort in knowing that peace efforts were proceeding elsewhere. As Thugut was bouncing along wintry roads on his way to Bucharest, Emperor Joseph had died and was succeeded by his brother Leopold, who had opposed the war from the beginning.[54] Leopold was determined to end it quickly and tactfully so that he could confront the other troubles plaguing the monarchy in relative peace. The reason the conflict was continuing, he believed, was Prussia's encouragement to the Ottoman Empire to fight on; to stop the war, then, it was necessary to contact not Constantinople, but Berlin. In March 1790, Leopold informed the king of Prussia, Frederick William II, of his willingness to reach an accord that would include a basis for ending the Austro-Turkish war. This proposal led to the Convention of Reichenbach in June 1790, which called for the mediation of Britain and Prussia in ending the war on the basis of status quo ante bellum.

It took time for the results of the Reichenbach agreement to reach the wilds of Walachia, where Thugut and the others were waiting. Not until August 11 did an official Prussian mediator reach Ottoman headquarters so that both the Austrian and Turkish field commanders could announce the end of military operations.[55] Shortly afterward, Herbert arrived in Bucharest, and that was the signal for Thugut to request his

[54] Upon hearing of Joseph's death, Thugut wrote to Jenisch, "You can conceive easily all of the distress that we have had here since the arrival of the news of the death of His Majesty; happily, the new master that heaven has granted us is quite likely to quiet our fears; he is just, good, and beneficent, and he will be able to establish in all the monarchy the same order that foreigners have so admired in Tuscany. The people have enjoyed prosperity there that certainly had been unknown to them." Thugut to Jenisch, March 11, 1790, ibid., 447.

[55] Golda, "Friede von Sistov," 78.

recall once again. His presence was no longer needed, he advised Kaunitz, because the important issues had already been decided at Reichenbach. Besides, his health (always convenient) was suffering from the pestilential environment of Walachia, and he was seriously concerned about his financial affairs in France, where the revolution had put his investments in considerable jeopardy.[56] Herbert could carry on alone, Thugut concluded, and he wished to return home.

On September 19, 1790, the armistice between Austria and the Ottoman Empire received formal approval by the two sides, and the fighting officially stopped. Shortly thereafter, Thugut left Bucharest for Vienna, and not too long after that he set out for Paris to assess the state of his investments. There he would meet the French Revolution in one of its tumultuous phases, and it would give him an experience that would both facilitate his advancement and change his perceptions of politics and policy for the remainder of his life.

[56] Ibid., 79. Thugut to Kaunitz, August 27, 1790, Vienna, HHSA, SK, *Friedensakten*, 104.

CHAPTER IV

REVOLUTION,

1791–1793

WHEN THUGUT arrived in Vienna in the autumn of 1790, the French Revolution had been underway for well over a year. But it had also reached a lull. The exciting events of June–October 1789 were a year old, and the Constituent Assembly that had come into being was still debating the details of the constitution that it would present to the citizens and their king. But few persons who mattered seemed content. The Jacobin clubs were meeting, conspiring, and debating what causes they should support or oppose; leaders like Abbé Sieyès, Mirabeau, and Lafayette were uttering platitudes while keeping wary eyes on one another's ambitions; the first émigrés were gathering in the German cities along the Rhine to utter threats and to issue pronouncements about what they were going to do to the rabble who had taken away their power and property; and the king and queen of France were publicly receiving all sorts of individuals while privately plotting either to restore their former authority or to run away. In other words, France appeared calm, but considerable turbulence remained beneath the surface.

Vienna's current policy toward the revolution was one of noninterference. Emperor Leopold still faced extraordinary difficulties in pacifying his own provinces, and he certainly did not intend to extricate Austria from a conflict with Turkey in order to plunge into another with France. Indeed, he looked upon the pacification of the Austrian Netherlands as so much more important than events in France that in August 1790 he ordered Marie Antoinette's most trusted friend and adviser, Mercy d'Argenteau, to leave Paris for the Hague, where he was to negotiate with representatives from Prussia, Britain, and Holland on how to restore Habsburg rule in Belgium.[1] Even after the talks ended, Mercy did not resume his old post in Paris but served instead as chief administrator of the Austrian Netherlands.

Even so, Mercy remained in close contact with the French king and queen, and in January 1791 they informed him that they were planning to flee Paris for the friendly confines of the Austrian Netherlands—and his authority. Mercy promptly passed this news to Vienna, where it generated little enthusiasm. Leopold advised his sister not to attempt such a flight except in close cooperation with foreign support that could come to the royal family's rescue in case of an emergency—foreign support that at that time seemed unlikely—while Kaunitz openly doubted that the royal family's departure from Paris would be beneficial to Austria, France, the conservative cause, or the family itself. Despite this cool response to their proposal, the king and queen were more determined than ever to escape after events in the spring of 1791 reminded them forcefully of their deteriorating status in Paris. Toward the end of May, Marie Antoinette informed her brother that the plans to flee were ready. Late in the evening on June 20, 1791, the king, queen, children, and a few servants left Paris in a huge carriage bound for Belgium. They rode without incident to the town of Varennes, where they were recognized, arrested, and escorted back to Paris. A new period of turbulence erupted in revolutionary France.

In the midst of all of this excitement was Thugut. He ar-

---

[1] Mercy "welcomed with joy" the opportunity to leave Paris. Claude, Comte de Pimodan, *Le comte F.-C. de Mercy-Argenteau* (Paris, 1911), 261.

rived in Paris in mid-May, witnessed with some anxiety the Parisian reaction to the flight to Varennes, and left in mid-August. For us the question is: what was he doing there? Some contemporary and later observers have assumed that he must have been involved in the royal family's plans to escape and probably in its conspiracies to return to power. Hormayr declared that Thugut was the man in charge of the negotiations with Mirabeau on behalf of Marie Antoinette and faulted him for not speeding the talks in anticipation of the Frenchman's demise in early April.[2] Later on, Hormayr continued, Thugut turned to Maximilian Robespierre and his brother Augustine to save the queen but achieved no success. The brothers accepted his bribes but did nothing for fear of the crowds.[3] Unable to negotiate or to bribe the royal family back into power, Thugut then helped them to escape. In his memoirs Hammer confirmed that Thugut prepared the flight, a contention endorsed by the British ambassador to the Hague, Lord Auckland, who wrote to his foreign minister in late June 1791 that "the Prince of Orange assures me that he has an absolute knowledge, in confidence, of a plan of *contre-révolution*. M. Thugut, an Imperial Minister, has been employed at Paris in this business, and also probably in the escape of the royal family."[4]

Actually, Thugut was not involved directly in any of this activity. In late August 1791 he sent to the influential court secretary in Vienna, Anton Spielmann, a report detailing his movements from May to August and offering observations on what he had seen during that time, observations that he would not soon forget. Indeed, perhaps no single document is more important than this one for understanding Thugut's later views of the French Revolution and the influence of these

[2] Hormayr, *Lebensbilder*, 1: 318.
[3] Ibid.
[4] Hammer, *Erinnerungen*, 175. Auckland to Grenville, June 25, 1791, in Great Britain, Historical Manuscripts Commission, *The Manuscripts of J. B. Fortescue, Esq., preserved at Dropmore* (London, 1894), 2: 106–107 (hereafter cited as *Dropmore Papers*).

views on his foreign policy.[5] In mid-May, began his report, he passed through Brussels on his way to Paris, where he hoped to salvage some of his personal investments from the financial chaos brought on in France by the revolution. He had no official duties either in Belgium or in France, but he planned to remain in touch with Mercy in Brussels and with the Austrian legation secretary in Paris, Count Franz Paul Blumendorf, who was conducting business there on the emperor's behalf. In Brussels Thugut learned that a plot of some kind involving Marie Antoinette and Louis XVI was afoot. "I was instructed in confidence that the aristocratic party planned some *coup d'é-clat*; Count Mercy even mentioned a project of escape for the royal family." Thugut remarked that he found the plot interesting, but foolish, especially considering the persons who now surrounded the queen. "It appeared to me a great danger," he told Spielmann, "that such an enterprise would have been undertaken by a party that possessed absolutely no brains and no sense." Perhaps an observation made with the benefit of hindsight, it nonetheless sounds like a point that would have occurred to the unromantic Thugut at the time.

Forewarned that something was about to happen, Thugut left Brussels for Paris. There he found that a forthcoming royal betrayal of the revolution and an imagined role for him in it were no secrets. The revolutionary broadsheets, Thugut noted, portrayed him daily as the villain in charge of clandestine negotiations, and "every step I took was watched by patriots." To discourage these suspicions as much as possible, Thugut avoided all contact with the royal family other than to notify the queen through Blumendorf that he was in town. He even declined to send letters outside the country for fear that they would only fuel rumors of royal plots and his involvement in them.

For the first month he concerned himself "with my own affairs and my own amusements." Then in mid-June he re-

[5] Thugut to Spielmann, August 25, 1791, Vienna, HHSA, SK, *Intercepte*, 2.

ceived a message from Blumendorf informing him that an event was coming that would "expose me to great risks" and advising him to prepare to leave Paris.[6] Thugut told Blumendorf that such preparations would only heighten suspicions of himself and the royal family and that he intended to carry on as if nothing unusual were happening. He still did not know what was planned and did not find out until all of Paris did. "Early one morning I understood by the general commotion in the streets that in effect the royal family had fled." He and Blumendorf, who had also remained in Paris, feared that the crowd would seize both them and the embassy, and "it was not until the king returned to Paris that things calmed down little by little." Thugut dared not leave right away, because a hasty departure "would have only confirmed the rumors that I had been involved in the flight of the queen." Since he had already told friends that he planned to leave Paris in mid-August, he decided to hold rather closely to that date. He departed the city for Brussels on August 11.

Having recounted for Spielmann his actions during the momentous days surrounding the flight to Varennes, Thugut then remarked on the Paris that he had seen and the new social and political system that he had observed. As to the city, it was certainly no longer the Paris he had grown fond of. "In spite of my predilection for a stay in Paris, I left this time not only without pain but without pleasure. This city, up to now the center of life's joys, has become in effect only a haven of scoundrels; individual security and tranquillity have ceased. There are efforts to restore a little order, but the lack of means available to the new regime makes it difficult." Especially cursed, he added, was the rule of the mob and its lack of re-

---

[6] Blumendorf wrote to Mercy: "One [Marie Antoinette] has ordered me to say to Baron Thugut that, circumstances not being advisable [for her] to see him personally but being afraid that he may encounter some troubles in Paris, he should be prepared to depart; she gave me the same advice in order not to be exposed to any affront by the people." Blumendorf to Mercy, June 14, 1791, in Florimund Mercy-d'Argenteau, *Le comte de Mercy-Argenteau et Blumendorf* (Brussels, 1919), 146.

spect for intelligence—an observation especially dear to Thugut, who realized that, given his common birth, his abilities and education were the keys to his success in life. The crowd made such a fetish of equality and democracy, he remarked, that any man with some talent or virtue was condemned to ridicule and scorn. "All disfavor is always against the man who is a little above the ordinary." And this foolishness seemed unlikely to cease in the foreseeable future. The "philosophers of equality and the French politicians" were outdoing one another in pandering to the feelings of the crowds in the streets, with almost continuous upheaval the result.

But, Thugut warned, this upheaval did not mean that France was in such chaos that it posed no danger to the rest of Europe. Should the revolution develop a system by which to promote its doctrines outside France, Europe, especially the Habsburg Monarchy, would have to undertake serious measures to overturn it. Wrote Thugut, "If the democratic regime there ever acquires any consistency and starts to spread the misfortune with which Europe is threatened, I would not hesitate to give all my support to the most vigorous means to pull this evil up by the roots, to make of these scoundrels an example that would dissuade forever those tempted to imitate it, and profit at the same time by the opportunity to deprive France of its former preponderance that it has so often abused vis-à-vis the other European courts." The dangerous France of old, reinforced by a new ideology that would appeal to the common people of all nations, was a fearful prospect for the stability and security of the rest of Europe.

These views of the French Revolution, as Thugut saw it in the summer of 1791, determined his interpretation of the revolution from then on. The revolution remained for him a menace in European affairs, a menace different from any before. While obsessed with the revolution, Thugut never carefully defined it in his own words. He relied on others for that, first Mercy and later the conservative Swiss observer Jacques Mallet du Pan. In Thugut's mind the revolution never represented a system of philosophical or political principles in action, nor was it a form of class warfare in which one could identify the enemy with particular social groups and their leaders. His favorite term to label the revolution and what it stood for was "democracy," which he used in no exact sense but as an epithet covering all the evils that the revolution represented in his mind. The revolutionary leaders—whether they be Girondists, Montagnards, Thermidorians, or Bonapartists—were "sans-culottes" or "Jacobins," labels that Thugut used as loosely as twentieth-century folk use "Bolshevik," "Communist," or "Fascist." For Thugut the revolution was a force that had somehow reinvigorated an old and usually threatening power, and had made it doubly dangerous by associating it with ideas that even non-Frenchmen found appealing. And these ideas, backed by French arms, could subvert the European order of things including the Habsburg Monarchy, if the monarchy and the rest of Europe did not take adequate precautions. Revolutionary ideology as such was a threat, but it was secondary to the threat of a new and mightier France that employed social revolution as inspiration and justification for aggression. For that reason, Thugut would rely less on propaganda and more on armed force when he later did battle with the France of the revolution.

In mid-1791, however, Thugut did not yet believe that Austria needed to engage in open warfare against revolutionary France. First of all, the monarchy was in no condition militarily or domestically for such a project; second, the revolution had not yet found the "consistency" that Thugut had mentioned in his report as necessary for it to endanger the rest of Europe. For the present, Thugut advised Spielmann, the Habsburg Monarchy should support as best it could the moderate leaders of the National Assembly, advise Louis XVI to accept the new constitution then being formulated, and seek through that constitution to encourage some moderating changes. This advice hints at a principle to which Thugut adhered throughout his days as foreign minister: although the revolution was indeed a force that must be resisted without respite from the outside, the only way to bring it under control permanently was from within France. Only when men of moderation and sanity assumed control in France would the country again be able to play a respectable role in the European society of states. And that clearly did not mean a thorough restoration of the *ancien régime*, which, Thugut believed, would be tantamount to restoring all of the causes of the French Revolution. Throughout the revolutionary period, Thugut had no use for the French pretender or the émigrés, and he always resisted suggestions from his allies—especially Russia—that the emperor announce his intention to restore the Bourbons to the French throne. Of the later French pretender, the Count of Provence and future Louis XVIII, Thugut wrote that the allies should not even try to return him to France because "The truth is that no one likes Monsieur, that no one wants to see him reign."[7] Of the émigrés he remarked with considerable contempt, "Why do the Jacobins shoot their émigré prisoners? They should let them all get together, and in a few days they would have imitated spiders and eaten each other."[8]

In concluding his observations to Spielmann, Thugut reflected upon the impact that his recommendations would have upon his own material fortune, a subject not without interest to Spielmann, who had loaned him money. "And so my dear and old friend," wrote Thugut, "when I advocate rigorous measures vis-à-vis France, it is out of pure conviction and zeal, since it is likely that, if France has to fight a war now, it will not be able to avoid bankruptcy and in the middle of that I will be reduced to penury." As to future plans, he wished to spend September in Brussels and then travel to Italy via Innsbruck.

Yet Thugut did not leave Brussels in the autumn of 1791. He remained there and joined a group that appeared to be a party promoting the cause of Marie Antoinette, but which really became something of a "think tank" for Austria on the

[7] Thugut to L. Cobenzl, September 6, 1795, Vienna, HHSA, SK, *Russland*, 2: 179.

[8] Quoted in Léonce Pingaud, *Un agent secret sous la révolution et l'empire: Le comte d'Antraigues* (Paris, 1894), 179.

French Revolution. Like so many "think tanks" of twentieth-century countries, it offered not only information and analyses but also specific points of view that it encouraged the government to accept. The group met most often at the Hotel Bellevue in Brussels, at the apartment of Quentin Crawford, an Englishman who had lived for some time in Paris and had become known to the fashionable and literary worlds there, including the society surrounding the French queen.[9] The core of the group—besides Thugut and Crawford—included Mercy, still in Brussels; Axel von Fersen, the romantic Swedish courtier who had planned the flight of the king and queen; Count Louis-Englebert de Lamarck, who had served as middleman between Mirabeau and the French court; Franz von Metternich, the great Metternich's father and after June 1791 Mercy's replacement as minister plenipotentiary of the Austrian Netherlands; Lord Auckland, British ambassador to the Hague; and Ivan Simolin, Russian ambassador to France, who joined the group after he left Paris in early 1792. But the heart, mind, and soul of the group was Mercy. After all, he had been Marie Antoinette's closest adviser, was in direct correspondence with the policy makers in Vienna, and, most importantly, was the most perceptive and persuasive of them all in his views of the revolution. Notably absent from the group were Frenchmen. Aside from de Lamarck and occasionally Baron Louis Auguste Breteuil, who served as Louis XVI's personal representative outside of France, these individuals by and large rejected association with the French émigrés and counterrevolutionaries swarming about Brussels. Mercy especially warned Vienna against listening to such persons, including the royal princes, whom he labeled a "swarm of intriguing fugitives." "It seems to me that the first condition to impose upon them," Mercy advised Kaunitz, "is that they play no role in anything that we undertake on their behalf."[10]

[9] William Eden, First Baron Auckland, *The Journal and Correspondence* (London, 1862), 3: 42; H. Arnold Barton, *Count Hans Axel von Fersen* (Boston, 1975), 138.

[10] Mercy to Kaunitz, July 18, 1791, Vienna, HHSA, SK, *Frankreich*, 180.

Mercy's essential message to Vienna was that the French Revolution had unleashed the irrational side of human nature and this made it impossible to predict accurately the course that it would take. The only certainty was that, whatever course it followed, it would be dangerous for the rest of Europe. In August 1791 Mercy sent Kaunitz an essay written by M. de Pellenc, a former secretary of Mirabeau and later associate of Thugut (some suspected him of being Thugut's most influential adviser), which Mercy characterized as conforming exactly to his view of the revolution and of what made it so difficult to comprehend. "It is the entire nation that is agitated," the essay read. "There are two thousand causes for every event, and so an analysis of all the causes becomes impossible. Each man who is only an instrument today becomes a leader tomorrow. When one restores calm at one place, troubles begin in another. . . . One thing only is constant: the nature of the illness, because there are really only changes in symptoms. The cause of the illness is in having given to the multitude an impact that public opinion has everywhere more authority than the administrators and tribunals."[11] Besides the observations of Pellenc, Mercy also sent the views of the famous British conservative, Edmund Burke, which he strongly recommended to Kaunitz.[12] The revolution, Mercy emphasized again and again, was a serious danger that must be studied carefully before it could be confronted effectively.

Despite observations and warnings such as Mercy dispatched, the group in Brussels only marginally influenced the policy makers in Vienna. When the revolution first erupted in 1789, Leopold had welcomed it as a victory for the constitutional principles that he had been promoting for most of his political life. The violent events of 1789 had tempered that positive view, but Leopold insisted on following a policy of noninvolvement despite complaints from his sister about the treatment that her family was enduring at the hands of the

[11] Mercy to Kaunitz, August 13, 1791, ibid.
[12] Mercy to Kaunitz, September 4, 1791, ibid.

revolutionaries. Kaunitz had certainly endorsed Leopold's policy, not only because he doubted that Austrian interference in French politics could accomplish any good, but also because, in terms of general European foreign affairs, the revolution had in his mind rendered France diplomatically and militarily impotent, a condition that might be exploited in some way to Austria's advantage.

The flight to Varennes, while not necessarily altering the views held by Leopold and Kaunitz, did require a response from Vienna, if only because the king and queen were actually made prisoners and because the events created such a sensation. The initial response was the Circular of Padua, issued on July 6 from the city where Leopold was vacationing. It invited the other great European powers to join the emperor in discussing how to assure the safety of the king and queen and how to maintain monarchical government in France.[13] The circular led rather quickly to a preliminary Austro-Prussian agreement on July 25, which was actually the culmination of earlier talks concerning Poland but which nevertheless bound both powers to cooperate in future policies toward France. This agreement in turn led a month later to the Declaration of Pillnitz, in which Leopold and King Frederick William II of Prussia warned the revolutionary leaders that events in their country were matters of concern to all the states of Europe and that Austria and Prussia would use military force to restore freedom of movement and authority to Louis XVI and to implement a new, moderate French constitution if (an important "if") the other states of Europe would assist Vienna and Berlin in doing so. As is well known, the purpose of this declaration was not to justify Austro-Prussian military intervention in

---

[13] What Leopold hoped to gain by the Circular of Padua and the subsequent Declaration of Pillnitz is subject to discussion if not to real debate. See especially Jacques Godechot, *The Counter-Revolution: Doctrine and Action, 1789–1804* (New York, 1971); Adam Wandruszka, *Leopold II* (Vienna/Munich, 1965), 2: 361; and Placid Genelin, "Leopolds II äussere Politik," *Dreizehnter Jahresbericht über die deutsche Staats-Oberrealschule im Triest* (1882–1883), 1–4.

France, but both to warn the revolutionaries that other powers were paying close attention to events in France and to moderate the "various, partly fantastic, partly exorbitant" statements about what monarchs should do to revolutionaries issued by the French émigrés, particularly by the king's brother, the Count of Artois. Leopold in fact emphasized in public statements that he planned no war and that, if Louis XVI accepted the new French constitution that was nearing completion, he would regard the whole affair as closed.[14]

Louis accepted the new constitution, but the affair was by no means closed.[15] The constitution created the Legislative Assembly in France, which was far more radical than the Constituent Assembly had been and just as eager to make its mark on the progress of the revolution. The Legislative Assembly decided that pronouncements such as the Circular of Padua and the Declaration of Pillnitz and the activities of the émigrés were in fact serious threats to the revolution. On November 29, 1791, it called upon Louis XVI to insist that the emperor and the elector of Trier (in whose lands many émigrés had congregated) disperse the fledgling armed force of émigrés and that states of the Holy Roman Empire cease their demands for compensation for various feudal lands in Alsace owned by German lords and confiscated during the course of the revolution. To show that it was serious, the assembly authorized the mobilization of an army on France's northeastern frontier. The resolution of November 29 represented the first step toward war, and over the next few months increasingly strident warnings and threats by both sides finally led to a formal declaration of war by the assembly against the king of

[14] Wandruszka, *Leopold II*, 2: 367.
[15] The new constitution, wrote Kaunitz, "makes France less dangerous for all of Europe than [it was] under the old government. If it is bad, it disturbs only France, and for the other states is of no importance. The perceived danger of an infection of other peoples by the bad example of the French is no more than a blind alarm and a phantom long laid to rest by events." Quoted in Viktor Bibl, *Kaiser Franz* (Leipzig/Vienna, 1938), 33.

Bohemia and Hungary on April 20, 1792. By omitting Prussia and the other German states, Paris hoped to keep them neutral.[16] In any case, the wars of the French Revolution were underway.

Throughout this steadily worsening international crisis, Thugut remained with the group in Brussels. The members had anticipated that war would erupt, but they had not necessarily looked forward to it. Mercy had repeatedly underscored the unpredictable nature of the revolution, and no one, he believed, could foresee the result if an international war were added to France's internal convulsions. In December 1791 Mercy had written to Kaunitz that "war is coming, as is a republic," but that it would be difficult to say what either would be like. The Jacobins, he speculated, probably wanted a war only against the émigrés, but other Frenchmen wanted a total war of peoples against their kings. Which side would win out—or whether some other faction would define the goals of the struggle—he did not know.[17] But regardless of internal French politics, Mercy warned, Vienna must be careful about what it announced it was fighting for and against. The French people might loathe the Legislative Assembly, but they would rise up to defend their country against an outside enemy no matter what government existed in Paris. And, Mercy went on, Vienna must not offer the French people the émigrés or the Bourbon princes as the only alternative to the revolutionary government. The revolutionaries might be widely criticized, but they were hated much less than the émigrés, who consisted of "nobles, clerics, parlementarians, former courtiers, and the former privileged: in other words a class of people whose personal interests are directly opposed to the

[16] There was no formal emperor at this time. Leopold died on March 1, and his successor would not be crowned until July. For a discussion of the steps leading to war, see T.C.W. Blanning, *The Origins of the French Revolutionary Wars* (Harlow, 1986), 69–130.

[17] Mercy to Kaunitz, December 24, 1791, Vienna, HHSA, SK, *Frankreich*, 180.

interests of the whole." A crusade to restore these elements to power in France would end in nothing but disaster.[18]

One should not, however, assume from Mercy's words that the Brussels group opposed war altogether. It favored action on the part of the emperor and his allies, especially as the months wore on and the Legislative Assembly became increasingly radical. Many in the group, including Thugut, complained that Leopold was not moving decisively enough and that his inaction was only making the French leaders more reckless in both their internal and foreign policies. Indeed, when Leopold died suddenly on March 1, 1792—an event judged by many since as a serious misfortune for the subsequent history of the Habsburg Monarchy—Thugut and others in Brussels were not unhappy. Fersen remarked in his diary, "In all the societies yesterday evening, the death of the emperor had little effect and did not stop the parties. The generals did not show the least chagrin but almost the contrary. Thugut told the Baron [Breteuil] that he was relieved."[19] Their hope was that the new ruler, Leopold's young son Francis, would take up arms quickly and decisively against the revolutionaries.

When the war began in April 1792, Vienna and Berlin were confident of victory. The king of Prussia, while obligated by treaty to provide only a limited number of troops because France had formally declared war only on Austria, decided nevertheless to mobilize a full army to make certain that at the peace talks he could demand indemnities suitable to his sacrifices.[20] Some Austrian officers referred to the upcoming campaign as a *Spaziergang*, a stroll, while a member of the war ministry suggested that, rather than mobilize the entire army, the emperor should send two regiments of Hungarian hussars

---

[18] Mercy to Kaunitz, January 7, 1792, in Ernst Herrmann, ed., *Diplomatische Korrespondenzen aus der Revolutionszeit, 1791–1797* (Gotha, 1867), 135–39.

[19] Quoted in Charles Kunstler, *Fersen et son secret* (Paris, 1947), 253.

[20] Lord, *Second Partition*, 220.

to Paris to disperse the revolutionaries with their lances.[21] Even Kaunitz had little doubt that Austro-Prussian arms would prevail; he feared only that the allies might have an early falling out and perhaps a scramble for spoils before victory was certain. To the Prussian ambassador in Vienna he wrote, "That we will win is obvious; we need only a bit of time to gather our strength. But we must do so! We must not give the enemy time to think, we cannot endure many campaigns; the war must end at one time, with convincing, decisive battles. Jealousy and mistrust must be banned from our circles; each must rejoice at the victories of the other; then our united victory is assured."[22]

Kaunitz's warning should have been heeded, but it was not. Both Prussia and Austria worked not to plan serious strategy but to determine the division of the spoils of war. The armies, each assumed, would face little resistance from the French, so that the efforts of the statesmen could focus from the beginning on compensation for the military efforts. Behind all of the talk of preserving monarchies, preventing the spread of revolution, and maintaining honor and tradition had always lurked the traditional objective of obtaining territory. When the war finally began in earnest, the allied statesmen brought this goal into the open. Vienna offered the first hint on May 4, 1792, when it asked Berlin whether they should ignore all indemnities until the war ended or begin talking about them right away.[23] Berlin responded not merely with an answer to the question, but with a firm offer: Prussia would annex a part of Poland, and Russia would take a portion as well; Austria could appropriate some territory of its choosing on the Rhine.[24] Vienna quickly replied with a proposal of its own: it would not object if Prussia and Russia acquired some Polish

---

[21] Hüffer and Luckwaldt, eds., *Frieden*, xviii.

[22] Quoted in Bibl, *Kaiser Franz*, 34.

[23] Karl Otmar von Aretin, *Heiliges Römisches Reich, 1776–1806* (Wiesbaden, 1967), 1: 263–64.

[24] Lord, *Second Partition*, 313.

land, but Austria had no use for any territory on the Rhine. It would be too far away from the Habsburg heartland, and its annexation would antagonize the French too much. Instead, Vienna revived a cherished project from days gone by: it would exchange Belgium with the House of Wittelsbach for Bavaria and the Upper Palatinate.[25] The Prussians, who had opposed such an exchange so vigorously in the days of Frederick the Great, were far more accommodating this time. To work out the details, they agreed to meet with the Austrians in western Germany in July, when Francis would journey to Frankfurt am Main for what was to be the last coronation of a Holy Roman Emperor.

Such was the talk when Thugut arrived in Vienna in June 1792. He came as an agent of Mercy, who knew that, with the war underway and a new sovereign on the Habsburg throne, Austrian statesmen would be eager to listen to the views and assessments of those who had witnessed the revolution at first hand. Thugut was his man to explain what Austria might encounter in the coming struggle.[26] Thugut was surprised by what he found. No one in Vienna seemed to care particularly about what was happening in France, and no one was eager to learn more about the revolution; rather, most were intent on discussing the gains Austria could achieve at the war's end. In mid-June Thugut had a long conversation with Kaunitz, but the old chancellor appeared largely uninterested in what he had to say.[27] In fact, to Thugut the general atmosphere in Vienna seemed to be one of misplaced interests and priorities, and the reason for it apparently was the accession of a young and inexperienced sovereign and the struggles for influence around him. To Mercy, Thugut wrote that the emperor appeared to mean well, but "unfortunately, the unbelievable piling up of business, the battle of the parties, and other troubles in affairs and measures have caused such complications and

[25] Ibid.
[26] *Allgemeine Deutsche Biographie*, 38: 144.
[27] Thugut to Mercy, June 21, 1791, in ibid.

confusions that one cannot make any sense of the whole and can count on nothing from one day to the next."[28]

No office reflected disarray more than Thugut's own, the chancellery. For the previous forty years the chancellery had been the province of Kaunitz, but, since Leopold's rapprochement with Prussia in mid-1790, the old chancellor had lost the preeminence that he had once enjoyed. Rising to challenge him in decision making were two of his subordinates, Philipp Cobenzl and Anton Spielmann. Neither aroused particular respect, even at the time. Robert Murray Keith, the British ambassador, described Cobenzl as a "superficial dabbler in politics, who possesses little understanding and no firm knowledge." Spielmann Keith portrayed—in a snobbish way—as a "man born in the lowest class of day laborers who has no more education than a common clerk," while Kaunitz "grows weaker year by year and is increasingly supercilious."[29] This view of the chancellery's leadership was endorsed by Archduke Charles, the emperor's brother and future war hero of the monarchy, who warned Francis as early as April 1792 that some changes in that department must be made for the sake of competent government. "It is only Cobenzl who does everything," he wrote, "and flatters himself that he can bring order out of chaos. He follows impulses which Spielmann gives him from time to time. For example, Spielmann says to him: If we go to war against France, we must try to bring order into the affairs of the Netherlands. So Cobenzl immediately goes to work, grabs ideas right and left, thinks he has found the means to solve everything, and has Kaunitz put his elaborate signature on it. Kaunitz no longer reads everything he signs and nobody shows it to the emperor so all is confusion. The crass ignorance that dominates the chancellery in all matters is scandalous." The only solution, he advised Francis, was

[28] Thugut to Mercy, July 4, 1792, in ibid., 145.
[29] Robert Murray Keith to Grenville, May 8, 1792, in Herrmann, ed., *Diplomatische Korrespondenzen*, 218–19.

"either to find the right men or to make them. All will go well as soon as you have competent men making policy."[30]

Francis did not immediately heed his brother's advice; instead, he followed the recommendations of Cobenzl and Spielmann, and they talked of nothing but annexations and compensation. It was Kaunitz who had regularly warned against trusting the Prussians too completely and against rushing into agreements dividing the spoils before the war was won. It was Cobenzl and Spielmann who encouraged the Prussian ties and eagerly sought accommodations specifying the territories that Austria would acquire. In fact, Cobenzl and Spielmann had made the offer to exchange Belgium for Bavaria without Kaunitz's knowledge, an act that infuriated the old man so much that he offered his resignation. Francis eventually accepted it, although he insisted that Kaunitz keep his titles and ordered that all important documents be sent to him for his perusal and advice.

Under the leadership of Cobenzl and Spielmann, the chancellery largely ignored the counsel of the Brussels group. The main concern of the two statesmen was to get firm commitments from Prussia concerning mutual gains. Shortly after the coronation of Francis as Holy Roman Emperor in mid-July 1792, Cobenzl and Spielmann placed the whole question of acquisitions before a conference of the most important Habsburg officials. The conference agreed that the exchange of Belgium for Bavaria was a good one but also instructed Spielmann and Cobenzl to try for more, especially the cession by Prussia of Ansbach and Bayreuth to Austria.[31] Upon hearing of this proposal, the Prussians rejected it but assured Vienna that transactions were possible and invited an Austrian delegation to come to Prussian headquarters to discuss them. Vienna accepted the offer and chose Spielmann as its plenipotentiary. Joining him to offer information and advice would be Mercy coming from Brussels, but since Mercy's

[30] Archduke Charles to Marie Christine, April 20, 1791, in Oskar Criste, *Erzherzog Carl von Österreich* (Leipzig/Vienna, 1912), 1: 47–48.
[31] Aretin, *Heiliges Römisches Reich*, 1: 265.

98

health was notoriously uncertain, on hand to take his place should he become ill would be another officer with firsthand knowledge of the "monstrosity" of the French Revolution, Baron Thugut.[32]

But what about the war against France? Did allied victories warrant confidence in haggling over various parts of Europe? As mentioned earlier, no one had doubted an Austro-Prussian success at the outset. Indeed, as rumors of the Austro-Prussian bargaining talks spread, more concern was expressed in Germany about possible Austrian and Prussian annexations than about the spread of revolutionary principles. In early September Austria and Prussia submitted a formal request to the Diet of the Holy Roman Empire for financial and military assistance in fighting France, but the representatives balked at it, fearing that they would only be aiding the two powers to fulfill their dreams of conquest.[33] Max Franz, elector of Cologne and uncle of Francis II, wrote to the elder Metternich, "All Germany is agitated; one fears the French less than these two powers [Austria and Prussia] and one believes generally that the cure will be worse than the disease."[34] Nothing could better illustrate the Austro-Prussian confidence toward the outcome of the war than the Brunswick Manifesto, issued on July 25, 1792, by the Duke of Brunswick, commander of the Prussian forces, preparatory to his invasion of France. The manifesto reflected perfectly—indeed was probably written by— the émigrés whom the Brussels group had condemned. It vowed to restore the old monarchy by force of arms and promised "an exemplary and unforgettable vengeance" if the progress of the allied armies into France were resisted.[35] Shortly after, the invasion began.

[32] P. Cobenzl to Reuss, September 9, 1792, in Vivenot, ed., *Quellen*, 2: 195–96.

[33] Aretin, *Heiliges Römisches Reich*, 1: 272; John G. Gagliardo, *Reich and Nation: The Holy Roman Empire as Idea and Reality, 1763–1806* (Bloomington, 1980), 142.

[34] Quoted in Max Braubach, *Maria Theresias jüngster Sohn, Max Franz* (Vienna/Munich, 1961), 278.

[35] J. M. Thompson, *The French Revolution* (Oxford, 1966), 310.

As the allied armies marched toward Paris, Mercy and Thugut prepared to join Spielmann to discuss future gains with the Prussians. But before they even set out, disaster struck. On September 20 at Valmy, not far from Varennes, the armed forces of revolutionary France turned back the oncoming Prussians. Of this battle Goethe wrote majestically, "From this place and day commenced a new epoch in the world's history."[36] Of it Edmund Burke wrote less reverently, "The military might of Europe fled before a troop of strolling-players."[37] Whether the battle deserved glorification or ridicule, it began an almost uninterrupted advance for the forces of revolutionary France. On October 4 Worms on the Rhine fell to French troops advancing from Alsace; on October 12 the Prussians fled Verdun; on October 21 the fortress of Mainz surrendered to the French; on November 6 the revolutionary army of Dumouriez defeated the Austrians at Jemappes in Belgium; and on November 14 the French occupied Brussels. The mighty armies of Austria and Prussia recoiled in defeat.[38]

On September 22, two days after Valmy, Thugut left Vienna to join Mercy and Spielmann at Prussian headquarters. He encountered the on-rushing French forces at Speyer on the Rhine and only by "a happy accident" was able to avoid capture.[39] On October 9 he reached Mercy's residence in Luxembourg city, and two weeks later the two of them and Spielmann met with King Frederick William at his headquarters near the village of Merle, an hour's ride from Luxembourg. The king invited the three to dinner on the evening of October 24 but refused to talk about serious matters. Instead he invited them to return the following day, when, he prom-

[36] Quoted in Gunther Rothenberg, *The Art of Warfare in the Age of Napoleon* (Bloomington, 1978), 11.

[37] Quoted in Harvey Mitchell, *The Underground War against Revolutionary France: The Missions of William Wickham, 1794–1800* (Oxford, 1965), 27.

[38] For a discussion of French military strategy from 1792 to Napoleon, see Steven T. Ross, *Quest for Victory: French Military Strategy, 1792–1799* (South Brunswick and New York, 1973).

[39] Thugut to Mercy, October 4, 1792, Vienna, HHSA, SK, *Grosse Korrespondenz*, 447.

ised, he would explain thoroughly Prussia's position on every issue. Mercy and Thugut were not certain what was coming, but Spielmann was. He told his fellow diplomats that he was a lost man.[40]

Spielmann's fears were soon realized. The following day Frederick William presented the envoys with the Verbal Note of Merle. He informed the Austrians that Prussia would continue the war against France but no longer as a major belligerent, only as an Austrian auxiliary. Although since 1791 Prussia had expressed more eagerness than Austria to make war on France and although in the face of defeat Prussian help was needed more than ever, the king now planned to pull most of his forces out of the conflict, leaving perhaps 20,000 to help the Austrians. Even to participate at these reduced levels, Frederick William went on, Prussia must have immediate compensation. Accordingly, he would annex part of Poland as soon as possible, but Austria would have to wait until some unspecified future point to exchange Belgium for Bavaria.[41] Spielmann was stunned. Not only would Austria have to fight on with significantly less assistance, it would have to be content with vague promises of future gains while Prussia annexed thousands of square miles of Poland. Prussia would expand as Austria made sacrifices.

While Spielmann tried to explain the Verbal Note to Vienna, Thugut offered his opinion of the whole business privately to Count Franz de Paula Colloredo-Wallsee, the emperor's old tutor and principal adviser and Thugut's future confidant.[42] The Verbal Note, commented Thugut, proved simply and openly that Prussia was untrustworthy. Since Austria could not depend upon the "frank and loyal cooperation" of Prussia, it must seek other allies as quickly as possible. But more important, Thugut wrote, the Verbal Note could not have come at a worse time, for now the political and military

[40] Lord, *Second Partition*, 355.

[41] Vivenot, ed., *Quellen*, 2: 292–93.

[42] For Spielmann's explanation, see Spielmann to P. Cobenzl, November 6, 1792, in ibid., 2: 338–48.

situations were both as bleak as could be. The Prussian armies were in flight, the Austrians were disorganized, and the French seemed obsessed with an irresistible enthusiasm for victory. "It is possible that I see too much black," summarized Thugut, "that my worries are exaggerated. But I declare to you, Count, that, when I think of our current state of affairs, my head whirls."[43]

Thugut remained in Luxembourg until the Austrian defeat at Jemappes, after which he journeyed to Liège and then to Maestricht to join Mercy again. On this trip he was caught up in the crowds of aristocrats, bureaucrats, émigrés, and common folk fleeing the oncoming French. All was confusion, disorder, and despair. Mercy joined in the flight as well and expressed his grief at what he saw about him. Of the soldiers he wrote, "It is necessary for the debris of the army to find shelter and rest and it will be hard to find either unless the Rhine is a barrier"; of the Habsburg administration in Belgium, "The government, which unfortunately has nothing more to govern, is established here [Wesel] as uncomfortably as it is ruined"; of the refugees in general, "I share with these unfortunates the profound ignorance of where we stand and of all that is going on around us."[44] To Mercy and Thugut, who participated in the Austrian debacle, the situation was black indeed.

To understand truly the emerging force and power of revolutionary France, Mercy believed Vienna must be told in clear and forceful terms of the allied disaster on the Rhine and in the Netherlands, and he knew of no better man to pass on such information than Thugut. To Cobenzl he wrote, "Baron Thugut is returning to Vienna; I am delighted he is going because he can tell you many details that are important to know

[43] Thugut to Colloredo, November 1, 1792, in Vivenot, ed., *Vertrauliche Briefe*, 1: 4–8.
[44] Mercy to Starhemberg, December 11, 1792, in A. Graf Thürheim, ed., *Briefe des Grafen Mercy-Argenteau an den Grafen Louis Starhemberg, 1791–1794* (Innsbruck, 1884), 26–27.

and which are almost impossible to express in writing."[45] Thugut reached Vienna in late December 1792 and, unlike his experience six months earlier, found this time people eager to listen to him. The emperor himself questioned him about the situation in Belgium and even expressed his wish to go there personally to seek the means to rectify it.[46]

Whether or not Thugut realized it as he arrived in Vienna, the events of the first three months of 1793 would vault him from diplomat and sometime political adviser to foreign minister of the Habsburg Monarchy. The conditions for that promotion came into being with the collapse of the foreign policy created by Cobenzl and Spielmann. Weakened by the Verbal Note of Merle at the end of 1792, that policy suffered a second serious blow in early 1793, this time at the hands of the British. Britain was not involved in the war against France in 1792, but the French conquest of Belgium late that year and the execution of Louis XVI in January 1793 convinced the British that they were facing considerable danger.[47] Therefore, on February 1, 1793, Great Britain (and Holland) declared war on France and immediately opened negotiations with Austria regarding a military alliance. In the first discussions, the British made it absolutely clear that they would never allow Austria to exchange Belgium for Bavaria. Keeping Belgium in Austrian hands was essential to British foreign policy, because it would assure the presence of a great power on France's northern border and create a barrier to French expansion northward along the coast of the North Sea.

[45] Mercy to P. Cobenzl, November 21, 1791, Vienna, HHSA, SK, *Frankreich*, 180.

[46] *Allgemeine Deutsche Biographie*, 38: 145–46.

[47] The foreign minister, Lord Grenville, and King George III were especially horrified by the execution of Louis XVI. The prime minister, William Pitt, was alarmed by the conquest of Belgium and the threat that it posed to Holland. McKay and Scott, *The Rise of the Great Powers*, 282–83; John M. Sherwig, *Guineas and Gunpowder: British Foreign Aid in the Wars with France, 1793–1815* (Cambridge, Mass., 1969), 2.

On March 11 a ministerial conference in Vienna considered the British statement, and for some days later its members exchanged position papers concerning it. The majority, led by the grand old man of the Austrian army, Field Marshal Franz Moriz von Lacy, agreed that an alliance with Britain was indispensable at this time and that the Belgian-Bavarian exchange should be abandoned to obtain it.[48] Indeed, Lacy now indicted the exchange in every way: Belgium for Bavaria was at best a poor trade because Belgium returned far more in revenue than Bavaria; Bavaria alone was worth very little strategically while Ansbach and Bayreuth remained in Prussian hands; thoughts of added compensation at French expense, such as Alsace, were extremely speculative; and Cobenzl's and Spielmann's obsession with the exchange was permitting Prussia and Russia a free hand in Poland.[49] Although Lacy's points won agreement from the majority of the conference, Cobenzl was not yet willing to give up his dream. He argued in response that an alliance with Britain was not worth Vienna's giving up the advantages it had painfully extracted from the other powers. Besides, in future negotiations he could persuade London (as he had others) that the exchange was vital to both Austrian security and the European balance of power. As to Poland, Cobenzl was certain that, despite various rumors, Prussia and Russia would do nothing behind Austria's back.[50] For the moment a compromise of sorts was reached. Vienna decided to pursue the British alliance while minimizing but not abandoning the exchange.[51]

Within a week after this compromise was agreed to, however, Cobenzl and Spielmann received the blow that proved absolutely fatal to their policy. On March 23 the Russian am-

---

[48] Supporting Lacy were Colloredo, Prince Georg Adam Starhemberg, and Prince Franz Xavier Rosenberg. Lacy's *Separatvotum*, March 15, 1793, Vienna, HHSA, SK, *Vorträge*, 153.

[49] Ibid.

[50] P. Cobenzl's comments on Protocol of March 11, 1793, ibid.

[51] Thugut's *Memoire* to Mercy, March 18, 1793, in Vivenot, ed., *Quellen*, 2: 504–507.

bassador to Vienna, Count Andrei Razumovsky, and the Prussian resident, M. Caesar, presented a joint statement announcing the Second Partition of Poland, an agreement reached by Russia and Prussia without the participation of Austria. The very thing that Cobenzl had assured the Conference would not take place—a Russo-Prussian arrangement concerning Poland that excluded Austria—had occurred. Cobenzl at first passed the statement to the emperor while declaring himself "in no condition" to present a full report of his own.[52] He quickly realized the peril to his policy, however, and submitted a memorandum pronouncing the Second Partition unfortunate but not serious enough to abandon the close friendship with Prussia or to sacrifice the Belgian-Bavarian exchange.[53] But in fact he and his policy were finished. On March 27 the emperor informed him that he was dividing the chancellery into a ministry of foreign affairs and an office for Italian domestic matters and that Cobenzl would be in charge of the latter.[54] Spielmann fared even worse. The emperor appointed him second delegate for Austria and Burgundy at the Diet of the Holy Roman Empire in Regensburg. He was to prepare to replace eventually the first delegate who was "very old."[55]

The man who assumed directorship of foreign affairs was Thugut, and for us the question is what circumstances in the above events enabled him to rise so high so quickly. In his memoirs, Cobenzl complained that, although his policies did suffer some reversals, he was primarily the victim of intrigue,

[52] P. Cobenzl to Francis, March 23, 1793, Vienna, HHSA, SK, *Vorträge*, 153.

[53] P. Cobenzl to Francis, March 23, 1793, in Vivenot, ed., *Quellen*, 2: 507–16.

[54] Francis to P. Cobenzl, March n.d. [27], 1793, ibid., 541. Thugut wrote on the tenth anniversary of the Second Partition that the Prussian foreign minister Haugwitz had "played with [Cobenzl] like a child." Thugut to Colloredo, January 23, 1803, in Vivenot, ed., *Thugut, Clerfayt und Wurmser*, xvii.

[55] Francis to Spielmann, March n.d. [27], 1793 in Vivenot, ed., *Quellen*, 2: 542.

specifically by a cabal composed of Colloredo, Rosenberg, Prince Ferdinand Trauttmannsdorff, and Thugut.[56] While this contention may reflect pique, other, less personally involved observers wrote at the time of conspiracies, parties, and the "intrigues of subalterns" in the chancellery that would lead to changes.[57]

Thugut was certainly in a good position to exert influence and to engage in intrigue. In late February the emperor appointed him political adviser to the commander of the Austrian armies in Germany, Josiah von Saxe-Coburg (Thugut's old associate from Walachia) and, in conjunction with that appointment, ordered Cobenzl to permit Thugut unlimited access to the chancellery's records, so that "he can learn the greatest detail about my situation vis-à-vis the different powers, the general system of my relations with them, and all of my political views." Moreover, Thugut was to be invited to all the ministerial conferences, not only to listen but so that "the political knowledge and experience acquired by him during his missions to many different foreign courts will enable him at times to present useful observations and ideas."[58] This order was issued by Francis, but it was composed by Thugut himself; the emperor merely approved and signed it. Obviously by late February Thugut had access to the emperor's inner circle.

Besides enjoying the favor of the emperor, Thugut was also winning the approval of other important figures. Mercy was the most eager to see him given a greater voice in foreign policy, but his influence was tempered by his being in Germany. Probably the most important official supporting Thugut in Vienna proper was the emperor's favorite, Colloredo, with whom Thugut was now beginning his extensive correspondence. But the decisive voice in the baron's advancement may

[56] Alfred von Arneth, "Graf Philipp Cobenzl und seine Memoiren," *Archiv für österreichische Geschichte*, 67 (1885): 154–57.

[57] Morton Eden to Grenville, March 23 and 30, 1793, London, Public Record Office, F07 (Austria), 33 (hereafter cited as London, PRO).

[58] Francis to P. Cobenzl, February 24, 1793, Vienna, HHSA, SK, *Vorträge*, 153.

have been that of Kaunitz. Upon announcing Thugut's appointment to the post of foreign minister, Francis wrote to the venerable chancellor, "I am informed of his feelings of admiration and attachment for you, and I realize that he has had the honor of being trained by your instructions and formed by your principles."[59]

It certainly appeared that Thugut represented a return to Kaunitz's principles, the most important being a profound distrust of Prussia. Since the mid-1780s Habsburg foreign policy had oscillated between those advocating hostility toward Prussia—represented by Kaunitz—and those advocating reconciliation and even cooperation with Prussia—represented by Cobenzl and Spielmann and endorsed by Joseph II and Leopold II. In the conference meetings debating the alliance with Britain and the Belgian-Bavarian exchange, Thugut argued persuasively that the latter had to be sacrificed for the former precisely because Austria had now to attach itself to Britain since Prussia had proved to be an utterly unreliable friend. In fact, Thugut contended, Prussia's recent actions had clearly shown that it was downright dangerous to be Prussia's friend. "Has not the court of Berlin twice guaranteed, by solemn treaty, the integrity of its ally, Poland?"[60] The news of the Second Partition convinced the conference that Kaunitz's suspicion of Prussia had been the correct position all along, and now Thugut had emerged as the most visible spokesman for that position.

But Habsburg policy toward Prussia was not the only issue on the conference's agenda at this time; indeed, it was not even the most important one. The primary issue was the French Revolution and what to do about it, and in this matter Thugut had recognized credentials as well. An extensive but anonymous memoir composed in early February 1793 analyzed the most important issues facing the Habsburg Monarchy and concluded that the paramount objective was "the defeat of de-

[59] Francis to Kaunitz, March n.d. [27], 1793, in Vivenot, ed., *Quellen*, 2: 543.

[60] Thugut's *Memoire*, March n.d. [27], 1793, in ibid., 498–501.

mocracy."[61] For this author, to defeat democracy meant first finding statesmen and military leaders who understood it. The men in power then, he wrote, "totally ignore that, in order to combat democracy, they must study it both to know its strengths and its weaknesses." After assessing the abilities and experiences of the more prominent Austrian figures and their capacity to deal with the threat posed by democracy, the author judged Mercy to be the best. He was a man "with an extensive perception, armed with a head of ice that no event can melt, no accident can disturb, no passion can alter." But his lack of ambition and reluctance to take charge were liabilities. He possessed, this observer continued, "a phlegmatic temperament that weakens his interest in affairs."

If Mercy would not assume leadership—and this author was convinced that he would not—then one must rely on Thugut, "after Count Mercy one of the most distinguished men in Austrian diplomacy." He possessed what Mercy lacked: energy. He was "the only one . . . whom one can call a man of spirit."[62] Moreover, he understood the threat posed by democracy "having personally observed the French Revolution and appreciated the danger it is preparing for its neighbors." But Thugut also was not without faults. "He gives in too often to a cynicism that often goes to contempt for affairs and that he justifies to himself by citing . . . those who call him visionary because he can see farther than they." Mercy and Thugut, he went on, to a great extent shared this cynicism, but "the court of Vienna had nevertheless better entrust to them its interests and those of the common cause . . . in order to obtain satisfactory success and to free us from the various factions

---

[61] Anonymous memoir, February 1, 1793, in ibid., 467–74. Vivenot attributes this document to Thugut's later antagonist, the Prince de Ligne. The author of Thugut's entry in the *Allgemeine Deutsche Biographie*, however, believes de Ligne's style to be quite different from this writer's. He names no one but calls the anonymous observer "high-standing, well-versed, and perceptive." *Allgemeine Deutsche Biographie*, 38: 147.

[62] The author cited Louis Cobenzl as another man of spirit but noted that he was unfamiliar with the French Revolution.

that sap so much of our strength by their opposition to each other."

At the end of March 1793 Thugut was the most attractive choice to succeed Cobenzl and Spielmann. He spoke for the policies favored by the majority of the emperor's advisers; he enjoyed the support of important officials; he possessed recognized talent and vigor; and he had witnessed firsthand the important events that had occurred in France and Belgium in 1791 and 1792. Intrigue was not essential. One question remains: did he want the job? It is not absolutely certain that the answer was yes. In late April 1793 his old associate from Brussels, Quentin Crawford, in summing up for the British ambassador at the Hague Thugut's likely policies, remarked that he was presenting Thugut's ideas as of December 1792 "when I believe he neither expected the place he now fills, nor even desired it."[63] He might not have desired the post in December, but he did not refuse it when offered to him three months later. He was appointed on March 27, 1793, again by a draft that he composed and the emperor signed.[64] He would guide Austria's foreign policy for the next eight turbulent years.

[63] Crawford to Auckland, April 29, 1793, in Auckland, *Journal and Correspondence*, 3: 44.

[64] Francis to Thugut, March n.d. [27], 1793, in Vivenot, ed., *Quellen*, 2: 544.

CHAPTER V

SUCCESS, 1793

FOUR DAYS after his appointment as director of foreign affairs, Thugut celebrated his fifty-seventh birthday. From the time he entered the Oriental Academy until this day, he had served the Habsburgs for forty years. Few likenesses of him exist. Five are in the Bildarchiv of the Austrian National Library, but only one is identifed as a portrait for which he actually sat. The likeness is in profile, and nothing is more prominent in his appearance than the enormous chin. It juts down and forward from his jaw line and prevents his lips from being even, suggesting that his teeth were not even either. One might say that it resembles a Habsburg chin, although it seems to go downward rather than outward as did the famous chin of Leopold I. Had Thugut's chin been less pronounced, his outstanding physical attribute would have been his nose, a feature also of considerable size. Despite his reputation for toughness and ill-temper, in this portrait he has a slight but pleasant smile on his face; his one eye in profile is calm, almost sleepy, and at the corner of his eye laugh lines are detectable. His face is lean, as is his torso, and his forehead high but not particularly sloped. He wears no wig, just white hair combed back with a ribbon tied at the base of the neck. His clothes are those of a gentleman, ruffled tie and well-cut jacket, the only decoration being the order of St. Stephen.

Although in this portrait Thugut does not reveal the qualities of cunning and shiftiness for which he was famous, one can see how a scowl or a sneer might bring such qualities to his appearance. Indeed, no contemporary writer found Thugut attractive physically. Hormayr described him as "of middling height; and in his advanced age . . . he stooped very much. His features were a mixture of a faun and a Mephistopheles. . . . No Austrian would have taken his likeness in a cabinet of wax figures for that of a countryman, but rather for that of a secretary to Louis XI of France, of Cesar Borgia, or one of the most confidential secretaries of Louvois."[1] Prince de Ligne wrote at a time when snobbish anti-Semitism was the rule: "Had Henry IV not been king of France and Navarre but king of the Jews, if instead of a free, spirited, and bright laugh, bitterness and scorn, arrogance and contempt had crossed his lips, then Baron Thugut would have resembled him."[2] Thugut's appearance was not an asset, and his manner when he received visitors did not enhance impressions of him. He rarely looked them in the eye, often listened to their requests or suggestions without saying a word, then smiled only a wry smile, made some pithy remark, and ushered them to the door.[3] No person who met him for the first time ascribed to him an open honesty or forthrightness, even when he was endeavoring to be honest and forthright. If anyone spoke of him, it was of his suspiciousness and sarcasm, which in turn usually inspired the observer to regard him with circumspection and scorn. That perceptive American, Gouverneur Morris, noticed that his appearance and manner rather than what he actually said might have been a major cause of the wariness with which so many viewed him. After noting how others regarded Thugut as cunning, indolent, and false, Morris added, "His countenance confirms this idea and perhaps gives rise to it."[4] A necessary attribute of all politicians at all times is to appear straightfor-

[1] Vehse, *Memoirs*, 2: 384.
[2] *Allgemeine Deutsche Biographie*, 38: 156.
[3] See Hammer, *Erinnerungen*, 35–36; and Oliver Bernier, *Lafayette: Hero of Two Worlds* (New York, 1983), 256.
[4] Morris, *Diary and Letters*, 2: 348.

ward even when being devious; Thugut's great misfortune was that he appeared devious even when being straightforward.

As director of foreign affairs, Thugut served in a government undergoing a number of changes. In the first year after his accession, Francis introduced many reforms, largely having to do with internal administration. In November 1792 came the most important, the uniting of the principal administrative and financial bureaus into a single body called the Directorium in cameralibus der hungarisch-siebenbürgischen und deutschen Erblanden under the directorship of Count Leopold Kollowrat, one of Thugut's later critics.[5] Generally historians have interpreted this reform as marking the end of the progressive and reformist governments of Maria Theresa and her two sons and the beginning of the backward-looking administrations that would characterize the monarchy through the remainder of Francis's days. At its beginning, however, this reform merely put more business into one office.[6]

As part of these administrative changes, the chancellery was restructured as well. Since early in Kaunitz's day the chancellery had been directly responsible not only for foreign affairs but also for the administration of the Austrian Netherlands and the Habsburg possessions in Italy.[7] In late February 1793, during the retreat of the Austrian armed forces from Belgium, the administration of the Netherlands was removed from the jurisdiction of the chancellery and granted its own office under the directorship of Trauttmannsdorff, another of Thugut's later foes. At the time of Cobenzl's removal and

[5] Friedrich Walter, *Die österreichische Zentralverwaltung* (Vienna, 1964), 5: 297–306.

[6] Ernst Wangermann, *The Austrian Achievement, 1700–1800* (London, 1973), 178; Ernst Joseph Görlich and Felix Romanik, *Geschichte Österreichs* (Innsbruck, 1970), 303.

[7] The official title of the chancellery before the reform in February 1793 was K. K. geheimen Hof- und Staats-Cantzley der auswärtigen, Niederländischen und Italiänischen Geschäfte.

Thugut's appointment, the administration of the Italian lands was separated from the chancellery as well and given to Cobenzl as consolation for his demotion. Thugut himself did not assume the title of chancellor nor did he become head of the chancellery; his official title was in French, *Directeur général des affaires étrangères*. Kaunitz continued to hold the title of chancellor until his death in June 1794. At that point Thugut was promoted to a higher position and granted a German title, *Minister der auswärtigen Geschäfte*. He never held the title of chancellor during his career.[8]

Thugut assumed leadership only of the section of the chancellery dedicated to foreign policy. He inherited a staff from Cobenzl's day and apparently thought so much of its members or had worked so often with them before that he did not remove or appoint a single senior officer (and none quit) during his entire eight years as foreign minister. At the head of his staff were four *wirkliche Hofräte*, or undersecretaries, who served as Thugut's immediate assistants. The closest to Thugut was his old school chum, Bernhard Jenisch, who was responsible for the office's correspondence with the Ottoman Empire and other Moslem governments and for matters of payroll and personnel within the ministry itself. Sybel named Jenisch the evil force behind Thugut, but there is no evidence that he had any significant influence upon Thugut's policies. Colloredo described Jenisch accurately in 1801 as "a perfect subordinate; full of zeal and diligence."[9] Second to Jenisch was Egydius von Collenbach, who guided the routine correspondence with the envoys in London and St. Petersburg and composed the office's advice on commercial and financial matters when the foreign ministry was involved in them. Colloredo

---

[8] Erwin Matsch, *Geschichte des Auswärtigen Dienstes von Österreich-Ungarn, 1720–1920* (Cologne/Vienna, 1980), 55. In April 1798 he was awarded the titles *Konferenzminister* and *General Kommissar bzw bevollmächtigten Minister für die neuen Besitzungen in Italien etc*. These new titles did not really signify a change in Thugut's position, however.

[9] Colloredo to Thugut, May 26, 1801, Vienna, HHSA, SK, *Grosse Korrespondenz*, 447.

wrote sympathetically of Collenbach as hard working but plodding, "always indecisive, a little slow."[10] Hormayr declared that he "spent most of his time during Thugut's ministry in public houses in the Prater working with equations, logarithms, and [mathematical] problems."[11] Karl Daiser von Sylbach was the German specialist on Thugut's staff, a man "particularly knowledgeable in imperial affairs."[12] He was assisted by the fourth undersecretary, the gifted historian Johannes von Müller, who with Daiser prepared most of the office's public announcements and statements. Daiser and Müller both possessed considerable literary talent, and Thugut exploited this talent by having them edit his memoranda to the emperor.[13] Below these officers served a number of secretaries, clerks, messengers, and notaries. What is most striking about them was that all continued to hold their posts from 1793 to 1801 with no changes except at the lowest level.[14] Such a minimal turnover suggests that, if one cannot directly prove that Thugut inspired loyalty among these men, at least none was dissatisfied enough to leave the service. Moreover, Thugut apparently ran his office with some budgetary restraint. In a report to Berlin in 1798, a Prussian agent remarked that even Thugut's critics admitted that he brought "order, efficiency, and economy to the department of foreign affairs. . . . He has annually saved his master seventy thousand florins simply by working harder than any of his predecessors."[15]

The task of the Foreign Ministry was not only to recommend policy to the emperor but also to maintain correspondence with the emperor's representatives abroad, and early in Thugut's career three of these became far more important than all of the others: Mercy; Louis Cobenzl (cousin of Philipp

---

[10] Ibid. [11] Hormayr, *Lebensbilder*, 1: 344.
[12] Colloredo to Thugut, May 26, 1801, Vienna, HHSA, SK, *Grosse Korrespondenz*, 447.
[13] Alfred von Vivenot, ed., *Zur Geschichte des Rastadter Congresses* (Vienna, 1871), xv.
[14] *Hofschematismus*, 1794 and 1800.
[15] Keller to Berlin, May 19, 1798, in Hüffer, *Rastatter Congress*, 1: 269.

Cobenzl), ambassador to Russia; and Louis Starhemberg, ambassador to Great Britain. As Mercy was the veteran in French relations, so Louis Cobenzl was the veteran in Russian affairs. Ambassador since 1779, he was perfect for the court of Catherine the Great. An inveterate libertine, he loved practical jokes, fun, teasing, food, and women. A corpulent figure with beady, laughing eyes peering out of a pudgy face, he was nevertheless an active and agile fellow who loved to perform in and to write for Catherine's private dramas. Indeed, Catherine found him so amusing and spirited that she dubbed him her "master of pleasures."[16] But Cobenzl was also a crafty diplomat, an imperturbable negotiator, and a dedicated servant of the Habsburg Monarchy. To him above all Thugut sent careful explanations of his policies, and from him he expected intelligent remarks and critiques. And when serious negotiating was required, as with Russia much of the time and with Bonaparte in 1797 and in 1800, Cobenzl was the man upon whom Thugut relied.

Cobenzl was Thugut's veteran; Starhemberg was his novice. He served as ambassador to the Hague in 1792 before being called to London to replace Johann Philipp Stadion about the time Thugut became director of foreign affairs. Because Stadion and Thugut were at odds throughout their careers and because Stadion himself would become foreign minister later on, some have suggested that Thugut removed Stadion because he distrusted him. In fact, Stadion resigned prior to Thugut's appointment because he resented Philipp Cobenzl's assignment of Mercy as special ambassador to London to negotiate an alliance with Great Britain.[17] In any case, Starhemberg's career as Stadion's successor lasted from 1793

[16] Hormayr, *Lebensbilder*, 1: 343.

[17] Matsch, *Geschichte des Auswärtigen Dienstes*, 56; Hellmuth Rössler, *Österreichs Kampf um Deutschlands Befreiung* (Hamburg, 1940), 1: 45. Stadion's expressed reason for his asking to be relieved was that his income was too low and that the French had overrun his family's possessions in the Rhineland. Hellmuth Rössler, *Graf Johann Philipp Stadion: Napoleons deutscher Gegenspieler* (Vienna/Munich, 1966), 1: 164–65.

to 1809, through the tenure of Thugut and for some time thereafter. Unlike Louis Cobenzl, Starhemberg was subjected to a good deal of criticism from both his Austrian superiors and his British hosts. In 1797 he made his greatest blunder, signing a subsidy treaty with Britain in the emperor's name that Thugut refused to have ratified and that caused considerable difficulty and ill will between the two countries for three years thereafter. Despite such gaffs and an inclination to overoptimism, Starhemberg did work hard at his job. He understood and appreciated the British constitution and the significant role of Parliament within it; he was well acquainted with the important people in the British government and in the opposition and tried to cultivate them; and he did his best to explain to Thugut the peculiarities and intricacies of British political life.[18] Thugut valued these gifts and kept him at his post despite the frequent ridicule directed at him. In late 1801, following his fall from power, Thugut revealed his warm feelings for Starhemberg when he wrote to his young associate Count Franz Dietrichstein of "our incomparable common friend Count Louis," and about the fidelity among the three of them formed "by our attachment to the same goals, true interests, and glory of Austria."[19] Thugut had other trustworthy officials besides his staff and these two ambassadors, but none remained as close to him during his tenure in office as they did.

Just as these subordinates had to please Thugut to keep their posts, so too Thugut had to please his superiors, none more so than the emperor himself, Francis II. A good deal of ink has been spilled by scholars trying to capture the personality of this man, who was important not only in the history of the Habsburg Monarchy but in the history of Europe during one of its truly formative periods. Born in Tuscany in 1768,

---

[18] A historian particularly impressed with Starhemberg as ambassador is Karl F. Helleiner, *The Imperial Loans: A Study in Financial and Diplomatic History* (Oxford, 1965).

[19] Thugut to Dietrichstein, December 28, 1801, Vienna, HHSA, SK, *Grosse Korrespondenz*, 447.

Francis II, Holy Roman Emperor
(Courtesy Bildarchiv, Austrian National Library)

Francis came to Vienna in 1784 to study statecraft under his uncle, Joseph II, and then remained in the city through the revolutionary wars, the Napoleonic occupation, the Congress of Vienna, and the era of administrative absolutism and conservative government preceding his death in 1835. Generally he is pictured as the stalwart sovereign behind the resistance to change that characterized, for better or worse, the Age of Metternich. Not particularly bright perhaps, he was nevertheless intelligent enough to appoint able men not only to carry out his conservative policies but also to give these policies intellectual foundation and justification.

In the days when Thugut served him, Francis was a young man, rather unsure of himself but already shcwing that stubborn streak that would remain with him all of his life. He was interested in reforms and admired those of his uncle, but his ideas of reform ran largely to switching duties around to different offices—changing one, abolishing another, creating a third. He did wish to be popular, and he thought that the best way to achieve popularity was to receive weekly the petitions of his subjects and to act upon those petitions if possible. It was a fine gesture, but many of his advisers believed that it did not enhance his popularity very much while it took considerable time away from his more important duties. He was a dedicated family man, devoted during Thugut's ministry to his second wife, Marie Therese, daughter of Maria Carolina of Naples and Sicily and thus his first cousin. Described in some contemporary accounts as a shrewd and manipulative woman, she seems to have had only a marginal influence on policy while dedicating most of her time to keeping her husband happy and contented.[20] One observer summed up Francis's personality as basically a boring one: "Without vices, without virtues, without notable passions, nothing can divorce him

[20] Walter C. Langsam, *Francis the Good: The Education of an Emperor 1768-1792* (New York, 1949), 164; Hüffer and Luckwaldt, eds., *Frieden*, xxv; Poteratz to Delacroix, February 1, 1796, in Sorel, "Poterat," 303; Nerciat to Guiraudet, December 14, 1796, in Hüffer and Luckwaldt, eds., *Frieden*, 102.

from his natural apathy."[21] Another described similar qualities as virtues: "We have never heard even the slightest suspicion of his mind being tainted with a propensity to any vice which would sully his fame either as a man or a monarch."[22]

Two characteristics of behavior that many ascribed to Francis in his early reign were an inability to distinguish between the important and the trivial in matters of state and a propensity, when making decisions, to follow the advice of the last man he talked to. These qualities prompted periodic admonitions from members of the Habsburg family and from his senior ministers to apply himself more diligently to subjects at hand and to pick men to serve him who were competent. Even his closest adviser and friend, Count Colloredo, who was by nature obsequious toward the emperor, felt called upon to scold Francis on occasion: "You must work. You must devote much more time to the abundant affairs that demand it. Your duty, your conscience insist upon it. If you are determined to work, it will become less difficult for you to do so, and it will become pleasant; your example will double the dedication of every officer, affairs will become orderly, you will gather the fruits of your labor, and you will soon hear a million voices sing your praises."[23] Regularly he was encouraged to appoint "a few sincere, solid, well-established, mature, unprejudiced, experienced men," but since he was unsure who among the contending individuals and factions around him possessed these qualities, he tended to rely on men he had known long before he became emperor, especially Colloredo and to a lesser extent his old military tutor, Franz von Rollin.[24]

Colloredo was Thugut's protector and confidant. Just as

[21] Poteratz to Delacroix, February 1, 1796, in Sorel, "Poterat," 303.

[22] Keith to Grenville, March 1, 1792, in Sir Robert Murray Keith, *Memoirs and Correspondence* (London, 1849), 2: 505.

[23] Colloredo to Francis, September 18, 1799, in Viktor Bibl, *Der Zerfall Österreichs* (Vienna, 1922), 1: 99. See also Colloredo to Francis, April 23, 1795, Vienna, HHSA, *Kaiser Franz Akten*, 78b (81).

[24] Colloredo to Francis, September 18, 1794, in Friedrich Walter, ed., *Die österreichische Zentralverwaltung* (Vienna, 1964), 5: 6.

Thugut confided in Louis Cobenzl concerning his policies and projects, so too he shared with Colloredo his intimate thoughts and concerns.[25] Colloredo's official position was *Konferenz- und Kabinettsminister*, and his functions included screening all information, advice, and correspondence that came to the emperor from governmental departments; scheduling the emperor's appointments and audiences; and advising the emperor on public and private matters. He had been with Francis longer than anyone else—since 1773 when Maria Theresa appointed him to serve as the then five-year-old archduke's tutor. Colloredo is often portrayed as the man who led Francis down the path of reaction, who persuaded him to abandon utterly the progressive reforms of Joseph II and even to overturn the compromising but egalitarian tendencies of his own father in order to turn state and society over to aristocratic conservatism. The Colloredo that emerges from the pages of Thugut's correspondence was substantially less than the dedicated reactionary suggested by such portrayals. He seemed a pleasant fellow, a little arrogant perhaps but not particularly passionate about any serious matter. While Thugut's letters to him sometimes rant and rave about the horrible consequences of particular actions for the monarchy, Colloredo's replies consist of soothing remarks, gossipy chatter, and general agreement, albeit with a tone suggesting that fate often prevents one from adopting the wise course no matter what demands or conditions exist. Others clearly doubted his abilities. Hormayr called him "a nullity in all foreign affairs, utterly ignorant of all great decisions made at this time, and forced to think only from one day to the next."[26] Gentz described him as "null and void, thoroughly reduced to depending upon what others tell him."[27]

[25] The two volumes of Thugut's *Vertrauliche Briefe*, edited by Vivenot, are almost exclusively letters from Thugut to Colloredo. The originals are found in Vienna, HHSA, SK, *Grosse Korrespondenz*, 444, 445. Checking the published copies against the originals, I found them practically complete.

[26] Hormayr, *Lebensbilder*, 1: 344.

[27] Gentz to Brinkmann, January 4, 1805, in Friedrich Carl Wittichen and E. Salzer, eds., *Briefe von und an Friedrich von Gentz* (Munich/Berlin/Oldenbourg, 1913), 2: 258.

Franz von Colloredo-Wallsee
(Courtesy Bildarchiv, Austrian National Library)

The finance minister Josef O'Donnell portrayed him as "foul and indolent but also insufferably arrogant"; the Russian ambassador to Vienna Count Razumovsky as "a byword for lack of ability, slow-witted and ponderous"; and Philipp Cobenzl as having "no knowledge of public affairs of any kind, a very restricted talent."[28]

He may have been Francis's closest adviser, but one can hardly imagine his personality forcefully dominating the young emperor. His written advice to Francis was couched in fawning phrases, generally preceded by a page or two of professions of devotion and repeated reminders that Francis always told him to speak his mind. When he finally made his points, they almost always began with the phrase, "In my poor opinion" and frequently concluded with an offer to resign if the emperor disapproved of his recommendations. And yet, Colloredo stayed by the emperor's side, and he protected Thugut. His support for the foreign minister suggests a certain strength of character because it brought him criticism not only from the Habsburg family but from the high aristocracy as well—a fact that casts some doubt on the contention that he was the uncompromising champion of that class. Colloredo's influence with Francis kept Thugut in his office through the sharpest intrigue and the most bitter defeats. Although it is difficult from the evidence to ascertain exactly why Colloredo supported Thugut for so long, there seems little doubt that the cabinet minister was greatly impressed by the man's intensity and dedication to his work, qualities that Colloredo appreciated even when he had to endure Thugut's sarcasm. Moreover, Colloredo was probably convinced that Thugut was right in his assessment of the French Revolution, that France must be contained by armed force if the monarchy and the rest of monarchical Europe were to survive. At times the emperor wavered in his support for Thugut, but on those occasions

[28] Quoted in Christian Sapper, "Josef Graf O'Donnell, Hofkammerpräsident, 1808–1810," *Mitteilungen des österreichischen Staatsarchivs*, 33 (1980): 174; Stella Musulin, *Vienna in the Age of Metternich* (Boulder, 1975), 20; Arneth, ed., *P. Cobenzl*, 154.

Colloredo strongly recommended that he be retained, at least until the catastrophic defeats of 1800 made it impossible for him to continue. Even after Thugut's disgrace, however, Colloredo corresponded with him, a correspondence interpreted by both Austria's friends and enemies to mean that Thugut was still manipulating the monarchy's foreign affairs with Colloredo serving as his puppet.

In the hierarchy of decision making, Thugut was solely answerable to the emperor through Colloredo. This procedure in itself marked a change; throughout most of the eighteenth century, foreign policy was discussed and often decided in the Privy Conference, a body of the most important officers in the Habsburg Monarchy. It was this group that overturned Philipp Cobenzl's policies in March 1793 and made possible Thugut's appointment. The conference met no more after March 1793, which was a great misfortune especially for historians, because the conference's minutes usually revealed the opinions on policy of each participant and whose ideas prevailed. Some of Thugut's contemporaries blamed him for ending the practice, declaring that his ego would not tolerate opposing views and that he wanted to present his policies to the emperor without allowing others to offer alternatives or criticisms. In fact, Thugut complained about the abolition of the conference, precisely because it prevented the dispassionate discussion of policy and the sharing of ideas. On one occasion, while expressing to Colloredo his pleasure that Francis wished his opinion on a matter, he vigorously protested the lack of conference meetings, a lack that only encouraged the emperor's propensity to follow the advice of the last man he consulted:

> It is necessary that, when His Majesty wants to hear our opinions, we all be together; because I always maintain that these separate and distinct conversations are the surest means of confusing all affairs and of perpetuating the state of uncertainty and irresolution that has caused all of our reverses. It is obvious that, when His Majesty speaks to one and then the other, the last speakers are able to

raise objections against the ideas of the first,—objections to which His Majesty perhaps cannot answer, because he cannot always have the sum of opinions at his fingertips, which is the case in which even the advisers find themselves.[29]

These then were Thugut's superiors and staff when he assumed his new office as director of foreign affairs at the end of March 1793. The policies that he believed the monarchy must follow were already set in his mind, and he explained them carefully in three major documents, one a memoir on the Holy Roman Empire written in early March 1793, one his position paper on the Belgian-Bavarian exchange composed in mid-March, and one a set of instructions he sent to Mercy and to Louis Cobenzl in mid-April. The overriding goal expressed in all three was to create an effective coalition against revolutionary France; the greatest immediate challenge was to overcome the crushing defeats Austria's forces had suffered at the hands of the revolutionary armies. Belgium had been overrun, the Rhineland invaded, and Holland threatened. Britain had entered the war on Austria's side, but Prussia seemed on the brink of leaving it. The states of the Holy Roman Empire were beginning to appreciate the danger they faced—in November 1792 the Reichstag had voted funds to raise an army and in late March 1793 had declared itself ready to protect Germany from France—but mobilizing an effective armed force among the German states would be a difficult task. Essentially, in late March Austria was combatting revolutionary France with little aid from others, and it was Thugut's duty to solicit more assistance.

This assignment, however, was compounded by certain difficulties, the most important being the Second Partition of Poland. The Second Partition had given Russia and Prussia substantial immediate gains, and it had included in its articles Russo-Prussian approval of the Bavarian-Belgian exchange as

[29] Thugut to Colloredo, August 8, 1800, in Vivenot, ed., *Vertrauliche Briefe*, 2: 256.

Austria's rightful compensation. But not only was the exchange now impossible owing to British opposition and the French occupation of Belgium, in the best of circumstances it did not represent a compensation for Austria equal to the Polish territories acquired by Russia and Prussia. To Louis Cobenzl Thugut wrote, "The only advantage the emperor will gain from the exchange would be the contiguity of his lands . . . but purchased with a diminution of a million in population and four million in revenue." Since Prussia would increase its holdings in Poland by almost two million in population and four to five million in revenue, the end result would mean "a difference of perhaps three million in subjects and eight-nine million in revenue to the detriment of His Majesty."[30] On these grounds alone, the Second Partition was unacceptable.

Thugut's task, then, was to create an effective coalition against revolutionary France while seeking to modify the results of the Second Partition without unduly antagonizing any potential member of that coalition. As the first step, Thugut believed that it was necessary to secure a firm alliance with Britain, and that meant renouncing—at least for now—the Belgian-Bavarian exchange. Since this decision had already been reached in the conference meetings in March, it posed no difficulties in principle. But in practice it meant keeping the Netherlands as an Austrian possession, and in the spring of 1793 that was no easy task. If Austria retained Belgium in the future, Thugut wrote to Mercy, the means must be found to defend it. The ease with which the revolutionary armies had overrun the Austrian Netherlands in the autumn of 1792 demonstrated that they were practically indefensible. When (and if) Austria reconquered Belgium, it must be protected by a "solid barrier," and that meant land and fortresses acquired from France. Although at this time Thugut did not specify

---

[30] Thugut to L. Cobenzl, April 14, 1793, in Alfred von Vivenot, ed., "Thugut und sein politisches System," *Archiv für österreichische Geschichte*, 42 (1870): 379–80.

what that barrier should include, he did insist that Great Britain help the emperor obtain it.[31]

An alliance with Russia was the second step. To Louis Cobenzl Thugut wrote that Russia must join in the fight against revolutionary France. The French Revolution had altered the fears and suspicions about Russia that Thugut had expressed to Kaunitz during the early 1770s. For Thugut Russia no longer represented a dark, mysterious threat looming in the East, but a source of salvation for a Europe suffering increasingly heavy blows from France. As time went on, Thugut became more and more convinced that France could be defeated only with Russian aid. Each hint from St. Petersburg that Russia would soon provide help buoyed Thugut's spirit, no matter how desperate matters seemed; each report that Russia probably would not send aid was always a great disappointment to him. As a consequence of this feeling, Thugut accepted Russian caprice far more tolerantly than he did that of any other power. A Prussian change of policy he greeted with cries of treason, a British change with accusations of selfishness, but a Russian change with expressions of hope for something better next time.

As much as he desired Russia's support in the West, however, Thugut still believed that Russian expansion in the East should be prevented if possible—especially if Prussian expansion accompanied it. For that reason, the Second Partition of Poland as it stood was unacceptable, and thus it represented an obstacle to an Austro-Russian accord against France. Not only had the partition enlarged Prussia far too much and diverted attention from the war against France, it had violated one of the principles of eighteenth-century Habsburg foreign policy that Thugut had personally worked to uphold: that Austria and Russia never share a common border. Fear of a common border had been a major reason for the short-lived Austro-Turkish concert of 1771 that Thugut had helped negotiate. The Second Partition created a common boundary by joining

<hr />

[31] Thugut to Mercy, April 14, 1793, Vienna, HHSA, SK, *Frankreich*, 182.

Austria and Russia along the Sbrucz River in Galicia and Podolia. In his first instructions to Louis Cobenzl, Thugut advised him to bring this point to Catherine's attention and to remind her that Vienna assumed continuing separation of Habsburg and Romanov lands to be Russian policy as well: "It has always been regarded as an irrevocable principle adopted by Austria and Russia that no circumstances might render the two empires neighbors, and that their possessions must constantly be separated by an intermediate barrier."[32]

Although the Second Partition violated a major precept in Austrian foreign policy, Thugut also knew that Vienna needed the Russians so much in the struggle against France that it could not be actively resisted, common boundary or not. In fact, Thugut was aware that he had to use great care not to oppose the Polish settlement in any way that might annoy St. Petersburg. But some effort had to be made if only to maintain principle and to satisfy the critics in Austrian policy circles who believed that the monarchy had been betrayed. After all, Thugut had become foreign minister in part because of his predecessors' failure to halt or to share in the Second Partition. Once in power himself, he could scarcely accept it with a shrug and move on to other matters. Therefore, while telling Cobenzl to couch his statements in elaborate professions of friendship, Thugut advised him to inform the Russian court that the emperor could not approve the Second Partition without adjustments.[33] In the meantime, Thugut called upon Mercy to ask the British to protest the partition openly and vigorously. The Russians might relent under British pressure, but "we are powerless to oppose it."[34]

If it could be crafted, a coalition of Britain, Russia, Prussia (Thugut planned on Prussia remaining in the war because that was a provision of the Russo-Prussian treaty of partition), and Austria would offer formidable opposition to France, but

---

[32] Thugut to L. Cobenzl, April 14, 1793, in Vivenot, ed., "Politisches System," 379.
[33] Ibid.
[34] Thugut to Mercy, April 14, 1793, Vienna, HHSA, SK, *England*, 130.

Thugut believed that the Holy Roman Empire had to play a role as well. And in his speculation about that role, he composed an astonishing document that called for a radical territorial rearrangement of the German states, especially those along the Rhine.[35] He argued that only Austria and Prussia could protect Germany from French aggression; therefore, Austria and Prussia had to create a new order in the Holy Roman Empire that would make that protection more effective. This new order would put all of the major fortresses in the Rhineland—Freiburg, Philippsburg, Mannheim, Mainz, Ehrenbreitstein, Trier, and Luxembourg—and their surrounding lands in the possession of three "powerful princes," namely, the ruler of Austria, the king of Prussia, and the elector Palatine. The ecclesiastical princes who would lose those fortresses and lands would be given possessions in the German interior as compensation. In that way the three major princes could maintain a military cordon from Basel to Luxembourg and garrison it with a united army of 200,000 men to protect Germany from the French.

On the face of it, this document suggests that Thugut wished to destroy or at least to alter radically the Holy Roman Empire as it then existed, and some have offered it as proof that the baron cared not at all for the territorial integrity of the lesser German states.[36] Moreover, since the plan called for sacrifices primarily on the part of the ecclesiastical princes, one might argue that, when secularization would become an issue later, Thugut would have no qualms about stripping those princes of their lands. The document does show a callousness toward the old German constitution, but it is curious that no plan like it appears again in Thugut's policies or proposals. Indeed, throughout his tenure as foreign minister, Thugut worked largely within the framework of the constitution of

[35] This document is published in Aretin, *Heiliges Römisches Reich*, 2: 249–55.

[36] Aretin especially promotes this thesis. See ibid. and his work *Vom Deutschen Reich zum Deutschen Bund* (Göttingen, 1980), 73.

the Holy Roman Empire and censured the Empire only when he believed that the other German states were themselves violating its principles.

In this document, Thugut's policies and attitudes toward the Holy Roman Empire are revealed less in the territorial adjustments he recommended than in the justifications he offered for making them. Such changes were needed, he wrote, because France was poised to destroy the Empire entirely. "Extraordinary conditions demand extraordinary measures: . . . the Netherlands already lost, the possessions of various imperial states in enemy hands, the whole Empire on the verge of extinction, [Germany] can only hope for salvation from Austria and Prussia." All of the German princes and their peoples, including the Austrians, had to realize that together they faced a struggle such as Europe had never seen in its history. Wars before had been fought for limited aims, argued Thugut, and each one had ended when both sides agreed that enough sacrifices had been made and that it was time for peace. But this war was different. It was a war for men's minds as well as their property, a war so frightening and so thorough that Germany's defenders were mesmerized by it. And, if Germany and Austria wished to survive, they must act. At the end of his memorandum Thugut summarized his views as clearly and forcefully as he could:

Austria has certainly fought more wars in which threatening danger was much closer. But one cannot compare those with such an all-embracing struggle that we are now in. . . . Just as [earlier] wars weakened us, so they weakened the enemy, and at the end military victory or a more or less advantageous peace would bring them to a halt. But now this House . . . must fight a nation which has not only become utterly fanatical but which tries to drag along with it other peoples and which has prepared its current efforts for a long time in all of Europe through the voices of its prophets.

For Thugut, Austria's cause was the Empire's cause, and it might be necessary to reorganize the Empire if the cause were to prevail.

An anti-French coalition of Austria, Russia, Britain, Prussia, and the Holy Roman Empire represented Thugut's highest aim when he took office. But, with or without such a coalition, he intended to continue fighting against France. In fact, as he assumed his new duties, the war was taking a turn for the better. On March 18, 1793, the Austrian army, commanded by Saxe-Coburg and inspired by the planning of Karl Lieberich Mack and by the leadership of Archduke Charles, defeated the French forces of General Dumouriez at Neerwinden. The victory stopped the intended French invasion of Holland and forced Dumouriez to evacuate Brussels.[37] On the Upper Rhine the Prussians, the agreement with Russia having cancelled their plan to weaken their forces as expressed in the Verbal Note of Merle, joined the Austrian forces to drive the French from Mainz. These military successes continued into the summer, leading to the allied conquest of the French border fortresses of Condé (July 10) and Valenciennes (July 28).

The confidence generated by the allied successes in the field was encouraged even more by news that France itself was in turmoil. The first direct evidence came from Dumouriez, who, shortly after his defeat at Neerwinden, offered Saxe-Coburg an armistice and revealed plans to turn his army against Paris and overthrow the government if the Austrians would relieve their pressure upon him. Saxe-Coburg endorsed the Frenchman's proposal, but Thugut heartily rejected it. In Thugut's mind, Dumouriez's suggestions were in themselves no more than symptoms that France was cracking under allied pressure, which, accordingly, had to be maintained. If France were ripe for counterrevolution, he advised the emperor, "then one has only the progress of Prince Coburg to thank" and not defections by republican generals.[38] When Dumouriez

[37] Gunther Rothenberg, *Napoleon's Great Adversaries: The Archduke Charles and the Austrian Army, 1792–1814* (Bloomington, 1982), 37.
[38] Thugut to Francis, April 7, 1793, Vienna, HHSA, SK, *Vorträge*, 153.

discovered that his army was unwilling to follow him to Paris, he and eight hundred of his men deserted and asked to join the struggle against the revolution. Thugut's reply to this request revealed his assumption that all those who deserted the French forces were forever infected by the disease of democracy and deserved no consideration or office. Do not allow these "constitutional deserters" any role in the Austrian forces, he told Colloredo, because Vienna would only be paying them "to disorganize our army and to indoctrinate our troops in the science of the rights of man and the unrestrained sovereignty of the people." Instead, "let the English transport this baggage to one of the rebellious provinces [in France]," and let them fend for themselves.[39]

Dumouriez's desertion was indeed a symptom of trouble in France. In March the first counterrevolutionary rising in the Vendée began; in May the struggle between the Girondists and Jacobins reached its climax, leading to the expulsion of the Girondists from the National Convention on June 2; and in June protests erupted against the revolution in Normandy, Brittany, Bourdeaux, the Gironde, and in the city of Lyon.[40] Vienna learned about these events from many sources, including French newspapers and observers such as Mercy in Belgium and others at Bern in Switzerland and at Turin in Piedmont. On the basis of the internal upheaval in France and continuing allied military progress, Vienna became increasingly confident that the war would be won and the revolution curbed. On August 7, 1793, Mercy concluded that the moment had come for the allies to strike the final blow. The French field armies were greatly weakened by defeats, desertions, and redeployment to fight internal enemies; the government in Paris would need at least three more months to raise another levy; and the French economy was collapsing. Given these troubles, Mercy surmised, France could not raise an army

---

[39] Thugut to Colloredo, June 2, 1793, in Vivenot, ed., *Vertrauliche Briefe*, 1: 17–18.

[40] Godechot, *Counter-Revolution*, 216ff.

large enough to stop the allies. The time had come to march on Paris.[41]

August 1793 would be the month that Austria was closer to defeating revolutionary France than it would ever be again during Thugut's tenure as foreign minister. At this time, however, Thugut seemed to be falling into the trap that had ensnared his predecessors: he was focusing more attention on Habsburg territorial gain than on final victory. Indeed, historians have criticized Thugut for steadfastly ignoring the true danger of revolutionary France and simply following the old policy of seeking to augment the possessions of the Habsburgs. And, some critics continue, he cared nothing about the value of potential acquisitions. He simply wanted territory, no matter what it was: a slice of Poland, a part of France, all of Venice; any place would do. One must admit that substantial grounds for this criticism are provided by Thugut's own writings composed while the allies were making progress during the spring and summer of 1793. He seemed concerned then primarily—almost exclusively—with securing territorial compensation for Austria. Yet, this criticism overlooks the fact that finding compensation was the major responsibility of his office during this period. Although he would later become involved in policy making in many areas, including finances and military strategy, those affairs were at first left to others in the Habsburg military and civil establishments. In the specific realm of foreign policy in the spring and summer of 1793, nothing appeared more important on a day-to-day basis than finding territory to counterbalance the expansion of Prussia and Russia resulting from the Second Partition of Poland.

From the perspective of the twentieth century, it is easy to condemn this concern as a failure of Thugut to appreciate truly the more serious matters at stake. It reflects the lessons that Thugut learned at Kaunitz's knee. For him and for his old mentor, balance of power really meant balance of territorial extent, population, and revenue. If any state acquired an

---

[41] Mercy to Thugut, August 7, 1793, in Pimodan, *Mercy-Argenteau*, 383–84.

unusually large amount of new land or resources—wherever it was—eighteenth-century diplomatic principles demanded that compensation be found for all of the other interested parties to maintain the previous balance. In the Second Partition of Poland, Austria had been the major party to receive nothing, and Thugut, as foreign minister, had to rectify the imbalance created by it. The one region where such compensation seemed likely to be found was France, particularly along its border with the Austrian Netherlands. Since Britain insisted so strongly that Austria retain Belgium, then it seemed only right that London would agree to an expansion of Austria's Belgian possessions to provide not only more revenue but also a more defensible frontier against France. Indeed, in early April 1793 the British foreign minister, Lord Grenville, told Lord Auckland at the Hague that the British would prefer to see the southern boundary of the Austrian Netherlands extend all the way to the Somme River rather than to permit Austria to exchange Belgium for Bavaria.[42] Auckland passed this idea on to Mercy, who not only agreed but also suggested a few other possibilities such as "our gaining possession of Alsace, Lorraine, the Bishoprics [Toul, Metz, Verdun], Flanders, and Hainault Française, providing there is no discussion of the exchange of the Low Countries."[43] In July the British told Starhemberg that they would not object to an exchange of Bavaria for Alsace and Lorraine, an idea discussed earlier by Mercy and Auckland, but they absolutely insisted that Belgium remain in Austrian hands.[44]

[42] Grenville to Auckland, April 3, 1793, and Auckland to Grenville, April 9, 1793, in Auckland, *Journal and Correspondence*, 3: 5, 14–15.

[43] Mercy to Thugut, May 2, 1793, Vienna, HHSA, SK, *Frankreich*, 181. I can find no evidence that Thugut first suggested extending the borders of the Austrian Netherlands to the Somme River or that he first suggested acquiring Alsace in order to trade it for Bavaria. Both suggestions either came from Auckland or came up in conversation between Auckland and Mercy. The evidence shows that Thugut was not enthusiastic about the acquisition of either place because he knew that they would be virtually impossible to pacify.

[44] Starhemberg to Thugut, July 12, 1793, in Vivenot, ed., *Quellen*, 3: 145–48.

Thugut actually did not like any of these proposals. Taking territory from France was a most difficult task, "where each bit of land must be purchased by blood and by the immense expenditures of a ruinous war," and Thugut doubted that the Austrian army was capable of it.[45] The army had made acceptable progress, but the progress was slow and painful. Austria needed land much easier to take and to hold than territory in France. The obvious place was Poland. In April Thugut had advised Francis that the Habsburgs would probably have to seek compensation in Poland because it was unlikely to be secured elsewhere.[46] By June he seemed ever more convinced. He advised Louis Cobenzl to explain to the Russians how difficult it would be for Austria to take land from France and to ask permission for the emperor to find compensation in Poland if none could be found in the West. Poland, after all, was paralyzed by the Second Partition anyway, and "It does not seem that the total partition of what remains would entail any great inconvenience." If a common border with Russia were unavoidable, there was no point in its being a short one. Cobenzl could work out the details; all Thugut insisted upon was that Cracow become a Habsburg city.[47]

All of this discussion about land in the West and land in the East strengthens the view that Thugut continued the search for territory begun by his predecessors, Philipp Cobenzl and Spielmann. And in the context of 1793—allied military success, reaction to the Second Partition, concern about Prussian,

[45] Thugut to L. Cobenzl, June 16, 1793, in ibid., 113. Curiously, Mercy had the same thoughts about the same time. After discussing the Austrian annexation of France to the Somme River with the Duke of York, Mercy wrote, "But alas! I fear that we will have much to back away from, and, if the French do not destroy themselves between us [the British and Austrian armies], they will retreat in order to lose three or four fortresses which will lure us into new wars and which they will be able to recapture in a few years. That is what has made me believe this idea of a vast barrier productive of revenue is exaggerated." Mercy to Thugut, June 15, 1793, in ibid., 112.
[46] Thugut to Francis, April 20, 1793, Vienna, HHSA, SK, *Vorträge*, 153.
[47] Thugut to L. Cobenzl, June 16, 1793, in Vivenot, ed., *Quellen*, 3: 113–17.

and, to a lesser extent, Russian gains—seeking a remedy for what he and others regarded as a serious injury to Austria's position was his legitimate concern. In this effort, however, Thugut wanted the other powers to recognize the principle of equal compensation (and for Thugut the key word was "equal") far more than he wanted specific territories. In practically every instruction he sent to Mercy, Starhemberg, and Louis Cobenzl, he avoided demanding particular lands, insisting instead that Austria's friends and allies acknowledge Austria's just claims to acquisitions equal to those of Prussia and Russia. Indeed, in July Mercy complained to him that, in demanding absolute equality, Thugut rarely suggested anything definite. He was too vague and circular, Mercy moaned; "It is absurd to pretend to hold ourselves in a labyrinth and to close to ourselves the straight routes."[48] In this case Mercy was right. Thugut's insistence on a general, imprecisely defined equality made the allies suspect that he wanted far more than they thought Austria deserved. In this matter he suffered from his old weakness of appearing devious when he was not trying to be.

Despite appearances, Thugut's major concern was not new lands even in 1793. He knew that far more was at stake in the war than acquiring territory. In fact, he worried that all the talk about compensation was distracting the allies from their primary goal, the defeat of France. He feared that the bickering among them would enable the revolution to escape destruction. In the midst of a letter about Poland, Thugut openly wondered if the attention paid to compensation might abort "the great and noble enterprise . . . of reestablishing order in France and of punishing the odious enemies of throne and religion."[49] Nevertheless, Thugut did little to remind the other members of the coalition to refocus their attention on the true purpose of their collective mission. He may not have thought it necessary, but he certainly should have. His assumption that everyone understood the goal of the coalition and always kept

[48] Mercy to Thugut, July 17, 1793, in ibid., 150.
[49] Thugut to L. Cobenzl, July 12, 1793, in ibid., 144.

that goal in mind was a false one, and he made it worse—and aroused suspicions of his own motives—by not insisting at all times that he was unhesitatingly pursuing the coalition's stated purpose himself.

Victory often threatens an alliance more than defeat, and this was certainly the case in 1793. The suspicions among the allies made evident in the discussions about territorial compensation carried over into other areas as well. In the spring and summer Britain had concluded treaties of alliance with practically every state fighting against the French (Sardinia on April 25, Naples on July 12, Prussia on July 13, and Austria on August 30), but all of them were vaguely worded, and only one, that with Sardinia, committed Britain to provide financial aid.[50] London was confident that victory was imminent and saw no reason to subsidize other powers that it did not really trust. Moreover, its own army had wandered away from the main allied force in northern France for Dunkirk, which seemed a prize that should be secured before joining the Austrians for the march to Paris.

If cooperation between the Austrians and the British was not the closest, relations between Austria and Prussia were bad and growing worse, and not simply on the diplomatic level. When Thugut sent Count Lehrbach to Prussian headquarters on a mission to discuss with the Prussian king Poland's future, he also instructed him to investigate reports of animosity between the Austrian and Prussian commanders of the combined Austro-Prussian army. Lehrbach discovered that relations were terrible. The Austrian commander, Dagobert Sigismund Wurmser, and the entire Prussian staff were absolutely at odds. "The Prussians and whoever takes their side blame Wurmser and his operations, and he and his supporters blame the Prussians for everything that goes wrong."[51] The disputes and recriminations reached such a point that Wurmser announced that his Austrian forces would simply leave the

[50] Sherwig, *Guineas and Gunpowder*, 22–25.
[51] Lehrbach to Thugut, August 30, 1793, in Vivenot, ed., *Quellen*, 3: 221.

Prussians and march into Alsace by themselves. The Prussians could do what they wished; he refused to be associated with them any longer.[52]

Success in war had given the allies the luxury of arguing about matters of compensation and cooperation, but that success soon came to an end. On September 8 French forces, inspired by the newly established Committee of Public Safety in Paris, attacked the British at the village of Hondschoote, relieved the siege of Dunkirk, and drove the enemy up the coast, thus exposing the right flank of the main Austrian army around Valenciennes.[53] Just as victory at Neerwinden led to a series of Austrian successes, so too victory at Hondschoote led to a series of French successes. In mid-October the French defeated the Austrians at Wattignies and in November forced Wurmser out of Alsace and back across the Rhine. Concurrently, the Prussians, who had moved slowly and hesitantly from Mainz to Kaiserslautern, retraced their steps from fear of a possible French counteroffensive.

None of the French successes was decisive, and none really posed a problem that the allies could not overcome in the next campaign. For Austria and for Thugut, the real blow of the autumn was delivered not by the French but by the Prussians. On September 22 the Prussian minister Girolamo Lucchesini presented to Lehrbach a formal statement that the king of Prussia faced serious problems in Poland with which he had

---

[52] Wurmser to Waldeck, September 1, 1793, in ibid., 242–43. Trouble had also erupted in the Austrian camp, especially between Wurmser and his chief of staff, Christian August Waldeck. To try to heal this trouble, Vienna sent yet another agent, Joseph Ferraris, to Prussian headquarters. Francis to Wurmser, September 7, 1793, in ibid., 261–62. Of all this animosity Thugut wrote, "It is most deplorable to see all the gentlemen jealous of one another, conspiring against one another, and creating their factions against one another; and in the middle of all these struggles of vanity and personal interest the monarchy proceeds at a speedy pace toward its own collapse." Thugut to Colloredo, September 10, 1793, in Vivenot, ed., *Vertrauliche Briefe*, 1: 40.

[53] Rothenberg suggests that Hondschoote was the first battle in which the draftees of the first *levée en masse* were engaged. Rothenberg, *Napoleon's Great Adversaries*, 39.

to deal personally. Therefore, he planned to leave his headquarters for the East and would reduce his army's efforts against France accordingly. Moreover, Prussia would not continue the war against France in 1794 unless the coalition provided it with the means to do so; in addition, the emperor would have to find indemnities and compensation at French expense without Prussian assistance.[54]

To Thugut, the statement represented "new proofs of duplicity," but he also realized that a Prussian withdrawal from the war would be a serious blow to Austria.[55] From Starhemberg in London, he discovered what Prussia wanted as payment to continue the fight: a total of twenty-two million écus, of which Britain would pay nine million, Austria three million, and the Holy Roman Empire ten million. Since the Empire would be unable to pay immediately, Berlin expected Austria and Britain to advance the Empire's share and then collect it from the German states later.[56] It was an enormous amount which resembled extortion rather than a request for financial aid. The British ambassador in Vienna wrote that the Prussians were "like Deal men, who avail themselves of the perilous situation of the passengers in a ship stranded on the Goodwins to drive a most unconscionable bargain." If the monarchies of Europe were overthrown, he remarked, he hoped that the Hohenzollern dynasty would be the first.[57]

Officially the Austrian response to the Prussian request was conciliatory. Thugut composed a letter from Francis to Frederick William expressing the hope that difficulties could be resolved so that the two monarchs could continue the "noble enterprise that concerns almost all thrones and especially the salvation, security, and future tranquillity of Germany, our

[54] Lucchesini's statement read to Lehrbach and Reuss, September 22, 1793, in Vivenot, ed., *Quellen*, 3: 190–95.

[55] Thugut to Starhemberg, November 4, 1793, and Thugut to L. Cobenzl, October 21, 1793, in ibid., 351–53, 333–40.

[56] Starhemberg to Thugut, November 8, 1793, in ibid., 366–67.

[57] Eden to Auckland, November 16, 1793, in Auckland, *Journal and Correspondence*, 3: 144.

common fatherland."[58] Lehrbach was dispatched again to the Prussian king with instructions to express the emperor's love of Prussia and to try to resolve all differences through negotiation.[59] Nevertheless, Thugut had no intention of paying Prussia any money. Prussia was an ally and had no right even to ask for special funds to carry out its solemn obligations. Moreover, no one could depend on Prussia to fulfill its promises anyway, whether the money was paid or not. Finally, Austria could not afford the sums demanded, for it had to finance its own army. While assuring Frederick William of Francis's good will and expressing hopes that they could defeat France together, Thugut set out to find more reliable sources of support elsewhere. He had to find such support if he wished to continue the war, and he certainly wanted to do that. As 1793 turned to 1794, that was the task he undertook.

[58] Francis to Frederick William, November 20, 1793, in Vivenot, ed., *Quellen*, 3: 400–401.

[59] Instructions to Lehrbach, November 22, 1793, in ibid., 387–95.

CHAPTER VI

DEFEAT, 1794

IN HIS SEARCH for dependable allies, the first power Thugut turned to was Russia. Catherine and her advisers had frequently condemned the revolution but thus far had done nothing practical to help stop it, and Thugut decided that, with Prussia wavering, the time had come to urge Russia to match its words with actions. He instructed Louis Cobenzl to request formally that Catherine honor her obligations under the Austro-Russian accord of 1781, which required Russia to send at least twelve thousand troops to support Austria in case of attack. Moreover, Cobenzl was to ask the Russians to use their influence in Warsaw to persuade the Poles to join the antirevolutionary cause by sending fifteen thousand men, a force for which Austria would gladly pay. Thugut acknowledged that the Austro-Russian agreement allowed St. Petersburg to supply a subsidy instead of men, but Cobenzl was to plead that "as much as this court [Vienna] needs monetary support, . . . the lack of soldiers is even greater and more difficult to overcome." If the Russians agreed, they must respond as quickly as possible; indeed they should send their troops stationed in Poland since they were already the closest to the Rhine.[1]

With the instructions to Cobenzl en route, Thugut turned to another source of additional aid: the Holy Roman Empire.

[1] Thugut to L. Cobenzl, December 18, 1793, in Vivenot, ed., *Quellen*, 3: 339–42.

The Reichstag of the Empire had declared war on France in 1793 but had provided little significant help during that year. Thugut believed that it could do much more; in January 1794 he, in the emperor's name, asked the Reichstag to provide additional assistance of a rather unusual kind: he called for an arming of the people—a *levée en masse* of the German citizenry living in the lands along the Rhine. The calling of all men to arms—in France, not in Germany—is judged one of the most important innovations introduced by the French Revolution to the modern world. First proclaimed by the Committee of Public Safety in the midst of defeat in August 1793, the levée en masse provided the French armed forces with so many recruits that they were able not only to regain the initiative in the war but to do battle with all of Europe for more than twenty years to come. The potential of the levée was brought to Thugut's attention within weeks of its pronouncement. In late October 1793 Pellenc warned Vienna that "The French have made a discovery more menacing to human existence than powder to cannon: make every man a soldier. If they had invented some new war machine, we could have made one just like it, but this dreadful secret . . . no one dares copy."[2] Pellenc was wrong; others would copy it or at least adopt a modified form of it, although none of their efforts would approach the success of the French.

But the idea of an armed citizenry was by no means exclusively French, even in 1793.[3] Before the French levée was proclaimed, some German territories had already attempted similar measures. In the spring of 1793, as the French approached the Upper Rhine, a few villages in the region had appealed to their inhabitants to take up arms. That appeal had so impressed the Austrian commander, General Wurmser,

[2] Pellenc to Mercy and transmitted to Vienna, October 29, 1793, in M. Ad. de Bacourt, ed., *Correspondance entre le comte de Mirabeau et le comte de la Marck pendant les années 1789, 1790 et 1791* (Paris, 1851), 3: 449.

[3] In the 1780s there had been discussion of a levée in Austria. Jürg Zimmermann, *Militärverwaltung und Heeresaufbringung in Österreich bis 1806* (Frankfurt, 1965), 114.

that he specifically requested civilian armed help in case the French invaded the Breisgau, one of the Habsburg provinces along the Rhine.[4] Such help was not needed then, but in September 1793 the governing body of the Breisgau announced a plan to arm fifteen thousand citizens to watch the Rhine so that regular forces assigned there could join the advancing army.[5] When the French launched their counteroffensive in the autumn of 1793, calls to arms in western Germany became widespread. Towns and villages in Baden, Württemberg, the Palatinate, and Electoral Mainz issued appeals, and in January 1794 the imperial defense circles of the Upper Rhine, Electoral Rhine, and Franconia also called their citizens to arms.[6] Thus the emperor's proposal for a general levée in the Rhineland was certainly not unprecedented. In fact, when justifying the call, Thugut wrote that it was not simply an imitation of the French practice, but the revival of an old tradition in Germany: "This kind of arming is no innovation in the Empire; it is based upon the spirit of the old imperial constitution; it is more or less always in effect from the old general call [*Aufgebot*], where in Germany every fifth man must enter the field against the barbarians while those left behind arm themselves to preserve internal order."[7]

It is not clear who actually thought of calling for a general mobilization. Given Thugut's view of the French Revolution, some scholars have suggested that he must have opposed the measure on the grounds that it would be akin to placing weapons in the hands of German sans-culottes, who might turn

[4] Reinhold Lorenz, *Volksbewaffnung und Staatsidee in Österreich (1792–1797)* (Vienna/Leipzig, 1926), 49; Wilhelm Wendland, *Versuche einer allgemeinen Volksbewaffnung in Süddeutschland während der Jahre 1791 bis 1794* (Berlin, 1901), 61.

[5] Lorenz, *Volksbewaffnung*, 50.

[6] Wendland, *Versuche*, 125–30; Aretin, *Heiliges Römisches Reich*, 1: 294. In November 1793 Archduke Charles recommended a levée of Rhenish farmers on a temporary basis. Helmut Hertenberger and Franz Wiltschek, *Erzherzog Karl: Der Sieger von Aspern* (Graz/Vienna/Cologne, 1983), 41.

[7] Thugut to Seilern, February 27, 1794, Vienna, HHSA, SK, *Regensburg, Kurböhmische Gesandtschaft*, 6.

them on their own rulers.[8] Although he may not have initiated it, Thugut did compose both the appeal itself and a long and careful rationale of it, in which he showed that he was by no means so undiscriminating that he categorized everyone into either upper-class traditionalists or lower-class malcontents. Thugut had no difficulty distinguishing among French revolutionaries, German peasants, Viennese bourgeois, and Tyrolean patriots; for him they were not all simply "the common people" to be distrusted or feared. The German citizen on the Rhine, he wrote, knew that his property and way of life were threatened, and, if the regular army proved unable to protect them, he would undertake the means to do so himself. "When the citizen farmer sees his home and his person left undefended, when he has to fear gruesome consequences from the enemy and uncertainty from the troops supposed to shield him, his arming will be difficult to stop." And this arming, Thugut went on, would not threaten a prince—providing he was a just and fair ruler—but actually furnish him with the means to save his throne; "and a sovereign must then seek his own salvation in it or be swept away if he can find no confidence in his own method of ruling and cannot depend on the loyalty of his own subjects." Those princes who could not depend on such loyalty, Thugut implied, deserved to be swept away. As to the emperor himself, he had complete trust in the people of Germany and no compunction about placing the fate of the Holy Roman Empire in their hands. "His Imperial Majesty can as head of the Empire only praise this patriotism and courage and, since it is so absolutely necessary, all the more appeal to it because, when the German nation once awakens, and individual citizens and farmers are ready to resist, then it will be so much easier to create an imperial defense force with armed civilians."[9]

Thugut sent these explanations to the Habsburg represent-

---

[8] Lorenz, *Volksbewaffnung*, 61; Anton Ernstberger, *Österreich-Preussen von Basel bis Campoformio, 1795–1797* (Prague, 1932), 430.

[9] Thugut to Seilern, February 27, 1794, Vienna, HHSA, SK, *Regensburg, Kurböhmische Gesandtschaft*, 6.

atives to use in the Reichstag at Regensburg. But did he really believe them? Did he really envision a struggle between the armed citizenry of France and the armed citizenry of Germany? One might doubt that he did, for in the proposals to arm the people he included an alternative: the creation of a Reichsarmee, an army to be established by the Reichstag independently of the Austrian and Prussian forces. If the Reichstag accepted this alternative, however, Thugut insisted that the German states must commit "the greatest energy" to raising the army and to making it a large and effective force.[10] The creation of such an army sounds like what Thugut had in mind all along. In fact, one could suggest that the proposal to arm the people was actually Thugut's way of pressuring the states of the Holy Roman Empire into contributing more substantially to the war effort. While such an interpretation is plausible, it must remain completely conjectural. Whatever his true intention, Thugut never expressed consistent contempt for or mistrust of the common folk of Germany and Austria. As we shall see, he was distressed when they seemed unable to comprehend the consequences of French victories, but he was likewise encouraged when they responded enthusiastically to calls to support the emperor's cause. He probably did, as Hormayr claims, refer to some citizens as *canaille*, but the targets of this epithet were persons who jeered and threw stones at him during the dark days of November and December 1800.[11] Thugut had no universal scorn for the masses, and he believed that they deserved sovereigns who ruled honestly and fairly. Indeed, he repeated on more than one occasion that the prince who ruled well need not fear the spread of revolutionary ideas—however much he should fear revolutionary France— and that the sovereign who did not rule wisely should not only fear those ideas but mend his ways.

The emperor's call for arming the citizens in the Rhineland was rejected by the Reichstag, because many states, especially Prussia, were indeed convinced that armed civilians were un-

[10] Ibid.
[11] Hormayr, *Lebensbilder*, 1: 320.

trustworthy. But the Reichstag did accept Thugut's alternative, the establishment of a Reichsarmee of 110,000 men that would act separately from but in cooperation with the forces of Austria and Prussia.[12] This army was placed under the command of Duke Albert of Saxe-Teschen, an Austrian field marshal with good imperial credentials and husband of Marie Christine, a daughter of Maria Theresa and aunt of Emperor Francis. The Reichsarmee was to protect the left flank of the allied cordon that stretched from the Netherlands to Switzerland. Coburg's British-Dutch-Austrian forces were stationed in Belgium, the Prussians under Field Marshal Wiehard von Möllendorf were based at Mainz, and the Reichsarmee was assigned to defend the Upper Rhine from Mainz to Basel. To protect such a long front with the forces available was a formidable task. Covering a distance of over two hundred miles with 110,000 soldiers would have been difficult in itself, but, because the German states failed to provide the men needed, Saxe-Teschen had to perform this duty with no more than 80,000, of whom 55,000 were his own Austrians. He had to spread his units so thinly that they were rendered ineffective. "Where is my army with which I will pursue victories?" he wrote upon taking command. "Everywhere and nowhere."[13] To make matters worse, when seeking men and supplies from the German states, the duke faced refusals, delays, unfulfilled promises, petty bickering, jealousy, and intrigue.[14] At the same time, he had to be sensitive to the constitutional restrictions upon his authority, and he did his best to abide by them. Com-

[12] Thugut explained that Vienna wished a Reichsarmee because (1) one already existed in the imperial contingents in the field; (2) many German states did not like their forces mixed with Austrians and Prussians; (3) a Reichsarmee would encourage the Empire to help the cause even more; and (4) many states, especially Hanover, Württemberg, and Mainz, had requested it. Thugut to Seilern, February 6, 1794, Vienna, HHSA, SK, *Regensburg, Kurböhmische Gesandtschaft*, 6.
[13] Quoted in Alfred von Vivenot, *Herzog Albrecht von Sachsen-Teschen als Reichs-feld-marschall. Ein Beitrag zur Geschichte des Reichsverfalles und des Baseler Friedens* (Vienna, 1864), 1: 82.
[14] Ibid., 75–78.

menting upon the instructions for Saxe-Teschen's political officer, Thugut declared that the duke must follow all of the laws and customs of the imperial constitution "as long as it can be done without disadvantage."[15] For Thugut the constitution was important, but not as important as victory.

In Thugut's mind the primary purpose of the Reichsarmee was to replace the Prussian force, which he assumed would be substantially reduced because the allies would not pay the exorbitant price Berlin demanded for keeping it at its previous strength. He had not, however, reckoned upon the Prussophilia of the British. Besides a fondness for Prussia that had weathered a number of storms since the Seven Years' War, the British had always harbored more respect for the military prowess of Prussia than they had for that of Austria. Consequently, they looked upon the announced reduction in Prussian forces as a truly devastating blow to the war effort. The British sent a special delegate, James Harris, Lord Malmesbury, to conclude an agreement by which Prussia would remain in the war with allied funding. The British hoped that Vienna would join them in providing the support, but Thugut steadfastly refused, inquiring openly why London would pay so much money for an army that had contributed little thus far and would likely contribute even less in the future.[16] Malmesbury proceeded anyway; on April 19, 1794, he concluded a treaty by which the British and Dutch governments agreed to pay to Prussia £150,000 per month, plus additional funds at the opening and closing of the campaign, for an army of 62,400 men, not including the 20,000 men Prussia owed as its obligation to the Holy Roman Empire.

The Prusso-British subsidy treaty guaranteed that Prussia would field a substantial army in 1794, but in every other respect it was unfortunate for future allied relations. As Thugut had warned, the Prussian performance in the campaign of 1794 was woeful. As the British-Dutch-Austrian forces in Bel-

---

[15] Thugut to Colloredo, March 19, 1794, in ibid., 58.

[16] Thugut to Lehrbach and Starhemberg, February 27, 1794, in Vivenot, ed., *Quellen*, 4: 104–12.

gium suffered defeat and Saxe-Teschen's Reichsarmee on the Upper Rhine struggled to hold its line, the Prussians in the center did nothing to aid either wing. To some extent this failure was the fault of the British themselves, who had demanded the creation of a joint Prusso-British military commission to plan strategy but had failed to specify its exact powers. Consequently, the Prussian army sat in its shelters while the commission debated military policy.[17] Not only did the treaty fail to achieve its purpose in the short run, it also created a legacy of suspicion and, at times, hostility between the Austrians and the British thereafter. London paid substantial sums for the Prussian army in 1794 and received nothing for its money. It was determined not to make the same mistake in dealing with Austria. Consequently, when answering later Austrian requests for funds, the British were far less generous than they had been with the Prussians and far more careful in exacting definite commitments from Austria in return. Thugut resented the attitude of the British and often reminded them that, after they had foolishly paid the Prussians handsomely when all the evidence had shown that Prussia was untrustworthy, they were now miserly toward the Austrians, who had fought hard in the past and would fight hard in the future. Such exchanges only enhanced the ill feelings of the British and the Austrians toward one another, feelings that remained throughout most of Thugut's tenure as foreign minister.

In the coming compaign, then, the Austrians and Prussians each placed substantial, though not always active, armies in the field, supported by the Reichsarmee of Duke Albert. The main theater for 1794 was Belgium, where the Austro-British-Dutch forces hoped to restore allied fortunes following the French victories of late 1793. But many officers believed that, after the defeats of the previous year, they and their men needed special inspiration provided by an appearance of the emperor himself on the field of battle. A trip to Belgium by the

---

[17] Sherwig, *Guineas and Gunpowder*, 41–42; Helleiner, *Imperial Loans*, 2.

emperor had been discussed and planned in 1793 but never undertaken. In 1794, however, appeals for his presence had become increasingly insistent. Archduke Charles implored him not only to show himself to the men but also to bring about some changes in the Austrian high command.[18] Coburg likewise requested Francis to visit the army, pleading that only his presence could improve cooperation between the Austrian and Prussian staffs. The most eloquent and wide-ranging plea came, however, from Mercy, who insisted that Francis escape his courtiers in Vienna in order "to listen to us who are here." In Vienna, he wrote, "one views this war as an ordinary war," and it was not. "One has never sufficiently appreciated the nature of this frightful French Revolution, not the detestable spirit of its authors, nor their future projects, nor their immense resources, nor the perils to which the very duration of this revolution exposes all governments; and this lack of appreciation has caused great errors and aggravated all the dangers of the moment." The emperor must personally inspect the battleground "where a few months will decide if the thrones of Europe have a future."[19]

Yet the man in Vienna who, Mercy believed, understood the revolution better than anyone else advised the emperor not to go to Belgium: Thugut. He opposed such a trip for a good governmental reason: in a time of trial a head of state should not leave his center of communications and administration, and for the emperor that center was Vienna. Wandering off to Belgium would cause delays in transmitting information and issuing orders that could be of considerable consequence.[20] As if to endorse Thugut's opinion, a few days before Francis was to leave for Brussels came the first news of serious trouble in

[18] Archduke Charles to Francis, January 4, 1794, in Vivenot, ed., *Quellen*, 4: 4–5; Thugut to Colloredo, January 7, 1794, in Vivenot, ed., *Vertrauliche Briefe*, 1: 70–72.

[19] Mercy to Francis, March 9, 1794, in Vivenot, ed., *Quellen*, 4: 128–31; Mercy to Francis, March 4, 1794, Vienna, HHSA, SK, *Frankreich*, 181.

[20] Thugut to Colloredo, January 2, 1794, in Vivenot, ed., *Vertrauliche Briefe*, 1: 68–69.

the remainder of independent Poland, the course and consequences of which were impossible to predict at that time. It seemed sensible for the emperor to remain in his capital at least until further information about the Polish rising could be gathered and evaluated and some decisions reached as to what to do about it. But with the news from Poland arrived Archduke Charles from the army in Belgium, carrying a special plea for his brother to return to the battlefields with him. Only the emperor's presence, Charles insisted, could at once inspire the troops, improve relations among the allied commanders, show the British Austria's true concern for the future of the Austrian Netherlands, and arouse the Belgian estates, officials, and populace to make sacrifices on the monarchy's behalf.[21] Francis could not resist such an appeal, and on April 2 he, Archduke Charles, Archduke Joseph, and a considerable entourage set out for Belgium. Thugut went as well, though waiting for news from Poland delayed his departure until April 9.

The Polish rising was that of Thaddeus Kosciuszko, a last, futile protest against the dismemberment of the country by the great eastern European powers. It would end in Poland's defeat and dissolution, a dissolution in which Thugut would play an important role. Some have described Austrian policy in the Third Partition as exemplifying the conduct of Thugut at his most cynical: loudly defending the rights of monarchs in the West while violating those rights in the East, complaining of the absence of Austria in the Second Partition while vengefully excluding Prussia from the Third, and taking time from his professedly dedicated struggle against the mighty and vigorous revolutionaries in France to liquidate a few pathetic patriots in Poland.

The evidence for Thugut's role in the Third Partition suggests that affairs were not quite as simple as commonly believed. Most importantly, Thugut did not view events in Poland as divorced from those in France. From the first he

---

[21] Criste, *Erzherzog Carl*, 1: 126–27; Hüffer and Luckwaldt, eds., *Frieden*, xiv–xvi.

suspected the Polish leaders to have ties with the revolutionary government in Paris. The first reports Thugut received were fragmentary. Some sources said that Kosciuszko was friendly toward Austria (which was true), and that the purpose of his revolt was only to end the influence of Russia and Prussia in Poland and to restore the famous reforming constitution of May 1791.[22] Kosciuszko's personal representative in Vienna wrote to Thugut assuring him that the Polish revolutionary leaders had no ties to Paris and wished only to establish in Poland a free state and society modeled on that of England.[23] But none of this information impressed Thugut as much as the evidence sent to him by the Austrian chargé d'affaires from his own days in Warsaw, Benedikt Caché. In early April Caché forwarded two of Kosciuszko's early manifestoes that spoke of the rights of the people in a way that left no doubt in Caché's mind that France was the model for the rising in Poland. "The whole business in Poland," he wrote succinctly, "is the same as the French Revolution"; the manifestoes could have been written in Paris. Besides, he continued, other evidence indicated the presence of "French money . . . and French officers and officials sent by the National Convention, the creation in Cracow of similar revolutionary tribunals, and the daily arrival of Polish émigré chiefs."[24] That was enough for Thugut. To Colloredo he wrote, "One sees in it [Poland] strictly the pattern of the French Revolution, and that it is from the hearth of Paris that the spark has come which has enflamed Poland and which will incinerate all of Europe; . . . it is war to the death between sovereignty and anarchy, between legitimate government and the destruction of all order."[25] For Thugut the rising in Poland was not an expression of Polish

[22] Kollowrat to Francis, April 9, 1794, in Vivenot, ed., *Quellen*, 4: 181–86; Kosciuszko to Brigido, Austrian governor of Galicia, April 28, 1794, in ibid., 226.

[23] Count Ossolinski to Thugut, May 2, 1794, in ibid., 202–208.

[24] Caché to Thugut, April 2, 1794, Vienna, HHSA, SK, *Polen*, 57.

[25] Thugut to Colloredo, May 29, 1794, in Vivenot, ed., *Vertrauliche Briefe*, 1: 103.

patriotism; it was the product of the intrigues of revolutionary France.

Despite his conviction that the Polish revolution was an extension of the French one, Thugut knew that Austria could not—and need not—commit substantial forces to crush it. Those forces would be provided by Russia. As indicated at the beginning of this chapter, Louis Cobenzl on Thugut's orders had been trying throughout the winter and spring to persuade Catherine to assist Austria in the war against France. In February 1794 he had even offered Austria's formal acceptance of the Second Partition of Poland in return for aid.[26] When the rising in Poland occurred, Thugut realized that the Russians would probably send no troops to the West for the time being because they would all be used to crush the Poles. And he also knew that the rising made a final partition inevitable. In fact, he expressed to Cobenzl his displeasure at such a prospect, indicating that his suggestion of the previous year to destroy Poland to compensate Austria might not have been altogether serious. "One cannot deceive oneself that the probable result of the events in Poland will be a new partition," he wrote. "As inconvenient for us as that would be, it is no less true that given the general situation, the emperor cannot oppose it." In the meantime, Thugut believed that Vienna must insist that the Habsburg portion match "our ruinous sacrifices" in the struggle against France.[27]

Whatever the result of a new partition, however, Thugut warned that Cobenzl must never allow the Russian court to forget that the real enemy was, is, and would be France. If Catherine really wished to combat an evil of substance, then it was France, not Poland, she had to fight. "Events in Poland, grave as one wishes to suppose them, can never detract the attention of Her Majesty from affairs in France, nor weaken the lively interest that she so often declares to have in them. The

---

[26] Thugut to L. Cobenzl, February 27, 1794, in Vivenot, ed., "Thugut und sein politisches System," 403–405.

[27] Thugut to L. Cobenzl, June 21, 1794, Vienna, HHSA, SK, *Russland*, 2: 178.

intervention of her efforts is without doubt the surest means of success of this great undertaking, in order to prepare for her a role worthy of her glory in the future peace."[28]

Thugut's appeal not to ignore France was heartfelt, because, as Poland rose in revolt, calamity struck the allies in Belgium, a calamity Thugut experienced firsthand. In early April he had followed the emperor to the Austrian Netherlands and there had witnessed Francis's efforts to inspire the Austrian soldiers and the Belgian citizenry.[29] But the enthusiasm the emperor instilled was short-lived. Using the enormous numbers of men made available by the levée en masse, the French went on the offensive in late April and early May and defeated the Austrians at Courtrai (May 11) and an Anglo-Austrian force at Tourcoing (May 18). The loss at Tourcoing, while substantial, was not catastrophic, but it set a tone of defeatism in the Austrian military that boded ill for the immediate future. That tone became more pronounced when Francis expressed his wish to return home to be with his wife, who was in the last stages of pregnancy. Thugut did not oppose that wish since he believed that the situation in Poland demanded that Francis be in Vienna anyway in order to monitor events more closely, but his departure, which took place on June 13 when the military situation was still in flux, was interpreted by many either as a sign of cowardice or as evidence that he and his advisers already regarded the loss of Belgium inevitable.[30]

As Francis set out for Vienna, the French maintained their pressure on the allied forces and by the third week in June were approaching Brussels. Thugut witnessed personally the difficulty and frustration of the Habsburg troops as they tried to stop the new, huge French armies. "Reduced to the defensive," he wrote, "we are continually harrassed on two flanks of our positions in Flanders and on the Sambre by innumerable hordes who are in fact constantly defeated and repulsed, but

[28] Ibid.   [29] Hüffer and Luckwaldt, eds., *Frieden*, xlvi.
[30] Starhemberg to Thugut, June 6, 1794, in Vivenot, ed., *Quellen*, 4: 255–56; Quentin Crawford to Auckland, June 3, 1794, in Auckland, *Journal and Correspondence*, 3: 214–16.

German Theater of Operations, 1792–1800

our army is vastly weakened by these partial victories while the enemy repairs its losses with the greatest ease."[31] When the French neared Brussels, panic set in among the Austrian officials and a substantial portion of the population, a panic that Thugut observed with a mixture of amusement and despair. Old Metternich, he told Colloredo, was making ready to flee and "had hoarded every horse and every vehicle in order to take along everything he owned down to the last table, last chair, and the last bottle of wine in his cellar." Field Marshal Johann Blasius Bender, who was supposed to provide for the city's defense, had "no information about and not even a good guess as to the troop dispositions of either ourselves or the enemy." And Mercy, his good friend, "always keeps his head," but was still bent on interpreting the approaching catastrophe rather than doing anything to mitigate it; he wants "to call numerous meetings to discuss the most absurd platitudes." "I despair at tiring Your Excellency with my ceaseless lamentations," Thugut concluded, "but finally our general situation worsens daily; we are at the edge of the abyss, and if His Majesty does not in his wisdom decide to make serious changes, there is no way to save us from irremediable loss."[32]

Thugut's call for changes could not halt the French onslaught, and on June 26 at Fleurus, southeast of Brussels, the French inflicted a crushing defeat upon the Austrians. Brussels was now indefensible. The army retreated past it to the north and east, the British fell back toward the Dutch border, and Belgium itself gave way to chaos. One observer wrote of the Belgian countryside: "Picture to yourself an immense country in promiscuous flight from Tournai to Breda, and from Breda to Liège; above two hundred thousand persons fleeing from their homes, carrying their effects; the roads swarming with priests, nuns, children, old men, covered with rags, bathed in perspiration, their spirits sinking under the

[31] Thugut to L. Cobenzl, June 21, 1794, Vienna, HHSA, SK, *Russland*, 2: 178.

[32] Thugut to Colloredo, June 23, 1794, in Vivenot, ed., *Vertrauliche Briefe*, 1: 108–111.

burden of the present and the future, defiling between two lines of wounded soldiers and military provisions in retreat."[33] Unlike 1792, when he joined the first exodus from Brussels, this time Thugut left the city two days before the battle of Fleurus and so missed the great surge of refugees. On July 9 he reached Vienna. Two days later Brussels fell for the second time to the armed forces of revolutionary France.

When Thugut arrived in Vienna, he discovered formidable opposition awaiting him. A peace movement, which had been simmering since late 1792, had burst into the open. It consisted of a variety of figures, many with considerable influence. Especially vociferous was Trauttmannsdorff, who had been an enthusiastic promoter of peace for over a year. In his mind, the whole premise for fighting the war was without foundation. "Just as groundless," he had written in 1793, "is the contention that recognition of the Jacobin system will overwhelm all of Europe and destroy every throne." In fact, Trauttmannsdorff maintained, continuing the war would cause such strains on the "wise and mild" Habsburg rule that they would actually stimulate the internal upheaval the monarchy claimed that it was combatting: "We are choosing the illness itself as the means to cure it."[34] As the Austrian troops fled Belgium in the summer of 1794, Trauttmannsdorff thundered against the war with renewed vigor, indicting especially Thugut, whom he accused of shielding the emperor from advice contrary to what he wished the ruler to hear. To reduce Thugut's influence, Trauttmannsdorff recommended the establishment of a policy-making state council representing all major departments and composed of men "of proven insight and honor."[35]

Earlier Trauttmannsdorff had found little open support for his calls for peace; in July and August 1794, support became

---

[33] Abbé du Pradt to Mallet du Pan, July 2, 1794, in A. Sayous, ed., *Memoirs and Correspondence of Mallet du Pan* (London, 1852), 2: 91.

[34] Trauttmannsdorff to Francis, n.d. (likely June 1793), in Aretin, *Heiliges Römisches Reich*, 2: 323–35.

[35] Trauttmannsdorff to Francis, n.d. (likely August 15, 1794), in ibid., 235–37.

not only open but enthusiastic. In the government itself Count Kollowrat, the head of the principal agency for internal affairs, argued that financially the monarchy would be unable to continue the struggle into 1795. To do so would cost 100,000,000 gulden, "a frightening sum"; and, with Thugut in mind, one of his aides told Francis that anyone who asserted that Austria could raise that much was either "a flatterer or a traitor."[36] Some of Francis's favorites joined the chorus for peace, notably his military adjutant, Rollin, who passed on an anonymous letter declaring that the entire army, "from the generals to the common soldiers," demanded peace, and *Staatsratkonzipist* Stahl, who contended that Vienna had forgotten the well-known principle that "an opinion opposed by bayonets augments the number of its followers."[37]

Even members of the Habsburg family insisted upon an immediate settlement, including Francis's nearest brother, Grand Duke Ferdinand of Tuscany, and his uncle, Max Franz, elector of Cologne.[38] But the most important figure to advocate peace and to continue advocating it even as his reputation for military victory rose was Archduke Charles. On August 9, 1794, he sent Francis a detailed analysis of the main Austrian forces in Belgium and a discussion of the aid that the monarchy's allies might offer in the future. On the basis of the evidence he judged that, to continue the war, Austria must have firm and substantial commitments in money, men, support, and planning from its allies; should these commitments not be forthcoming—and he believed that they would not be—then Vienna must conclude peace. Such a peace, the archduke concluded, would not encourage the spread of the "French system" in Europe, but sapping the strength and will

[36] Viktor Bibl, *Erzherzog Karl: Der beharrliche Kämpfer für Deutschlands Ehre* (Vienna/Leipzig, 1942), 58; Josef Karl Mayr, *Wien im Zeitalter Napoleons* (Vienna, 1940), 23.
[37] Quoted in Bibl, *Kaiser Franz*, 99.
[38] Ferdinand to Francis, June 24, 1794 in Vivenot, ed., *Quellen*, 4: 299–301; Braubach, *Max Franz*, 319–20.

of the Austrian people through an unwinnable war certainly would.[39]

It was Thugut who opposed seeking peace most vigorously. One should never conclude a settlement in the midst of serious defeat, he told the emperor, especially a defeat at the hands of revolutionary France. One should right the situation as best one could and then summon the means to regain one's losses. And that was exactly what Thugut urged. The monarchy, he argued, had to follow three courses of action: first, it needed to raise much more money to carry on the war. To that end, Vienna had to resort to a number of measures, including reducing expenditures drastically, issuing new currency, finding new and varied ways to increase revenue, and obtaining substantial subsidies from the British. Second, the emperor had to find new commanders for the army, especially to replace Coburg, who had become a whining, pathetic old man, and his chief of staff Waldeck, who was prone to excuses, exaggeration, and intrigue. Third, relations among the allies needed again to be altered and improved. By keeping its British-subsidized army at Mainz and avoiding contact with the enemy throughout the campaign, Prussia had revealed even to London that it deserved no confidence. It was now imperative to ignore Prussia and to seek closer cooperation with Britain. Moreover, Vienna should not abandon its resolve to gain more support from the Holy Roman Empire and should double its efforts to bring Russia into the war.[40]

The emperor sided with Thugut. In fact, from this time on, the emperor not only allowed but encouraged Thugut to give

---

[39] Archduke Charles of Francis, August 9, 1794, in Vivenot, ed., *Quellen*, 4: 381–84. Of Austria's allies Charles wrote, "Prussia wishes to do nothing and actually seems to be in contact with the enemy; the agreement of the Empire to form an army is a chimera; Holland does not have enough troops to garrison all of its fortresses and defend itself; Spain needs, wants, and seeks peace; Piedmont is in no condition to defend even its own borders; and England can scarcely mobilize 30,000 men."

[40] Thugut to Francis, August 16, 1794, in ibid., 387–88.

advice on matters other than those strictly related to foreign policy. To be sure, Thugut had for some time expressed firm views on financial, military, and administrative policies to confidants such as Colloredo, Mercy, and Louis Cobenzl, but he had not extensively interfered in matters outside the province of the foreign minister. Although Trauttmannsdorff had believed for some time that Thugut possessed too much influence in too many areas and in mid-1793 Princess Eleonore Liechtenstein had complained of Thugut's "haste in bringing all business to himself," so far he had not really done so.[41] Beginning in August 1794, however, Thugut took a far more active role in areas outside the normal limits of foreign policy but related directly to the war effort, notably in finance and in military appointments and affairs.

In financial matters Francis specifically asked him to recommend new sources of revenue and, as part of the charge, to undertake negotiations with the British to obtain substantial sums for the Austrian war effort.[42] From that point on, Thugut was involved deeply in Austria's efforts to raise funds both internally and externally. Even then, however, he mostly offered suggestions, not orders, for increasing domestic revenue, while in his capacity as foreign minister he negotiated with Britain and other foreign states regarding loans and subsidies.

In military affairs Thugut played a more direct role. He not only began corresponding with the commanders in the field but began to compose most of the emperor's letters to them as well. Some contemporaries and historians have judged Thugut's growing participation in military decisions at this time to have been detrimental ultimately to the monarchy's cause, but, given the failures of the Austrian army in 1792 and 1794, one can hardly blame Thugut for seeking a greater say in matters involving the army. He believed that leadership was the key to

---

[41] Eleonore Liechtenstein to her daughter Josephine, September 14, 1793, in Adam Wolf, *Fürstin Eleonore Liechtenstein, 1745–1812* (Vienna, 1875), 238.

[42] Francis to Thugut, August 1 and August 10, 1794, Vienna, HHSA, SK, *Vorträge*, 154.

military success and that it was the emperor's duty to find competent leaders, to provide them with the best forces possible, and to encourage them in their duties. Indeed, Thugut took to heart Mercy's conception of civilian responsibility in military affairs: "It is the role of the military to assess the places and means," Mercy had written, "but it is to us political advisers to emphasize to [the generals] the need to act promptly and with energy; it would cripple our policy if the army did not take advantage of the most favorable moments, the most precious the current war offers us, and which will not recur again if we let them slip by."[43]

Mindful of this conception, from this time on Thugut beseeched commanders to move quickly, to seek out the enemy, and to destroy him. When he offered suggestions regarding strategy, he couched them in phrases indicating that the details of what he recommended were less important than undertaking some kind of offensive action. Thugut grumbled most bitterly about officers who avoided engagements while whining about shortages of supplies, manpower, and ammunition—complaints that seemed to him mostly excuses for inaction. As in nonmilitary affairs, Thugut believed that failure on campaign was largely a failure of will. Soldiers, materiel, and planning were important, but in the end it was the determination and skill of the commander that counted most. Consequently, aside from the levée en masse, he barely noticed the innovations in warfare introduced by the French because he assumed that an able and vigorous commander could overcome any surprises that he encountered. There is no evidence that Thugut read any military writings, not even Archduke Charles's *On War Against the New Franks* composed in late 1794 and early 1795. If he had read it, he probably would have agreed with its conclusions, because Charles himself argued that the "ignorance, indolence, and egotism" of the generals were mostly at fault for Austria's defeat.[44] Of all the Austrian com-

---

[43] Mercy to Starhemberg, August 4, 1793, in Pimodan, *Mercy-Argenteau*, 382–83.

[44] Quoted in Rothenberg, *Napoleon's Great Adversaries*, 43.

manders, Thugut admired General and later Field Marshal Wurmser the most because he breathed confidence, decisiveness, and eagerness to attack. Most of Wurmser's undertakings ended in defeat, but that did not affect Thugut's admiration and affection for him. He was a man of action, and Thugut appreciated that. The true Austrian military genius of the time, Archduke Charles, received Thugut's respect but also his criticism, because each time the archduke won a battle—which Thugut always praised—he seemed to recommend that the emperor conclude an armistice or even a peace—which Thugut found unconscionable.

In August 1794 Thugut, as well as many others, knew that the first step toward salvaging the military situation in Belgium had to be replacing the two commanders, Coburg and Waldeck. Not only had they lost most of the Netherlands, but they had also created serious distrust of Austria among the allies. After Fleurus British, Prussian, and Dutch officers had begun to speak of Austrian betrayal, to complain that secret orders had been issued to the Austrian commanders in June to abandon Belgium. This treachery was the reason, they believed, for the emperor's hasty departure in mid-June and for the Austrian army's poor showing before Brussels later in the month.[45] Thugut initially expressed disgust that the allies would believe the emperor capable of such a decision, but then he became disturbed by reports that Coburg and Waldeck themselves had actually been responsible for the misunderstanding.[46] Mercy reported being asked on one occasion by the two commanding officers if it were truly the emperor's policy to abandon Belgium, a question he found odd especially when he noticed that both officers were "highly embarrassed" when they heard that "His Majesty had always determined to de-

[45] Duke of York to Henry Dundas, June 28, 1794, in Biro, *German Policy*, 1: 239; Starhemberg to Thugut, July 1, 1794, in Vivenot, ed., *Quellen*, 4: 309–12; Dohm to Frederick William II, July 8, 1794, in Ludwig Häusser, *Deutsche Geschichte vom Tode Friedrichs des Grossen bis zur Grundung des deutschen Bundes* (Berlin, 1861), 1: 569.

[46] Thugut to Starhemberg, July 23, 1794, in Vivenot, ed., *Quellen*, 4: 351.

fend his provinces as vigorously as possible."[47] Then in mid-
August Thugut received a personal letter from Waldeck declaring that the generals had "believed for a long time that His
Majesty attached no value to the Low Countries" and therefore had seen no reason to protect them.[48] Thugut was outraged. Immediately the emperor recalled both Coburg and
Waldeck, replacing the former as commander in chief with
Franz Sebastian Clerfayt and the latter as chief of staff with
Johann Peter Beaulieu. Clerfayt's first orders were to restore
discipline and spirit among the soldiers, to purge the officer
corps of those too ill to fight or persistently absent, and to make
certain that those remaining "understood fully their duty."[49]

Believing the army now in competent hands, Thugut
turned his attention to the next important task: seeking closer
cooperation with Britain. In 1793, when the allies were winning, strong, mutual ties between Austria and Britain were
not particularly desirable to either party. London had not
wanted to entrust significant resources to a state that it believed likely to misuse them, and Vienna had no wish to solicit
aid that would encourage the British to try to exert greater influence over Austrian policy. But the defeats of 1794 forced the
two states together. Since both sides (especially Thugut, Colloredo, and the emperor on the one and the ministry of the
younger Pitt reinforced by the Portland Whigs on the other)
wished to continue the war, an alliance was needed to bind
them more formally in a crusade against the French.[50] But
reaching an agreement was not easy. Each party had specific
ideas about what it wished from the the other and was reluctant to offer much in return.

[47] Mercy to Thugut, July 3, 1794, in ibid.

[48] Waldeck to Thugut, August 2, 1794, in Vivenot, ed., *Vertrauliche Briefe*,
1: 389.

[49] Francis to Clerfayt, August 21, 1794, in Vivenot, *Thugut, Clerfayt und
Wurmser*, 1–4; Thugut to Colloredo, August 21, 1794, in Vivenot, ed., *Vertrauliche Briefe*, 1: 126.

[50] John Ehrman, *The Younger Pitt. Volume II: The Reluctant Transition*
(Stanford, 1983), 343–44.

Since both sides were now at least more eager to talk, they exchanged special delegations to open negotiations. The British chose Lord Earl Spencer, keeper of the privy seal, and Thomas Grenville, brother of the foreign minister, both described by Starhemberg as men "of great influence."[51] Their orders were to coordinate with Vienna ways to stop the French advance in the Netherlands, to relieve the frontier fortresses then under siege, and to resume the offensive before the year was out.[52] These initial instructions did not authorize the envoys to offer the Austrians money or troops to aid in achieving such goals, suggesting that the mission might have been primarily a means of testing Austria's commitment to the cause.

On his part, Thugut selected Mercy to go to London to seek specific British commitments of troops and, above all, cash. Since Prussia had proven unreliable, Mercy was to tell the British that they must find a way to make up for the 62,000 Prussians who had conspicuously failed to contribute to the campaign. Britain should send men of its own, pay for armed forces raised in the Holy Roman Empire, and help Austria persuade the Russians to commit themselves to the cause. Most importantly, Britain should provide direct monetary assistance to Austria.

Vienna had previously avoided asking openly for British funds, not only because it wished to avoid the conditions London would invariably place upon them but also because, prior to 1794, Habsburg policy makers had not thought they would be needed. By August 1794, however, Austria was desperately short of money. When the war began in 1792, the monarchy had enjoyed two years of peace during which it had achieved a rough budgetary balance between income and expenses. Indeed, the national debt had reached 390,730,000 gulden in 1791, but all the expenditures in 1792, including service on the debt, had not added to the deficit. In 1793, however, as the in-

---

[51] Starhemberg to Thugut, July 18, 1794, in Vivenot, ed., *Quellen*, 4: 347.
[52] Lord Grenville to Spencer, July 19, 1794, London, PRO, FO7, 38; Sherwig, *Guineas and Gunpowder*, 57.

tensity of the war against France increased, the debt rose sharply. Expenses exceeded revenue in that year by 28,590,000 gulden and in 1794 by 55,613,000 gulden, an enormous deficit for the time.[53]

At the outset of the conflict, the emperor had assured his subjects that no new taxes would be imposed because the war could be financed by regular taxes, by continuing the war tax (a variety of small excise taxes that had not been discontinued at the conclusion of the Austro-Turkish war in 1791), by revenue from the imperial domains, and by Habsburg family income.[54] Some voluntary contributions, including offerings by individual cities and towns, and the collection of silver and gold from private citizens helped the cause, but these efforts did not produce nearly enough income, especially after the defeats of 1794.[55]

A number of new schemes to raise money were offered by various officials in August and September 1794. Thugut himself suggested selling domain land to Polish aristocratic refugees fleeing Prussian and Russian reprisals, imposing a forced loan on Jews, and paying all soldiers serving outside the Habsburg lands in scrip rather than in specie.[56] There were, however, only two recognized means of raising truly significant sums: the issuance of paper money (always called the last ex-

[53] Adolf Beer, *Die Finanzen Oesterreichs im XIX Jahrhundert* (Prague, 1877), 390. In 1793 expenses totalled 93,434,000 gulden while income reached 68,854,000; in 1794 expenses rose to 113,247,000 of which 85,357,000 was spent on the military.

[54] Lorenz, *Volksbewaffnung*, 45–46.

[55] Ibid., 70–71. The British ambassador believed that those Austrians who sold their unminted precious wares were well paid. He reported that they received a good price at the outset, then got a premium of 4 percent, and, if they invested that money in state bonds (available at the place where they took their gold and silver), they could get a 4.5 percent rate of interest paid in six years. He also reported that the response "infinitely surpassed what was expected." Eden to Grenville, April 7 and 10, 1794, London, PRO, FO7, 33. By 1796 the government collected eleven million gulden in unminted silver and gold and an additional eleven million in the next three years.

[56] Thugut's "Unofficial Thoughts" on raising revenue, September 2, 1796, in Vivenot, ed., *Quellen*, 4: 417–19.

pedient and almost always the first one adopted) and procuring money from Britain.[57] Securing British funding had already been tried in 1794 through private, not public, means, and it had failed miserably. The Austrians had sought to raise three million pounds (approximately thirty million gulden) on the London money market by offering bonds through Boyd, Benfield, & Company, the parent company of Thugut's old investment house in Paris. These bonds were supported but not guaranteed by the British government. Unfortunately, the collateral offered was the revenue from the Habsburg lands in Belgium, and the bonds appeared on the London market just as the French were expelling the Austrians from those lands. After the battle of Fleurus, the bonds were withdrawn, having raised only one-tenth of the anticipated amount.[58] When Mercy received his orders to depart for London in August 1794, his primary charge was to request a guarantee from the British government for the three-million-pound loan which would be reissued, to solicit advances on that loan, and to discuss subsidies for the future, all in order to alleviate "the present penury of our finances."[59]

It was generally recognized by both London and Vienna that Mercy had the best chance of successfully negotiating an Austro-British agreement because he was not only a skilled diplomat but one known and admired by the British. Unfortunately, he became seriously ill during the crossing of the North Sea and died in London on August 25, 1794. Although Thugut did not express it abundantly, the death of Mercy caused him considerable sorrow, for Mercy was not only his best diplomat but also his patron and friend. Normally Thugut wrote very little about the deaths of others—nothing at all on the execution of Louis XVI, a few remarks about protocol on the demise of Marie Antoinette, comments primarily about

[57] Mayr, *Wien*, 37.
[58] Sherwig, *Guineas and Gunpowder*, 55–56; Helleiner, *Imperial Loans*, 4–9.
[59] Thugut to Mercy, June 30, 1794, in *Dropmore Papers*, 3: 513–16.

papers being preserved upon the death of Kaunitz in June 1794—but he expressed "profound regret" when he heard of Mercy's passing.[60]

With Mercy gone, negotiations in London became the province of Starhemberg, but in fact it was understood that the serious discussions would now take place in Vienna between Thugut on the one hand and Grenville and Spencer on the other. The talks went poorly. The British offered to guarantee the loan of three million pounds and to pay Austria the subsidy previously given to Prussia, but they requested substantial concessions in return, notably that Austria place in the Netherlands 160,000 men, that it persuade the Holy Roman Empire to assume payment of the British subsidy to Prussia, and, the most insulting proposal in Thugut's eyes, that the emperor appoint the British general Lord Cornwallis commander in chief of the allied armies.[61] Thugut found these demands "truly unacceptable"; Britain was demanding far too much for its gold.[62]

To aggravate the differences over issues, the negotiators themselves found that they disliked each other. Spencer and Grenville acknowledged Thugut to be "the only efficient Minister here," but, because he did not accept London's view of things, they branded him "without the disposition or capacity to see the present great crisis of Europe upon the large scale."[63] They wrote that in the talks Thugut behaved "more like a haberdasher of small wares than the minister of a great Empire."[64] Thugut was equally displeased by his British counterparts, complaining of their "imperious attitude"; in this

---

[60] Thugut to Dietrichstein, September 22, 1794, in Vivenot, ed., *Vertrauliche Briefe*, 1: 136–37.

[61] Sherwig, *Guineas and Gunpowder*, 59–60.

[62] Thugut to Colloredo, September 14, 1794, in Vivenot, ed., *Vertrauliche Briefe*, 1: 134.

[63] T. Grenville to Lord Grenville, September 1, 1794, in *Dropmore Papers*, 2: 626–28.

[64] T. Grenville to Lord Grenville, September 15, 1794, in ibid., 631.

context he expressed his greatest tribute to Mercy: "In general the death of Mercy is an irreparable misfortune."[65] Given the feelings and attitudes of the negotiators, little could be accomplished, and on October 7 Grenville and Spencer left for home.

Something still had to be done, however, for the allied war effort was faring no better. Despite the change in command, the Austrian army had continued its retreat, crossing the Rhine at the end of October. Since the Prussians withdrew as well, by November the left bank of the Rhine from Basel to Rotterdam—with the exceptions of Mainz and Luxembourg city still held by Austrian garrisons—was in French hands.

Now that the French stood on the Rhine, the German states began to waver. In August, Thugut had issued new and more passionate appeals to the Diet of the Holy Roman Empire, proclaiming "the fatherland in danger" and calling for sacrifices of considerable proportions.[66] The Reichstag had responded initially quite satisfactorily, passing on October 13 a bill to create an army of 200,000 men.[67] But on October 24 the elector of Mainz shattered the facade of anti-French unity by submitting a plan for peace with France that would restore the territorial status quo of 1792 in exchange for imperial recognition of the French republic and a mutual guarantee of noninterference in each other's affairs.[68] With this proposal, a respected German state had openly rejected Austria's official view of France as an irreconcilable enemy and had called for compromise with the revolution itself. To Thugut's chagrin, the peace plan met an enthusiastic response among most of the other German states.

The Mainz proposal was a serious challenge both to Thu-

[65] Thugut to Colloredo, September 25, 1794, in Vivenot, ed., *Vertrauliche Briefe*, 1: 139.

[66] Colloredo-Mansfeld to the *Reichstag*, August 13, 1794, and Thugut to all ministers, August 3, 1794, in Vivenot, *Herzog Albrecht*, 1: 203, 186–96. Thugut to Seilern, August 5, 1794, Vienna, HHSA, SK, *Regensburg, Kurböhmische Gesandtschaft*, 6.

[67] Vienna, Kriegsarchiv, *Krieg gegen die Französische Revolution* (Vienna, 1905), 1: 116.

[68] Vivenot, *Herzog Albrecht*, 1: 351–60.

gut's policies and the assumptions behind them. For Thugut, revolutionary France represented the greatest threat to the Holy Roman Empire in its history. Indeed, when appealing to the Empire for support in August, the emperor's official delegate had proclaimed in ringing terms that the war against France was no ordinary war but a struggle for "religion, property, civil peace, international order, honor, virtue, sovereignty of the German fatherland, for self-preservation and self-determination."[69] The favorable reception of the peace proposal showed that the German states had in fact no strong commitment to defeating revolutionary France and were now eager to end hostilities.

Thugut had to formulate a response to the peace plan quickly. He knew that Austria could not reject it outright. To do so would give credence "to the perfidious insinuation that, while having insufficient means to protect the Empire, we do not hesitate to sacrifice it to the interests of Austria and to perpetuate its dangers and misfortunes by our particularist views."[70] Thugut advised the emperor to express his own yearnings for peace, but to argue that there was no one in France with whom to discuss a serious settlement. France was governed by criminals, who replaced each other with such speed that a peace concluded on one day would mean nothing by the next. "When there exists in France an authority or a power with which one can enter into negotiations, we . . . will not refuse to join our co-estates in finding the means to conclude a just and honorable peace."[71] Such an approach would testify to the peace-loving nature of the emperor but at the same time would make it impossible to reach a settlement with a French government identified by Vienna as revolutionary. In the meantime, Austria's delegates to the Reichstag were simply to delay a decision on the peace proposal as long as possible.

[69] Colloredo-Mansfeld to the *Reichstag*, August 13, 1794, in ibid., 203.
[70] Thugut to Starhemberg, October 26, 1794, Vienna, HHSA, SK, *England*, 135.
[71] Ibid.

While struggling with the problems of a British alliance and imperial wavering, Thugut also had to keep watch on the talks with Russia regarding the future of Poland. The issue there was whether to leave a small portion of the country independent or to eliminate it altogether. For Thugut the latter course was preferable. "If circumstances seem to make a new [partition] inevitable," he wrote to Cobenzl in mid-September, "then a partition of all that remains of Poland seems to conform more to the interests of His Majesty." A partial dismemberment "would be advantageous only to the courts of Petersburg and Berlin by keeping their borders apart." If Austria had to have Russia as a neighbor, then Prussia would have to as well; when it came to worrying about the Russians, Berlin should be subjected to the same anxiety as Vienna. As to details, Thugut absolutely insisted that Cracow, seized in mid-June by the Prussians shortly before an Austrian occupation force reached it, be given to Austria because it was strategically vital to the protection of Galicia; the remainder of Poland was negotiable. Most important, the ambassador was to make certain that any agreement included "positive promises of aid from both courts [Prussia and Russia] for His Majesty during the duration of the war against France."[72] A final partition of Poland was inevitable in Thugut's mind, and he hoped that he could use it somehow to manipulate Russia into playing a role in the war against the revolution.

In the final month of 1794 Thugut faced four vital questions: Would the British and Austrians be able to agree on a treaty of cooperation that would provide Austria needed funds? Would the Reichstag pass a resolution demanding peace? Would a third partition of Poland take place? And would Prussia conclude a separate peace with France? Remarkably, in just three weeks between December 16, 1794, and January 3, 1795, the first three questions were answered. On December 16 the British, greatly worried now by the on-

---

[72] Thugut to L. Cobenzl, September 11, 1794, in Vivenot, ed., *Quellen*, 4: 437–41.

going French conquest of Holland, offered Austria a guaranteed loan of six million pounds as part of a general bond sale of twenty-four million pounds that the Pitt ministry was offering to the British public. On December 22 the Reichstag approved a resolution calling upon the emperor to seek an end to the war first by an armistice and then by a settlement with France based upon the Treaty of Westphalia (1648). On January 3, 1795, Cobenzl concluded with the Russians only—excluding the Prussians—the Third Partition, thus snuffing out the independent state of Poland for 123 years to come. While unknown to Thugut, even the fourth question was answered in this three-week period: on December 28 the Prussian envoy Bernhard von der Goltz arrived in Basel to begin secret negotiations with the French that would lead to a separate Franco-Prussian peace. Yet a fifth question and the one that concerned Thugut most was whether Russia would join in the war against the revolution. To his anxiety, in 1795 the Russians would still offer no firm answer.

CHAPTER VII

FRUSTRATIONS, 1795

FOR THE FIRST three months of 1795, Thugut struggled with the details of resolving the questions posed at the turn of the year. The one that presented the least difficulty was the Third Partition of Poland. Cobenzl had arranged a satisfactory territorial settlement, which gave to the monarchy West Galicia, the land between the Bug and Pilica rivers. It was almost as large as Bohemia and contained, besides Thugut's coveted prize of Cracow, the city of Lublin, the upper reaches of the Vistula River, and 1,250,000 inhabitants. It was, however, a poor region, offering a rather meager two million gulden in annual revenues.[1] In addition to the territorial division, Cobenzl and the Russians agreed that Austria would adhere to the provisions of the Second Partition, including the Bavarian-Belgian exchange although with the restriction "that it conform to the interests of the two courts." That wording enabled Austria to declare that the exchange did not in fact conform to its interests at the time, since the exchange would alienate the British. Therefore, discussion of it could be dropped. In a "most secret" article, Austria agreed to Catherine's famous Greek Project, which consisted of establishing two new Christian kingdoms in the Balkans should the Ottoman Empire collapse, a proposal first presented to Joseph II in 1782. Cobenzl

[1] Hermann Günther Meynert, *Kaiser Franz I* (Vienna, 1872), 136.

170

described the project as still her "favorite idea" but added that even her advisers now regarded it as largely fantasy. In exchange for supporting the Greek Project, Catherine agreed to use "all means in her power" to help Austria win additional compensation in the West, "at the expense of France, of the Venetian Republic, or elsewhere."[2] Although the mention of Venice in the Third Partition agreement seemed to add something new to the various talks about compensation and acquisition, it had been discussed a few times earlier. In fact, the addition of Venice to the Habsburg patrimony had been one of Kaunitz's well-known dreams in the 1780s.[3]

The real surprise of the Third Partition was the omission of Prussia as one of the signatory powers. Many have argued that Prussia's exclusion was Thugut's long-planned revenge for Austria's being left out of the Second Partition.[4] The insult and injury to Austria in 1793 Thugut paid back in 1795. Such an interpretation, while acknowledging Thugut's diplomatic adroitness if not necessarily his wisdom, is, nonetheless, incorrect. Prussia's exclusion from the final agreement (although the treaty provided some Polish land for Prussia) surprised Thugut as much as it did anyone else. Indeed, Louis Cobenzl felt called upon to offer an explanation of why he agreed to a separate Austro-Russian arrangement. He began, "I realize that I was authorized to conclude a partition only with the two courts of St. Petersburg and Berlin at the same time, that the work is imperfect until one is certain that the court of Berlin will adhere to it . . . and that I must render to Your Excellency an exact account of the reasons that motivated me in this re-

---

[2] L. Cobenzl to Thugut, January 5, 1795, in Vivenot, ed., "Thugut und sein politisches System," 430–45; Robert Howard Lord, "The Third Partition of Poland," *The Slavonic Review* 3 (1925): 494–95. The treaty is published in Miliutin, *Geschichte des Krieges Russlands*, 1:296–98.

[3] Karl A. Roider, Jr., *Austria's Eastern Question, 1700–1790* (Princeton, 1982), 179.

[4] Sybel, *Geschichte der Revolutionszeit*, 4:28–88; Hugo Hantsch, *Die Geschichte Österreichs* (Graz/Vienna/Cologne, 1962), 2:252; Uhlirz, *Handbuch*, 1:438.

gard." Cobenzl went on to explain that he had advised Thugut earlier of a possible separate settlement but had received no firm orders to resist one. Moreover, the Russian ministers had warned him that, if he balked at signing a separate treaty with them, they would immediately request the Prussian envoys do so instead. Anyway, the Russians now assured him that they would assume responsibility for persuading the Prussians to accept the partition, including the cession of Cracow to Austria since that city was still occupied by Prussian troops, so that Austria would not have to take on this task. Finally, Cobenzl wrote that, if what he had done would prompt the emperor and Thugut to "disavow me personally, . . . my zeal and my devotion for the service and interests of my august master will make me not hesitate at all to be the victim."[5]

Thugut was clearly not distressed by Cobenzl's actions; he was delighted. When the news reached Vienna, he remarked that Cobenzl had performed "quite marvelously." He had indeed gained revenge on Berlin, which Thugut found quite satisfying even if he had not planned it. "The king of Prussia finds himself thwarted in the same way we were two years ago." Moreover, any closer association between Russia and Prussia was now out of the question, while the "old intimacy" between Vienna and St. Petersburg could be restored.[6] Curiously, in his various writings at the time, Thugut wasted no ink either in applauding the acquisition of West Galicia or in speculating on its importance for the monarchy's future. The annexation of Polish land for its own sake (except for Cracow) had played only a small role in Thugut's policy regarding a final partition, and he did not concern himself with its significance now that it had been achieved.

From the beginning, his primary goal had been not to acquire territory in Poland but to enlist Russia in the cause against France. Now that the partition was complete, he

[5] L. Cobenzl to Thugut, January 5, 1795, Vienna, HHSA, SK, *Russland*, 2:81.
[6] Thugut to Colloredo, January 22, 1795, in Vivenot, ed., *Vertrauliche Briefe*, 1:175.

hoped that Catherine would at last join in the fight. Although he acknowledged that St. Petersburg would have to devote some resources to persuading Prussia to accept the Third Partition, he believed that the Polish issue was resolved and that the empress had no more excuses to hold back her support. His first instructions to Cobenzl following the news of the partition show that Thugut simply assumed that Russia would now eagerly enter the struggle against France: "Perhaps it would be best to insist upon the greatest number of men that Her Imperial Majesty will employ in the common cause, but it is utterly necessary that some number of troops begin their march immediately to join the allied armies, and finally [it would be best] to regulate the real role and the active cooperation of Russia in the efforts against the enemy."[7]

As Thugut depended upon Russia to contribute men to the cause, so he ardently hoped that Britain would contribute money. He was extremely pleased with the first news that the British government would guarantee a loan of six million pounds to the monarchy, but his delight turned to disappointment when he read the details. Although the British had offered the Austrians a loan of six million pounds in conjunction with a domestic loan of eighteen million pounds, the interest rates were to be computed differently. The Austrian bonds would be sold at a rate of 7.5 percent on their return and the British bonds at a rate of 4.5 percent. Since the bond sale would be presented to the public as a single package, the Austrians would in effect be underwriting a portion of the British loan rather than the other way around. To Starhemberg Thugut wrote, "We will in fact be supporting a part of the cost of the British loan which at bottom means we will be paying a form of subsidy to England."[8] That thought infuriated Thugut, especially when he recalled what seemed to him the obscene generosity of the British toward Prussia. In 1794 London had fairly lavished funds on Berlin but this year offered Vi-

[7] Thugut to L. Cobenzl, February 4, 1795, Vienna, HHSA, SK, *Russland*, 2:179.

[8] Thugut to Starhemberg, January 15, 1795, ibid., *England*, 135.

enna only a loan, "under the most unfavorable terms," while demanding "that the exact and scrupulous reimbursement be assured by the pettiest precautions."[9] He advised the emperor not to accept an offer, "so ruinous for the finances of Your Majesty," but to return it to London for negotiations. Accordingly, Francis appointed Joseph Pergen, son of the head of the police and an official in the Finance Ministry, to join Starhemberg in London in finding better terms.

Another remaining concern for Thugut from 1794 was the peace resolution passed by the Reichstag on December 22. When the news of its adoption reached Vienna, the immediate question was whether the emperor should ratify it or not, and in this matter Thugut encountered someone in an important official position to oppose his views. Although Thugut was minister of foreign affairs, he was not the principal correspondent with the emperor's delegates to the Reichstag. The Habsburg monarch had four such delegates. The one with the most prestige held the office of *Principal-Commissär*, whose primary function was to represent the emperor on formal occasions and to read official proposals and declarations to the Diet. The most influential post, however, was that of *Concommissär*, held in 1795 by the able Aloisius von Hügel. His task was to lobby the representatives to the Diet and the College of Electors on the emperor's behalf. According to accepted practice, the Concommissär did not report to or receive instructions from the foreign minister but the imperial vice-chancellor, who at that time was Prince Franz von Colloredo-Mansfeld. A stalwart aristocrat who would later become one of the baron's outspoken critics, Colloredo-Mansfeld deeply resented the upstart Thugut's encroaching upon his authority in imperial matters. Thugut himself had the right to correspond formally with the other two delegates, one who represented the emperor in his position as king of Bohemia and one who represented him in his position as archduke of Austria. Generally, however, these two officers were instructed not to

[9] Thugut to L. Cobenzl, April 2, 1795, ibid., *Russland*, 2:179.

174

embark on policies at variance with those of the Concommissär—and thus of the imperial vice-chancellor.

Colloredo-Mansfeld and Thugut had a sharp difference of
opinion regarding the peace resolution of December 22, 1794.
Colloredo-Mansfeld argued that it must be rejected out of
hand because it diverged so widely from current Habsburg
policy. Thugut took a more subtle approach, not unlike the
one he developed when the proposal was first presented to the
Diet in October of the previous year. First of all, he recommended that Francis accept the resolution in his capacity as
emperor. Not only would that enhance his peace-loving image, it would enable him to control any forthcoming peace negotiations and, if necessary, frustrate them. However, Thugut
recommended that the emperor also remind the Reichstag
that, in his capacity as king of Bohemia and archduke of Austria, he had the right and responsibility to serve the best interests of the House of Habsburg. Thus, if the Reichstag
concluded a peace of which Francis disapproved, he would accept it as emperor, but he would still be entitled to continue
the war with France as king of Bohemia and archduke of Austria. To justify this approach, Thugut advised the emperor
that the war was not being fought solely to protect Germany
from revolutionary principles "because neither peace nor war
can protect against those—only a wise and intelligent government." Instead, Austria was fighting to preserve its "present
and future status as a leading European great power."[10]

This argument implies that Thugut was at this time separating Austrian policy from policy of the Empire. In fact, that
was not true. Within weeks he was soliciting imperial support
even more assiduously than before while expressing ever
greater concern that the Empire on its part might desert Austria. Rather, the words he expressed here to the emperor reflected both Thugut's frustration regarding the peace
resolution and his recommendation that the emperor find a

[10] Thugut to Francis, January 26, 1795, in Vivenot, *Herzog Albrecht*, 3:32–
33.

course less offensive to German sentiments than Colloredo-Mansfeld's recommendation that Francis reject the peace proposal outright. In the end Francis followed Thugut's advice. In early February he ratified the Reichstag's resolution in his formal capacity as emperor.

The Third Partition, the British loan, and the imperial peace resolution consumed Thugut's attention through the first three and a half months of 1795. Then came a blow that added a new urgency to his concerns yet strengthened his determination to continue the struggle with France: the conclusion of a separate peace between France and Prussia at Basel on April 5. Rumors of a forthcoming Franco-Prussian settlement had been circulating since late 1794, but none had fully convinced Thugut that a treaty would actually be signed. A principal reason for his doubts was that Berlin had repeatedly assured Vienna that it would not make peace with France. Moreover, the Austrian ambassador at the Prussian court, Prince Heinrich Reuss, had given Thugut the impression that the question of war or peace depended upon the intrigues of various royal advisers and court factions, of which currently none had sufficient influence to persuade the king to desert the emperor.[11] Indeed, as late as April 12, a week after the treaty had been concluded, Thugut wrote to Colloredo that an agreement was unlikely because the Prussian ministers were not sufficiently united to accept one and because coming elections in France would distract the French government from any important diplomatic step.[12]

---

[11] There were indeed factions, but all of them favored peace by this time. Only the king himself expressed serious concern about fulfilling his obligations to the emperor. Willy Real, *Von Potsdam nach Basel* (Basel/Stuttgart, 1958), 122.

[12] Thugut to Colloredo, April 12, 1795, in Vivenot, ed., *Vertrauliche Briefe*, 1:203. The British likewise did not believe that the Prussians would conclude a separate peace. On April 8 the British cabinet approved a proposal from Pitt to offer again large subsidies to Prussia based on Malmesbury's conviction that Berlin was now eager to rejoin the fight. Sherwig, *Guineas and Gunpowder*, 65–67.

Thugut had misjudged both the Prussians and the French. When he heard of the treaty, he knew that it could have repercussions of monumental proportions. First of all, he feared that France and Prussia might now ally against Austria. In eighteenth-century diplomacy, a common sequel to a treaty of peace between powers was a treaty of alliance. In 1762 Austria had almost been the victim of such a step when the Russo-Prussian settlement in the Seven Years' War had led immediately to a Russo-Prussian alliance against Austria. In 1790 the Austro-Prussian reconciliation had been followed by the armed coalition of the two powers against France. And just as there had been rumors of a separate Franco-Prussian peace, so too there were rumors of a forthcoming Franco-Prussian accord against Austria. One report even hinted at an alliance that would unite France, Prussia, Denmark, Sweden, the Ottoman Empire, and Russia for the purpose of establishing Prussia as master of the Holy Roman Empire.[13]

But Thugut also realized that Prussia could easily disrupt the Austrian war effort without formally allying with France. As Thugut wrote to Cobenzl, the Prussians might "conspire with the French to interdict our supplies and transport, intercept our movements, and thereby try to force us into inactivity and put us at the mercy of the enemy."[14] Indeed, it appeared that the Prussians intended to do exactly that, for on May 27, 1795, they concluded another agreement with France establishing a neutrality zone embracing all of Germany north of the Main River, where no fighting or troop movements would be allowed. The measure was obviously aimed at Austria, not only because it permitted the German states north of the Main to withdraw their forces and funds from the imperial army without fear of reprisal, but also because the region declared neutral was the staging area for the Austrian forces stationed

[13] Lehrbach to Thugut, April 15, 1795, in Ernstberger, *Österreich-Preussen*, 123.
[14] Thugut to L. Cobenzl, May 16, 1795, Vienna, HHSA, SK, *Russland*, 2:179.

along the Lower Rhine. Those troops might be unable to procure supplies and might suffer harrassment if they remained where they were.

The Treaty of Basel was a blow to Thugut for another reason too. At the time of its announcement, he was convinced that revolutionary France was on the verge of collapse. This conviction was based not only on raw news from France but also on analyses provided by a new source whom he had found to replace Mercy: Jacques Mallet du Pan. Mallet du Pan had been a firm supporter of the French Revolution in its moderate phase. In fact, from 1789 to 1792 he directed the political writing of the great newspaper of the revolution, *Le mercure de France*.[15] In mid-1792, however, he had left France and, after some travels, published his most famous work, *Considérations sur la révolution française*, in which he argued that the revolution was not caused by the rationalist writings of enlightened thinkers—as Edmund Burke contended—but by a displacement of power "effected by necessity every time the old power no longer has the strength to protect the commonwealth or the courage to protect itself."[16] In other words, the old regime collapsed because it had become too weak internally to continue. Mallet du Pan and his work had come to Mercy's attention in Brussels, and he had recommended both highly to Vienna. After Mercy's death in 1794 Mallet du Pan began to furnish Vienna with observations regarding the revolution as he followed it from his residence in Bern, Switzerland. These reports were syntheses and interpretations of information that he received regularly from a vast network of correspondents in France, many of whom served in national, provincial, and local offices and many of whom were members of counterrevolutionary organizations.[17]

In the first half of 1795 it was Mallet du Pan who convinced Thugut that France would collapse internally, providing the

[15] Godechot, *Counter-Revolution*, 72.

[16] Quoted in ibid., 78.

[17] Jacques Mallet du Pan, *Correspondance inédite de Mallet du Pan avec la cour de Vienne (1794–1798)* (Paris, 1884), 1:v.

allies maintained their military pressure. In early February he reported that the fate of the revolution depended wholly upon whether there was peace or war. If war, "the position of the Convention will become as difficult as it is dangerous, and the view of the people will collide with that of their pretended representatives"; if peace, "the Convention is assured of [the support of] the people and can eternalize the revolution."[18] Events in France seemed to confirm Mallet du Pan's assessment. In February 1795 a white terror began in Lyon that led to popular agitation against the government elsewhere. By early March Mallet du Pan reported that France had become "an anarchy of parties, sentiments, and interests which each day strain harder to strike one another and to change themselves."[19] Above all, the coalition must stand firm at this time, Mallet du Pan advised, and "the General Will will force the Convention to disarm."[20]

Then came the Treaty of Basel, which, in Mallet du Pan's eyes, was devastating to allied interests. "If the cabinet of Berlin . . . had only waited a few weeks," he wrote to Vienna, "the Convention would have vanished, the monarchy established by acclamation, and all the conquered lands restored."[21] Now the Convention could present itself to the people as a peace-seeking government, and that might preserve it much longer than it would have survived had there been no treaty.

Thugut was aware of these consequences, and he feared the treaty's effect on France in other respects as well. When he first heard about it, he bitterly complained that the settlement would now give the revolutionaries new heart because they would interpret it as evidence that the coalition against them was disintegrating.[22]

And Thugut feared that the coalition might indeed col-

[18] Mallet du Pan to Francis, February 1, 1795, in ibid., 1:94–107.
[19] Mallet du Pan to Francis, March 7, 1795, in ibid., 133–39.
[20] Mallet du Pan to Francis, February 28, 1795, in ibid., 124–33.
[21] Mallet du Pan to Francis, April 22, 1795, in ibid., 177–85.
[22] Thugut to L. Cobenzl, April 20, 1795, in Vivenot, ed., *Quellen*, 5:180–83.

lapse. In fact, Thugut's immediate concern over the Treaty of Basel was the example it set for the other German and even non-German members of the coalition. Prussia had shown that a state could end the war with France with a minimum of sacrifices; perhaps others might do the same. Thugut feared that the Prussian precedent could precipitate a rush among the smaller allied powers and especially among states of the Holy Roman Empire to conclude their own separate agreements with France as quickly as possible. His anxiety was certainly justified. The news of the treaty caused a sensation among the German states and in Sardinia, Naples, and Spain. Spain quickly opened negotiations of its own with the French at Basel and concluded a treaty there on July 22. The settlement won for Manuel Godoy, the Spanish minister who negotiated it, the title of "Prince of Peace" from his queen, which prompted the Prince de Ligne to remark in polite Viennese circles that, if Godoy deserved the sobriquet "Prince of Peace," then Thugut assuredly deserved that of "Baron of War." The nickname became popular in Vienna, and Thugut hated it. His long, unconcealed resentment toward de Ligne for coining it prompted the prince to remark later that Thugut "carries a grudge to excess."[23]

Before discussing Thugut's policies in response to the real and potential consequences of the Treaty of Basel, one must consider why he himself did not seize the opportunity to arrange a Franco-Austrian peace.[24] After all, there were certainly many advocates of peace in Vienna at the time. In March Trauttmannsdorff had submitted another of his vigorous memoranda urging a settlement, a document Francis

[23] De Ligne, *Fragmente*, 1:179.

[24] The historians Leopold von Ranke and Karl Otmar von Aretin condemn Thugut for not seeking a settlement in 1795. They contend that peace would have preserved not only a strong Austria but also a viable Holy Roman Empire and might have prevented the subjugation of both to Bonaparte later on. Leopold von Ranke, *Denkwürdigkeiten des Staatskanzlers Fürsten von Hardenberg bis zum Jahre 1806* (Leipzig, 1877), 245–47; Aretin, *Heiliges Römisches Reich*, 1:321–22.

read "with gusto" and passed on to Thugut for comment.[25] Many others joined Trauttmannsdorff in pressing for an end to the war, including the young Pergen who had been sent to London to negotiate the loan with the British.[26] In fact, the whole Ministry of Finance seemed so bent on peace that at one point Thugut implied that the emperor should sweep out the whole office staff: "If the complex management of finances continues according to the whims of people whose foggy brains are not capable of a consequential idea and who have regularly expressed the view that His Majesty should finish the ruination of the monarchy by a quick and ill-considered peace, even that he should disband his armies, that he has no more resources, then it is useless to battle against the torrent, and we should join his other servants in awaiting with resignation and stoic tranquillity the final blow that will stop the machine."[27]

Thugut would not seek peace because, as the above quotation indicates, he had changed none of his views of revolutionary France. It was still a dangerous force that threatened to destroy the social and political fabric of Europe. In fact, it mystified him that the Prussians, regardless of their feelings toward Austria or toward him, still did not comprehend the true danger of revolutionary France. In response to a report from Berlin that the Prussians no longer feared the revolution because of the turmoil in France, Thugut expressed bewilderment that they could be so blind. Even now the French were sowing "the seeds of discontent, insubordination, unbelief, false freedoms everywhere," and they were taking root, "disturbing and weakening the security and power of the princes." If allowed to continue by a Franco-Prussian peace, the result would be "the destruction of the general European balance of

[25] This document is printed in Aretin, *Heiliges Römisches Reich*, 2:284–92, and in Vivenot, ed., *Quellen*, 5:125–35.

[26] Starhemberg to Thugut, April 27, 1795, in Vivenot, ed., *Quellen*, 5:170–72; Helleiner, *The Imperial Loans*, 44.

[27] Thugut to Colloredo, June 20, 1795, in Vivenot, ed., *Vertrauliche Briefe*, 1:227.

power" and the endangering "to the utmost of all monarchical forms of government," including Prussia's.[28]

Thugut had also not abandoned his belief that the powers of Europe must continue to resist the French Revolution with armed might. To fail to do so would be tantamount to turning Europe over to France to be remade in its new image. The treaty had strengthened Thugut's will to press on to defeat revolutionary France, and to that end he now began to work with an even greater intensity. Adversity only prompted Thugut to greater effort.

Thugut focused his attention first on the sensation he knew the Treaty of Basel would cause in the Holy Roman Empire. It might encourage the Empire to withdraw from the war as a body, or it might inspire individual German states to withdraw separately. Both of these possibilities Thugut set out to thwart. His first effort was directed at the Empire as a whole. To his delegates of the Reichstag he wrote that their task was to keep the representatives "on the right path, hold them tightly together, and maintain an imposing, unified body so that in any peace the Empire appears as an independent power."[29] To achieve these goals, he ordered the delegates to persuade the Diet that Germany's only salvation was to persevere with the emperor. If the Reichstag followed Prussia's lead, it would be yielding Germany to French dictatorship. The emperor wanted peace too, they were told, but a peace based on unity and integrity, not one based on division and concession, and it was the latter kind of peace that Prussia was promoting.[30]

As a by-product of Thugut's effort, he assumed full control of the correspondence with the emperor's envoys at the

[28] Thugut to Reuss, February 25, 1795, in Vivenot, *Herzog Albrecht*, 3:74–76.

[29] Thugut to Seilern, April 24, 1795, Vienna, HHSA, SK, *Regensburg, Kurböhmische Gesandtschaft*, 7.

[30] Thugut to Francis, April 29, 1795, ibid., *Vorträge*, 155; Thugut to Buol, May 2, 1795, ibid., *Regensburg, Österreichische Gesandtschaft*, 10.

Reichstag, eclipsing Colloredo-Mansfeld completely. For a month after the news of the Treaty of Basel, Thugut sent instructions to all of the Habsburg delegates at the Reichstag, including the Concommissär, thereby ignoring constitutional formalities. The practice aroused some protest at Regensburg, where delegates from other German states complained to Hügel that Vienna was not observing proper form.[31] In response, Thugut explained his policy to Colloredo-Mansfeld and requested the imperial vice-chancellor to approve it and to authorize the Foreign Ministry to send instructions from now on to all the Habsburg delegates without interference or advice from any other office in Vienna.[32] Whoever or whatever persuaded Colloredo-Mansfeld to agree to this request is unknown (more than likely the emperor told him to do so), but he consented to it.[33] From then on all matters of foreign policy, including those relating to the Empire, were in Thugut's charge.

Maintaining support for the emperor in the Reichstag was only a part of Thugut's effort to keep the German states in line. On April 29 he recommended sending Count Lehrbach on a tour of the most important German courts outside of the Prussian neutrality zone to listen to complaints, explain Habsburg policy, and persuade the rulers and statesmen to support Austria and to reject Prussian efforts to mediate separate settlements on their behalf.[34] Lehrbach had served as Thugut's representative before. Born of a Hessian knightly family, he had risen in imperial posts before becoming first Austrian ambassador to Sweden and then Habsburg envoy to various German courts. Although Thugut ridiculed him frequently, calling him on one occasion "verbose, garrulous, and precipitate in his judgment of men and events," Lehrbach was Thugut's

---

[31] Ernstberger, *Österreich-Preussen*, 142.
[32] Thugut to Colloredo-Mansfeld, June 2, 1795, Vienna, HHSA, SK, *Vorträge*, 155.
[33] Thugut to Francis, June 10, 1795, ibid.
[34] Thugut to Francis, April 29, 1795, ibid.

diplomatic specialist in matters relating to the Holy Roman Empire.[35] He knew intimately the imperial constitution, laws, and customs, and he was also familiar with the personalities and policies of the greater and lesser German states. He was the best man available for the task at hand.

Lehrbach set out on his mission right away, stopping first at Munich and then at nine other south German capitals before reaching Regensburg, where he joined the Habsburg delegation in its lobbying efforts at the Reichstag. For Thugut, Lehrbach's reports from the German courts brought encouraging news. With the exception of Hesse-Cassel, which was eager to conclude peace with France and would do so under Prussian auspices in late August, the south German princes promised to stand with the emperor, but on the (to them) very important condition that he honestly and sincerely seek peace with France. That was what Thugut wanted to hear. While he had no intention of advising the emperor to seek peace honestly and sincerely, he had no objection to striking that pose if it meant keeping the Empire collectively in the war.[36] And that was the pose the emperor struck. In his official response to the Treaty of Basel, Francis declared his determination to continue to defend the Empire and expressed his expectation that the other German states would do so too. However, he also announced that he would follow the wishes of the Reichstag set forth in the resolution of December 22, 1794, and seek peace with France, even accepting Danish services in opening talks.[37] Prussian offers to mediate were ignored.

The Reichstag, however, had still not made up its mind as to whether it should follow Prussia's lead in seeking peace. The month of June was a time of intense politicking at Regensburg as the Austrians tried to hold the German states to the original resolution of December 22—which granted to the emperor the leading role in concluding a settlement—while

[35] Thugut to Colloredo, May 28, 1795, in Vivenot, ed., *Vertrauliche Briefe*, 1:219.

[36] Thugut to Francis, May 19, 1795, Vienna, HHSA, SK, *Vorträge*, 155.

[37] Aretin, *Vom Deutschen Reich*, 79; Vivenot, *Herzog Albrecht*, 3: 480.

the Prussians tried to persuade them to allow Prussia to have a major share in all future peace negotiations. On July 3 the Reichstag made its decision. It was a compromise of sorts, but one that clearly favored Austria. The vote censured Prussia for making a separate treaty with France and reaffirmed belief in the unity of the Empire under the leadership of the emperor. It also reaffirmed the resolution of December 22 in favor of peace by constitutional means—that is, disallowing separate agreements between individual states and France and demanding that the territorial integrity of the Empire be maintained. Then it called upon the emperor to guide the peace negotiations, with the important proviso that he seek Prussian assistance (but not joint mediation) in doing so. Various interpretations have emerged regarding the long-term impact of the Diet's decision. One has labelled it a significant defeat for Prussia, which led ultimately to Prussian isolation in later years, an isolation that really did not end until Prussia was welcomed back into the antirevolutionary coalition in 1813.[38] Another contends that the rivalry between Austria and Prussia for influence in Germany simply switched issues after July 3, from the question of peace itself to the choice of the peace delegation that would represent the Reichstag at future talks with France.[39] Still another regards the decision as essentially meaningless because it called for maintaining the territorial integrity of the Holy Roman Empire, a condition Paris would never accept anyway since the Treaty of Basel itself had given imperial lands on the Rhine's left bank to France.[40] Thugut's reaction to the resolution is clear: "It is truly not as bad as we feared it would be," he wrote to Colloredo. "And it is susceptible to interpretations that we might give it."[41] In other words, Thugut was reasonably satisfied that his effort to

[38] Aretin, *Heiliges Römisches Reich*, 1:331. Real, *Von Potsdam nach Basel*, 137; Gebhardt, *Handbuch*, 3:17.

[39] Ernstberger, *Österreich-Preussen*, 148.

[40] Albert Sorel, *L'Europe et la révolution française* (Paris, 1892), 4:402.

[41] Thugut to Colloredo, July 7, 1795, in Vivenot, ed., *Vertrauliche Briefe*, 1:238.

thwart the Prussian campaign for a general peace and to keep the Empire formally behind the emperor had succeeded—at least for the time being.

As part of his endeavor to rally the Empire during the spring and summer of 1795, Thugut became involved for the first time in the art of swaying public opinion. Thugut had always been aware of the need for public support of governmental policies and had often expressed concern that the people might not be sufficiently sophisticated or informed to appreciate the policies he wished to follow. But Thugut was reluctant to explain his policies to the public, largely because he did not really know how to do so effectively. In the debate following the Treaty of Basel, however, appeals to the German literate public became necessary. Prussian officialdom was quite aware that the Treaty of Basel would tarnish respect for Prussia in Germany because the settlement smacked of betraying the Empire; accordingly, when the treaty was signed, Berlin hired writers to defend it. Indeed, the treaty opened a *Federkrieg* in Germany, in which publicists argued bitterly back and forth as to whether Prussian withdrawal from the conflict was justified.[42] When the journalistic debate began, Thugut's agent with Clerfayt's army, Count Dietrichstein, implored Thugut to employ writers in Austria's cause to refute the slander flowing from pro-Prussian presses. "All the world has writers," Dietrichstein pleaded; "Why don't we have any?"[43]

In the chancellery the best man for the task of writing pamphlets was Johannes von Müller. Thugut assigned that job to him and hired as his assistant Karl Kolbielski, political adventurer, publicist, and early economist. Müller and Kolbielski mounted an impressive assault on the Treaty of Basel that proved to be only the beginning of a surge of pamphlets over the next five years defending Austria's—that is, Thugut's— policies and ideas and ridiculing all policies and ideas at vari-

[42] Gagliardo, *Reich and Nation*, 167–70.
[43] Dietrichstein to Thugut, April 30, 1795, in Vivenot, *Herzog Albrecht*, 3:309–10.

ance with them.[44] Thugut allowed these men to work without supervision, and he never commented on the results of their endeavors. He must have been satisfied, however, because he financed their ongoing efforts without complaint.

Besides keeping the German states in the war, Thugut's response to the Treaty of Basel included resolving if possible the outstanding issues with Britain and Russia. Not only did Prussia's place in the coalition need to be filled, but precautions had to be taken in the event that Berlin adopted a policy actively hostile to Austria. The obvious power both to take Prussia's place and to neutralize a potential Prussian threat was Russia. Despite all of Thugut's previous attempts to convince Russia to take an active role in the war, St. Petersburg had so far offered nothing substantial. The Treaty of Basel required Thugut to double his effort to solicit Russian help. On April 20 he sent new proposals to Cobenzl to present to Catherine and her ministers. The first two were expected: he asked Catherine to use her influence among the small German states friendly to Russia—specifically Baden, Württemberg, and Saxony—to keep them in the emperor's camp, and he requested that she put "the largest army possible" on the border with Prussia as a warning to Berlin to keep the peace with Austria. It was Thugut's third suggestion that caused surprise. Since Prussia had ended its war with France, Thugut mused, then Berlin would probably reject the Third Partition of Poland, which it still had not approved. In that event, Russia and Austria should reconstitute Poland as a kingdom, restore some of its lands, and then promise to help the new Poland reconquer the territories seized by Prussia since 1771. In this way, Poland would be revived (and presumably the Austro-Russian border created by the Second Partition eliminated), and all the parties within the country, including Kosciuszko and his followers, would be grateful to Vienna and St. Petersburg and hostile to Berlin. As to the new Poland's government, the Poles could

[44] Hermann Freudenberger, "Kolbielski," *Neue Deutsche Biographie* 12 (1980): 455–56. The titles of twenty-two of Kolbielski's anti-Prussian pamphlets are printed in Vivenot, *Herzog Albrecht*, 3: 418–19.

write their own constitution subject to Catherine's arbitration, and they could choose their own king, subject to her approval.[45]

The proposal to restore Poland is so remarkable that one wonders if Thugut genuinely believed Russia would even consider it. If he did, then it reveals either wishful thinking on his part or a complete misunderstanding of Russian policy. More than likely, however, it reflects his anger at the Treaty of Basel and a fundamental misreading of the Prussian motives for it. Thugut had always believed that Berlin was untrustworthy. This is not to say that he wished to abandon the Austro-Prussian alliance against France or that he wanted to end the war with France in order to attack Prussia. He simply regarded Prussian policy as unpredictable and potentially treacherous. There was clearly a basis for his suspicion because some of Frederick William's ministers, notably Karl August von Hardenberg, were recommending an anti-Austrian course of action. However, the most pressing reason for Prussia's withdrawal from the war—and one that Thugut never fully appreciated—was that the king and the majority of his advisers genuinely believed the state's resources to be exhausted and Prussia to be in need of a long period of tranquillity to recover. By the spring of 1795 Berlin had spent the entire war chest accumulated by Frederick the Great and had floated loans on the money market in Frankfurt that had attracted few subscribers, strong evidence that Prussian credit was weakening badly.[46] It was this financial weakness and concern about preserving order and stability in its new Polish possessions that led Prussia to make peace.[47] Nonetheless, from the Treaty of

[45] Thugut to L. Cobenzl, April 20, 1795, in Vivenot, ed., *Quellen*, 5:180–83.

[46] Real, *Von Potsdam nach Basel*, 85; William W. Hagen, "The Partitions of Poland and the Crisis of the Old Regime in Prussia, 1772–1806," *Central European History* 9 (1976): 122–23.

[47] The French had no illusions about why Prussia had concluded peace. By the autumn of 1795 the new Prussian ambassador was complaining that the French now regarded Prussia as timid, obliging, and servile. "Flattering words do not help here; in fact they betray our weakness which people here

Basel to the end of his service Thugut worried about a potentially aggressive Prussia, even though Berlin showed repeatedly that it was reluctant to risk any major military undertakings.

Thugut's proposal to restore Polish sovereignty reflected his immediate wish to retaliate against Prussia in some dramatic way; it was not a carefully considered plan for an improved state system in eastern Europe. In fact, Louis Cobenzl's initial response was to return the proposal for clarification, because he knew that Catherine would not only dismiss it as unacceptable, but object so much to the very thought that it might actually harm Austro-Russian relations.[48] Fortunately, the proposal was not needed, because St. Petersburg offered numerous assurances that it would act against Prussia for any attempt to interfere seriously with the Austrian war effort.[49] Besides, in late February 1795 the Russians and the British had concluded a treaty of cooperation, which made Russian participation in the common cause against France more likely than ever.

While seeking assurances from Russia, Thugut also strove to resolve the outstanding differences that he had with the British, specifically those concerning money. After the Treaty of Basel, instead of relying further on Starhemberg and the Finance Ministry's agents in London, Thugut opened talks himself with the British ambassador in Vienna, Morton Eden. On May 4 he and Eden concluded an agreement by which the British government would guarantee a loan of £4,600,000 in exchange for an Austrian commitment to place 200,000 men in the field against France. The interest on the loan was adjusted in a rather complicated fashion that still made it higher than the 4.5 percent to be paid on the British bonds but below the 7.5 percent originally requested. Neither side was partic-

---

regard as great." Gervinus to Hardenberg, October 23, 1795, in Ernstberger, *Österreich-Preussen*, 217.

[48] L. Cobenzl to Thugut, May 16, 1795, in Vivenot, ed., *Quellen*, 5:208–14.

[49] L. Cobenzl to Thugut, June 16 and July 9, 1795, in ibid., 248–51, 279–87.

ularly pleased by the arrangement. The British regarded Austria as a poor credit risk, and the Bank of England openly warned about the loss of specie the loan would necessitate and emphasized that the British government itself would be ultimately responsible for the interest payments.[50] On the Austrian side Thugut told Cobenzl that the financial aid was "not a subsidy but a loan made by English capitalists with conditions that are frankly usurious."[51] Nevertheless, the resolution of the financial differences made possible a formal Austro-British military alliance, concluded in Vienna on May 20, that provided for mutual guarantees of possessions and an invitation to Russia to form a triple alliance to preserve the European state system.

By his energetic efforts, Thugut had for the moment neutralized most of the ill effects of the Treaty of Basel. But he knew that ultimate success depended on military victory. Austria needed to win on the battlefield to convince its various supporters that their decisions to remain committed to the war effort were right. By July 1795 the Austrian army had as yet achieved no victories in its campaign, but it had suffered no defeats either. Indeed, it had done practically nothing.

The strategic plan for 1795 called for the Reichsarmee to hold the Upper Rhine while Clerfayt crossed the Lower Rhine to relieve the fortress of Luxembourg, still in Austrian hands but besieged by the French. To facilitate this operation, the emperor had appointed Clerfayt commander of the entire theater, placing the Reichsarmee under his control and removing Saxe-Teschen. But all Clerfayt did was offer excuses not to act. Initially he advised remaining on the defensive because of rumors of the coming Franco-Prussian settlement; then, when the Treaty of Basel was announced, Clerfayt proclaimed offensive action out of the question for many reasons: Prussia could cause considerable confusion in the supply system, the

[50] John Ehrman, *The Younger Pitt. Volume I: The Years of Acclaim* (New York, 1969), 557.
[51] Thugut to L. Cobenzl, June 16, 1795, Vienna, HHSA, SK, *Russland*, 2:179.

imperial contingents were now unreliable, and the creation of the neutral zone along the Main would preclude operations north of Mainz and Frankfurt, particularly on the Lower Rhine.[52] Thugut, through the emperor, rebuked him for his excuses: "You must pay no attention to anything the Prussians say regarding neutrality, lines of demarcation, projects of pacification, and other affairs of this kind. You must not even enter discussions with them about these points." If Clerfayt found his supplies insufficient, he should badger his supply officers and deal severely with civilian provisioners. In any case, he must take whatever action necessary to begin the march toward Luxembourg.[53]

These urgent demands produced no results, however, and Thugut knew why. Since the beginning of the year Count Dietrichstein had been at Clerfayt's headquarters reporting on the condition of the army and its commander. In Dietrichstein's view, Clerfayt himself lacked the physical and psychological strength to advance. He complained always of ill health and was far too unsure of himself and his abilities. The officer corps only reinforced Clerfayt's timidity. It was made up of an "excessive number of officers of fortune, aging noncommissioned officers, and of our own people of quality who possess a poor education," who "gossip a lot, discussing politics and suggesting indecent and treacherous proposals in front of the soldiers and sometimes with them, the generals providing the examples."[54] Yet, Dietrichstein could not recommend a new commander; he was "unfortunately convinced" that Clerfayt was the best man available. Although clearly inferior to the generals of Maria Theresa's time, Clerfayt was better than any of the other senior commanders the monarchy now had. "That, dear Baron, is the actual state of things, which makes me say we will never do anything."[55]

[52] Clerfayt to Francis, April 20 and 24, 1795, in Vivenot, ed., *Thugut, Clerfayt und Wurmser*, 109–15.

[53] Francis to Clerfayt, May 21, 1795, in ibid., 133–35.

[54] Dietrichstein to Thugut, April 30, 1795, in ibid., 115–22.

[55] Dietrichstein to Thugut, May 15, 1795, in Vivenot, ed., *Quellen*, 5:205.

Thugut was by no means willing to accept this conclusion. In June he sent Lehrbach and a military financial expert to Clerfayt's headquarters to investigate the reasons for his inaction. Before either could report, however, Luxembourg fell to the French (June 22), an event that convinced Thugut to make a change. On July 30 the emperor ordered Clerfayt to transfer 75,000 of the Austrians under his command to the old warhorse, Wurmser. Wurmser would take the offensive with these men by crossing the Upper Rhine into Alsace from a base at Freiburg, while Clerfayt would remain on the defensive along the Lower Rhine between Mainz and Düsseldorf.[56] Clerfayt was shocked by the orders. He complained that the troops selected for Wurmser's army were the only ones "upon whom we can really depend," and he offered his resignation if the orders were not changed—an offer rejected out of hand by the emperor.[57] As for Wurmser, he found his forces "a numerous army, brave troops, . . . capable but in need of absorbing a little élan." As soon as preparations were complete, he advised Thugut, he would march forward. "I have taken care not to consult my generals about advancing but rather to familiarize them with the idea."[58] Thugut was delighted to have a general who would attack.

Before Wurmser could cross the Rhine, however, the French—who had been almost as inactive as the Austrians—suddenly seized the initiative. Detecting the division of the Austrian forces between Clerfayt and Wurmser, the French launched a pincers movement against Clerfayt's army. Jourdan crossed the Rhine at Düsseldorf and struck Clerfayt's right, driving him southward to the Main River. Then a second French army under Pichegru crossed at Mannheim between Clerfayt and Wurmser and threatened both to turn Clerfayt's left and to seize the huge Austrian supply depot at Heidelberg. The fortress of Mannheim itself surrendered on

[56] Francis to Clerfayt, July 30, 1795, in Vivenot, ed., *Thugut, Clerfayt und Wurmser*, 173–77.
[57] Clerfayt to Francis, August 12, 1795, in ibid., 183–86.
[58] Wurmser to Thugut, August 26, 1795, in ibid., 191–93.

September 20, after the representative of the elector Palatine, who ruled the city, persuaded the Austrian battalion in the garrison to depart and then ordered the remaining Palatine troops to fire not upon the approaching French but upon an oncoming Austrian relief column.

Thugut's reaction to these reverses was typical: he encouraged the generals to fight back with all their might. On September 23 and 25 Thugut wrote to Clerfayt through the emperor that he must not withdraw from the Lahn River (which Clerfayt was then doing) "under any pretext whatsoever," and that Vienna would hold him personally responsible for the loss of the important fortification of Ehrenbreitstein at the mouth of the Lahn unless he fought "more than once, if necessary with all the energy and stubbornness that the crisis demands."[59] To Wurmser Thugut wrote that, if rumors proved true that the elector Palatine had surrendered Mannheim without a fight, then the general should treat the Palatinate "as an enemy country," requisitioning supplies and men but avoiding needless devastation that would "only complicate more and more those matters that are already too confused."[60]

Even as Thugut was forwarding these orders, the tide was turning. On September 24 at Handshuhsheim south of Mannheim, Wurmser's advance column under Peter Quosdanovich attacked a French force four times its size, inflicted serious losses, and scattered the enemy.[61] That victory, combined with vigorous encouragement from Wurmser, inspired Clerfayt to turn on Jourdan. On October 3 his forces defeated the French at Weilmünster on the Main, initiating a series of Austrian

[59] Francis to Clerfayt, September 23 and 25, 1795, in ibid., 231–33.

[60] Francis to Wurmser, September 25, 1795, and Thugut to Wurmser, September 25, 1795, in ibid., 234–39, 240–41.

[61] Biro, *German Policy*, 1:395–96. The victory was such an unusual one that some French historians blame it on Pichegru's budding treason that would later come to flower. Curiously, when Thugut heard the news of the battle, he interpreted it as proof of Austrian military superiority and strong evidence that Clerfayt's retreat could only be the result of treason on his part. Thugut to Colloredo, October 1, 1795, in Vivenot, ed., *Vertrauliche Briefe*, 1:264.

successes that eventually forced Jourdan to withdraw behind the Rhine. To everyone's surprise, Clerfayt did not halt when he heard of Jourdan's retreat but crossed the Rhine himself by night, attacked the French siege works at Mainz, and captured the whole artillery park as well as over three thousand Frenchmen including one hundred officers and two generals. In the meantime Wurmser had besieged Mannheim, shelling the city mercilessly for over a month until it surrendered on November 22 with two-thirds of its buildings reduced to ashes.

Wurmser's taking Mannheim gave Thugut the opportunity to make an example of undependable allies who had abandoned their obligations to the Empire too quickly in the face of a French advance. With Thugut's blessing, Wurmser treated Mannheim as a conquered enemy. He quartered his troops in those houses still standing, confiscated the treasures belonging to the elector Palatine, and imposed an indemnity of four hundred thousand gulden upon the inhabitants. He also arrested the elector's delegate, Count Franz Albert Oberndorff, and the envoy of the duke of Zweibrücken, the elector's heir, and threw them both into prison. Not only did Thugut approve Wurmser's rough treatment of Mannheim and the representatives of its German ruler, but he also informed the Reichstag that the emperor would not restore the Palatinate to the elector without the latter's conceding that Austrian troops now be responsible for the Palatinate's defense; that its citizens contribute substantially to the maintenance of those troops, including restoring the appropriate Palatine contingents to the imperial army and supplying recruits for the Austrian forces; and that military authorities in the Palatinate have the right to arrest and punish anyone believed to be interfering with Austrian efforts to defend the region. As to the two imprisoned officials, both would remain confined for some time, and Oberndorff especially would be subject to criminal prosecution.[62] When the elector Palatine

---

[62] Ernstberger, *Österreich-Preussen*, 202; Francis to Wurmser, December 4, 1795, in Vivenot, ed., *Thugut, Clerfayt und Wurmser*, 392–96. Oberndorff

194

protested such harsh treatment as violating imperial law, Thugut reminded him that he had violated that law first by making peace with the enemy. "Now that Mannheim has been reconquered," Thugut wrote to Francis, "the Palatinate wants all those laws that it flouted strictly enforced."[63]

Public opinion in the Rhineland did not seem to resent the harsh treatment meted out to Mannheim. Dietrichstein reported that Rhenish citizens generally welcomed the Austrian troops and denounced vehemently the aggression of the French and also the perfidy of the Prussians. The people of Frankfurt especially vilified the Prussians, who had refused for twelve hours to admit Austrian wounded into the city until the populace forced them to do so. Wrote Dietrichstein, "The hatred shown toward the French and the Prussians and the enthusiasm for us are now at such a pitch that in all this country we could make our own revolution if we wanted to. . . . Even the Jews are openly for us and against the Prussians."[64]

Thugut felt especially satisfied by the Austrian victories and the outpouring of affection for the Habsburgs, not only because they dealt a blow to the French but also because they helped to embarrass Prussia. In the fighting of September and October, the Prussians had been clearly unable to defend their line of neutrality from either French or Austrian incursions, a revelation that seriously damaged Prussian prestige. Because the line was obviously only a paper barrier and because he wanted to suffer no more loss of face, Frederick William announced the withdrawal of the neutrality line from the Main River northward to the Ruhr and east to Hesse-Cassel and Saxony, where he hoped no one would challenge it. The king also decided to resolve the outstanding differences among Prussia, Austria, and Russia regarding Poland, and in late Au-

---

was released in March 1796, but the representative of the duke of Zweibrücken remained in prison until the autumn of 1797.

[63] Thugut to Francis, December 12, 1795, Vienna, HHSA, SK, *Vorträge*, 155.

[64] Dietrichstein to Thugut, October 18, 1795, in Vivenot, ed., *Thugut, Clerfayt und Wurmser*, 300–30.

gust he offered to concede Cracow to Austria in exchange for a small territorial concession on Austria's part near Warsaw, the principal city in the Prussian zone.[65] Thugut hastened to agree. A settlement was signed on October 24, exactly at the time when Frederick William ordered his troops northward to the new line of demarcation. Thugut could not help but gloat. To Cobenzl he reviewed Prussia's recent diplomatic defeats and its discovery that France was an unreliable friend. There was even talk, he noted, that Prussia, now ashamed of its earlier defection, was seeking to rejoin the coalition against France. "There is no doubt that [Prussia's] return would be useful, if it is sincere," Thugut sneered, "but how [can it be] after the sad experience of the past and after so many new proofs of the blackest perfidy on the part of such a weak prince guided by a ministry of the most profound perversity?"[66]

Besides, it no longer appeared that additional help from Prussia would be needed, for in St. Petersburg on September 28 Britain and Russia concluded a treaty of alliance which Cobenzl endorsed in the emperor's name. It required Russia to contribute thirty thousand men or an equivalent in money to the war against France, certainly not the strong commitment that Thugut had hoped for, but one that would nudge the Russians closer to ever more active participation in the war. A firm coalition of Britain, Russia, Austria, and the Holy Roman Empire would bring imposing strength to bear on France in 1796.

By the end of November 1795 Thugut was absolutely buoyant over recent developments. The army was winning victories after two years of defeats. The German states—at least in the south—had by and large resisted the pressures from Prussia and others to desert the emperor's cause, and the carrot of military victory and the stick of Austria's treatment of the Palatinate would keep them in the Habsburg camp. Prussia was

[65] L. Cobenzl to Thugut, September 1, 1795, in Vivenot, ed., *Quellen*, 5:343–44.

[66] Thugut to L. Cobenzl, October 27, 1795, Vienna, HHSA, SK, *Russland*, 2:179.

disgraced by the French disregard of the neutrality zone, and Russia was on the verge of joining the fight, a goal for which Thugut had wished and worked for some time. Finally, reports still portrayed France as falling to pieces. On October 26 the National Convention dissolved itself in favor of the Directory, which Thugut interpreted as further evidence of French internal collapse. Nevertheless, the good news was tempered somewhat by a slowing of Austria's military progress, which, as usual, Thugut attributed to a weakness in command, particularly to "marshal cacadubio," Clerfayt, who after Mainz had "buried himself in his old anxieties, seeing in all directions enemies about to pounce on him, enemies who at the moment certainly do not exist."[67]

Aside from that, however, Thugut was so confident that the tide had turned in the coalition's favor that he thought it time to share some ideas about the future. In a confidential letter to Cobenzl, Thugut revealed what he had in mind for the next campaign. The first step would be to switch Austria's principal effort from Germany to Italy, not because Italy was more important—Thugut had largely ignored the Italian theater up to now—but to take pressure off the German states and to relieve some of the anxiety in the Holy Roman Empire. While Austria conducted offensive operations in Italy, British and Russian troops should undertake "formidable landings" on the western coast of France and "penetrate into the French interior," lending support to counterrevolutionary forces and eventually taking Paris. But Thugut did not stop there. His confidence was so great that he went on to discuss proposed Austrian gains, the most unusual being a modified version of the old Bavarian-Belgian exchange. The emperor had shown that he would fight France vigorously even when not possessing Belgium, so that Britain no longer need fear that Austria would ignore French aggression in the Low Countries if

---

[67] Thugut to Colloredo, November 18, 1795, in Vivenot, *Vertrauliche Briefe*, 1:271. Relying on scholars whose knowledge of Italian is superior to mine, I chose the most acceptable translation of "cacadubio" as calling Clerfayt an "irresolute piece of dung."

they did not belong to the monarchy. Thus, London could confidently allow the emperor to annex Bavaria and to rid himself of Belgium. Belgium would this time not be given to the House of Wittelsbach, but to a prince acceptable to both Austria and Britain. Should London still insist that the monarchy share a border with France, Vienna would annex Alsace and Lorraine.[68]

This document is a curious one, not only for its scope and optimism, but because it appears to be a throwback to the correspondence of 1793. After all, the allies were still far from imposing their will on Paris, and it seems unusual that a cautious man such as Thugut would have been so carried away by an upturn in fortune that he would formulate highly speculative plans for the future. There seem to have been two factors that influenced the views voiced in this unusual document, one relating to the military discussion and the other to the new proposal about Belgium. As to the military plans, the recent successes in arms and diplomacy may well have persuaded Thugut that the campaigns he proposed for 1796 were possible, but the true intent of his suggestions appeared aimed primarily at encouraging the other allies to bear the brunt of hostilities for the coming year. For the first three years of the war, the Austrians had done most of the fighting and had suffered most of the losses. If Austrian troops advanced into Italy while a Russo-British invasion force invaded France, the French would undoubtedly concentrate their efforts on defending their own soil. The Austrians would then incur fewer losses in men and resources, while Russia and Britain assumed the major burden of the war effort. Thugut had no intention of taking Austria out of the struggle, but he wished that the allies would share the sacrifices more equally.

In respect to Belgium, Thugut's proposal probably reflected less a renewed infatuation with Bavaria than his desire at the time to punish the Wittelsbachs further for their desertion of

---

[68] Thugut to L. Cobenzl, November 23, 1795, Vienna, HHSA, SK, *Russland*, 2:179.

the imperial cause at Mannheim. The elector Palatine and the elector of Bavaria were the same person, Charles Theodore, and his heir to both titles, the duke of Zweibrücken, was pro-French and anti-Austrian. Those men, in Thugut's mind, had authorized the surrender of Mannheim to the French and ordered the city to resist the Austrians. They were thus traitors to the emperor and deserved little consideration in any future peace. It seemed perfectly just to award Bavaria to Austria and to give Belgium not to a Wittelsbach, as called for in the original plan for an exchange, but to another, more loyal prince. In that manner Britain would receive an Austrian-backed sovereign in Belgium, the emperor would acquire Bavaria, and the House of Wittelsbach would be punished for its betrayal.

These plans were dispatched to Cobenzl when Thugut was feeling his best, but one can reasonably doubt that even he thought them workable. He warned Cobenzl not to communicate any of his reflections, especially those involving Bavaria and Belgium, to the British or even to Starhemberg, an order which suggests that Thugut knew they would be most unwelcome in London.[69] Such an assessment of British views would have been correct. In November a special British emissary arrived in Vienna to talk about additional loans; in the course of a conversation dealing with the future of the Netherlands, Thugut remarked that this question could now be discussed only jointly with a Russian representative. On that meager hint alone, the British envoy judged that Vienna was contemplating the Bavarian-Belgian exchange again and warned London to be prepared to oppose it.[70]

In any case, Thugut's dispatch to Cobenzl reflects his unusual optimism about the outcome of the war against France in the fall of 1795. After so many adversities, one can scarcely fault him for indulging in overly sanguine speculation. But soon disturbing news arrived from the quarter where he expected progress next year: Italy. The peace that France had

[69] Thugut to L. Cobenzl, January 26, 1796, ibid., 180.
[70] Ehrman, *The Younger Pitt*, 2:594–95.

concluded with Spain during the summer had freed French troops for service on the Italian front. On November 23 and 24 a reinforced French army in northern Italy inflicted a serious defeat upon the Austrians and Sardinians at Loano, which led to French occupation of the Genoese Riviera. When Thugut heard the news, he expressed his disappointment but also his hope that the situation could be saved "by redoubling our zeal and efforts."[71] Little did he realize that the defeat at Loano was a prelude to disaster in Italy, a disaster that would make him forget for a time Wittelsbach matters and Russo-British landings on the French west coast. It would ultimately force him to undertake the unthinkable: a peace settlement with revolutionary France.

[71] Thugut to Colloredo, December 4, 1795, in Vivenot, ed., *Vertrauliche Briefe*, 1:275.

CHAPTER VIII

VICTORY IN GERMANY,

DEFEAT IN ITALY, 1796

BEFORE 1796 Italy had played almost no role in Thugut's efforts to defeat France. Many of the Italian states, including the kingdoms of Sardinia and Naples, the Habsburg secundogeniture of Tuscany, and the Papal States, had declared war on France in 1792, and in 1796 most were still in the struggle. The rather surprising exception was Tuscany, whose ruler, the brother of the emperor, Grand Duke Ferdinand, had made peace in the spring of 1795. Despite the formality of declared war, however, the fighting in Italy had been desultory, consisting largely of Austro-Sardinian operations to win control of the Riviera between Nice and Savona and an unsuccessful British attempt to occupy the French port of Toulon in 1793. Other than that, little serious action had occurred, and Thugut did not mind. For him, Germany had always been far more important than Italy in the struggle against France.

It was the Franco-Spanish treaty that brought Italy to the forefront. The Italian allies realized that Spain's withdrawal from the war would allow the French to transfer arms and men to the effort in northern Italy; that prospect made them quite unhappy, and they told the emperor so. Not long after the treaty, Thugut sketched an analysis of Austria's allies in which he briefly and rather impressionistically characterized the Italian states and their weakening dedication to the common cause: "The sovereigns of Italy, easily daunted by this dangerous example [Spain's defection] and by the insidious mediation offered by the court of Madrid, intimidated by the gathering of considerable [French] forces coming from the Pyrenees to the Alps; the king of Sardinia . . . remaining in the coalition only out of fear of our army, greatly disposed to join the enemy as soon as the occasion offers considerable advantages; Naples cooperating, as it were, only because of its wants, remaining faithful only because of the poor success of its opening negotiations [with France]."[1] Should the French achieve a significant victory in Italy, Thugut believed, these wavering allies would race one another to conclude peace.

Thugut feared that the French success at Loano in late November 1795 might be that victory. In the wake of the battle, reinforcements from the Tyrol were sent to shore up the Austrian forces in northern Italy, and Vienna encouraged the Italian courts to remain in the coalition.[2] But the news from Italy remained disquieting. Reports of large numbers of French troops arriving in Italy continued to reach Vienna, so many in fact that Thugut became convinced that the enemy army there might soon become as strong as either of the two French armies on the Rhine. And the increased French presence was having its predicted unsettling effect on the Italian states. The Papacy concluded a truce with France at Tolentino in mid-February, and Thugut was sure that most of the other southern allies wished to follow the Papal example. These developments bothered Thugut sufficiently so that he pleaded with Cobenzl to resolve quickly the last details regarding the Prussian evacuation and Habsburg occupation of Cracow to enable

[1] Thugut to L. Cobenzl, September 6, 1795, in Vivenot, ed., *Quellen* 5:349–52.
[2] Francis to Wurmser, January 19, 1796, in Vivenot, ed., *Thugut, Clerfayt und Wurmser*, 417. Thugut to Starhemberg, January 22, 1796, Vienna, HHSA, SK, *England*, 141.

the Austrian forces watching Prussia to be transferred to Italy before the campaigning season commenced.[3]

As spring approached, Thugut did not know who would command the ever-increasing French army in Italy. Early reports indicated that it would be Pierre Beurnonville, a former minister of war, but in late March Mallet du Pan wrote from Bern: "The commander in chief of the [army in Italy] is not yet known. One has spoken of Beurnonville and of a Corsican terrorist named Bonaparte, the right arm of Barras and commander of the armed forces in and around Paris."[4] The commander would indeed be the "Corsican terrorist," and he would cause Thugut considerable grief to the end of his days in the Foreign Ministry and his successors even more grief for years thereafter. Mallet du Pan's report was not the first to bring Bonaparte to Thugut's attention, but it was probably the first to make a serious impression upon him. In July 1794 the Habsburg envoy in Genoa had informed Thugut of the arrival of five Frenchmen, one particularly noteworthy: "A young man of twenty-seven [Bonaparte was actually twenty-five at the time] who is afraid of going stale, of an ardent republican spirit, of vast knowledge of military affairs, of great energy, and of a courage demonstrated in his plan for executing the repression of Toulon."[5] In early October 1795 Bonaparte had fired his famous "whiff of grapeshot" to put down the rising of the Parisian sections against the National Convention, but Thugut was probably unimpressed by the young man's role in the incident, simply because Mallet du Pan did not point it out to him.

Throughout his tenure as foreign minister and even after-

[3] Thugut to L. Cobenzl, February 14, 1796, Vienna, HHSA, SK, *Russland*, 2:180.

[4] Mallet du Pan to Francis, March 17, 1796, in Mallet du Pan, *Correspondance*, 2:32. Mallet du Pan's assessment is repeated word for word in Gherardini (Turin) to Thugut, March 30, 1796, Vienna, HHSA, SK, *Sardinien*, 25.

[5] Giovanni Girola to Thugut, July 17, 1794, in Vivenot, ed., *Quellen*, 4:340.

ward, Thugut steadfastly refused to admit openly that Bonaparte was a genius. His stunning victories in the field Thugut
generally attributed—as he had done before when discussing
victories of other French generals—to the incompetence and
lack of will of the Austrian general officers and their staffs.
Bonaparte's youth did not suggest to Thugut that he might be
a man of remarkable ability, but rather that the Habsburg
high command was more anemic and pathetic than he had
imagined. In November 1796, toward the end of the series of
stunning French victories in Italy, Thugut wrote, "When one
realizes that Bonaparte, a young man of twenty-seven years,
with no experience, with an army which is only a heap of brigands and volunteers, with half the strength of ours, defeats all
of our generals, one must naturally bemoan our decadence and
debasement."[6] Not even the negotiations of 1797 or the campaign of 1800 persuaded Thugut to acknowledge that he was
up against a man of truly remarkable talents, and, after Bonaparte's victories led to Thugut's retirement and exile in 1801,
he still referred to his nemesis for some time only as the "Corsican usurper." Outwardly Thugut lumped Bonaparte together with the other leaders of the French Revolution, all of
them bandits, thieves, and scoundrels.

But Thugut did at times indirectly reveal that he recognized Bonaparte to be a person of special talents. In late 1797
he did not entrust serious negotiations with Bonaparte to any
of his lesser and younger diplomats, but to the most skilled
man available, Louis Cobenzl, whom he recalled from Russia
for that purpose. In a situation that developed in 1798, he again
displayed his underlying respect for the "Corsican usurper."
In April of that year, Austrian policy had reached an impasse.
Fighting had ended six months earlier, but efforts to negotiate
a formal peace were making no progress. At the same time
Russia and Britain, though expressing eagerness to create another anti-French coalition, were encountering difficulties

---

[6] Thugut to Colloredo, November 17, 1796, in Vivenot, ed., *Vertrauliche
Briefe*, 1:357–58.

working out the details. Increasingly frustrated, Thugut went so far as to submit his formal resignation as foreign minister, only to withdraw it when a message from Bonaparte arrived promising that all Austro-French differences could be resolved through a personal meeting between himself and Cobenzl. Resuming his duties, Thugut briefed Cobenzl quickly and dispatched him to confer with Bonaparte. As we shall see later, the meeting between the two never occurred, but that is not the point here. The point is that Thugut believed Bonaparte to be the only Frenchman with whom Austria could negotiate sincerely and whose decisions would be honored by the government in Paris no matter who composed that government. Essentially, by 1798 Thugut recognized Bonaparte as the outstanding political and military personality in France and the only person who could enforce his will upon other revolutionary leaders.

When Bonaparte took command of the French army in Italy in April 1796, however, all of that was in the future. His initial Italian operations immediately revealed his uncommon abilities. His army of sixty thousand men was based along the shoreline of the Gulf of Genoa with headquarters at Savona, facing thirty thousand Sardinians under the command of General Michael Colli and an equal number of Austrians under Beaulieu in the mountains to the north. Although the allied forces held the high ground and the French had their backs to the sea, the allied position was weakened by a strict separation of the two armies, the Sardinian opposite Bonaparte's left wing and the Austrian opposite his right. Bonaparte proposed to thrust between these two forces, drive them apart, and then advance on the Sardinian capital of Turin, where he hoped to force the king to conclude peace. The action began on April 10, and the fighting and maneuvering went on relentlessly for the next ten days, during which Bonaparte achieved both his tactical and strategic objectives. On April 28 the Sardinian king accepted an armistice, renounced Sardinian rights to Savoy and Nice, granted to the French control of the Alpine passes, and ceded to them the use of

Coni, Tortone, and Valenza as bases of operations against the Austrians, who had retreated behind the Po River. In his *Memoirs*, Napoleon wrote that between April 10 and 25 he won six victories, captured twenty-one colors and sixty-six pieces of artillery, and inflicted casualties upon his enemy numbering fifteen thousand prisoners and ten thousand dead and wounded.[7]

To the surprise of the Austrians, Bonaparte wasted no time in crossing the Po and carrying the fight to them. The Austrian and French armies met at Lodi on May 10, where Bonaparte defeated Beaulieu and drove him in retreat toward the great Austrian fortress at Mantua, leaving Milan and practically all of Lombardy at the mercy of the French. As Thugut had feared, the French victories precipitated a rush among the Italian states to make peace. The duke of Parma concluded an armistice on May 9, and shortly thereafter Naples—to Thugut's special disgust—opened negotiations with Bonaparte as well. While talks proceeded, Bonaparte continued his offensive. He forced Beaulieu back across the Oglio River while sending some units north to Lake Garda to threaten the Adige River valley and the entrance to Habsburg Tyrol. Other French units pushed into neutral Venetian territory, where they seized Peschiera, Verona, and Legnano. At this point, however, Bonaparte realized that he could make no progress farther northward without consolidating his gains and capturing Mantua. Having blockaded the city, he spent the month of June securing for France all three of the Legations—Bologna, Ferrara, and Ravenna—and marching through Tuscany to take the port of Livorno, where he confiscated a considerable cache of English supplies and goods. By mid-July he had secured his hold on Italy south of the Po and was prepared to begin the siege of Mantua in earnest.

The swiftness of Bonaparte's success in Italy shocked con-

[7] Somerset de Chair, ed., *Napoleon's Memoirs* (New York, 1949), 59. For a study of Bonaparte's Italian campaigns of 1796 and 1797 see Guglielmo Ferrero, *The Gamble: Bonaparte in Italy, 1796–1797* (1939, reprinted London, 1961).

temporary observers, and none more than Thugut. To Cobenzl Thugut bemoaned the desertion of the Italian states
from the coalition, the relentlessness of Bonaparte's progress,
and the consequences of both for the monarchy. In his mind,
there was no doubt that Vienna now faced a crisis greater than
any yet encountered. "Since the beginning of this disastrous
war, Austria has never been in such a critical situation; Austria
may not only lose its possessions in Lombardy but see the enemy march even into the Tyrol and carry its devastation to the
heart of His Majesty's German provinces." Given such a prospect, one might assume that at last Thugut would attempt to
salvage the monarchy by seeking peace. But such a thought
was for him still out of the question. He wrote to Cobenzl that
"in spite of all this we are not discouraged by these defeats, and
we are thinking only of what measures to take to repair the
misfortune and to prevent any serious consequences."[8]

The chief measure envisioned by Thugut and the other
Austrian leaders was to reinforce the army in Italy as quickly
as possible. The only sufficiently large body of veterans that
could be sent in a short time was stationed along the Upper
Rhine where Wurmser held command. Although Vienna had
planned for Wurmser to invade Alsace, the situation in Italy
was so critical that those plans had to be abandoned and
twenty-five thousand of Wurmser's troops moved southward.
Since a fiery, aggressive leader was needed to restore Habsburg fortunes in northern Italy, Wurmser himself was given
command.[9] The seventy-two-year-old Wurmser was setting
out to challenge a French commander born four years after
Wurmser himself had reached the rank of general in the
Habsburg army. The age difference may have been great, but
no Habsburg officer was more eager to undertake such an assignment.

The Austrian forces who remained behind on the Upper

[8] Thugut to L. Cobenzl, May 21, 1796, Vienna, HHSA, SK, *Russland*,
2:180.

[9] Francis to Wurmser, May 29, 1796, in Vivenot, ed., *Thugut, Clerfayt und
Wurmser*, 447–52.

Rhine were placed under the command of Archduke Charles, who had replaced Clerfayt in February 1796. With Wurmser's departure, all of the Austrian and allied forces in Germany were assigned to the archduke. For the first months of 1796 the German theater had been quiet owing to an armistice arranged in the last week in December 1795, but, as Bonaparte fought his way through northern Italy, Vienna determined that the army in Germany should undertake some action against the French to prevent them from sending him additional troops.[10] Consequently, the emperor ordered Charles to notify his French counterpart that the armistice would end on May 21 and to undertake measures to relieve the pressure in the Italian theater, suggesting that "a push into Upper Alsace might work."[11]

Before the archduke could begin his offensive, however, the French struck first. In early June Jourdan and seventy-six thousand Frenchmen crossed the Rhine at Neuwied, followed by the crossing of Moreau and seventy-eight thousand more at Kehl. Commanding only one hundred thousand effectives, Charles clearly could not challenge both of these armies simultaneously, so he withdrew into Germany. As he did so, he and his staff composed a plan to confront the two French armies separately and to defeat each one in turn. It consisted of allowing Jourdan to advance rapidly up the Main valley while delaying as much as possible Moreau's march down the Danube. Then, when the two French armies were too far apart to help each other, the Austrians would fall upon one and then the other. The plan worked to perfection. Archduke Charles withdrew slowly before Moreau until mid-August when he rushed northward with all available forces toward Jourdan. On August 24 he defeated Jourdan at Amberg, just east of Nürnberg, and then for the next month drove him back all the way to Düsseldorf where, on the last day of September, the

---

[10] Thugut had opposed the armistice but accepted it when persuaded to do so by Wurmser, whose aggressiveness he did not question. Wurmser to Francis, December 29, 1795, in ibid., 413–17.

[11] Francis to Archduke Charles, May 6, 1796, in ibid., 437–44.

Archduke Charles
(Courtesy Bildarchiv, Austrian National Library)

battered French forces crossed the Rhine. With Jourdan defeated, the archduke then turned on Moreau, but he, not wishing to suffer the same fate as Jourdan, retreated to the Rhine before the Austrians could inflict a serious defeat upon him.

Just as the battle of Neerwinden in 1793 had established Archduke Charles's reputation as a field commander, so the campaign of 1796 proved him to be a master of bold and well-executed strategy. However, the brilliance of his generalship was by no means obvious to all as he put his plan in motion. Indeed, in June, July, and August, it appeared to most Germans that the French armies were marching irresistably through their land while the Austrians were in full retreat. In the Empire, where Thugut had struggled so hard in 1795 to keep the princes in the war, the apparent Austrian withdrawal led to widespread panic. Some rulers immediately rushed to conclude peace. On July 17 the duke of Württemberg purchased an armistice from Moreau for four million livres in indemnities and a promise not to aid any power at war with France regardless of his constitutional duty. A week later Baden concluded a similar agreement at approximately the same cost, in addition to ceding permanently to France the important bridgeheads over the Rhine at Kehl and Hüningen. Within the next few days, the princes of the Swabian and Franconian Circles (July 27 and August 7) also reached terms with France and broke off hostilities. While these princes capitulated as the French advanced, others simply fled. The ecclesiastical electors along the Rhine and the landgrave of Hesse-Darmstadt abandoned their lands for safety behind the Prussian neutrality line, and on August 22 Charles Theodore evacuated Munich, leaving instructions to the officials who remained to conclude an armistice with the French as quickly as possible.[12] In the last week of July the elector of Saxony, although not threatened personally, ordered his troops to leave the archduke's command and to come home. At the end of August even many of the delegates to the Reichstag left Re-

[12] Aretin, *Heiliges Römisches Reich*, 1:339.

gensburg for fear that they would be captured when the French arrived.[13] Princes were not the only persons fleeing the invaders. The roads of western Germany were crowded with refugees of all classes, not unlike the roads of Belgium in 1794. The exodus was a difficult and heart-rending affair for those who took part, and it made such an impression on Goethe that he immortalized it in his poetic masterpiece "Hermann und Dorothea."

Thugut rushed to counter this desertion within the Empire by the only means he could think of: he again sent Lehrbach on a tour of the south German capitals to persuade the princes to remain committed to the cause.[14] This time the effort was hopeless. From his first stop in Munich Lehrbach wrote, "In the Empire there is no longer merely a desire for peace but a lust for peace, a lust that clouds all thought and no longer asks if the terms are acceptable or possible." Moreover, there was no point in his continuing his mission because it had no chance of success. "I can assure Your Excellency that it is frightful to be in the Empire at this time . . . . Clear-thinking men have utterly lost their heads, and all declare that, if they can obtain peace, why should they concern themselves with Austria." Vienna now must choose either to take over the Holy Roman Empire or to abandon it, Lehrbach believed, for to talk about preserving its structure and its customs had become meaningless.[15] And most persons had no doubt as to who was responsible for the disaster overwhelming Germany: Thugut himself. Many imperial officers, including Austrians, had told Lehrbach, "We should put all the ministers opposed to peace on the forward outposts and load Baron von Thugut and the whole chancellery into a mortar and shoot them out of it." Lehrbach described such talk as "impudent" but widespread nonetheless.[16]

[13] Ernstberger, Österreich-Preussen, 359.

[14] Thugut to Francis, July 30, 1795, Vienna, HHSA, SK, Vorträge, 156.

[15] Lehrbach to Thugut, August 19, 1796, in Ernstberger, Österreich-Preussen, 337–38.

[16] Lehrbach to Thugut, August 24, 1796, in ibid., 339.

The lust for peace described by Lehrbach was by no means confined to the region invaded. As Archduke Charles withdrew in Germany and Bonaparte advanced in Italy, the clamor for peace reached new highs in Vienna itself. As usual there was Trauttmannsdorff, who said of Thugut, "We are totally delivered up to the madness of this man," but he was gaining ever more numerous and influential partisans.[17] High aristocrats who opposed Thugut had now grouped themselves around Duke Albert of Saxe-Teschen and his wife Marie Christine, who pointed to Thugut's commonness as a reason behind his desire to continue the war. Why should he care about losses since he had nothing to lose, being a man "without land or standing?"[18] Thugut labeled these persons "frondeurs," after the French aristocrats who rose against Cardinal Mazarin in the seventeenth century, and the British ambassador, Morton Eden, called the most vociferous of them "archfrondeurs." To London Eden wrote, "Never was there a more degenerate race of nobility; there is not amongst them a grain of public spirit, and but little talent, and still less application."[19]

Aristocratic opposition had pursued Thugut before, but now that opposition pervaded not only the salons but the government itself. In June a reorganization of the ministries dealing with internal affairs took place, including a revamping of the central body, the Staatsrat. In its first meeting, the members specifically excluded Thugut from attending any sessions "so that he could have no influence in the statements that the Staatsrat would issue criticizing his decisions."[20] In May, in an effort to improve morale and efficiency in two vital areas, the emperor, with Thugut's understanding, had appointed Procop Lazansky head of the Finance Ministry and Thugut's friend Field Marshal Count Friedrich Moriz Nostitz-Rieneck

[17] Aretin, *Heiliges Römisches Reich*, 1:342.
[18] Hüffer and Luckwaldt, eds., *Frieden*, cvi.
[19] Eden to Auckland, May 15, 1796, in Auckland, *Journal and Correspondence*, 3:334.
[20] Karl Hock and Hermann Bidermann, *Der österreichische Staatsrat (1760–1848)* (Vienna, 1972), 649.

chief of the War Ministry, but by the beginning of August both were recommending immediate peace as the only solution to the monarchy's problems.[21] Nostitz particularly disappointed Thugut, who described him as taking up "the cry of all our marshals and the War Ministry that all is lost, that we are absolutely at the end of our rope, and that all that remains for us to do is to surrender."[22]

The pressure on Thugut from the aristocrats both within and without the government was intense, but for the first time it was reinforced by protests of the Viennese people. Outbursts of popular opinion, at least of informed popular opinion, were rather new in Vienna. In the 1780s a combination of factors—influences of the Enlightenment, an increase in the size of the reading public owing to educational improvement, the lifting of censorship, and the expansion both of population and of the number of places where affairs could be studied and discussed—provided the populace of the capital with a more sophisticated understanding of major issues. Indeed, a modern author has described the Vienna of 1785 with its publishing establishments as well as coffee houses, beer gardens, and wine cellars where the literate public gathered as "the only true urban center of the German-speaking world in the eighteenth century."[23]

Joseph II had stimulated the formation of public opinion by establishing freedom of the press, but when he found that a free press could not only endorse but criticize policies, he began to reimpose restrictions on it. With the accession of Leopold II and the outbreak of the French Revolution, these restrictions became increasingly severe. On September 1, 1790, a new law placed a sweeping ban on all materials that criticized laws or decrees from the sovereign, all publications call-

---

[21] Zinzendorf's diary, mid-August, 1796, in Hüffer and Luckwaldt, eds., *Frieden*, 484.

[22] Thugut to Colloredo, July 21, 1796, in Vivenot, ed., *Vertrauliche Briefe*, 1:319–20.

[23] Bodi, *Tauwetter*, 45. The population of Vienna in 1796 was 215,000. Mayr, *Wien*, 84.

ing for public disobedience of any kind, and all foreign literature that conveyed distortions or falsehoods.[24] In late 1791 the Censorcommission was revived, this time not with Josephinist elements at its head but the more conservative members of the Hofkanzlei. As a result, the bureau "changed from an educational body to a police establishment."[25]

But the reimposition of censorship by no means meant that the Viennese public ceased to talk about governmental affairs. The number of newspapers declined to only two by 1794, the official *Wiener Zeitung* and Josef Richter's *Eipeldauer Briefe*, a paper aimed to some extent at explaining Habsburg policy to the common folk. But selections from the *Eipeldauer Briefe* demonstrate that discussion of foreign and domestic policy was widespread and intense, not only in coffee houses and wine cellars but in such places as tailor shops and hairdressing establishments as well.[26] And there was still plenty to read. Richter wrote in 1793 that his tailor subscribed to the famous French revolutionary paper the *Moniteur*, "which comes every day from Paris on an extremely long sheet and printed with such small type that one might believe the French plot to blind us all with reading it."[27] Moreover, the upper classes still enjoyed the *Schmähschriften*, the lampoons that appeared in spite of the censor, while the lower classes read the *Spott- und Stachelversen*, which poked the same kind of fun at public policies and officials.[28] Ernst Wangermann writes that the appeals to the ministers and to the emperor to change their policies were sufficiently numerous and sophisticated in the late eighteenth century to constitute the first knowledgeable political opposition in the Habsburg Monarchy outside the privileged estates.[29]

[24] Bodi, *Tauwetter*, 399; Bibl, *Zerfall*, 1:35.

[25] Bodi, *Tauwetter*, 399.

[26] Joseph Richter, *Briefe eines Eipeldauers über d'Wienstadt* (Munich, 1970), passim.

[27] Ibid., 53–54.

[28] Criste, *Erzherzog Carl*, 2:185.

[29] Ernst Wangermann, "Josephiner, Leopoldiner und Jakobiner," in Reinalter, ed., *Jakobiner in Mitteleuropa*, 236.

In 1794 the government had begun to take popular expression very seriously, for the police uncovered what was called the Jacobin conspiracy, a broad label for a few cells of persons favoring thorough changes in the government. The discovery led to a number of arrests beginning in July, trials in the autumn, and the first execution of a conspirator in January 1795. A great deal has been written about the Jacobin trials; the general consensus of scholars is that the so-called conspirators posed little threat to the well-being of the Habsburg state, but the government, especially the head of the police, Johann Anton Pergen, vastly overrated their plotting and overreacted to it.[30] In the wake of the trials in 1795, the government issued decrees warning that anyone advocating revolution would be tried for treason; that the authorities would hold the author, publisher, printer, and bookseller liable for the publication of any uncensored manuscript; and that all remaining Freemasonry lodges would be closed.[31] The trials and the police measures to deal with future trouble clearly had an impact on the Viennese. In her memoirs Caroline Pichler wrote that the incident of the Jacobins had a significant dampening effect on what she described as a previously carefree city. During and after the trials, she noted, one heard the word "Jacobin" used "often and regularly" to describe anyone opposed to one's own ideas. "It is a word to hurt honest people." The accused party would retort by calling his antagonist "an aristocrat, a bigot, or an enemy of the Enlightenment." This name calling, Pichler complained, only intensified bitterness in the political conversations in public places, but she also noted that such conversations did not cease.[32]

At least before the crisis in the summer of 1796, Thugut had paid little attention to Viennese popular opinion. Censorship

[30] See especially Ernst Wangermann, *From Joseph II to the Jacobin Trials*, 2d edition (Oxford, 1969); Paul P. Bernard, *Jesuits and Jacobins* (Urbana, 1971); and Bodi, *Tauwetter*.
[31] Bodi, *Tauwetter*, 422–25.
[32] Caroline Pichler, *Denkwürdigkeiten aus meinem Leben, 1769–1844* (Munich, 1914), 1:180–81.

he apparently thought of little value. Upon hearing that Francis wanted the *Moniteur* forbidden in his crownlands, Thugut remarked to Colloredo that, under such a ban, the newspaper "would simply become more desirable and valuable." Besides, copies would still go to the important government agencies and to the foreign embassies, and from there they would reach "everyone else."[33] When censorship was tightened, Thugut complained now and again that the censorship commission confiscated materials addressed to him, an annoying practice because the materials often carried necessary news from France. At one point he pleaded with the emperor to order the commission "to pass without exception not only all publications but all packages that contain published or unpublished writings that come to the post office with my address on them."[34] As to the police, Thugut had considerable respect for the vice-president, Count Saurau, but virtually none for the president, Pergen, whom he described on one occasion as seeing conspiracies everywhere, especially where they did not exist, and on another as "truly an embarrassment."[35] There is no evidence that Thugut played a role in the Jacobin trials or that he thought the persons accused posed any danger to the state. On the day of the execution of the most prominent Jacobin, Lieutenant Franz Hebenstreit, he remarked that the Viennese "apparently applauded the harsh justice" meted out, but he voiced no opinion on the trials themselves. He did express concern that another of the convicted, "a Hanoverian or Brunswickian," was being exiled to his own country, a sentence Thugut regarded as unfortunate because the fellow would be free to spread ill will against the emperor by "venemous discourse and writings" about his mistreatment by Habsburg authorities. Thugut recommended that the man be held until peace was concluded although "I have paid no at-

[33] Thugut to Colloredo, November 19, 1793, in Vivenot, ed., *Vertrauliche Briefe*, 1:58.
[34] Thugut to Francis, May 23, 1795, Vienna, HHSA, SK, *Vorträge*, 155.
[35] Thugut to Colloredo, December 15, 1795, and January 10, 1797, in Vivenot, ed., *Vertrauliche Briefe*, 1:276–77, and 2:2–3.

tention to his affair and have no idea if this treatment is just."[36]

In his general appreciation for the intertwining of domestic and foreign matters, Thugut was different from Kaunitz and from Metternich. Both of the others were keenly aware of the close connection between foreign and internal affairs, and their foreign policies reflected concerns about matters at home. This was less true of Thugut, who in his writings commented rather infrequently on domestic problems and how they influenced his policies toward other states. To some extent this can be explained by the position he held. He was director of foreign affairs exclusively (until April 1798 at least) and as such was supposed to present his recommendations to the emperor as they dealt with foreign policy alone. Only when domestic affairs affected foreign policy—and they did so in his time primarily in matters of finance and the military—did he voice formal opinions about them. He did not have the broader responsibilities for internal policy as did Kaunitz and Metternich. Moreover, Thugut had been a diplomat for all of his life and viewed affairs with a special eye to their foreign implications. In other words, for Thugut domestic matters had remained largely secondary to foreign matters. Generally, Thugut believed that the greatest danger to the Habsburg Monarchy and its people came from abroad, not from home, and before 1796 his obsession with that threat made him less sensitive than he might have been to the monarchy's internal stresses and strains and less sympathetic to those who tried to call them to his attention.

Thugut's observations on public opinion in Vienna prior to the summer of 1796 reflected an uncertainty about its importance not unlike that he felt about German public opinion before the Franco-Prussian Treaty of Basel. And just as that treaty impressed upon him the need to respond to the literate public in Germany, so too popular opposition to his policies in 1796 impressed upon him the need to influence the literate public in Vienna. Early in the summer Eden reported that the

[36] Thugut to Colloredo, January 8, 1795, in ibid., 1:169.

cry for peace, any peace, was now as loud in the streets as it had been in the salons, and in July and August Thugut was personally subjected to jeers and catcalls as he walked to and from the chancellery.[37] Thugut responded to these demonstrations in the same way that he responded to popular opinion after the Treaty of Basel: he set Müller and Kolbielski to writing stirring pamphlets. The most dramatic was "The Dangers of our Time," in which Müller vigorously warned the people of the horrors of the oncoming French and exhorted young men to join the army.[38]

But even Thugut was aware that the open hostility displayed toward him by the public added a new and serious dimension to the opposition to his policies. He was not certain of the depth or pervasiveness of that hostility, but he knew that it mattered a great deal and that measures had to be taken to quiet it. In a rare but revealing admission of the importance of domestic opinion, he wrote to Colloredo: "It will undoubtedly be important . . . to find some means of quelling and calming the unbelievable babbling of this city. I always fear Vienna more than the furor of the enemy, and it is from here that will come our ruin! I propose to have a conference with Saurau tomorrow concerning this subject because, after all, it is the police especially who must provide the means of directing public opinion particularly in public places."[39] He even began to appreciate censorship. In November he expressed his delight that Colloredo would be charged with monitoring "spectacles" so that he could "purge the theater of all pieces tending to scorn religion and favor democracy," especially owing to "the extreme danger in this crisis."[40] It is doubtful that Thugut had changed his mind about the efficacy of censorship as a general policy, but he certainly thought it necessary in an emergency.

---

[37] Hüffer and Luckwaldt, eds., *Frieden*, cvi.

[38] Johannes von Müller, *Sämmtliche Werke* (Stuttgart/Tübingen, 1835), 39:101–13.

[39] Thugut to Colloredo, July 24, 1796, in Vivenot, ed., *Vertrauliche Briefe*, 1:323.

[40] Thugut to Colloredo, November 19, 1796, in ibid., 1:354.

In his study of Metternich, Henry Kissinger argued that the true test of a foreign policy is not its application to the foreign scene but its "ability to obtain public support" at home, defined by approval within the bureaucracy, conformity to "domestic experience"—that is, acceptance by public opinion—and an effectiveness in educating those who might find it wanting.[41] Thugut did not comprehend these ideas in such concise terms, but he knew that such influences existed and must be confronted in some way. Thus he assigned Müller and Kolbielski to write popular tracts and fretted about public concern over his policy. One would like to think that, had he served in a state with a true public forum—such as Parliament in England—he might have had the opportunity to explain his policies, to answer criticisms in the open, and to win the support of the concerned public. At the same time, however, one wonders if his own personality, so tough-minded but so taciturn toward all but close associates, would have prevented him from effectively enlisting popular support.

As it was, the extent of the criticism and opposition to him and to his policies made him less, rather than more, willing to defend them personally before others. In fact, it made him withdraw from the public almost altogether. When he became director of foreign affairs in 1793, Thugut had participated fully in the Viennese social scene, dining at the homes of the high-born, visiting salons, attending the theater, and generally making himself as pleasing as possible to the people who mattered. Indeed, he remarked on one occasion that, when he assumed office, he had only friends and no enemies.[42] In the summer of 1793 the Prussian ambassador complained that Thugut was often hard to find at work, since he "spends only four or five hours at the chancellery; the greater part of the day he spends visiting the great families in Vienna and spreading the often contradictory views of the various Austrian minis-

[41] Henry Kissinger, *A World Restored: Europe after Napoleon* (New York, 1957), 326.
[42] Thugut to Colloredo, January 7, 1794, in Vivenot, ed., *Vertrauliche Briefe*, 1:72.

ters."[43] As the military and political misfortunes mounted in 1794, 1795, and 1796, bringing with them increasingly widespread criticism, Thugut became progressively withdrawn. He spent more and more time at his office, frequented the homes of others less and less, and sought no entertainment. In April 1796 Axel von Fersen visited Vienna to discuss some personal matters with his old acquaintance and found Thugut a retiring, antisocial figure. "He never meets with them [the high nobility] and is seen nowhere," wrote Fersen. "He does not own his own horse, has no servants, visits no one and never invites anyone to dinner. No one knows where he lives. He is in the state chancellery from 7:00 [a.m.] to 3:00 and from 6:00 to 10:00; there he works and receives visits."[44] Later in the year a French agent in Vienna echoed Fersen's description of Thugut's way of living and added: "With this schedule he sees only whom he wants to. . . . He hears everything said to him but he confides in no one."[45]

Thugut's withdrawal into the routine of the chancellery reflected both an aversion to open criticism and his self-righteous conviction that others did not appreciate the danger that threatened them and his efforts to save them from it. Unfortunately, his retreat from the public also deprived him of opportunities to persuade others of the correctness of his policies. He failed to appreciate what most politicians and statesmen know by nature, that, with or without an open forum, circu-

[43] Caesar to Frederick William, June 20, 1793, in Herrmann, ed., *Diplomatische Korrespondenzen*, 377–81.

[44] Quoted in Barton, *Fersen*, 211. During the eight years he guided Habsburg foreign policy, Thugut lived at five different addresses in Vienna: Obern Bräunerstrasse 1172 in 1793 and 1794, Judenplatz 373 in 1795 and 1796, Mariahilf 49 in 1797, Alstergassen 155 in 1798, and Wahringerstrasse 243 in 1799 and 1800. *Hof- und Staats-Schematismus* for those years. These are the old street numbers.

[45] Nerciat to Guiraudet, November 24, 1796, in Hüffer and Luckwaldt, eds., *Frieden*, 87–89. Eden wrote in 1798: "He lives so totally secluded from all society and has done so since his return from the Low Countries, that there is no opportunity of meeting him except at his office." Eden to Grenville, May 7, 1798, in *Dropmore Papers*, 4:188.

lating among one's constituents is as important to effective policy making as keeping abreast of the news. While admittedly more inclined by personality to social activity, both Kaunitz and Metternich recognized the importance of participation in social events to influence people and to hear criticism and complaints. Thugut willfully deprived himself of these opportunities. De Ligne noted that weakness: "If Thugut knew that one conducted more affairs in a salon than in an office, if he had respected and consulted people's opinions, if he wanted to know people more in a position to judge them than anyone, he would have been a great man. . . . But, living as he lived, he did not know [these people and their concerns]."[46]

Thugut was able to confine himself most of the time to his office in the chancellery—called later by Suvorov his "infernal cavern"—because his position and policies were protected by the emperor and by Colloredo. But, as the military situation seemed to deteriorate in 1796, Thugut detected signs that the support of both men was eroding. In late July Thugut complained to Colloredo that Francis had invited Prince Starhemberg, one of the peace party, to dinner at his country palace at Laxenburg and expressed concern that he would entertain other persons who "are known here and in foreign courts to advise peace and defection from the common cause." While he warned that such meetings would create doubt about the emperor's policies among the allies and in Austria, his real fear was that Francis might indeed change his mind about continuing the war.[47] Three weeks later Thugut's anxiety seemed justified when Colloredo in an unusually formal letter advised him that the emperor was calling a meeting of Prince Starhemberg, Colloredo-Mansfeld, and Field Marshal Lacy—all now vigorous foes of Thugut—to discuss "if the war should continue or if it is necessary to make peace." Francis was particularly upset by the course of the war, Colloredo noted, "es-

[46] Prince de Ligne, *Fragments de l'histoire de ma vie* (Paris, 1927), 1:179–80.
[47] Thugut to Colloredo, July 30, 1796, in Vivenot, ed., *Vertrauliche Briefe*, 1:325–26.

pecially as one bad and unforeseen piece of news follows another."[48]

There is no evidence that this meeting ever took place, probably because either Colloredo or Thugut was able to talk the emperor out of it. But the incident shows that in August 1796 Thugut, his policies, and his perception of revolutionary France as the monarchy's irreconcilable foe were on the verge of rejection. And nothing shows more clearly Thugut's desperation than an appeal that he composed for the emperor to Catherine of Russia and a letter of instruction he wrote to Cobenzl to accompany that appeal. Despite the assurances of the year before, Russia had still sent no aid, and in Thugut's mind such aid had become Austria's only salvation. In the emperor's letter, Thugut described the desertion by the German princes, the open malevolence of Prussia, and the retreats of the Austrian armies. In the face of these misfortunes, the emperor's appeal read, "without prompt and effective assistance, the only alternative will be to see myself exposed to the imminent danger of total ruin."[49] If this document reflected discouragement, Thugut's own letter to Cobenzl smacked of desperation. "In this terrible state of things only the most prompt and effective support of Her Imperial Majesty of all the Russias can sustain the confidence of His Majesty." Vienna was no longer asking Russia to defend "some far-off province" but "the core of the monarchy. The frontiers of Bohemia, Austria, and the Tyrol are under attack, and the slightest reverse will bring the enemy into the center of the hereditary lands and destroy us all." The monarchy was doing its best to defend itself, Thugut continued, but it could not succeed without assistance from the Russians.[50]

With the news of Archduke Charles's victories in late August and September, however, Thugut's despair turned to ju-

[48] Colloredo to Thugut, August 21, 1796, in ibid., 331.
[49] Francis to Catherine, September 2, 1796, Vienna, HHSA, SK, *Russland*, 2:180.
[50] Thugut to L. Cobenzl, September 3, 1796, ibid.

bilation. Upon hearing of the Austrian success at Amberg, Thugut wrote, "Thank God for the victory of Archduke Charles. Bohemia is saved." After a win at Würzburg he rejoiced, "God bless our Archduke Charles. He does not let us take a holiday from good news and his victories are truly glorious."[51] As the extent of the archduke's triumph became known, the mood of Vienna was transformed from anxiety to celebration. Patriotism flourished as hundreds of volunteers enlisted in the army and contributions poured into the treasury. Poets, pamphleteers, and composers rushed to turn out patriotic tracts and jingles celebrating Archduke Charles and his achievements. A cantata entitled "Retter in Gefahr" (Savior in Danger) attracted three thousand enthusiastic listeners, including the emperor, to the Redoutensaal in the Hofburg and reportedly inspired them to contribute three hundred thousand gulden to the war effort.[52] In summing up all of the enthusiasm, the *Eipeldauer Briefe* printed simply, "It is not possible to describe the happiness and joy that fill Vienna."[53]

If Thugut's spirits were lifted by Archduke Charles's victories, they absolutely soared with news from Russia. On August 18 (long before Thugut had dispatched his pleading letters of early September) Catherine notified Louis Cobenzl that she was immediately dispatching sixty thousand troops to reinforce the Austrians in Germany and Italy. When Thugut read that report, he wrote enthusiastically to Starhemberg that victory over revolutionary France was assured at last. "The preponderance of the union of the three allied powers [Austria, Russia, and Britain] will rebuke the aggression of the wicked; it will encourage the well-intentioned to show their true sentiments and end their timidity; and . . . not only will [France] be obliged to seek a peace honorable to the allies, but its current distress may trigger those events that will change its monstrous government and replace it with a regime less

[51] Thugut to Colloredo, August 28 and September 7, 1796, in Vivenot, ed., *Vertrauliche Briefe*, 1:332, 335.
[52] Richter, *Briefe*, 122. [53] Ibid., 119.

dangerous for the other powers and which promises to its neighbors lasting tranquillity."[54]

The victories in the Rhineland and the commitment from Russia inspired an outburst of pro-Austrian sentiment in Germany. Many peasants and townspeople joined the Habsburg forces in following the French westward, and, as the pursuit became more intense and the numbers involved larger, the civilians began to inflict acts of frightful savagery upon French stragglers and small units. One eyewitness recorded: "Husbands and fathers, whose wives and daughters had been raped often before their eyes, were inspired to castrate the Frenchmen alive and then to butcher them as one would butcher hogs."[55] Princes who had rushed so eagerly to reach accommodations with the French now crept back shamefacedly to apologize and to try to explain their earlier behavior. But Thugut was unwilling to forgive easily. The archduke, he declared, had the right to requisition whatever he needed from the south German states without regard to customs, laws, payment, or devotion. "It does not matter that Hesse-Darmstadt offered its congratulations immediately, that Baden renounced its special treaty [with France] and proclaimed its loyalty to the *Kaiser* and *Reich*, or that the Swabian Circle gave thanks for its liberation and apologized for concluding an armistice under stressful circumstances."[56] Even the Reichstag did not escape Thugut's resentment. When it passed a resolution of thanks to the emperor and to the archduke for Germany's salvation, the Austrian delegates responded that thanks were no longer enough. If the German princes really cared about protecting Germany, the Reichstag would provide money and men, and it would pronounce any member's claim to neutrality as treason to the Empire.[57]

---

[54] Thugut to Starhemberg, September 10, 1796, Vienna, HHSA, SK, *England*, 141.

[55] Quoted in Criste, *Erzherzog Carl*, 1:353.

[56] Thugut to Archduke Charles, September 16, 1796, in Ernstberger, *Österreich-Preussen*, 342.

[57] Ibid., 360.

These acts and pronouncements provoked outcries from other German princes, some of whom claimed that the Austrians were treating them and their lands as severely as the French had done. The French had come proclaiming themselves liberators and had pillaged the countryside and violated public order; the Austrians now seemed to be doing the same. One German official complained, "Only the name of the oppressor has changed; the oppression remains."[58] Even the principal Habsburg delegate to the Reichstag warned Thugut that the archduke lacked the constitutional authority to carry out forced requisitions, and that both he and Vienna should avoid any openly unconstitutional action. If Thugut wished to contrast effectively Habsburg morality, religion, and political virtue with French rapine and plunder, then the emperor must prohibit outright violations of imperial laws and customs. Moreover, strict observance of the constitution now would demonstrate the emperor's moral superiority not only over the French but over those German princes who had deserted the common cause. In the moment of crisis they had abandoned the sacred constitution of the Empire; in his moment of crisis—and of triumph—the emperor had to show that he continued to respect it.[59] As much as he wished to seek revenge, Thugut acknowledged the persuasiveness of these arguments and curbed his eagerness to punish the German states.

The turn in Habsburg fortunes was not, however, as complete as Thugut would have wished it to be. In contrast to the good news from Germany, bad news continued to come from Italy. While Bonaparte had spent July solidifying his hold south of the Po River, Wurmser had gathered his forces in the Tyrol for a counteroffensive to relieve Mantua. In an effective strategic move, Wurmser succeeded in drawing Bonaparte away from the city and was able to relieve it for a time, but a

<hr />

[58] Hofkanzler Albini of Mainz to Strauss (Regensburg), November 5, 1796, in ibid., 344.
[59] Fahnenberg to Thugut, November 6, 1796, in ibid., 360.

subsequent defeat at Castiglione on August 5 compelled him to retreat back to the Tyrol while the French siege of Mantua was resumed. In mid-September Wurmser again marched south but was so badly outmaneuvered this time by Bonaparte that he and half of his army ended up within the walls of Mantua with the original garrison while the other half fled back to the Tyrol. In November yet another relief force under General Josef Alvinczy almost trapped Bonaparte at Verona before suffering defeat at Arcola on November 15–17 and withdrawing. Thus, between July and November 1796 not only had all three major efforts undertaken by the Austrian army to relieve Mantua failed, but the Habsburg commander in chief and most of his fighting men in the theater of operations were now themselves inside the besieged fortress they were supposed to have freed.[60]

If the news from Italy dampened the joy inspired in Thugut by Archduke Charles's victories, news from Britain did away with it altogether. At the end of September the British informed Thugut that they were opening peace negotiations with the French. Many reasons lay behind London's decision, not the least of which was the Austrian military failure in Italy. The British had become convinced that Austria could not achieve a military victory on the continent and that now perhaps the only way to halt French aggression would be to end hostilities. Moreover, a Franco-Spanish alliance concluded in August 1796 led Spain to declare war on Britain, forcing London to withdraw the British fleet in the Mediterranean so that it would not be caught by combined French and Spanish naval forces. The departure of the British fleet encouraged the remaining Italian allies to reach accommodations with France, which made the military situation even more hazardous for Austria. Assessing these troubles, the British government judged the prospect of military success for the coalition so dim that in mid-October it dispatched Lord Malmesbury, who in 1794 had concluded the Prusso-British subsidy treaty over

[60] David G. Chandler, *The Campaigns of Napoleon* (New York, 1966), 99–113.

Thugut's vigorous objections, to France to begin talks. The British assured Thugut that Malmesbury was not authorized to conclude any agreement without Austrian participation and advised him to support conditions under which the emperor would accept peace.[61]

To Thugut the British initiative seemed the prelude to betrayal. The choice of Malmesbury was particularly disturbing, because Thugut considered him the spokesman for the Prussophiles in London and therefore the person most likely to seek a settlement to Austria's disadvantage. Besides, notwithstanding the protests about Austro-British solidarity, the very willingness of the British to send a negotiator to France without an Austrian representative suggested to him that London planned to make peace "on conditions of its own convenience, and it will not grant the particular interests of its allies any consideration."[62] Referring to what he considered past British betrayals, Thugut advised Cobenzl that the Malmesbury mission "looked like Utrecht [1713] and Aix-la-Chapelle [1748] all over again."[63]

By early December 1796 Thugut's confidence following Archduke Charles's victories had given way utterly to frustration. Deeply disappointed by the military setbacks in Italy and apparent British desertion, Thugut began to lash out rather unfairly at others for various failings. His favorite target was the army, which, despite repeated efforts, had been unable to defeat the French in Italy. To Colloredo Thugut wrote that the army had become so burdened with "details and military pedantries" that it had "become one of the worst armies in Europe, which scarcely offers battle even when it outnumbers the enemy two to one."[64] Four days later, when news of Alvinczy's

[61] The Cambridge History of British Foreign Policy, 1783–1919 (New York, 1922), 1:566; Ehrman, The Younger Pitt, 2:628–30.
[62] Thugut to L. Cobenzl, October 23, 1796, Vienna, HHSA, SK, Russland, 2:180.
[63] Thugut to L. Cobenzl, November 30, 1796, ibid.
[64] Thugut to Colloredo, November 25, 1796, in Vivenot, ed., Vertrauliche Briefe, 1:358.

retreat reached Vienna, he complained, "The fact is that we have no army, we have no officers, that generals rise according to age and that the order of ranks has rendered the commanders utterly incapable. God alone knows how this confusion in Italy will end."[65] In another letter not only the army but the whole Habsburg system was the target of his frustration, especially "the conflict of authority where each has his own protector who defends him despite the impunity of all his faults." If the emperor did not resort to wholesale changes in the government, Thugut warned Colloredo, "Austria will not be able to avoid becoming what Italy has become and what happens to every country where one cannot decide to sacrifice petty considerations for the greater needs of the general good."[66]

On December 8, however, came the worst news of all: the death of Catherine of Russia. For almost four years Thugut had pressed for Russian participation in the war against the French Revolution, and in August Catherine had finally given her consent. Indeed, at the time she died, Austrian and Russian staff officers were charting the march routes, filling supply depots, and coordinating strategy. Now all was uncertain. Thugut had no firm perception of Paul, Catherine's successor, because he had always focused attention solely on the empress. Upon hearing of her death, Thugut wrote to Colloredo, "Your Excellency can easily sense the incalculable consequences that could result from this fatal event, and in what embarrassment we might find ourselves in the midst of the great changes that might result: without an army, without finances, and with all of the internal disorder in the bureaucracy." But Thugut had by no means lost his nerve. Official reaction, he told Colloredo, must not appear overcome by despair. Although Thugut had been pressing for the immediate return of the emperor from a visit to Pressburg, at the news of Catherine's death he now advised a delay in that return, "in order to display tranquillity to the public."[67] Displaying outward calm, however, could not

---

[65] Thugut to Colloredo, November 29, 1796, in ibid., 361–62.
[66] Thugut to Colloredo, December 2, 1796, in ibid., 364.
[67] Thugut to Colloredo, December 10, 1796, in ibid., 371.

fool careful observers. Wrote the Prussian ambassador to Berlin, "The death of Empress Catherine is the greatest misfortune Austria has yet suffered. Thugut himself, who has very sensitive nerves anyway, is supposed to have become ill at the news."[68]

Catherine's passing was a devastating blow to Thugut, but, like so many disappointments in the past, it in fact strengthened his determination to continue. Once again he drew upon his inner toughness to pursue the path that he believed was right: Austria would fight on. He wrote: "Firmness, deliberation, order, and additional means of help will appear later. Mantua is still ours and our good but old friend Wurmser will eat everything down to his old boots before he surrenders."[69]

It was appropriate that Thugut should cite Mantua as the symbol of continued Austrian resistance. The city did indeed still belong to Austria, and Wurmser would practically eat his old boots before surrendering. But his situation was growing more precarious daily. At the end of December the field marshal reported that the garrison in Mantua would not surrender "as long as a horse, a dog, a cat, or a piece of bread is available," but he added that his supplies were disappearing quickly and that the Austrians must send help soon.[70] In response to such appeals the War Ministry formed yet another army to relieve Mantua, which in December and January gathered in the Alpine passes, battling snow, ice, and cold in preparation for a new advance into Italy. In the first week of 1797, Alvinczy led this force southward, where it collided with Bonaparte's troops at Rivoli near Lake Garda on January 13. The ensuing battle lasted three days and ended in complete victory for the

[68] Lucchesini to Frederick William, December 14, 1796, in Hüffer and Luckwaldt, eds., *Frieden*, cxxiii. Paul countermanded Catherine's orders to prepare the army to march against France. Hugh Ragsdale, "Russia, Prussia, and Europe in the Policy of Paul I," *Jahrbücher für Geschichte Osteuropas* 31 (1983): 81–82.

[69] Thugut to Colloredo, December 10, 1796, in Criste, *Erzherzog Carl*, 1:390.

[70] Wurmser to Alvinczy, December 30, 1796, in Vivenot, ed., *Thugut, Clerfayt und Wurmser*, 548–49.

French. In a tone that seemed to anticipate criticism from Thugut, Alvinczy wrote to the emperor on the day after the battle, "I did my best! I promised—I threatened—I pleaded—I punished even with death—and I served as an example." But it was not enough.[71] When the news of the defeat reached him, Thugut wrote, "My opinion is undoubtedly worth little, but I tell you I am feverish."[72]

Thugut's remaining hope was that Wurmser could hold Mantua a bit longer, but on February 2 the city surrendered to the French. Wurmser informed Thugut that he was surprised his troops held out as long as they did, and he noted that they had consumed three thousand horses during the siege.[73] Remarked Thugut, "Although we have had a long time to prepare for this event, my heart is no less afflicted in thinking about it."[74] Now the crownlands themselves were open to Bonaparte and his Frenchmen. The Corsican terrorist was about to invade the heart of the monarchy.

[71] Alvinczy to Francis, January 16, 1797, in ibid., 574.

[72] Thugut to Colloredo, January 22, 1797, in Vivenot, ed., *Vertrauliche Briefe*, 2:5.

[73] Wurmser to Thugut, February 2, 1797, in Vivenot, ed., *Thugut, Clerfayt und Wurmser*, 587–89.

[74] Thugut to Colloredo, February 11, 1797, in Vivenot, *Vertrauliche Briefe*, 2:16.

CHAPTER IX

PEACE, 1797

AGAIN SERIOUS DEFEAT demanded dramatic measures. Reinforcements from the Rhine were dispatched to Italy, but, more important than that, the emperor appointed Austria's hero, Archduke Charles, commander of all the Habsburg armies. As commander of all fronts, he could move troops from Germany to Italy and back again as conditions required.[1] One author has suggested that these measures were largely Thugut's doing on the grounds that, as misfortune followed misfortune, the foreign minister steadily took control of all phases of the war effort, including the formulation of strategy and the selection of commanders.[2] In fact, Thugut's influence in military matters was now marginal. When Archduke Charles was directed to take over in Italy, Thugut, although not opposing the decision, had recommended that it remain secret, so that the enemy would not be alerted to the Austrians' plan to focus their efforts beyond the Alps. He had suggested that the archduke be sent to the Tyrol, so that the French would not know whether the Austrians planned to attack in Germany or in Italy.[3] Whatever he advised, however, received scant attention;

[1] Francis to Archduke Charles, January 25, 1797, in Criste, *Erzherzog Carl*, 1: 495–98.
[2] Hüffer and Luckwaldt, eds., *Frieden*, cxxxvi.
[3] Thugut to Colloredo, February 8, 1797, in Vivenot, ed., *Vertrauliche Briefe*, 2: 13–14.

by this time in military matters at least the emperor and his officers were scarcely listening to him.

Official Austria expected the archduke to save the day, but when he inspected the troops assigned to the Italian theater, he was dismayed by what he saw. He rushed to Vienna to tell the emperor personally that the army could not continue the war and to advise him to seek peace. Nothing could have endangered Thugut's policy more seriously. Archduke Charles's arrival in the capital generated enormous enthusiasm. The people cheered him wildly in the streets, and, when he appeared with the emperor at the Hofburgtheater on the evening of February 21, he was greeted with thunderous applause. The city was illuminated in his honor for two days. As everyone in Vienna knew, the archduke enjoyed this reception not only because of his military exploits but also because he wished to end the war. The peace party at last had at hand a champion worthy to pit against Thugut. Charles, after all, was "not a subject who wished to make some proposals; he was the savior of the state who demanded to be heard."[4] Noted one historian, "From all sides, from the nobility, from the court, from the administration, the discontented rushed to his side."[5]

Could Thugut resist such formidable pressure? Apparently he did so, although how he accomplished it is not clear from the documents. The evidence does not indicate how often he and the archduke met while the latter was in Vienna, if they had face-to-face confrontations, or if discussions took place in the presence of ministers. It is clear, however, that the archduke argued vigorously for peace. The army in Italy, "disorganized and in the most pitiable state," could not defeat the oncoming French. Should the war continue, the enemy could march all the way to Vienna, and the Austrian forces would be unable to stop them. For that reason alone, the archduke emphasized, peace was essential.[6]

[4] Caesar to Frederick William II, February 20, 1797, in Heigel, *Deutsche Geschichte*, 2: 229.

[5] Hüffer and Luckwaldt, eds., *Frieden*, cxxxix.

[6] Zinzendorf's diary, February 20–22, 1797, in ibid., 486. Hertenberger and Wiltschek, *Erzherzog Karl*, 76.

Thugut disagreed on both diplomatic and military grounds. Diplomatically, a treaty with France would constitute a separate peace and as such would violate Austria's solemn promise to Britain not to conclude an independent settlement. If Austria disregarded this promise, the emperor could expect no help of any kind from Britain in the future.[7] Besides, peace was not even necessary militarily. If Bonaparte were to invade Austria, he would encounter serious logistical and strategic difficulties, since he would be advancing farther and farther from his source of supplies and reinforcements, while the Habsburg troops would be drawing nearer and nearer to their own. Eventually the Austrians would become stronger than the French; then they could turn on the enemy and inflict a crushing defeat upon him.[8] Thugut's analysis was certainly reasonable; indeed, Bonaparte himself echoed it later. When he concluded the preliminary peace at Leoben in mid-April 1797, he justified his action to the Directory by explaining that his strategic situation was becoming increasingly perilous as he approached Vienna, and he admitted that he could not have attacked the city itself without risking the total destruction of his army.[9] In his memoirs, Napoleon noted that, even if he had taken Vienna, he could not have held it.[10]

However spirited the discussions, the emperor continued to agree with Thugut that the war should continue. On February 28 Archduke Charles left the capital for his headquarters at Udine with orders to try to stop Bonaparte. His parting may not have been a pleasant one, for, when an aide expressed surprise at seeing him at headquarters so soon, the archduke responded, "I was thrown out of Vienna."[11] Nonetheless, Thugut seemed confident that Charles would revive the fighting spirit of the army in Italy. "The presence of the young hero," he wrote to Starhemberg, "is without contradiction the best means of restoring the ardor of the troops and of reestab-

[7] Heigel, *Deutsche Geschichte*, 2: 230.
[8] Hüffer, *Österreich und Preussen*, 237.
[9] Ferrero, *The Gamble*, 208–13.
[10] Chair, ed., *Napoleon's Memoirs*, 177.
[11] Quoted in Criste, *Erzherzog Carl*, 1: 401.

lishing order in those units where indiscipline has spread owing to successive defeats."[12] Like so many others, Thugut believed that the archduke would save Austria. But unlike the others, he thought that Charles would do so by winning the war, not by asking for peace.

Charles above all needed time to restore the morale and strength of the army, and Bonaparte would not give him time. In late February the French leader had paused in his pursuit of the Austrians to force the Papal States to conclude a "disastrous and humiliating peace," but the respite lasted only a few days.[13] On March 10 the forward units of his army of sixty-five thousand appeared on the Piave River, where they surprised the archduke, whose reinforcements from Germany had not yet arrived. The Austrians fell back to the Tagliamento River, but on March 16 Bonaparte pushed across that waterway while the Habsburg forces withdrew toward the city of Villach in Carinthia.

With Bonaparte's crossing the Tagliamento, the archduke warned that the situation was becoming truly serious. He advised the emperor that "the most critical and decisive moment is the present. If the enemy attacks us quickly, it will disintegrate my army before I have a chance to unify and reorganize it. It will prevent the linking of the Rhine army and the one here, and, if not utterly destroy us, . . . make it impossible for us to win."[14] Eight days later Charles reported that to defend Carinthia was impracticable and proposed instead to gather all available forces from all theaters—the Rhine, Tyrol, and Carinthia—at assembly areas near Linz and Schärding in Upper Austria and to deploy them in a defensive line along the Danube with strong points at Vienna in the east and Ingolstadt in the west.[15] On the day that this message was sent, Bonaparte

[12] Thugut to Starhemberg, March 1, 1797, Vienna, HHSA, SK, *England*, 141.
[13] Thugut to Starhemberg, March 8, 1797, ibid.
[14] Archduke Charles to Francis, March 16, 1797 in Criste, *Erzherzog Carl*, 1: 501.
[15] Archduke Charles to Francis, March 24, 1797, in ibid., 509–13.

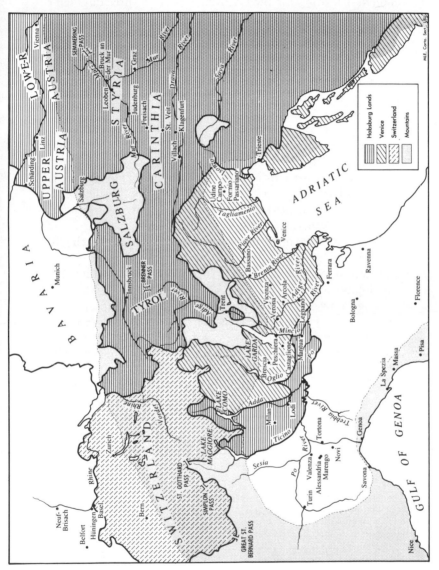

Italian Theater of Operations, 1796–1800

Habsburg Lands
Venice
Switzerland
Mountains

ADRIATIC SEA

GULF OF GENOA

LOWER AUSTRIA
UPPER AUSTRIA
STYRIA
CARINTHIA
SALZBURG
BAVARIA
TYROL
SWITZERLAND

Vienna
SEMMERING PASS
Bruck an der Mur
Leoben
Judenburg
Graz
Freisach
St. Veit
Klagenfurt
Villach
Schärding
Linz
Salzburg
Munich
Innsbruck
BRENNER PASS
Trent
Udine
Campo Formio
Passariano
Tagliamento
Trieste
Bassano
Venice
Vicenza
Arcola
Verona
Legnano
Ferrara
Ravenna
Bologna
Florence
Pisa
Massa
La Spezia
Peschiera
Mantua
Brescia
Castiglione
Oglio
Milan
Lodi
Genoa
Tortona
Ravenna
Adda
LAKE COMO
LAKE MAGGIORE
LAKE GARDA
Zurich
Bern
ST. GOTTHARD PASS
SIMPLON PASS
GREAT ST. BERNARD PASS
Neuf-Brisach
Belfort
Hüningen
Basel
Nice
Turin
Valenza
Alessandria
Marengo
Novi
Savona
Sesia
Po River
Ticino
Mincio
Trebbia River
Rhine
Adige River
Brenta River
Piave River
Mur River
Drava River
Sava River

MI.E. Carto. Sect. 1969

entered Tarvisio near the Carinthian border; three days later he invaded Carinthia proper. By April 4 he had established his headquarters at Judenburg in Styria, 141 miles from the Habsburg capital.

As Bonaparte drew closer, Vienna became increasingly tumultuous. Since the crisis of mid-1796, the police especially had devoted themselves not so much to censorship and other restrictive measures as to positive measures to boost patriotic spirit. This effort produced one lasting achievement when Saurau commissioned the great composer Joseph Haydn and the mediocre poet Lorenz Haschka to create a stirring anthem to inspire the Austrians in the same fashion as "God Save the King" did the English.[16] The result was the "Kaiserlied," which was performed for the first time on February 12, 1797—the emperor's birthday—and which remained the Austrian anthem until the dissolution of the monarchy in 1918. It was specifically intended to arouse everyone's spirits, and Saurau made certain that his agents gave it the widest circulation possible.

Songs, however, would not stop Bonaparte. As the French drew ever closer to Vienna, feelings of loyalty and determination inspired by such devices as the "Kaiserlied" paled before the citizens' growing anxiety. Already refugees were arriving in substantial numbers from Carinthia and Styria, so many in fact that at the end of March the emperor ordered Pergen to steer the flood of people around Vienna proper and toward Hungary and Bohemia so that they would not add to the confusion within the city. On that same day Pergen issued orders to the bureaucrats that, for the sake of public confidence, they must act quickly and competently in their duties "so the people will see that purposeful activity is taking place and that pressing matters will not be treated in a dilatory fashion."[17] By order of the police, official Vienna had to obviate its famous *Schlamperei* for the duration of the crisis.

[16] Karl Hafner, "Franz Josef Graf von Saurau," *Zeitschrift des historischen Vereins für Steiermark* 7 (1909): 29.
[17] Quoted in Lorenz, *Volksbewaffnung*, 96.

As March turned to April, the tumult in Vienna intensified and many of the city's inhabitants fled. Emilie Weckbecker, who experienced the evacuation as a young girl and therefore viewed it as something of an adventure, described the crowds of people in the streets, all getting in one another's way, all short of temper, and all making a great deal of noise. She and her family, riding in wagons from their residence on the Hoher Markt, needed two hours to get to the gate on the Danube Canal, a distance of only three blocks. After leaving the city behind, they stopped at an aunt's house on one of the main roads from Vienna toward Bohemia, where the young people "could not leave the window" as they watched what seemed to them a traveling circus heading northward. The younger and female members of the Habsburg family joined the exodus, but the emperor and empress remained in the capital.[18]

Most of the citizens staying behind demanded peace. And for them there was no question who symbolized unwavering dedication to war: Thugut. Wrote the Prussian ambassador, "Widespread defeatism spreads daily; the discontent of the aristocracy in sharp criticism and that of the people in open attacks are expressed routinely against Baron Thugut." Whenever he left the chancellery in the evening, Thugut was followed by a crowd shouting insults and threats. Indeed, the outpouring of wrath against him was such that Saurau told him that the police could not guarantee his safety.[19] As the crowd tormented him in the streets, his aristocratic foes denounced him in the courtyards and offices. The cries against him from Trauttmannsdorff, Prince Starhemberg, Kollowrat, and Colloredo-Mansfeld became shrill, Kollowrat publicly branding him "a rogue" and "a rascal."[20] Thugut reacted to this vilification with his usual obstinacy and doggedness. Wrote Eden, "In the midst of these accumulated calamities M.

---

[18] Weckbecker, *Die Weckbeckers*, 103–104.

[19] Caesar to Frederick William II, April 2, 1797, in Hüffer, *Österreich und Preussen*, 237–38.

[20] Zinzendorf's diary, April 2, 1797, in Hüffer and Luckwaldt, eds., *Frieden*, 487.

de Thugut retains his firmness and, determined not to be the instrument of concluding a disgraceful peace, continues to struggle against the united voice of the nobility and amongst the numerous other adversities which at present press upon him."[21]

The excitement in the city reached its height on April 2–3, when rumors spread that the British might be unable to make good on their promises to pay subsidies to Austria in specie. Since the government had for some time been issuing steadily increasing amounts of paper currency to pay its bills and meet its payroll, the prevailing feeling in the streets and counting-houses was that, given a British default, Austrian paper money would be worthless. Consequently, people rushed to redeem their paper notes for hard currency. The banks could not meet the demand and closed their doors. On April 3 the Staatsrat promised to redeem the paper at 10–20 percent of its value, a promise that simply caused the anxiety and uncertainty to worsen.[22] In the midst of it all, Francis wrote to Archduke Charles, "You would not believe the chaos here and behind the army, but we are doing all we can to maintain order. We are putting Vienna in a state of defense, but the people are not only reluctant but positively unwilling; we need time to get things right since the largest magazines in the whole monarchy are here."[23]

At the height of the commotion on April 3, a courier from Archduke Charles arrived in Vienna carrying a letter from Bonaparte. The letter, addressed to the archduke, blamed the entire Franco-Austrian struggle on British intrigue and avarice and called upon Charles to conclude an armistice "in the interests of humanity."[24] From Poteratz's first visit to Vienna in the autumn of 1795, a number of French agents had come to Thugut or had written to him proposing to restore peace

[21] Eden to Grenville, April 1, 1797, in ibid., 153–55.
[22] Ibid., cxliii.
[23] Francis to Archduke Charles, April 2, 1797, in ibid., 157.
[24] Bonaparte to Archduke Charles, March 31, 1797, in Napoleon Bonaparte, *Correspondance* (Paris, 1859), 2: 436–67.

between Austria and France on behalf of the Directory. But to Thugut they were all disreputable characters representing a disreputable—and distant—government. This offer, unlike the others, came not only from the French military hero of the moment but from his headquarters within striking distance of Vienna. The Habsburg army was disorganized, the citizens of the capital almost riotous, the monetary system in confusion, and the governmental offices in turmoil. To refuse this proposal might lead to total disorder within the armed forces and insurrection among the populace.

For the first time Thugut conceded that the emperor should reach some sort of peace with the French. He hoped that it would be temporary, but he knew that it was unavoidable. As much as he disliked it, on April 4 Thugut submitted to his sovereign a letter to be sent to Archduke Charles on the emperor's behalf. "His Majesty has no good opinion of the seriousness of French intentions or their pacific pronouncements," the letter read, "but in the present unfortunate situation of our affairs, it would be impolitic to give France another chance . . . to say that their overtures have been utterly rejected." The archduke was then instructed to arrange for an armistice followed by a "frank and loyal discussion of terms that the French wish to serve as the basis for a future peace." Although Charles should make the arrangements, he should not conduct the talks himself, for his haggling with a "Corsican usurper" would be too great an affront to Habsburg dignity.[25] Besides, Thugut wanted a negotiator sent to Bonaparte's headquarters who would unhesitatingly follow orders, and the archduke was clearly not that kind of man.

This letter set in motion a whirlwind of meetings and correspondence that led, just two weeks later on April 18, to the preliminary peace concluded at Leoben in Styria, which in its turn produced the Treaty of Campo Formio in October and

[25] Thugut to Francis, April 4, 1797, in Criste, *Erzherzog Carl*, 1: 427–28. On April 9 Thugut explained to L. Cobenzl that it was the emperor's wish, not necessarily his own, to respond favorably to Bonaparte's letter. Thugut to L. Cobenzl, April 9, 1797, Vienna, HHSA, SK, *Russland*, 2: 181.

an end to the Austro-French portion of the War of the First Coalition. As those two weeks began, however, Thugut intended the forthcoming talks not necessarily to reach a settlement but to serve instead to give the army a rest and to placate the public. In fact, he instructed the two delegates sent to meet Bonaparte, Lieutenant General Heinrich Josef Bellegarde and Major General Maximillian Merveldt, to conclude first a ten-day armistice and then to use those ten days to negotiate the arrangements for future talks and the establishment of a second, much longer armistice.[26] Thugut's hope was that, as the talks dragged on, the Austrians could take advantage of the cease-fire to muster additional resources and to revitalize their means of defense.

In fact, the revitalization was already underway as Bellegarde and Merveldt left for Bonaparte's headquarters. In Vienna on April 6 Saurau appealed to a specially gathered group of citizens in front of the old Rathaus to contribute funds to volunteer to serve in a citizens' army to protect Vienna. Given the whining and wailing of the previous few days, no one expected the response that followed. The citizens not only enthusiastically enlisted in the new forces themselves but also encouraged enlistment by their sons, servants, apprentices, and journeymen, whom they clothed and armed. The rector of the university rallied the students to arms by raising the flag carried by their predecessors during the siege of Vienna in 1683, and the director of the Academy of Art set an example for his budding painters by serving as flag bearer himself. Musicians, including Beethoven, composed songs and poets wrote ditties to inspire the volunteers, while offerings of money poured into the treasury. A sixteen-year-old student wrote at the time, "I cannot describe the enthusiasm to defend the fatherland that has affected young and old, rich and poor, high and low. . . . I saw many of my schoolmates crying because they had been rejected by the army as too young and too weak."[27]

[26] Francis to Archduke Charles, April 4, 1797, in Hüffer and Luckwaldt, eds., *Frieden*, 157–59.

[27] Quoted in Richard Kralik, *Geschichte der Stadt Wien* (Vienna, 1926), 366.

Although such an outpouring of support after so much despair is hard to explain, the emotional impact of the official appeals, the emperor's willingness to seek peace, reports of a rising of the Tyroleans against the French, and Saurau's promise that enlistment would be short and intended only to defend the city all apparently encouraged it. Thugut, as comforted as he was by the response, certainly played no positive role in inspiring the citizenry. He was still the despised warmonger, and Zinzendorf noted in the midst of the patriotic fervor that "many say Thugut does not leave the chancellery for fear of the people."[28] Thugut's part in strengthening the war effort was confined to another anguished plea for Russian assistance and requests to Eden and London to dispatch currency to undergird Austria's failing banks.[29] To the people he remained out of sight.

For these efforts to have a chance of succeeding, time was necessary, the very thing Bonaparte was in no mood to grant. When Merveldt and Bellegarde offered the ten-day armistice that Thugut hoped to turn into long, leisurely, and probably fruitless negotiations, Bonaparte insisted upon a six-day armistice and the dispatch from Vienna of a bona fide diplomat to conduct serious talks. He even offered the outline of a permanent peace: France would obtain the left bank of the Rhine, and the two powers together would reach an understanding regarding Italy.[30] To make certain that Vienna did not delay its response, he kept his army moving northward. Between March 31 and April 7 Bonaparte moved his headquarters from Klagenfurt (209 miles from Vienna) to Leoben (110 miles from Vienna), his vanguard to Bruck an der Mur (100 miles away), and his reconnaissance patrols to the Semmering Pass (75 miles distant).

With the French still advancing, Thugut decided to comply with Bonaparte's request. As the diplomat to represent Aus-

[28] Zinzendorf's diary, April 10, 1797, in Hüffer and Luckwaldt, eds., *Frieden*, 489.

[29] Francis to Paul I, April 7, 1797, in Vivenot, ed., "Thugut und sein politisches System," 123–25.

[30] Hüffer and Luckwaldt, eds., *Frieden*, cxlii–cxlviii.

tria, Thugut chose the ambassador from Naples, Marzio Nas-
trilli, Duke of Gallo. Gallo was a curious choice, a choice
questioned even at the time. He was not an official in the
Habsburg government, and Thugut himself had ridiculed
him for the earlier peace treaty that he had negotiated with
France on behalf of Naples. The selection of a foreigner raised
doubts everywhere. Zinzendorf sneered, "Gallo, the negotiator of peace, ho-ho, as if one could not find someone in this
country."[31] When Gallo first mentioned the Holy Roman Empire to Bonaparte, the French general responded, "Are you a
German? Your name does not sound German." "I am a Neapolitan, General." "Really? Since when am I negotiating with
Naples? Does the emperor not know a German gentleman
with whom I can discuss German affairs?"[32]

Various factors may have influenced Thugut to make this
unusual choice. One possible reason was that the empress
forced it upon him. The ambassador from Naples was the confidant of the empress and her mother, the Neapolitan queen,
and inasmuch as the empress wanted peace above all—Zinzendorf attributed the emperor's decision to negotiate to the
tears of his wife—Gallo was the one who could reach a settlement in accordance with the imperial couple's wishes.[33] Even
Thugut's own correspondence partially supports this interpretation, for he wrote to Louis Cobenzl that, although Gallo represented a neutral court, he was selected because he was
"attached to the emperor by the thinnest ties of blood."[34]

A more likely explanation, however, is that in Thugut's
opinion no one else in Vienna at the time was as qualified as

[31] Zinzendorf's diary, April 16, 1797, in ibid., 490.

[32] Quoted in Heigel, *Deutsche Geschichte*, 2: 237.

[33] "Someone said that the empress cried so much on Friday and Saturday
[March 31 and April 1] that finally the emperor decided to approve negotiations." Zinzendorf's diary, April 5, 1797, in Hüffer and Luckwaldt, eds.,
Frieden, 488. Hüffer and Luckwaldt promote the idea that Gallo's appointment was the empress's doing, as does Napoleon in his memoirs. Ibid.,
cxlvii–cxlviii; Chair, ed., *Napoleon's Memoirs*, 175.

[34] Thugut to L. Cobenzl, April 30, 1797, in Vivenot, ed., "Thugut und
sein politisches System," 125–26.

Gallo. As the confidant of the empress and the ambassador from a power deeply concerned about the fate of Italy, Gallo had been briefed regularly on events and policy during the first months of 1797, so that he was quite familiar with official Austria's hopes and fears. Moreover, he was the one person near high-ranking circles who had experience in negotiating with French revolutionaries. Finally, the men whom Thugut might have preferred as representatives were out of town and unable to return quickly enough to be useful. Egid Josef Fahnenberg, rapidly becoming Thugut's favorite in imperial matters, was in Regensburg; Lehrbach was helping to organize civilian resistance in the Tyrol; Dietrichstein had been sent as special envoy to Russia in December to congratulate the new tsar; Starhemberg was in London; and Cobenzl, the best of them all, was still in St. Petersburg. When Thugut heard of Bonaparte's objections to Gallo, he wrote to Merveldt, "We are greatly concerned because, given our real lack of people versed in policy here, it will not be easy to replace him with anyone whose experience and diplomatic skills can give you equivalent help."[35] Thugut did send as a substitute Karl Vincent, a young man who would later serve as Austrian ambassador to France, in the event that Bonaparte absolutely refused to talk with Gallo.

Bonaparte, however, wasted no time quibbling over the credentials of the men on the other side of the table. He wished to conclude a peace as quickly as possible according to his own needs and perceptions, especially before instructions or agents from the Directory reached him and circumscribed his authority. On April 13 Bonaparte offered Merveldt (Gallo would reach Leoben only on the 15th) two alternatives: France would make the Rhine River its northern and northeastern border (thus annexing not only the Austrian Netherlands but the lands of the Holy Roman Empire on the river's left bank), re-

[35] Thugut to Merveldt, April 15, 1797, in Hüffer and Luckwaldt, eds., *Frieden*, 170–71. Gallo saw himself not as an Austrian advocate but as a mediator. B. Maresca, ed., "Memoire del Duca di Gallo," *Archivio storico per le Province Napoletane* 13 (1888): 250–51.

turn Lombardy and Mantua to Austria, and arrange for the monarchy to acquire the Venetian Republic to the Tagliamento (including Istria and Dalmatia) as compensation for Belgium. Or, France would annex only the Austrian Netherlands but make a republic of Lombardy and arrange for Austria to receive Venice, this time with its boundary at the Adige or Mincio River.[36] When Thugut received this proposal, he sensed that the talks were progressing much faster than he would have liked and that, without immediate instructions, his delegates might agree to terms that were truly unacceptable. Consequently, he advised Merveldt and Gallo to concede Belgium in exchange for Venice (an easy concession since Belgium had long since been lost), but to try to acquire a few additional territories and to save Milan for the monarchy. Above all, they were not to make any other concessions without consulting Vienna.[37]

Good diplomats appreciate the value of delay; good soldiers appreciate the value of speed. Thugut's instructions expressing the need for caution and care had barely reached the Austrian representatives when they concluded with Bonaparte the Treaty of Leoben on April 18. The provisions of this preliminary treaty began with both powers promising to promote the internal tranquillity of the other; France would not try to revolutionize Austria, and Austria would not try to restore the monarchy in France. From there, the public articles provided for the cession of Belgium to France and the formal recognition of the French Republic by the emperor. The secret articles then ceded Lombardy to Bonaparte's various Italian republics (Mantua was to remain in Habsburg hands) and provided for Venice and its Adriatic provinces to serve as compensation to Austria. Both sides agreed to send plenipotentiaries to Bern, Switzerland, where a general congress would meet within three months to conclude a definitive peace. Bonaparte per-

[36] Merveldt to Thugut, April 13, 1797, in Hüffer and Luckwaldt, eds., *Frieden*, 168–70.
[37] Thugut to Merveldt and Gallo, April 15, 1797, in ibid., 171–74. See also Biro, *German Policy*, 2: 749.

sonally promised to withdraw his troops from Austrian lands as soon as the emperor ratified these articles.

On April 19 Merveldt sent the letter explaining why he and Gallo had reached an agreement so quickly. News had come not only that the French armies were about to invade Germany (on April 18 Moreau's forces crossed the Rhine at Strasbourg and Jourdan's old army, now under Hoche, crossed at Neuwied), but also that couriers were on the way from Paris to add new and possibly outrageous conditions to the terms of the settlement. Consequently, Merveldt believed it necessary to take advantage at once of "the good will of General Bonaparte" to conclude an acceptable peace. Besides, Merveldt considered the agreement a favorable one: Venice had become a Habsburg possession, and Bonaparte had promised to remove his forces from the center of the monarchy. The crownlands were safe again, and the Habsburgs still possessed a large part of northern Italy. Belgium was lost, but it had been for some time.[38] Merveldt the soldier was confident that he had performed well. Gallo the diplomat was less certain. Upon arriving in Vienna on April 20, Gallo's personal secretary reported that his master was "sick with anxiety; he is not able to conceal that he has much to explain, at the very least the way the articles were drafted and the quick way Bonaparte shortened our negotiations which in effect will result in a chaos of discussions and difficulties."[39]

Thugut was quite unhappy with the preliminary peace. He had envisioned an extended truce and ongoing negotiations while Austria resolved its military and financial problems. Instead, he was confronted by a complete settlement whose results he found unsatisfactory. One might think that, given the crushing defeats of the Austrian army, the loss of Belgium and Lombardy and the acquisition of Venice were quite lenient terms—indeed, the Directory itself believed Bonaparte had

[38] Merveldt to Thugut, April 19, 1797, in Hüffer and Luckwaldt, eds., *Frieden*, 179–81.
[39] Thugut to Colloredo, April 20, 1797, in Vivenot, ed., *Vertrauliche Briefe*, 2: 34.

been far too generous toward a defeated Austria. However, for Thugut it was not a favorable peace at all, because in terms of the kind of balance he had learned from Kaunitz, it weakened Austria not only relative to France but relative to the ever-treacherous Prussia as well. As he explained to Cobenzl, Austria would lose the three million subjects of Belgium and the one million of Lombardy, while gaining the two and a half million of Venice, for a combined loss of one and a half million souls and the revenue they paid. Combined with Prussia's large and Austria's small gains in Poland as a result of the Second and Third Partitions, the net effect of the war effort from 1793 to 1797 would be a vast loss of Austrian strength compared to that of France and Prussia. Moreover, in Thugut's opinion, Gallo was clearly right about the treaty's phrasing, which in places was vague and confusing. Thugut blamed the uncertain prose upon the faulty French of two Italians, Gallo the Neapolitan and Bonaparte, "more Corsican than French," whose use of language resulted in "even some errors in grammar that we will try to correct if possible."[40]

Given the serious faults that he found with the treaty, did Thugut recommend that the emperor reject it? The evidence is not clear on this issue, but he may have done so. In the note to Gallo informing him that Francis would likely accept the treaty, Thugut was careful to point out that the articles were "certainly susceptible to different interpretations," but that "the sincere desire to terminate the evils of war . . . prevail in the heart of His Majesty over all other considerations."[41] Three days later the emperor sent a formal order in his own hand to Thugut to send the ratification of the treaty to Leoben, "being persuaded by the urgency of circumstances that the love of my subjects and the desire to allow them to enjoy to the fullest the benedictions of peace must surpass all other consid-

[40] Thugut to L. Cobenzl, April 30, 1797, Vienna, HHSA, SK, *Russland*, 2: 181.

[41] Thugut to Gallo, April 20, 1797, in Hüffer and Luckwaldt, eds., *Frieden*, 182–83.

erations."[42] Both of these statements hint that Francis accepted the treaty against Thugut's advice. If so, it was the first time that the emperor had openly rejected his foreign minister's counsel in a serious foreign policy matter. The acceptance of Bonaparte's initial offer on April 4 had generated no significant disagreement between Thugut and his master, because Thugut regarded it as a device to gain a respite from the unstinting French advance. Acceptance of the settlement at Leoben may have been different, however, for the treaty recognized revolutionary France as a legitimate power in European affairs and made serious territorial concessions to it. As necessary as it might have been in terms of immediate political and military concerns, the treaty violated the principles Thugut had followed since 1791; in fact, for him Leoben represented a Habsburg surrender to revolutionary France. As a result, he may have even offered to resign. According to the British ambassador, Thugut submitted his resignation in late April but was persuaded by the emperor himself to carry on the duties of his office until the final peace was arranged.[43] Thugut's resignation seems unlikely, however, because no document in the Austrian sources attests to it. He may have told Eden that he had resigned to excuse himself from a role in breaking the Austrian promise to London not to conclude a separate peace with France.

It is difficult to define Thugut's exact reaction to the establishment of peace itself. His comments in various letters were for him rather subdued; he included no jeremiads about creeping democracy, wholesale social upheaval, or the potential destruction of the entire European monarchical system. Instead, in his writing he focused on carefully explaining what had happened, justifying the Habsburg decisions in light of events, and speculating about the outcome of the further ne-

[42] Francis to Thugut, April 23, 1797, in Vivenot, ed., *Vertrauliche Briefe*, 2: 34.
[43] Eden to Grenville, April 22, 1797, in Hüffer and Luckwaldt, eds., *Frieden*, 183–84.

gotiations called for by the treaty. Perhaps he was really persuaded that ending the war was now necessary. With Bonaparte so close to Vienna and the Austrian army and finances in disorder, he may have believed that continued resistance would prove futile and possibly harmful. It is also possible that, despite all of his previous warnings about the inexorable dangers posed by revolutionary France, he hoped that the old diplomacy of Kaunitz—trading lands while talking of balance—would work to avert future danger. After all, it was the French and not he who had proposed the terms, so perhaps France would now end its ideological and political aggression against other powers in exchange for territory. By bartering lands as Kaunitz and his peers would have done, the French themselves might set limits to the revolution. Whether or not Thugut reasoned in this way, he was willing now to continue the peace process on the emperor's behalf, and that claimed most of his attention as April ended and May began.

In the eighteenth century the conclusion of an armistice and a preliminary peace represented an understanding between powers that a rough status quo had been reached, a status quo to be maintained while negotiations leading to a final settlement were underway. On this occasion, the status quo was not maintained, and that disturbed Thugut a great deal. On May 1 Bonaparte declared war on Venice, not in itself a surprise because he would have to conquer the republic to meet his commitment to give it to Austria. When Venice surrendered after offering no practical resistance, however, Bonaparte set about revolutionizing the republic, establishing a government propounding French principles while stripping the countryside of needed supplies. Thugut was scandalized. The French were "depriving [Venice] of its last *sou*, massacring all opposed to democracy, leaving us . . . with a land peopled by democrats and consequently most susceptible to troubles and revolts and capable of infecting by their doctrines and examples the remainder of His Majesty's lands."[44] And that was not all. A cri-

[44] Thugut to Colloredo, May 26, 1797, in Vivenot, ed., *Vertrauliche Briefe*, 2: 37.

sis in Genoa in mid-May led to French occupation of the city and the establishment of the Ligurian Republic, which made Genoa a French satellite. Even in peace revolutionary France was extending its influence, and that was a frightening prospect.

Thugut soon became even more upset. On May 24 Gallo and Bonaparte met at the latter's sumptuous palace at Montebello near Milan to exchange the formal ratifications of the preliminary peace. But here Bonaparte announced that he was no longer content with the terms reached at Leoben and offered others in their place. The general now demanded not just Belgium but the entire left bank of the Rhine, in return for which Austria would be allowed to annex the archbishopric of Salzburg and the bishopric of Passau in the Holy Roman Empire. Austria could also keep Venice but not Mantua. The congress of Bern, which, according to the Treaty of Leoben, would include all of the warring powers, would be transferred to Rastadt but restricted to delegates only from France and the Holy Roman Empire. Although these terms diverged considerably from those reached at Leoben, Gallo, out of timidity and awe, signed them anyway. Bonaparte knew that Gallo's signature was worthless without the endorsement of Thugut, but the Frenchman's instincts told him that Thugut would agree. "The Viennese cabinet is led now by a single man," he advised the Directory, "who is apparently mediocre, frightfully slow, lacking in vision, and devious at every opportunity. He follows no system, but sways with the rumors from all of Europe. In the last analysis he has only one idea that I believe to be correct: he does not want to renew the war."[45]

Bonaparte's opinions about Thugut's reaction to the new terms were both right and wrong. As Bonaparte assumed, Thugut had no wish to reopen the war, but he also had no intention of accepting the terms agreed upon at Montebello. He initially expressed outrage: "What chicanery! What pretension on the part of the French! To what humiliation we have

---

[45] Bonaparte to the Directory, May 27, 1797, in Bonaparte, *Correspondance*, 3: 73.

descended!"[46] He explained to Gallo why none of the changes was acceptable and ordered him not to concede anything to France in the future without consulting Vienna. Thugut even sent Merveldt to join Gallo for all later talks, ostensibly to assist him in the negotiations but actually to prevent him from bowing to new French demands.[47] Notwithstanding these precautions, Thugut also decided that Gallo must be replaced in the ongoing diplomatic negotiations. To deal effectively with the talented Bonaparte, the emperor would need a much more skilled representative, in fact, the most adroit, imperturbable, and perceptive diplomat in his service. That man was Louis Cobenzl. On June 12 Thugut sent orders to Cobenzl to leave St. Petersburg as soon as possible and to return to Vienna.[48]

For the order to reach the Russian capital, for Cobenzl to ready his departure, and for him to travel to Vienna required almost two months. In the meantime, since neither side wished to resume hostilities, negotiations continued in a spasmodic effort to resolve the rather wide differences that had emerged between the French and Austrian positions. On June 19 Gallo, accompanied by Merveldt, met Bonaparte again at Montebello and delivered Vienna's rejection of the terms reached on May 24, as well as Thugut's insistence on a strict adherence to the articles concluded at Leoben. Bonaparte of course refused to return to the earlier agreement, and it appeared that the talks had reached an impasse.

Nevertheless, Bonaparte had no intention of breaking off negotiations because events at home seemed about to undermine his authority. Elections to the National Convention in March 1797 had featured a decided swing to the royalists who, although divided between those loyal to prerevolutionary ab-

---

[46] Thugut to Colloredo, June 6, 1797, in Vivenot, ed., *Vertrauliche Briefe*, 2: 38.
[47] Thugut's conversations with Gallo, June 5, 1797, in Hüffer, *Österreich und Preussen*, 336.
[48] Thugut to L. Cobenzl, June 12, 1797, Vienna, HHSA, SK, *Russland*, 2: 181.

solutism and those supporting constitutional monarchy, were united in their desire not merely for peace but for an immediate peace with no annexations. Moreover, in the constitutional rotation of the five members of the Directory, the French diplomat and prominent member of the peace party Barthélemy had been chosen, so that the Directory now consisted of two republicans (Reubell and Larévellière), two closet royalists (Barthélemy and Carnot), and one waverer (Barras). The revival of royalist and pacifist sympathies inspired hope for peace and stability among many Frenchmen, and in the summer of 1797 antirepublican demonstrations had become increasingly numerous. Bonaparte feared that a seizure of power by conservative forces would destroy his career and his dreams utterly. Securing a quick, favorable settlement with the Austrians would undermine the contention that he and his republican friends were unwilling and unable to end the war.

Yet to achieve peace by offering concessions would suggest weakness; being Bonaparte, he used threats instead. He continued to spread republicanism in the Venetian lands, warning that, if Vienna did not accept his wishes, he might renege altogether on the cession of Venice to the monarchy and create a French-sponsored republic there. Moreover, he implied that Paris was trying to enlist the Prussians and the Turks in the war against the monarchy and attempting to persuade the Russians and the British to remain neutral in any renewed conflict. If these menaces were not sufficient, he even proposed sending his associate, General Henri Jacques Clarke, to Vienna ostensibly to talk directly with Thugut but in fact to resurrect past French threats to expose the Austrian foreign minister as a traitor and spy if he did not accede to Bonaparte's demands.[49]

Thugut believed that his opponent was bluffing. He had also been keeping abreast of events in France, largely through the reports and analyses of Mallet du Pan, and those reports

[49] Gallo and Merveldt to Thugut, July 1, 1797, in Hüffer and Luckwaldt, eds., *Frieden*, 241–43.

persuaded him that changes in the French government were in the offing and that for now he should remain steadfast and await developments. To his delegates he wrote, "While the French engage in all of these efforts to confuse, browbeat, and cajole, we will simply stand by our demand to fulfill [the preliminaries of] Leoben."[50] Consequently, neither side conceded a point in exchanges that began in late June. The only agreement reached was to move the site of the talks from Montebello to Udine in order to improve communications with Vienna. Bonaparte, seeing no immediate progress likely, decided not to participate personally, and Gallo used the opportunity of Bonaparte's absence to journey to Vienna to consult with Thugut. Clarke and Merveldt took up residence at Udine to preserve the pretense of a peace conference, but everyone involved knew that nothing would be decided at least until Bonaparte and Gallo returned.

Since Thugut was now depending on events in Paris either to make Bonaparte more conciliatory or to remove him from the talks altogether, he decided to dispatch a representative to the French capital to gather firsthand information on events and conditions there. He selected I. Baptiste, an adept man who had served as Gallo's secretary during his negotiations with revolutionary France on behalf of both Naples and Austria. Thugut instructed Baptiste first to call upon Barthélemy, the leader whom Thugut believed most sympathetic to a moderate settlement, and to inform him that Bonaparte alone was delaying peace and that only his removal would lead to a treaty satisfactory to both sides. Then Baptiste should visit the French foreign minister and present to him the conditions under which Austria would conclude peace: strict adherence to the articles signed at Leoben, an informal Austro-French agreement that would define the joint policies to be followed at the forthcoming general peace conference at Rastadt, and an invitation to Russia to participate in the talks. In addition, Thugut ordered Baptiste to keep his eyes open, to assess the

[50] Thugut to Merveldt, July 7, 1797, in ibid., 248–50.

political situation in Paris, and to report who the men of power and influence seemed to be.[51]

For Thugut, Baptiste's reports brought discouraging news. On visiting Barthélemy, Baptiste learned that, contrary to Thugut's hopes, Barthélemy had virtually no power in the Directory and clearly no influence with Bonaparte. Barthélemy himself told Baptiste that, if he tried to sway Bonaparte in any way, he would only draw ridicule upon his own head. Baptiste also visited the new foreign minister, Thugut's old acquaintance from his Parisian days and the soon-to-be-famous Talleyrand. When he presented Thugut's principles to Talleyrand, they were not only rejected but answered with conditions even more unacceptable to Vienna than those Bonaparte had proposed on May 24. Baptiste's conclusion from these two interviews and his other observations was that the majority of the Directory was actually "more eager for [a resumption of the] war than Bonaparte himself." If Thugut wanted peace, "it is not with the Directory but with Bonaparte that it is necessary to negotiate and to conclude [a treaty]. People here do not cease in repeating [that] to me." In fact, Baptiste speculated that his mission might have done more harm than good, because it might have annoyed Bonaparte that Vienna was conniving with the Directory behind his back and thus might make him even more difficult than before.[52]

These reports seemed to dash Thugut's hopes of securing a better peace for Paris. Indeed, he was most irritated by the unwelcome news, calling the Directory "a gambling-den of brigands" and recommending that the army prepare for a resumption of hostilities.[53] But he knew that further conflict was impossible. Each time Merveldt enjoyed a few days' res-

---

[51] Thugut to Baptiste, July 31, 1797, and Thugut to the foreign minister of France, July 31, 1797, in ibid., 273–78. When Thugut dispatched Baptiste, he did not know who currently served as foreign minister of France, so he addressed his letter to the office and not the man.

[52] Baptiste to Thugut, August 12 and 15, 1797, in ibid., 291–300.

[53] Thugut to Colloredo, August 25, 1797, in Vivenot, ed., *Vertrauliche Briefe*, 2: 50.

pite from the peace talks, he visited the camps and assembly areas of the Austrian forces north of Udine and reported on their condition to Thugut. His opinion was that the army could not take the field again for some time to come. "The greater part of the army still lacks the most necessary clothing, a large number of recruits has not arrived, some grenadier battalions lack thirty or forty rifles each."[54] Even if these logistical problems were overcome, the army would be incapable of fighting because "the subaltern officers lack instruction," and the regular officers "live in an unmilitary and often scandalous manner."[55]

While not abandoning hope that change was still possible in France, Thugut realized that conditions left him no alternative but to turn his attention back to the negotiations at Udine. On August 18 Gallo returned to the city, and the following day he and Merveldt were joined by another Habsburg delegate, Ignaz Degelmann, a German specialist whom Thugut sent because it was obvious that the fate of at least part of the Holy Roman Empire would figure in the talks from now on. When Bonaparte learned that Gallo had returned to Udine, he too joined the discussions. He was still persuaded that the best way to insure his future in Paris was to conclude a settlement with Austria so that he might pose as master of both war and peace. The renewed talks began on August 31 with a slight modification in format; as a concession to Bonaparte, who claimed that he was somewhat ill, the site of the sessions alternated between his magnificently appointed headquarters in a former doge's palace at Passariano and the comparatively modest merchant's home where the Habsburg delegates resided in Udine.

As before, Thugut instructed his delegates to insist upon a congress rather than a definitive Austro-French peace and to demand that the articles of Leoben be the basis for any future settlement. Such instructions could not lead to a treaty, and

[54] Merveldt to Thugut, July 19, 1797, in Hüffer and Luckwaldt, eds., *Frieden*, 265.
[55] Merveldt to Thugut, August 19, 1797, in ibid., 302–304.

Thugut knew it. However, he still believed that changes in Paris might temper Bonaparte's revised demands. Despite Baptiste's pessimism, Thugut now expressed a hope that the promotion of Talleyrand might lead to a compromise: "His insights, which I myself applauded a few times during my trips to Paris, are only able to make me confident of his influence on the great work of pacification."[56]

In short, Thugut's purpose was still to delay, and nothing could have been more frustrating to Bonaparte. The Frenchman knew that the three Habsburg representatives in Udine were mere surrogates of little consequence. Gallo he described as "a foreigner. Although supported by the empress he dares nothing, as a foreigner, to counter the intentions of Thugut." Merveldt "is a colonel of a cavalry regiment, personally very brave. . . . But when he says 'these are our instructions,' he has said it all." Degelmann "is of no consequence, an indecisive character, a hypochondriac." Bonaparte was perfectly aware that his actual diplomatic opponent was Thugut. "When alone, they [the Austrian delegates] say to you very softly, after having looked right and left to see if anyone is listening, that Thugut is a scoundrel who should be hanged; but Thugut is the true sovereign in Vienna."[57] Yet Bonaparte could think of no way to circumvent the pawns and to reach Thugut directly; for now the only pressure that he could envision was a return to threats. To Paris he wrote, "The emperor and the nation want peace; Thugut does not want peace, but dares not want war. Show him war like the head of Medusa, and we will bring Thugut to his senses."[58]

In the end, it was not Bonaparte's threats of war that convinced Thugut to come to terms at Udine; it was news from Paris. On September 4 (18 Fructidor by the French revolutionary calendar) the republicans, with the help of the army,

---

[56] Thugut to Baptiste, September 1, 1797, in ibid., 316.

[57] Bonaparte to the minister of foreign affairs, September 6, 1797, in Bonaparte, *Correspondance*, 3: 265.

[58] Bonaparte to the minister of foreign affairs, September 3, 1797, in ibid., 260–61. Biro, *German Policy*, 2: 836.

staged a coup. They arrested or called for the arrest of the two moderate Directors, Carnot and Barthélemy (Carnot escaped), fifty-three members of the two legislative houses, and the owners, editors, managers, and writers of forty-two royalist newspapers. The coup dashed Thugut's hopes for a more accommodating regime in France.[59] He realized that his choices had narrowed either to resuming hostilities or to negotiating seriously with Bonaparte, and war was out of the question. Although the Habsburg civil and military establishments had known since Leoben that a resumption of the fighting was possible, in fact neither had undertaken any serious preparations for it. To Colloredo Thugut wrote, "Unfortunately we have deluded ourselves too long so that [war] is impossible and nothing can be done about it."[60] The only practical choice was to negotiate seriously, and that could not be done by Gallo, Merveldt, and Degelmann. The time had come for the seasoned negotiator who could not only resist Bonaparte's threats and blandishments but employ a few tricks of his own to win concessions for Vienna. That man was at last in the capital: Louis Cobenzl.

Cobenzl had reached Vienna on August 8. Thugut, who had not seen him in eighteen years, observed: "I had heard that in Russia he had become a monster of corpulence, that he was overloaded with unhealthy fat, that he was menaced with being struck by apoplexy from one day to the next; I found nothing of any of it. He looks well, his figure appears to me nothing out of the ordinary, and he looks like any other man."[61] After his arrival, Cobenzl remained in Vienna studying dispatches, agreements, memoranda, and proposals in preparation for the time when he might depart to conclude a settlement with the French. By September 20 that time had come. Thugut's faith in him was so great that Cobenzl took

[59] Gallo, Merveldt, and Degelmann to Thugut, September 12, 1797, in Hüffer and Luckwaldt, eds., *Frieden*, 346.
[60] Thugut to Colloredo, September 17, 1797, in Vivenot, ed., *Vertrauliche Briefe*, 2: 57.
[61] Thugut to Colloredo, August 8, 1797, in ibid., 46.

Louis Cobenzl
(Courtesy Bildarchiv, Austrian National Library)

with him no formal instructions, only a collection of notes, ideas, and recollections from his discussions with the foreign minister. His authority was complete and unrestricted. His formal orders were "to conclude and to sign" a definitive peace with France.[62] When he reached Udine, Cobenzl summed up his assignment: "I ask your indulgence and compassion. You have sent me to the galleys. I will row with all my might, and I hope that I will not wreck."[63]

The talks between Bonaparte and Cobenzl began on September 27 and continued intensely for the next three weeks. Each man resorted to many diplomatic tricks to bend the other to his will. Bonaparte complained of Cobenzl as a man "not accustomed to negotiating but always to having his own way," and in his memoirs described him as "positive and intractable in business," intentionally being imprecise while "talking loudly and using imperious gestures."[64] Cobenzl in his turn complained of Bonaparte's unpredictable moods, of his theatrics, and especially of his ill manners; he conducted himself "like a man from a hovel."[65]

By October 10 they had reached an agreement, and it was indeed different from Leoben. Austria still ceded the Austrian Netherlands to France, and, although it did not recognize French control of the left bank of the Rhine, the agreement provided for the emperor to summon a peace congress at Rastadt between France and the Holy Roman Empire, where he would use his good offices to secure most of the left bank for France. In exchange for those good offices, the emperor would receive the archbishopric of Salzburg and a small portion of Bavaria east of the Inn River. In Italy the emperor would give up Lombardy, Brescia, and Mantua to the French-sponsored

[62] Francis to L. Cobenzl, September 20, 1797, in Hüffer and Luckwaldt, eds., *Frieden*, 367.

[63] L. Cobenzl to Thugut, September 27, 1797, in ibid., 374.

[64] Bonaparte to Talleyrand, September 28, 1797, in ibid., 375; Chair, ed., *Napoleon's Memoirs*, 254.

[65] L. Cobenzl to Thugut, October 14, 1797, in Hüffer and Luckwaldt, eds., *Frieden*, 460–61.

Cisalpine Republic and allow Modena, a part of Venetia, and the Legations to be incorporated in it as well. Austria would annex Venice proper and its possessions of Istria, Dalmatia, the Adriatic islands, and Venetia to the Adige and Po rivers. France would win the Ionian Islands and the Albanian coastline dependent upon them. Lesser compensation would be offered to the Duke of Modena, the House of Orange, and Prussia.[66] Although the articles were agreed upon by October 10, a bit more verbal pushing and shoving were needed before they became the definitive treaty. When all was completed, Cobenzl suggested the town hall of Udine as the appropriate site for the signing, but Bonaparte declined because Udine was the location of the Austrian delegates' residence. Since Bonaparte's headquarters at Passariano were then unacceptable on the same grounds, the two men agreed upon the village of Campo Formio (now Campoformido), halfway between Udine and Passariano. There on October 17 the treaty ending the Austro-French war was concluded.

The Treaty of Campo Formio was clearly in the eighteenth-century tradition of balance-of-power-cum-acquisition diplomacy. Austria had lost the war to France and therefore gave up territory as a consequence of that defeat. However, it was incumbent upon the Austrians to arrange for compensation at someone else's expense to preserve at least the illusion of balance, and the eighteenth-century diplomatic tradition required Bonaparte to allow them to do so—a tradition Bonaparte clearly followed.

The major Habsburg acquisition at Campo Formio was Venice and its possessions along the Adriatic Sea. One might imagine that Thugut would have been pleased with this gain because it gave the monarchy not only territorial compensation but also the opportunity to become a significant commercial and perhaps even naval power in the Adriatic, an opportunity never quite realized with only the port of Trieste.

---

[66] L. Cobenzl to Thugut, October 10, 1797, in ibid., 445–52; Bonaparte to the Directory, October 10, 1797, in Bonaparte, *Correspondance*, 3: 374–76.

In fact, Talleyrand had argued vigorously against ceding any part of Venice to the Habsburgs for fear that maritime competition between Austria and France would intensify their traditional rivalry on land.[67] One could even have faulted Cobenzl for giving in so readily to Bonaparte's demand for the Ionian Islands, which in French hands would block Austrian naval expansion into the Ionian and Mediterranean seas.

But Thugut cared nothing at all for naval strength, either military or commercial. Indeed, to suggest that he found the treaty at all acceptable on the basis of gains and losses misses the point. He found the treaty repulsive, but not because he believed that under the circumstances either he or Cobenzl could have secured a better one.[68] Thugut was distressed that he had been forced to end Austria's resistance to France and the revolution. He was not certain what course revolutionary France would follow in the future, but he feared that it would not bode well for the monarchy. When he formally submitted the treaty to Colloredo for presentation to the emperor, he described it as "a peace treaty truly unfortunate, whose ignominy will be epoch-making in the annals of Austria, that is, if those annals themselves do not cease to exist."[69]

Thugut was especially grieved that the Viennese people did not understand that their government had just concluded a humiliating and potentially dangerous settlement. To Colloredo he wrote:

That which crowns my despair is the shameful debasement of our Viennese, who are intoxicated with joy at the simple name of peace, without considering the conditions good or bad; no one thinks of the honor of the monarchy,

[67] Talleyrand to the Directory, August 13, 1797, in Hüffer and Luckwaldt, eds., *Frieden*, 296.

[68] Thugut to Dietrichstein, November 2, 1797, in Vivenot, ed., *Vertrauliche Briefe*, 2: 66. Thugut admitted to Dietrichstein that the treaty was probably the most favorable that Vienna could hope for: "The only consolation I can see is that Count Cobenzl made it, and it is certain that he obtained all that was humanly possible at the time."

[69] Thugut to Colloredo, October 22, 1797, in ibid., 63.

or what will become of it in ten years providing that for the moment he can stroll the bastions and quietly eat his fried chicken. How can such sentiments challenge the energy of a Bonaparte, cheerfully overcoming all obstacles? Peace! Peace! But where is it? I do not see it in the treaty; at least if a rapid reading has not misled me. I find no security for us, and the execution of it will perhaps be only a second volume of the preliminaries.[70]

Some historians have called the Treaty of Campo Formio merely an armistice and have suggested that Thugut especially viewed it as such. This interpretation implies that Thugut eagerly looked forward to rekindling the war and plotted to arrange it from the moment of the settlement. To be sure, Thugut believed that a renewed war between Austria and France would come, but to say that he eagerly sought it is misleading. He feared the coming of a new conflict, because he wondered if the monarchy would survive it.

[70] Thugut to Colloredo, October 22, 1797, in ibid., 64.

CHAPTER X

PEACE OR WAR?

1798

WITH PEACE restored, Thugut seems to have pondered seriously submitting his resignation. It would have been customary for him to do so, since the policies he had championed had ended in failure. Again the archives contain no formal letter of resignation, but on January 1, 1798, Thugut sent a circular notifying various officials that his offer to resign had been rejected by the emperor and that he would continue at his post.[1] In mid-February he complained to Dietrichstein that the embarrassment of Campo Formio, the burden of day-to-day work, and the heavy responsibilities of his office were too much for his "physical and moral forces" and that he wished to step down. "I do not know what arrangement His Majesty will make for my replacement, but I am certain that, of the infinite number of those who will rejoice to see me leave the department of foreign affairs, none will be happier than I."[2]

Whether he wished to retire or not, he believed that he must remain until he had insured that the Congress of Rastadt, which began in December 1797, carried out the terms agreed

[1] Thugut to all ministers, January 1, 1798, in Vivenot, ed., *Rastadter Congress*, iv–v.
[2] Thugut to Dietrichstein, February 17, 1798, in Vivenot, ed., *Vertrauliche Briefe*, 2: 86.

upon at Campo Formio. The imperial delegation to the congress had been selected in the wake of the Reichstag's peace
resolution of July 3, 1796, and included ten formal delegates
representing each major interest in the Empire.[3] The emperor
himself sent three ministers: the elder Metternich representing
him in his capacity as emperor, Louis Cobenzl in his capacity
as archduke of Austria and king of Bohemia, and Lehrbach in
his capacity as leader of the Austrian defense circle. In addition, ninety other German states sent envoys to observe the
proceedings and to advise the official delegation. In all, about
nine hundred German representatives and their staff members descended upon Rastadt, thus placing a considerable burden on the ability of that city to provide lodging, sustenance,
and entertainment.[4]

Bonaparte represented France. He arrived in the city on
November 25 and immediately became the center of attention.
Not merely the newspapers but the diplomats themselves
rushed to record his every glance, word, and gesture.[5] Bonaparte had no intention of staying long, however. Aside from
awing the imperial delegates, his purpose at Rastadt was to exchange the formal ratification of the Treaty of Campo Formio
with Cobenzl and to arrange the transfer from Austria to
France of Mainz and the corresponding transfer of the Republic of Venice from France to Austria. The news that Mainz
would be surrendered caused a sensation among the German
delegates, who, still ignorant of the actual terms of Campo
Formio, feared that other territories might be ceded to France
as well. But that was all Bonaparte wanted, and on December
3 he left the city.[6] Remaining behind to negotiate for the Directory were Ange Bonnier and Jean-Baptiste Treilhard,

---

[3] The delegates included two from the college of electors, six from the college of princes, and two from the imperial cities. Five were Protestant and
five Catholic.

[4] Joseph Helfert, *Der Rastadter Gesandtenmord* (Vienna, 1874), 36.

[5] Lehrbach to Thugut, November 29, 1797, in Hüffer, *Rastatter Congress*,
1: 6.

[6] Gagliardo, *Reich and Nation*, 189; Hüffer, *Rastatter Congress*, 1: 12.

whom Bonaparte prophetically described as "arrogant, muddle-headed, and . . . likely to quarrel between themselves and to negotiate fruitlessly with the Germans."[7] On December 9 the formal talks began.

Thugut had little doubt that, although some tough negotiating lay ahead, the congress would restore formal peace between France and the Empire. The principal Habsburg negotiator was Cobenzl, and his instructions were to hold the French strictly to the provisions of Campo Formio and to resist any efforts to change them as Bonaparte had earlier changed the terms agreed upon at Leoben. As anticipated, such an effort was made. On January 18, 1798, the French delegates formally demanded surrender of the entire left bank of the Rhine River, a clear violation of Campo Formio, whose articles had specifically excluded from French control the left-bank lands of the archbishop of Cologne from Crefeld to Bonn along with various possessions of the king of Prussia.[8] Now the French intended to overturn those exclusions and thus once again undermine a covenant that they had solemnly concluded just a short time before.

The new demands annoyed Thugut, but he had come to expect French efforts to revise agreements already signed. What troubled him far more were French initiatives elsewhere. As with Leoben, Thugut had hoped that the settlement reached at Campo Formio would halt attempts by France to conquer more lands. The treaty might not have been a favorable one, but he expected that it would at least check the expansion of the warring powers. As 1798 began, however, news reached Vienna that revolutionary France was continuing its conquests as if no agreement had been reached at all.

Rome was the first victim. On December 28, 1797, demonstrators for and against the creation of a republic in the city had clashed in a Roman street near the French embassy. A

---

[7] Quoted in Sorel, *L'Europe*, 5: 266.

[8] Hüffer, *Rastatter Congress*, 1: 88. The lands denied to France were those east of the Nette and Vanloo rivers. T.C.W. Blanning, *The French Revolution in Germany: Occupation and Resistance in the Rhineland, 1792–1802* (Oxford, 1983), 79.

French general named Duphot happened to be at the embassy for the purpose of marrying the sister of the wife of Joseph Bonaparte, who was serving as French ambassador. Upon hearing the ruckus in the street, Duphot went out to try to quell it and was shot dead. Outraged, Joseph Bonaparte and his entourage left Rome for Florence, where he called upon the Directory to exact revenge for the general's demise. A French army under Louis Berthier promptly marched on Rome and occupied it by the second week in February 1798. Berthier deposed the pope and on February 15 proclaimed the establishment of the Roman Republic with a government modeled upon that of the Directory in Paris.[9]

As the Papal States fell to revolutionary France, so did Switzerland. For some time the revolution had found sympathetic admirers in Switzerland, and now and then the cantons had protested what seemed to them provocative French efforts to exploit these sentiments in order to undermine the existing governments there. Owing to Bonaparte's successes in Italy in 1796, the routine interest that the revolutionary governments had previously shown toward Switzerland was joined by strategic considerations, for it was now important for the French to secure the shortest Alpine routes between France and northern Italy's new Cisalpine Republic, especially the roads over the Simplon and Great St. Bernard passes in Switzerland.[10] In January the French took advantage of appeals from so-called Swiss patriots in the cantons of Vaux and Basel to occupy Switzerland militarily and to impose on that country a new political order modeled after that of France. The lower Swiss lands resisted the French hardly at all, but the invaders encountered some hostility in the highlands, where the mountaineers carried on guerrilla activity against them for some time thereafter.

The French subversion of Rome and Switzerland seemed to

---

[9] Godechot, *Counter-Revolution*, 312; Bernard Nabonne, *La diplomatie du Directoire et Bonaparte d'après les papiers inédits de Reubell* (Paris, 1951), 125–26.

[10] Raymond Guyot, *Le directoire et la paix de l'Europe des traités de Bâle à la deuxième coalition (1795–1799)* (Paris, 1911), 637–38.

vindicate Thugut's conception of revolutionary France as a power that could be stopped only by unrelenting force. In peace or in war, France would expand with equal determination. As he pondered the events in Rome and Switzerland, Thugut became ever more convinced that no lasting security was possible with such a power.

As if to strengthen Thugut's conviction, in February 1798 the arrogance, aggressiveness, and bumptiousness that characterized the revolution came right to the foreign minister's doorstep in the person of General Jean-Baptiste Bernadotte, the first ambassador to Austria from revolutionary France. The restoration of peace between France and Austria at Campo Formio had again made possible the customary exchange of embassies between the two powers. But Thugut had no intention of allowing a "Jacobin" official status in Vienna, for he (and many others) looked upon French envoys not as diplomats but as conspirators and spies, who stirred up local malcontents to destroy confidence in the governments to which they were accredited.[11] When Louis Cobenzl notified Thugut that Bernadotte was coming, the foreign minister simply declared it impossible. He would not treat with a revolutionary at the ambassadorial level, and he certainly would not allow a French representative to reside in Vienna. Austria and France should instead appoint envoys of the second rank, and the monarchy would receive the chosen Frenchman in Rastadt only.[12]

Thugut composed this statement on February 3; to his astonishment, five days later Ambassador Bernadotte and his entourage appeared in Vienna.[13] When Bernadotte had reached the Austrian border on his way from Milan, he had simply told the Habsburg commanding general that, although he had no passport, France would assuredly consider it a hostile act if anyone barred his way, and the general let him pass.

[11] L. Cobenzl to Thugut, January 24, 1798, in Hüffer, *Rastatter Congress*, 1: 243–44.

[12] Thugut to L. Cobenzl, February 3, 1798, in ibid., 244.

[13] Bernadotte to Talleyrand, February 10, 1798, Paris, Archives, *Autriche*, 368.

Thugut knew that Bernadotte's presence in the capital portended trouble. He told Dietrichstein, "Owing to the negligence of a few of our civil and military officers, General Bernadotte, after crossing our borders without first requesting or receiving passports, has presented himself unexpectedly here as ambassador of the French Republic. It is easy to see that disagreements, pettiness, and intrigue of all kinds will result from the establishment of such a mission in Vienna."[14]

Thugut was right; Bernadotte immediately became the center of turmoil. His status as an official of revolutionary France alone attracted considerable attention, and Eden especially complained that elements of Viennese society lionized him as an extraordinary and therefore attractive character. "The conversation for the last week runs entirely upon him, and I am weary with it, and all the nonsense of a set of gaping blockheads who either cannot or will not see their danger, and so for a dinner will treat him with the vilest adulation."[15] Bernadotte contributed to his notoriety by his own arrogance and that of his subordinates, who walked the Viennese streets wearing revolutionary caps and tricolor cockades and then bitterly complained when they suffered affronts from the local citizenry or when they encountered émigrés wearing the insignia of Bourbon France. A riot almost erupted in the Hofburgtheater when members of the French mission whistled and jeered at the audience, which was shouting "Long live the king of France."[16] As expected, Bernadotte also engaged in conspiratorial activity. He gathered about him a small group of local sympathizers and helped to establish contact between discontented Poles and the Polish exiles in Paris and in Italy, an act that not only disturbed Thugut but worried the ministers from Prussia and Russia as well.[17]

---

[14] Thugut to Dietrichstein, February 17, 1798, in Vivenot, ed., *Rastadter Congress*, 136–39.

[15] Eden to Auckland, March 8, 1798, in Auckland, *Journal and Correspondence*, 3: 387.

[16] Hüffer, *Rastatter Congress*, 1: 254.

[17] Thugut to Dietrichstein, April 5, 1798, in Vivenot, ed., *Rastadter Congress*, 156.

Thugut avoided official contacts with Bernadotte as best he could. He generally excused himself from formal audiences for one reason or another, but he was now and then surprised by Bernadotte in the chancellery itself when the Frenchman would suddenly appear to engage him in impromptu talks.[18] Generally, when Bernadotte wished to communicate with Thugut, he sent his secretary to the chancellery with the message and with instructions on how to answer questions that Thugut might ask. When Thugut wished to reply, he dispatched either Degelmann or Baptiste to deliver a response orally. Thugut wrote little of his dealings with Bernadotte, but Bernadotte's reports of his Viennese experiences run to more than 350 folio pages.[19] Not until April 11 was the young French general confident that he had observed the foreign minister carefully enough to offer an assessment of Thugut's personality to the Directory, and then his report stressed mostly the usual faults soldiers find in diplomats. "Never does one see in him the man of force," Bernadotte wrote. "He never admits that which systematic logic demands be done . . . or demands be rejected. . . . When discussion becomes truly serious, he always has no plan other than to attack it with detailed objections; it seems that he wants to deflect rather than to refute rationally what one has told him." Thugut was "without doubt immoral in a number of ways" and insufficiently sincere or resolute "to produce an impression of talent."[20] The diplomat's refusal to argue vigorously and forthrightly on all major points Bernadotte interpreted as a sign of weakness and dissipation.

If Bernadotte found Thugut contemptible, Thugut found Bernadotte frightening. In Thugut's eyes, Bernadotte was not simply the ambassador of another great power; he was a vision of terrifying force, revealing to Vienna firsthand how revolutionary France was subverting European government and so-

[18] A. Hollaender, "Zur Gesandtschaft Bernadottes in Wien, 1798," *Monatsblatt des Vereines für Geschichte der Stadt Wien* 15 (1929–1933): 143.

[19] Paris, Archives, *Autriche*, 368.

[20] Bernadotte to Talleyrand, April 11, 1798, ibid.

ciety. "The Directory in Paris pursues with an unheard-of enthusiasm the consummation of its projects to destroy Europe," Thugut wrote to Dietrichstein, and Bernadotte's actions were part of those projects. "Bernadotte and his mission haughtily reckon on the coming explosion in all the corners of Europe. The mean and secret maneuvers that they employ to seduce and to corrupt the multitude are so varied that, if one delays in putting into effect a common accord, a deplorable catastrophe will inevitably envelop all thrones."

For Thugut the news from Rome and Switzerland and Bernadotte's behavior in Vienna brought back into sharp focus the need for unceasing resistance against revolutionary France. Every delay in that resistance permitted some success that strengthened France and weakened the traditional monarchies. "Each day witnesses the ravages of general upheaval. A revolution in Spain seems near and unavoidable. The king of Sardinia will be obliged to descend his throne at the first order of a French general. The court of Naples believes itself near to utter ruin, and a considerable number of troops have actually embarked at Genoa, and one supposes them to be on the way to attack Sicily." As monarchies toppled, Thugut speculated, a momentum would take hold, convincing many that revolution was the wave of the future and orderly government a thing of the past. The tragedy of such thinking was that, by creating an aura of inevitability about coming upheaval, it gave hope and confidence to the revolutionaries and spread despair and defeatism among the traditionalists. "The continuous overthrow of all governments agitates the people and weakens their respect for their sovereigns, whom they regard as becoming unable to protect them in any effective way, and it is only too true that, in proportion to the strengthening of democracy, the means of resistance left to monarchical government diminish."[21] Therefore, the monarchies must unite their collective efforts immediately, or all would perish at the hands of revolutionary France.

[21] Thugut to Dietrichstein, April 5, 1798, in Hüffer, *Rastatter Congress*, 1: 227–28.

Thugut continually pondered how to halt the growing strength of France. After all, Austria had fought hard against France for five years and lost. During the war, Thugut had appreciated the need for a united front among the great powers, but in his mind the monarchies, instead of committing themselves to the same cause, had either pursued narrow self-interest or rushed to make peace at the first sign of ill fortune. Notwithstanding these impressions, Thugut could imagine no other way to defeat France and to restore order and stability to Europe than by calling again upon the great monarchies to join in a coalition. And it must include all of them, even his old nemesis, Prussia; a union of Prussia, Austria, Russia, and Britain had to be formed immediately. "There is not an instant to lose," he told Dietrichstein; "Without a sincere accord among the different powers for the preservation of their respective governments, all of Europe shall perish."[22]

Despite his conviction that only a mighty coalition could counter revolutionary France, Thugut was by no means certain in April 1798 that such a coalition could be created. Austria was not on the best of terms with any of the other three great European monarchies, especially Great Britain, the only state still at war with France. The treaties of Leoben and Campo Formio had soured Vienna's relations with London, but that bitterness had deepened significantly because of a disagreement that had a far greater impact than it should have had: the rejection by Austria of a substantial British loan negotiated by Starhemberg in 1797.

As mentioned earlier, in May 1795 Thugut had concluded the first major loan with Britain on terms that he and other Habsburg ministers found decidedly prejudicial to Austria. Nevertheless, the Austrian officials signed the agreement anyway because they desperately needed the money. As one would expect, within a short time the Austrian war effort required even more funds, and in 1796 negotiations began in London for a second major loan. Since 1796 was a year of great

[22] Ibid.

concern and urgent need, the Pitt government consented to pay the monarchy non-interest-bearing advances to help finance the ongoing war on the assumption that these advances would be included in the larger loan when its terms were finally accepted by both parties. The agreement was duly concluded by Starhemberg and British officials in London on May 16, 1797, and shortly thereafter approved by Parliament.[23] It gave Austria £4,600,000 on generally the same terms as provided for in the loan of 1795. Since London had already advanced £1,600,000 before the signing, the Austrians would receive an additional £3,000,000 but pay interest on the whole £4,600,000. By the time Starhemberg concluded the loan, however, the Treaty of Leoben had effectively ended the war for Austria. When the terms of the agreement reached Vienna, therefore, Thugut advised the emperor not to ratify it. In announcing Vienna's rejection of the loan, Thugut assured London that the monarchy would repay the advances but without any interest since there had been no commitment to do so.

Thugut's action infuriated the British; indeed, it cast a pall over Austro-British relations for the next three years. It prevented any formal Austro-British military agreement until 1800, precluded all British monetary support for the monarchy, contributed to significant mistrust during the important military campaign of 1799, and created an atmosphere of animosity and suspicion between London and Vienna that was not easily dispelled. The charge that each government leveled at the other was that of bad faith. Grenville contended that the British cabinet had concluded an honest—indeed generous—financial arrangement with Austria, had paid interest-free advances, and had passed it through a skeptical Parliament by assuring the members that the monarchy was a loyal ally and a good credit risk. Then the arrangement had been repudiated. For his part, Thugut argued that the British had se-

[23] Piers Mackesy, *Statesmen at War: The Strategy of Overthrow, 1798–1799* (London, 1974), 10–11; Gustav Otruba, "Englands Finanzhilfe für Österreich in den Koalitionskriegen und im Kampf gegen Napoleon," *Österreich in Geschichte und Literatur* 9 (1965): 84–87.

duced Starhemberg into accepting the loan at a time of crisis in Habsburg affairs "in order to turn us over pitilessly to the capitalists of London who almost ruined His Majesty's finances by conditions of our first loan."[24] Now Austria did not need the money so urgently, especially on terms that promised not merely sacrifices but possible bankruptcy.

Curiously, the bad feelings over the loan persisted mostly because neither side truly appreciated the position of the other, and that in turn prevented them from reaching an acceptable compromise. The British cabinet was less concerned with the money as such than with the prestige it had sacrificed for Austria's sake in Parliament. Even as it was being negotiated, the Austrian loan was unpopular in Britain. The Bank of England had been warning for some time that Austria was a poor credit risk and that Britain's own monetary resources could be jeopardized if the government supported a large loan to a country that might be unable to repay it. When a financial panic occurred in February 1797, many members of Parliament blamed it squarely on the uncertain return on Austrian loans. Despite the widespread sentiment against it, the Pitt ministry presented the new loan to Parliament anyway and, amidst much grumbling from the members, managed to secure its passage. Under the circumstances, the Pitt ministry was deeply aggrieved and embarrassed when Vienna rejected the loan. Moreover, Pitt now had to explain to Parliament that he had advanced £1,600,000 in British currency to Austria without either Parliamentary approval or a formal promise from Vienna to pay it back by a specific time with interest.[25] The money-conscious squires in Parliament considered the Pitt ministry to have been duped by Vienna, and, more seriously, they would be reluctant to approve loans to any of Britain's allies in the future. The issue for the Pitt ministry was not merely the money, but its reputation with Parliament.

On Thugut's side, there was no question that the loan was

[24] Quoted in Helleiner, *The Imperial Loans*, 101.
[25] Mackesy, *Statesmen at War*, 11.

a bad one for Austria. The interest charged was exorbitant and Austria's financial situation so perilous that the sums necessary to pay it could not be collected. As Thugut wrote to Starhemberg, Vienna had so many other "pressing needs" that nothing could justify accepting a loan on such terms. But immediate cost was not the only consideration. Should the terms of the British loan be published—and they would have to be to encourage subscriptions—the publicity would "absolutely destroy" any chance of the emperor's borrowing money from any other source because every banker in Europe would see "the enormity of our debt" and label Austria the poorest credit risk.[26] Moneylenders would assume that future Austrian revenues would be dedicated exclusively to paying the British with no money remaining to repay anyone else, and Austria's credit would collapse. If they accepted the British loan as negotiated by Starhemberg, Thugut and the Finance Ministry feared that they would never be able to raise another penny anywhere in Europe.

To resolve the misunderstandings over the loan, Starhemberg tried to explain to London the precarious state of Austrian finances while at the same time illustrating for Vienna the unusual problems facing a British cabinet when working with Parliament. Despite his efforts, each side remained convinced of the rightness of its position and refused to consider seriously the explanations of the other. Consequently, the issue of the loan remained for some time the major obstacle to improvement in Austro-British relations.

The other two powers that Thugut envisioned as members of a new, dedicated coalition—Prussia and Russia—appeared marginal candidates as well. Of the two, Russia seemed the more likely to join, because in early 1798 Tsar Paul had expressed increasing concern about the threat to all monarchies posed by revolutionary France. Prussia, on the other hand, was

---

[26] Thugut to Starhemberg, November 2, 1797, Vienna, HHSA, SK, *England*, 141. For a list of agents seeking loans in other cities, see ibid., *Interiora*, 82.

still an object of Thugut's loathing, although he did want it included in his projected united front. In 1798 there was a chance that Prussia might rejoin the cause, because in November 1797 Frederick William II had been succeeded by Frederick William III, and the first careful overtures to the new king had yielded hints that he might be enticed into a coalition. Preliminary negotiations would, of course, be necessary to resolve outstanding Austro-Prussian differences, but Thugut could not overcome his disgust at Prussia's past betrayals to open talks directly. Consequently, when Russia offered to mediate a settlement between the two German powers, he agreed to it. Lest the Russians overlook Vienna's true feelings, however, Thugut told them that the emperor was seeking a reconciliation with Berlin, "despite just motives of defiance in regard to a court that has on so many occasions shown such little good faith."[27] Given all of the points of disagreement among the potential members, Thugut seriously doubted that the coalition of monarchies he desired would become reality.

While he was reflecting on these problems, an extraordinary event took place in Vienna that threatened to rekindle war between Austria and France immediately, whether Austria was ready for it or not. As mentioned before, Bernadotte and his associates had aroused a good deal of commotion in the Habsburg capital, some of it favorable to them, but most of it decidedly hostile. Shortly after he arrived, Bernadotte took up residence in a house on the Wallnerstrasse, about two blocks from the chancellery. Around the house was always a small gathering of curiosity seekers, who frequently engaged in arguments among themselves and with passersby about the virtues and faults of the revolution. At 6:00 P.M. on April 13, for reasons not entirely clear, someone in the embassy raised a large French tricolor emblazoned with "Liberty, Equality, Fraternity" in gold letters on the flagpole of the residence. The onlookers spread the word of the flag's appearance, and within a short time a large crowd gathered, so that at 7:00 P.M. the

[27] Francis to Paul, March 9, 1798, in Vivenot, ed., *Rastadter Congress*, 140–42.

police requested that Bernadotte take the flag down because it was inciting a riot. Bernadotte refused, declaring that the police were responsible for maintaining order and that, if they could not, he would protect the banner himself. The crowd continued to swell, and at 8:30 a Frenchman, perhaps Bernadotte himself, appeared at the doorway, drew his sword, and yelled at the crowd to disperse. In response, the people began to throw cobblestones at the house. As the excitement grew, a young man climbed the front balcony, pulled down the flag, and threw it to the mob. It was ripped apart, one portion taken to a nearby square and burned and another carried to the Hofburg and presented to the captain of the watch for delivery to the emperor. Back at the embassy, the crowd still held sway and, at the sound of a few shots, broke down the door of the house and began to ransack the rooms. Shortly after, however, troops arrived and restored order. By 11:00 P.M. the crowd dispersed, singing patriotic songs and shouting "Long live the emperor."[28]

The destruction of the flag and the assault on the embassy provoked a crisis. Bernadotte had no doubt that the whole affair was instigated and orchestrated by Thugut and the ambassadors of Britain and Russia. To Talleyrand he wrote, "These villains had planned to murder the French embassy, to stick our heads on pikes, and to carry them through the streets. The Russian, as dastardly as he is barbaric, can conceal neither his plans nor his hopes; the vile and worthless Thugut, bent by the weight of his crimes and of his years, waited every moment for news that we had perished. The English envoy attributes to himself the plan of that day and reproaches those who actually carried out the effort with being satisfied with only half

[28] This story is told in a number of places with some variations. See Eden to Auckland, April 14 and 16, 1798, in Auckland, *Journal and Correspondence*, 3: 405–408; Thugut to Reuss, Starhemberg, and Dietrichstein, April 15, 1798, in Vivenot, ed., *Rastadter Congress*, 14–20. For Bernadotte's side, see Paris, Archives, *Autriche*, 369. At the centennial of the event in 1898 the short street connecting Wallnerstrasse and Herrengasse between Regierungsgasse and the Kohlmarkt was renamed Fahnengasse or Flag Street, the name it carries today.

a success. Our death was the aim of these three tigers."[29] On the day following the incident, Bernadotte formally complained that Thugut had ignored his appeals for protection, and he demanded immediate satisfaction, including the arrest and trial of the ringleaders and the dismissal of Thugut and of Pergen, the head of the police. If his demands were not met, he wished for his passports in order to return to Paris. Colloredo responded on behalf of the emperor by requesting Bernadotte to show some patience while an investigation could be conducted and by promising him that the guilty parties would be punished.[30] Bernadotte would tolerate no delays, however, and on April 15 he and his entourage left Vienna not at dawn, as the police had suggested, but at high noon in four ostentatious wagons. An armed troop escorted them out of the city, and no additional trouble occurred.[31]

Despite Bernadotte's suspicions, Thugut had not arranged the demonstration nor had the Russian and British ambassadors. It had been provoked by the behavior of Bernadotte and his entourage.[32] That also was the formal explanation that Thugut sent to his envoys abroad. He declared Bernadotte without "the necessary education and experience for his post but plucked instead from the raw, wild, arrogant French officer corps," deficiencies that virtually compelled him to pro-

[29] Bernadotte to Talleyrand, April 16, 1798, in Hüffer, *Rastatter Congress*, 1: 261–62.

[30] Colloredo to Bernadotte, April 14, 1798, Vienna, HHSA, *Kaiser Franz Akten*, 78b (81).

[31] Hüffer, *Rastatter Congress*, 1: 261.

[32] Some of Thugut's opponents believed all of the rumors. On April 15 Zinzendorf, upon hearing that Bernadotte demanded the removal of Thugut and Pergen, speculated that the demonstration was arranged by Bernadotte, Louis Cobenzl, and Saurau so that the latter two could replace Thugut and Pergen. Three days later Zinzendorf seemed certain that Thugut himself began the demonstration to prevent Bernadotte from flying the tricolor, but then Eden and Razumovsky had thrown gold coins to the crowd to turn the affair into a riot. "So Thugut's schemes failed because the canaille overstepped the bounds he thought would hold them." Zinzendorf's diary, April 15 and 18, 1798, in Wagner, ed., *Wien von Maria Theresia bis zur Franzosenzeit*, 67–68.

voke and antagonize others.[33] To be sure, this is the view one would expect from Thugut, but his assessment was echoed by two leading Frenchmen, Talleyrand and Bonaparte. When the Directory heard of the incident and began to plot revenge, Talleyrand reminded the members that Bernadotte himself was "frivolous and imprudent" and likely to be as much to blame as anyone for the desecration of the flag.[34] In his *Memoirs*, Bonaparte remembered that, when called upon to lead an army against Austria to avenge the insult to the flag, he advised the Directors that Bernadotte, rather than the Austrians, was in the wrong, because he had "suffered his temper to master his judgement."[35]

No matter who was at fault, Thugut clearly did not want this incident to precipitate a break with France. Austria was in no condition either militarily or diplomatically to resume hostilities, and Thugut feared that the Directory might declare war immediately over the insult to the flag. He quickly adopted two alternative policies to deal with the crisis. The first one aimed at conciliating the French. The day after Bernadotte left Vienna, Thugut dispatched a letter reassuring Talleyrand that the emperor wished only peace and notifying him that an Austrian delegate would arrive shortly in the French capital to resolve the issue. Then, as if to prove how sincerely he wanted to avoid trouble, Thugut announced that he would resign his post as Habsburg foreign minister in favor of Louis Cobenzl, who at that moment was being recalled from Rastadt.[36] Thugut understood that Paris regarded him as a serious obstacle to improved relations, so he would remove himself from power. With him absent, the French and the Austrians could then settle not only the issue of the flag but all of their other outstanding differences.

[33] Thugut to Reuss, Starhemberg, and Dietrichstein, April 15, 1798, in Vivenot, ed., *Rastadter Congress*, 14–20.
[34] Georges Lacour-Gayet, *Talleyrand, 1754–1838* (Paris, 1930), 1: 294.
[35] Chair, ed., *Napoleon's Memoirs*, 273.
[36] Thugut to Talleyrand, April 16, 1798, in Hüffer, *Rastatter Congress*, 1: 261–67.

It is uncertain whether or not Thugut really intended to resign at this point. On April 29 he did compose a letter for Colloredo to send formally to him requesting his resignation as well as a letter to Cobenzl appointing him foreign minister; as the reason for the change, the second letter cited Thugut's "weakness of health and multiplication of work."[37] Moreover, as early as April 25 Cobenzl had assumed the task of corresponding with Austria's diplomats abroad and had sent forth several notes explaining possible Austrian reactions to a resumption of war with France.

But other evidence suggests that Thugut's apparent resignation was a tactic to appease Paris. While Cobenzl assumed the title of minister of foreign affairs, Thugut was given a new one of "minister of conference" with responsibility for administering Venice and its lands, naval matters, and "those affairs regarding the Low Countries"—in other words, the duties of those offices previously taken out of the chancellery administratively but still close by physically. By moving to offices down the hall, Thugut would be readily available to advise Cobenzl on any matter that came up.[38] Moreover, in his first dispatch to Dietrichstein, Cobenzl remarked that he had not returned to Vienna to assume leadership of the Foreign Ministry, but "to lighten the burden on Thugut in his numerous and important occupations." In that same letter he referred to Thugut as "our common chief" and suggested that Thugut would still determine the course of Habsburg policy.[39] Finally, in a private missive to Dietrichstein, Thugut informed him that, while assuming the duties of foreign minister, Cobenzl would retain his post of ambassador to Russia and would return to St. Petersburg "as soon as one has decided if we have peace or war."[40] More than likely, Thugut's retirement was a

[37] Thugut to Colloredo, April 29, 1798, in Vivenot, ed., *Vertrauliche Briefe*, 2: 97–98.

[38] Ibid.

[39] L. Cobenzl to Dietrichstein, April 27, 1798, in Vivenot, ed., *Rastadter Congress*, 159–65.

[40] Thugut to Dietrichstein, April 27, 1798, in Vivenot, ed., *Vertrauliche Briefe*, 2: 96.

pretended concession to the Directory, which, it was hoped, would provide adequate proof of Vienna's remorse over the flag incident to forestall a declaration of war. At the same time, however, Thugut would retain sufficient influence and rank to continue to mold foreign policy after his own ideas; Cobenzl, though not necessarily Thugut's puppet, would act only in consultation with him.

Thugut's first policy was to appease the French; his second was to find help in case the French would not be appeased. To that end he began by seeking a reconciliation with Prussia. To Dietrichstein he wrote, "In the urgency of the dangers that menace Germanic Europe and the necessity of not losing a moment to stop the destructive progress adopted by the French, we have decided to propose to Berlin to agree without delay to common measures." Although "the acquisition of a few bits of land cannot compare with the goals upon which rest the ultimate existence of the two monarchies and the rest of Europe," Thugut was perfectly aware that Prussia would not join Austria against France without the promise of territorial gain. Therefore, Thugut proposed that the House of Hohenzollern receive the bishopric of Hildesheim; that the related House of Orange be awarded the bishopric of Paderborn; that the duke of Modena win the archbishopric of Salzburg; and that other minor shifts of territory be made, with the important restriction that the changes should not be made at the expense of Catholic ecclesiastical lands alone.[41] This offer was not sent directly to Berlin but through St. Petersburg, since the Russian court was still mediating the improvement in Austro-Prussian relations. Thugut hoped that these concessions would satisfy the Prussians enough for them to join in resisting further French expansion and, incidentally, make a sufficiently good impression on the Russians to encourage them to join as well.

While Thugut was attempting to deal with the crisis in Austro-French relations, there arrived in Vienna something

---

[41] L. Cobenzl to Dietrichstein, April 27, 1798, in Vivenot, ed., *Rastadter Congress*, 159–65.

he never anticipated: a personal letter from Bonaparte to Cobenzl offering not only to resolve the dispute over the flag but
also to clear away all the other differences remaining between
Austria and France. Wrote Bonaparte, "It will be easy for us
to harness all the passions, to destroy all the troubles, to con-
ciliate all interests, to deflect the evil intrigues of the foreign
powers on the continent." And to Thugut's surprise and pleasure, Bonaparte proposed these objectives "to maintain the
good rapport established by the Treaty of Campo Formio."[42]
   Thugut's reaction to this letter was remarkable. Instead of
treating it cautiously, Thugut seized upon it as a great opportunity not only to resolve the flag issue but to restore the terms
of Campo Formio and in doing so finally to halt persistent
French expansion without resorting to a monarchical coalition
and without resuming the war. Thugut's enthusiastically positive response reflected no change in his attitude toward revolutionary France but his growing respect for Bonaparte as a
political figure. Thugut was convinced that at last he would
negotiate with the one man capable of forcing his will upon all
the elements of revolutionary France, including conniving Directors in Paris, arrogant delegates at Rastadt, and willful republican army officers like Bernadotte. An agreement reached
with Bonaparte, Thugut believed, was an agreement that
would be kept. Whether or not he correctly judged either
Bonaparte's influence or his ambition at this time is open to
question, but no one could doubt Thugut's eagerness to accept
the general's offer as a means to preserve peaceful relations
with France on what he thought would be terms satisfactory
to both sides.
   With the arrival of Bonaparte's letter, Thugut withdrew his
resignation and set to work on instructions for Cobenzl to follow in the forthcoming discussions. Cobenzl was to treat the
flag episode as unimportant and to focus the talks on the territorial adjustments necessary to create a stable relationship

[42] Bonaparte to L. Cobenzl, April 25, 1798, in Bonaparte, *Correspondance*,
4: 84–85.

between France and Austria. First he would insist on a restoration of the entire European status quo as it existed at Campo Formio, but, if that now proved unacceptable to Bonaparte—and Thugut assumed that it would—he would demand Habsburg equivalents for the new French acquisitions in Switzerland and Italy, equivalents that would include either the three Legations (Bologna, Ferrara, and Ravenna) or the left bank of the Po River to the Oglio or Chiese River. Elsewhere in Italy the Pope must be restored to Rome or at least guaranteed a respectable income, and Naples and Tuscany must be promised complete independence. Should Bonaparte wish to annex Tuscany to the Ligurian Republic, then Vienna would accept Lombardy in exchange as the Italian secundogeniture for the Habsburg family. In Germany, France must have nothing on the right bank of the Rhine; aside from that, Cobenzl could agree to small adjustments in order to bring Austria's policies into harmony with any agreements already reached between France and Prussia.[43] Thugut intended to restore the spirit if not the letter of Campo Formio and to do it in the old way, with territorial adjustments. Armed with these terms, on May 8 Cobenzl set out for Rastadt where he was to meet with Bonaparte. He was so eager to begin talks that he travelled "as fast as a courier," arriving during the night of May 11–12.[44]

In Rastadt Cobenzl found no Bonaparte and no preparations for his coming. The prevailing rumor was that the French general had left Paris eight days earlier for Toulon. If so, wrote Cobenzl, "the letter he sent to me was a lie."[45] Shortly thereafter Cobenzl received a message from Bonaparte dated May 4, in which the Frenchman declared that he had heard that Cobenzl had left Rastadt for Vienna (this referred to Cobenzl's earlier departure from Rastadt on April 15), and, since he had other pressing matters to attend to (the fleet he was joining at Toulon was the one that would sail for

[43] Instructions to L. Cobenzl, May 7, 1798, in Hüffer, *Rastatter Congress*, 1: 272–73.
[44] Hüffer, *Rastatter Congress*, 1: 274.
[45] Ibid.

Egypt), he could not wait for Cobenzl's return. But he assured Cobenzl that the Directory would send a representative to Rastadt in his place who would be as eager to accommodate Vienna as he was.[46]

Cobenzl and Thugut both had doubts about negotiating with anyone other than Bonaparte, but, since no alternative seemed promising, they decided to see what this other Frenchman had to offer. He was Nicholas François de Neufchateau, a former member of the Directory, described by the historian Albert Sorel as "a fop of letters, poet without talent, dramatist without genius" whose only contribution to diplomacy had been the publication of a seven-volume set of bureaucratic documents dedicated to "the spirit of Vergennes."[47] As a former director, François was forbidden to leave French territory; thus the talks did not take place at Rastadt as originally planned, but at Selz, a town directly across the Rhine from Rastadt that had suffered considerable damage during the war. François resided in the house where the talks were held while Cobenzl commuted from the Austrian diplomatic residence in Rastadt. The talks began on May 30, and the first session revealed how they would go. François explained exactly what compensation and restitution the Directory demanded for the insult to the tricolor and to Bernadotte, to which Cobenzl replied that flags were of little importance compared to a restoration of the spirit of Campo Formio and an adjustment of Austrian and French acquisitions to insure a stable European peace. Thereafter, François refused to discuss anything but the flag, and Cobenzl talked of nothing but Campo Formio; the negotiations ended without result on July 5.[48] One observer noted that the envoys departed "after five weeks of dinners, debates, civilities, and comedy," while another wrote, "All that they agreed upon was that the rosé wine of Épernay

[46] Bonaparte to L. Cobenzl, May 4, 1798, in Bonaparte, *Correspondance*, 4: 93.

[47] Sorel, *L'Europe*, 5: 325–26.

[48] See Karl Mendelssohn-Bartholdy, "Die Conferenzen von Seltz," *Historische Zeitschrift* 23 (1870): 27–53.

is one of the premier wines of France."[49] Cobenzl was not so flippant about the consequences of the failure: "There is nothing more for Your Majesty to do but take up arms; France will not undo what has happened in Italy and Switzerland and will not extend our borders. . . . For the rest, treaties will never prevent the French from attacking us. Small or great powers, France treats them all the same."[50] In Cobenzl's opinion, Thugut had been right about France all along.

The meeting at Selz confirmed Thugut's perception of revolutionary France as an insatiable power with which there could be no peace. In sending along copies of documents relating to Selz, Thugut told Dietrichstein that "things have reached a point . . . that we must either accept the status quo in Italy and in Switzerland or come to a new rupture with France." But, even accepting the status quo probably would not provide a permanent solution because, given the nature of revolutionary France, the status quo would soon be upset again. The French would not be content with the current situation in Italy, but "augmenting day-by-day the partisans they have in Tuscany and in the Kingdom of the Two Sicilies, they will without effort destroy those weak governments before the news of the enterprise even reaches Vienna." And they would not likely stop after securing Italy. They would cross the seas to even greater conquests. "Nothing can prevent them from becoming masters of Turkey and exploiting from there indefinitely the ravages of a general upheaval." They would overturn the governments of the Near East and then perhaps move on to India. Just as the French possession of northern Italy would lead naturally to the conquest of the entire peninsula and of the eastern Mediterranean, so too French possession of Switzerland would lead to the subversion of Germany. "If the French continue to hold Switzerland, other than the formidable increase of forces that their armies will get from this valorous and marshal nation, revolution in the Swabian Circle

[49] P. Montarlot and L. Pingaud, eds., *Le congrès de Rastatt* (Paris, 1912), 1: 132, 9.

[50] L. Cobenzl to Francis, July 6, 1798, in Sorel, *L'Europe*, 5: 327.

first and then in all of Germany is inevitable . . . whose ruin will lead to the upheaval of all of Europe."[51] Thugut's analysis was an eighteenth-century version of the domino theory, and he was convinced that, without concerted resistance, his prophecy would come to pass. With the collapse of the talks at Selz, Thugut believed that the emperor must resume the fight against France. Failure to do so would sentence all of Europe and many lands beyond to French domination. Yet Thugut did not find renewing the war an exhilarating prospect; the very thought of it, he confided to Dietrichstein, had reduced his health "to the most pitiable state."[52]

One reason for Thugut's depression was that Austria could not face France without significant help, and in early July 1798 hopes for such help remained dim. The negotiations in Berlin to create an understanding among Russia, Prussia, and Austria were not progressing, and to complicate them the great revolutionary figure, Abbé Sieyès, had arrived in Berlin in June, his mere presence fomenting Prussian fears about the possible consequences of anti-French activity. Likewise, improvement of Austria's relations with Britain remained utterly stymied by the deadlock over the loan of May 16, 1797. On July 8 Lord Grenville emphatically told Starhemberg that ratification was a sine qua non for a new Austro-British agreement and that Vienna was simply wasting its time by offering explanations as to why ratification was impossible.[53]

Confronted by these obstacles, Thugut could think of no other way to break the diplomatic deadlock among the monarchies than to resort to the old and not always successful device of sending a special agent to the critical courts. He selected Louis Cobenzl, whose assignment was to visit Dresden, Berlin, and St. Petersburg to see if some agreement could be arranged for an alliance against France. Cobenzl carried with him no instructions; he was empowered to conclude any ac-

---

[51] Thugut to Dietrichstein, July 7, 1798, in Vivenot, ed., *Rastadter Congress*, 186–90.

[52] Thugut to Dietrichstein, July 7, 1798, in Vivenot, ed., *Vertrauliche Briefe*, 2: 109.

[53] Grenville to Starhemberg, July 8, 1798, in *Dropmore Papers*, 4: 252.

cord he thought appropriate. No one seriously believed that Prussia or Saxony would be receptive to Habsburg appeals, but Cobenzl and Thugut both hoped that Russia would be; indeed, they considered Russia "more than ever the arbiter of the destinies of Europe."[54]

Before Cobenzl even reached St. Petersburg, Thugut's dream of Russian assistance, which he had cherished since 1793 and for which he had struggled so hard, was suddenly realized. In late July Tsar Paul informed Dietrichstein that he would send Austria not only the auxiliary corps provided for in Austro-Russian treaties, but also an army of "60–70,000 men in which would be 11,000 Cossacks" to fight the French.[55] Dietrichstein attributed this sudden enthusiasm for the cause to the influence of the tsar's brother-in-law Ferdinand of Württemberg, who had eloquently persuaded Paul that the emperor was in fact bearing the whole burden of defending monarchical principle against social and political disorder. After listening to his brother-in-law's arguments, Paul agreed with him and dictated to him as he would to a secretary the promises of support that Dietrichstein forwarded to Thugut.[56] The words of Ferdinand of Württemberg may have impressed the tsar (and Dietrichstein) at the moment, but historians have cited other, more compelling reasons for Paul's decision. One was the French occupation of the Ionian Islands and Egypt, which threatened traditional Russian interests in the Near East; another, personally important to the tsar, was Bonaparte's conquest of the island of Malta and the expulsion of the Knights of St. John of Jerusalem, an old crusading order of which Paul had become enamored as a boy and over which he was determined to become grand master.[57]

[54] L. Cobenzl to Bezberodko, July 17, 1798, in Vivenot, ed., *Rastadter Congress*, 199–202.
[55] Hüffer, *Rastatter Congress*, 2: 51; Dietrichstein to Thugut, July 27, 1798, Vienna, HHSA, SK, *Russland*, 2: 88.
[56] Dietrichstein to Thugut, July 27, 1798, Vienna, HHSA, SK, *Russland*, 2: 88.
[57] Norman Saul, *Russia and the Mediterranean 1797–1807* (Chicago, 1970), 23–77; Hugh Ragsdale, ed., *Paul I: A Reassessment of His Life and Reign* (Pittsburgh, 1979), 31–75; Ragsdale, "Russia, Prussia, and Europe," 86.

The report of Paul's commitment to help Austria in a war against France reached Vienna on August 8, and Thugut was delighted to receive it. His enthusiasm was somewhat dampened, however, by the memory of previous empty Russian promises and by the awareness that Paul was an unstable personality who could change his mind at any moment. To Colloredo Thugut praised the Russian decision as promising virtual salvation for Austria, but he warned "that with a prince of his character [Paul], one can never be entirely without concern." Thugut was nevertheless sufficiently pleased that he even thought of personally delivering the news to the emperor at his retreat in Baden bei Wien but decided against it for fear that "it would excite the curiosity of the public."[58]

The Russian commitment was the first of several pieces of encouraging news that reached Thugut in the late summer and early autumn of 1798. France's occupation of Switzerland and the Italian states had not generated the enthusiastic support for republicanism hoped for by Paris and feared by Vienna. It had instead aroused significant popular resistance. In the mountains of eastern Switzerland many local inhabitants took up arms, ambushing French patrols and at times fighting pitched battles against small French units. Likewise, anti-French activity increased in Italy, especially in the former Papal States, where bands of antirepublicans often led by priests carried out raids against French outposts and murdered French sympathizers. Moreover, the great powers were stirring. Following Bonaparte's invasion of Egypt in the summer of 1798, the Ottoman Empire declared war on France; as a result, Constantinople reached an accord with St. Petersburg to allow Russian warships and troops through the Straits to combat the French in the eastern Mediterranean. The major naval success of the year, however, was achieved by the British under Nelson, whose fleet destroyed the French ships supporting Bonaparte at the Battle of the Nile on August 1. The victory not only boosted the morale of the anti-French courts, but it

---

[58] Thugut to Colloredo, August 9, 1798, in Vivenot, ed., *Vertrauliche Briefe*, 2: 114.

rendered the Kingdom of the Two Sicilies downright arrogant toward France, especially after Nelson was accorded a hero's welcome when he landed at Naples in late September.

By mid-August 1798, Thugut was committed to preparing for renewal of the struggle against revolutionary France, but he had no intention of overseeing a new war that would simply repeat the defeats of the past. Thugut believed that the fundamental error in the war waged by the First Coalition was the lack of joint planning among the allies. Despite high-sounding pledges of mutual support, each power had pursued only its own perceived interests and had left the others to fend for themselves. Discussions among the allies had been numerous, but they had focused far more on territorial acquisitions and compensation than on the coordination of military efforts and goals. As a result, the French had scored victory after victory by fighting the allies essentially one at a time. In the coming effort, Thugut was determined not to let that happen again, especially since the monarchy had borne the brunt of the defeats in the previous war. In a new conflict Austria would probably be the major French target once more—whether the main theater was Germany, Switzerland, or Italy—and defeat would bring ruin. Unlike Austria, Britain "with the uncontested superiority of its navy," and Russia, "by the still intact preponderance of its army and its distance away," would be protected from serious injury.[59] Therefore, Thugut believed that comprehensive plans must be laid, the right objectives chosen, and the proper timing selected so that the coalition would achieve victory with the least risk to Austria. In early 1799 Razumovsky summarized for the tsar Thugut's policy: "The court of Vienna is absolutely convinced that there is only one way to defeat the Directory and to snuff out the revolution: it is war. [But the allies must] strike only when their plans burst in simultaneous explosion with the result a decisive victory for their cause." Above all, the allies must not act separately. "The minister told me," Razumovsky contin-

[59] Thugut to L. Cobenzl, January 24, 1799, in Vivenot, ed., *Rastadter Congress*, 377–84.

ued, "that it would be a great mistake for [our armies] to act singly since it would correspond exactly to the enemy's strategy which has always been to defeat our troops piecemeal and then to carry disorder, disorganization, and ruin of government and authority in the wake of their victories."[60]

Thugut was seeking a new kind of coalition to do battle with revolutionary France. He envisioned a concert whose purposes would be careful planning, full cooperation, victory, and finally a peace that would include provisions acceptable to all. At the same time he knew Austria could no longer bear the brunt of the fighting and that some arrangement had to be made to insure that the British and the Russians assumed a full share of the effort. Thugut was at least hinting at the concert that would later emerge under Metternich's auspices in 1814. It was only a hint, and one still seriously qualified by an inability to escape from traditional views of diplomatic and military affairs, but he knew that the great European monarchies could not pursue the coming war in the way they had pursued the last one and retain any hope of success. For Thugut, improved cooperation was at least a first step to a new and different kind of effort—yet vaguely conceived in his mind—against revolutionary France.

Achieving the cooperation he envisioned represented a difficult task. A formidable obstacle from the beginning was the continuing poor relations between Austria and Britain. Throughout the autumn of 1798, the diplomatic stalemate with London over ratification of the loan agreement continued. The intransigence of both sides and the refusal to explore avenues of compromise on this issue led the Pitt ministry to break off negotiations for an Austro-British alliance altogether and focus all of Britain's attention—and money—on Russia.[61] As a result, there was no formal Austro-British agreement throughout the campaign of 1799.

Both London and Vienna believed that they could keep their distance from each other because both looked to Russia

[60] Razumovsky to Paul, January 23, 1799, in Miliutin, *Geschichte des Krieges*, 1: 70–72.

[61] Grenville to Pitt, October 28, 1798, in *Dropmore Papers*, 4: 354.

for ultimate salvation, and in the autumn of 1798 Russia seemed to be willing to fulfill that assigned role. On October 24 the advanced units of the promised Russian auxiliary corps crossed into Austrian territory, and by the end of December a force of sixteen thousand had reached Brno (Brünn) in Moravia, where it was inspected by Francis. Even with this army, however, problems had emerged. A dispute over the amount of supplies Austria was to provide to the Russians had led to ill feeling, and already there was growing evidence that discipline among the Russian troops left much to be desired.[62] Moreover, Dietrichstein and Louis Cobenzl were sending frequent reports of the tsar's psychological instability and of the possibility that it might affect his judgment regarding the coalition. Thugut himself noted anxiously in mid-November that "The barometer in Petersburg always points to change."[63]

But the least important member of the coalition turned out to be the most unreliable one, Naples. On May 18, 1798, Austria had concluded an alliance with the court of Naples, and afterward Thugut had emphatically reminded the king and queen that the accord was defensive only and that Austria would not support Naples if it acted precipitously against France or the Italian satellites. In the autumn of 1798, however, the enthusiasm generated by Nelson's victory, his subsequent arrival in Naples, and British pressure to join in the struggle against France spread war fever at the Neapolitan court. Thugut was adamant in warning Naples to wait until all was ready before opening hostilities. A premature attack would not only alert the French to the coalition that was forming against them but likely lead to a Neapolitan defeat, after which "they [Naples] will accuse us of disloyalty and bad faith, cry out against us and weep and lament when they find themselves victims of their own folly."[64] Enthusiasm carried the day, however, and a newly reformed Neapolitan army at-

[62] Thugut to L. Cobenzl, November 26, 1798, in Vivenot, ed., *Rastadter Congress*, 259–61.
[63] Quoted in Hüffer, *Rastatter Congress*, 2: 249.
[64] Thugut to Colloredo, October 3, 1798, in Vivenot, ed., *Vertrauliche Briefe*, 2: 127.

tacked the French-sponsored Roman Republic on November 24—with disastrous results. The Neapolitans fled in the face of French counterattacks, and on December 23 the royal family, to avoid capture, embarked on one of Nelson's warships for evacuation to Sicily.[65] Thugut was absolutely disgusted with Naples's folly but decided not to take action. He had to focus his attention on the defeat of France and could divert neither time nor resources to aid those who went off on their own.

Not only was cooperation with the other members of the coalition difficult to achieve, but Thugut could not be certain of cooperation within his own government either. As he prepared for war, Thugut began to complain about resistance to his efforts within Austrian officialdom. "Our machine has become a warehouse of inextricable confusion," he grumbled to Colloredo, caused by "internal and external enemies who conspire against the monarchy."[66] Thugut encountered opposition in the army as well. Because of the need to coordinate operations with foreign armies closely, Thugut intended to play a much greater role in military planning during the upcoming campaign than ever before, and that incurred resistance from Habsburg senior officers. In the first war conferences of December and January, Archduke Charles grew so angry over Thugut's interference in planning that he resigned; although withdrawn quickly, Charles's resignation warned Thugut that he would face considerable disagreement from his commanders in the months to come. Yet, as the great campaign of 1799 approached, Thugut remained convinced that success depended upon proper direction at all levels, direction

[65] A French royalist described the Neapolitan troops: "A quarter of the men were trained; the rest hardly dared pull the trigger and turned away their faces as they fired." Comte Roger de Damas, *Memoirs of the Count Roger de Damas (1787–1806)* (New York, 1913), 256. King Ferdinand had no illusions about his army, reformed or not. "Dress them in red coats or green coats, they'll run away just the same." Quoted in A. B. Rodger, *The War of the Second Coalition, 1798–1801* (Oxford, 1964), 76.

[66] Thugut to Colloredo, October 9 and 11, 1798, in Vivenot, ed., *Vertrauliche Briefe*, 2: 125–26.

vastly improved from previous years, and he intended to provide that direction at every turn.

No one would deny that the Second Coalition needed far better cooperation and coordination than were evident in the First, but one might question if Thugut were the right man for the task. He did possess the necessary determination and energy, and he appreciated the causes and consequences of the past failures. But his personality and reputation seriously handicapped his efforts to manage the coalition. Ministers at other courts and many leaders within the Habsburg government simply distrusted him. When he spoke of cooperation and planning, they often believed either that his words hid other aims considerably less noble than those he professed or that he really wanted others to conform their ideas to his own instead of engaging in a respectful exchange of views. For the coalition to achieve success, it not only needed plans upon which all could agree but also a spirit of trust that would make it possible to pursue or even adjust those plans for the common good. Hidden away in his "infernal cavern" and poring over his papers, Thugut would have great difficulty inspiring that trust.

CHAPTER XI

WAR, 1799

IN HIS EFFORTS to control the allied military and diplomatic campaigns in 1799, Thugut had a rival, the British secretary of state and London's chief advocate for fighting France on the continent, Lord Grenville. In terms of commitment, Grenville was the best British partner Thugut could have had. Like his Austrian counterpart, Grenville viewed revolutionary France as the scourge of the times, a threat not only to the existence of his own country but to the entire social and political fabric of Europe. And like Thugut, Grenville believed that the only way to resist this daemonic force was to enlist all of the monarchies in a just and honorable struggle for their mutual salvation. There, however, Grenville's empathy with Thugut ended. Grenville was high-principled and high-minded, but he did not appreciate or understand those who disagreed with him—especially if they were foreigners. One recent author has depicted Grenville as "the Englishman at his worst. Loyal, clever, parochial, and suspicious of knowledge, he collected both foreign shrubs and maps while neither knowing nor wishing to learn anything of the world."[1] Confident not only in the rightness of his cause but in his own ability, Grenville expected his allies to do as they were told and, when they did

[1] Edward Ingram, *Commitment to Empire: Prophecies of the Great Game in Asia, 1797–1800* (Oxford, 1981), 24.

not, railed at their treachery, untrustworthiness, and incompetence.

Grenville was as keen to direct the forthcoming war effort as was Thugut, and, like Thugut, he planned to do so in part through influence over the Russians. At the end of December 1798, Britain concluded a subsidy agreement with Russia by which London would pay for a Russian army of forty-five thousand men to participate in the war in Europe; this force was to supplement the Russian troops already bound for Austria. From the beginning Grenville referred to these soldiers as "our Russians," and he intended for them to fulfill British strategic goals and not to be used in any way to support Habsburg schemes.[2] In respect to the Austrians themselves, Grenville would cooperate with them if their efforts conformed to British wishes, but he absolutely refused to conclude any formal agreement until the emperor ratified the loan of May 16, 1797.[3] As for Thugut, Grenville had no respect at all for this shifty Austrian, who not only counseled against ratification of the loan but also thought so little of his commitments to his allies that he had signed a separate peace with France in order, as Grenville thought, to seize Venice.

While Thugut and Grenville were equally intent upon guiding the war effort, the Russians, especially the tsar, had ideas of their own, which frequently did not conform either to British or to Austrian wishes. As the military effort began in 1799, the Russians put into the field three separate armies that set out in three different directions, one toward northern Italy, one generally westward toward Germany, and one toward Naples. At any moment all three could be diverted elsewhere by the mercurial tsar in St. Petersburg. As early as mid-January Thugut prophesied disaster if the Russian armies assigned to western Europe remained subject to the whims of an authority so far from the scene. "It is inevitable that all the efforts

---

[2] Grenville to Whitworth, March 15, 1799, in Hermann Hüffer, *Der Krieg des Jahres 1799 und die zweite Koalition* (Gotha, 1904), 1:67.
[3] Helleiner, *The Imperial Loans*, 114–17.

of the allies will collapse if one believes one can change plans daily according to directives issued from an enormous distance away in St. Petersburg without being familiar with local circumstances that vary from one moment to the next."[4] Little did Thugut know that within a few months others would be making similar complaints about him.

The conceptions and egos of the three strong-willed men obviously posed obstacles to allied cooperation in the War of the Second Coalition, but the obstacles might have been diminished by harmony among the commanders of the allied armies and the officers attached to their staffs. Unfortunately, the antagonism and faultfinding among the various headquarters and between them and the capitals were often more intense than those among the statesmen. Thugut in particular was the target of frequent complaints from Archduke Charles (again in command of the Austrian forces in Germany), while the British and later Russian liaison officers attached to his staff often relayed the carpings and laments they heard about Thugut and others to their governments, which only exacerbated the suspicions of Austrian intentions there. Indeed, when the British dispatched a special officer to the archduke's headquarters to coordinate military planning in Switzerland and Germany, Thugut requested that he come to Vienna instead because of the enmity toward the foreign minister found in "the archduke's character and the disposition of those who surround him."[5] The hostility between Thugut and the archduke was only one example of many. The commander of the Austro-Russian army in Italy, the famous Field Marshal Alexander Suvorov, was endlessly at odds with most of the Austrian generals in his command and with the War Ministry in Vienna, and he did not get along with the archduke either. Liaison officers everywhere championed to their capitals the causes of their favorite generals and criticized the causes of

---

[4] Thugut to L. Cobenzl, January 12, 1799, Vienna, HHSA, SK, *Russland*, 2:182.

[5] Eden to Grenville, August 3, 1799, London, PRO, FO7, 55. Minto to Grenville, August 3, 1799, in *Dropmore Papers*, 5:235–36.

those they disliked. It seemed at times as if everyone were complaining about everyone else.

One by-product of this mistrust was the recall of both the British and Russian ambassadors to Vienna on the grounds that they were insufficiently critical of Thugut. In January Razumovsky received notice to return to St. Petersburg, but the order was rescinded in March after Thugut and the emperor appealed to the tsar to allow him to stay.[6] Nonetheless, St. Petersburg dispatched another minister to Vienna, Count Stepan Kalichev, to make certain that Razumovsky kept his positive analyses of Thugut's policies to a minimum. The British ambassador, Eden, was accused by London of being in the "coat-pocket of Thugut," and his ongoing efforts to explain Thugut's policies in a favorable light led to his replacement in August 1799.[7]

As the campaign was beginning in 1799, the suspicions, jealousies, and stubbornness of the most important policy makers did not bode well for the cooperation that all of them claimed was so necessary for the success of the coming effort. On March 11 Razumovsky reported that, because of the rancor being exchanged, Thugut was already despairing of the coalition's chances for success: "I have noticed in him a profound impression of discontent, of concern, and even of discouragement such that I have never seen in him even in the most painful circumstances of preceding years. He complains of the lack of cooperation existing among the allies in the Empire, Berlin, and England at a time when the powers should be deploying their forces against an enemy whom they will doubtless defeat if they can agree [on what to do]."[8]

[6] Hüffer, *Krieg des Jahres 1799*, 1:366–67; Thugut to L. Cobenzl, February 27, 1799, Vienna, HHSA, SK, *Russland*, 2:183.

[7] T. Grenville to Lord Grenville, April 3, 1799, in *Dropmore Papers*, 5:515. Grenville suspected that Thugut harbored secret plans of all kinds, a suspicion Eden ridiculed in his reports. Eden to Grenville, June 4, 1799, London, PRO, FO7, 55.

[8] Razumovsky to Paul, March 11, 1799, in Miliutin, *Geschichte des Krieges*, 1:472.

Discouraged or not, Thugut had no thought of quitting; he intended to prosecute the war as best he could. The major difference between the War of the Second Coalition and that of the First was the length of the front on which the opposing sides would fight. Until 1796 Belgium and the Rhine had occupied almost everyone's attention, while Spain and northern Italy served as secondary theaters and Switzerland remained neutral. Bonaparte's campaigns of 1796 and 1797 in northern Italy had made that front as important as the one in Germany, but hostilities could still be confined primarily to the Rhine and Po valleys. By 1799 French armies were established in Holland, along the Rhine, in Switzerland, in northern Italy, in the former Papal States, in the Kingdom of the Two Sicilies, in the Ionian Islands, on Malta, and in Egypt, thus creating a front of twenty-four hundred miles over land and water.

The question facing Thugut and the Austrian planners was the choice of a point along this line where the allies could strike the French most effectively while exposing Austrian lands to a minimum of danger. Archduke Charles recommended that the target be Switzerland. Control of Switzerland enabled the French to transfer troops and resources easily between Italy and Germany and even provided them a base from which to launch offensives into the Tyrol or down the Danube toward Vienna. Taking Switzerland from the French would deprive them of all those advantages. The archduke proposed to station a small defensive force in the Tyrol, to strike with a small army in northern Italy to freeze the French there, and then, with the largest force possible under his command, to launch the major offensive into Switzerland from bases in southern Germany. Thugut opposed this plan for two reasons: it would again put the major burden of the allied war effort on Austrian shoulders, and it overlooked the recent French occupation of southern Italy, which had placed the full human and material resources of the peninsula at French disposal. In Thugut's view, victory in Switzerland would mean little as long as the French controlled Italy, from which they could strike northward toward Switzerland, the Tyrol, or even Vienna.

Thugut preferred a plan put forward by Bellegarde that called for maintaining the defensive on the Rhine and in the Tyrol (with a larger force than the archduke had recommended), while launching a combined Austro-Russian offensive in northern Italy that would push the French back toward Savoy and force the French troops in central and southern Italy to withdraw northward to avoid being cut off. Bellegarde believed that the allies could defeat the French in northern Italy first and then crush the French coming up from the south, thus driving them from all of Italy in one campaign.[9]

Over the archduke's objections, Francis accepted the plan put forth by Bellegarde and endorsed by Thugut. He did so not because he necessarily judged it superior in terms of its strategic concept but because he believed that it offered greater protection for the Vorarlberg and the Tyrol, and for him the defense of the hereditary lands was of primary importance. The strategy having been chosen, the next task was to find a commander of skill and daring to lead the allied army in Italy. Archduke Charles was not chosen, largely to free him for assignment on the German front where he had considerable experience. Thugut picked for Italy another young general, Frederick of Orange, a twenty-four-year-old scion of the Dutch princely house who "raised hopes no less than did his friend Archduke Charles."[10] Appointed commander on November 30, 1798, Frederick was busily preparing for the coming campaign when he suddenly died on January 6, 1799. Thugut was grieved at the loss. To Starhemberg he wrote that the prince was "cut down . . . just at the time when circumstances seemed to make ready for him a glorious future."[11]

Thugut had no confidence that he could find a replacement for Frederick of sufficient quality in the Habsburg ranks; ac-

---

[9] Rothenberg, *Napoleon's Great Adversaries*, 55; Criste, *Erzherzog Carl*, 1:34–36; Manfried Rauchensteiner, *Kaiser Franz und Erzherzog Carl: Dynastie und Heerwesen in Österreich, 1796–1809* (Munich, 1972), 44–45.

[10] Hüffer, *Krieg des Jahres 1799*, 1:7. Wurmser had died in August 1797.

[11] Thugut to Starhemberg, January 12, 1799, in Hermann Hüffer, *Die Schlacht von Marengo und der italienische Feldzug des Jahres 1800* (Leipzig, 1900), 28.

cordingly, he sought out the most illustrious non-Austrian commander available: Field Marshal Suvorov, victor over Turks and Poles and certainly the most colorful military figure of his day. An unusually sly, clever, and able officer, Suvorov cultivated an image that, along with his skills, inspired his men, frightened his enemies, and confounded his detractors. Everyone who observed him noted his bizarre behavior: he hated mirrors and broke any he saw; he slept on straw because Christ was born in a manger; at elegant parties he would stuff himself with pastries and then jump on tables and sing obscene songs; and in battle he often stripped to a peasant shirt so that he would be comfortable as he issued orders. And yet Suvorov was not "the perfect Bedlamite" or "follower of Attila's hordes" as two observers in Austria described him.[12] He was an extraordinarily well-read officer, especially but not exclusively in military matters. He could converse in German, French, Greek, and Turkish as well as in Russian, and he could read Latin, the language of the great Roman military commentators, who were his favorite authors.[13] Although he publicly scorned the military arts of transport, supply, and planning and although he proclaimed his belief in speed and the bayonet ("Steel in the belly of the enemy, that is my reconnaissance; thrust, speed, vigor, those are my maneuvers"), he nevertheless admitted confidentially that no Russian army fighting against the French could function without Austrian transport, Austrian artillery, and a planning section of Austrian staff officers.[14] Suvorov had a firm grasp of the strengths and weaknesses of his own army and of other armies as well.

Tsar Paul gladly complied with Thugut's request to put Su-

[12] Minto to Lady Minto, January 3, 1800, in Countess of Minto, ed., *Life and Letters of Sir Gilbert Elliot, First Earl of Minto from 1751 to 1806* (London, 1874), 3:107–10; Lulu Thürheim, *Mein Leben: Erinnerungen aus Österreichs grosser Welt, 1788–1852* (Munich, 1913), 1:83.

[13] Christopher Duffy, *Russia's Military Way to the West: Origins and Nature of Russian Military Power, 1700–1800* (London, 1981), 193–95.

[14] Wickham to Grenville, October 17, 1799, in William Wickham, *Correspondence* (London, 1870), 2:277; Suvorov to Paul, January 4, 1800, in Hüffer, *Krieg des Jahres 1799,* 2:278; Sorel, *L'Europe,* 5:405.

Field Marshal Alexander Suvorov
(Courtesy Bildarchiv, Austrian National Library)

vorov in command of the Austro-Russian forces in Italy, and, on his way to the front in late March 1799, the old warrior stopped in the Habsburg capital, where he made a stunning impression. When he visited the Hofburg, people lined his way shouting "Hurrah Suvorov" and "Hurrah Paul," to which he would shout back "Hurrah Emperor Francis." Upon entering St. Stephen's cathedral on one occasion, he reportedly responded to the crowd's acclaim with "Long live Emperor Joseph." When reminded that Joseph had died nine years earlier, he merely shrugged and said that he had forgotten that times had changed. Residing in the Russian embassy, Suvorov refused all invitations to dinner on the grounds that he was fasting for Lent; however, one observer wrote that at the receptions given at the embassy in his honor, he "ate like a glutton of all the delicacies on the table without waiting for anyone."[15]

While in Vienna Suvorov met Thugut, whom he called, among other things, "the head rooster of the Austrian flock of scribblers."[16] The meeting was a formal affair in the presence of the emperor and the Russian ambassador, and the two masters of the art of appraising others while revealing little of themselves practiced their skills to the utmost. As the Russian ambassador related to his sister-in-law, Suvorov was introduced first to the emperor and then to Thugut.

> After numerous bows on both sides, Thugut led him [and the others] into his office and wanted now to begin discussions. But Suvorov bowed almost to the ground and called out "Great minister! Great minister!" Thugut felt that he had to make his most elegant bow in response. Scarcely had he begun his presentation when the general repeated his former words in his most resonant voice. The emperor finally became impatient and said to Suvorov: "The baron wishes, Field Marshal, that you reach an understanding with him about the campaign plan."

[15] Thürheim, *Mein Leben*, 1:83–84.
[16] Quoted in Kralik, *Geschichte der Stadt Wien*, 371.

"Ah, Your Majesty!" replied the general and crossed himself and bowed even lower. "Your Majesty is an Alexander the Great—Baron Thugut an Aristotle! Great minister! Great minister!" More they could not get out of him.[17]

Another witness noted that, when the meeting ended, Suvorov and Thugut, both full of smiles and bows toward one another, came down the steps to Suvorov's carriage and there exchanged their final good-byes. As Thugut turned to ascend the steps back to his office, Suvorov "hastily executed all those innumerable signs and crosses which [Orthodox] priests employ in exorcizing the devil."[18] Thugut himself only remarked of the encounter that he had met Suvorov and was pleased.[19]

Because Thugut attempted to discover Suvorov's plans during this visit and because Suvorov complained frequently and bitterly during the campaign about Vienna's interference in his command, some scholars have suggested that from the beginning Thugut intended to control the field marshal's operations completely, and, in doing so, he fettered the very genius that the monarchy needed to save itself. In fact, Thugut wanted the Russian to have a free hand militarily because he knew that Suvorov would act with speed and determination. Before the commander reached Vienna, Thugut told Colloredo: "We have to admit that our army will make progress with astonishing rapidity under Suvorov, who will bring about extraordinary results whether good or bad; we just must try to make sure they are not the latter."[20] Originally, Archduke Joseph was to command the army in Italy with Suvorov as senior adviser, but on Thugut's advice the emperor placed Suvorov in full charge and assigned him the rank of field marshal in the Austrian army.[21] In oral and written orders the em-

---

[17] Thürheim, *Mein Leben*, 1:84–85.

[18] Vehse, *Memoirs*, 2:397.

[19] Thugut to Colloredo, March 26, 1799, in Vivenot, ed., *Vertrauliche Briefe*, 2:153.

[20] Thugut to Colloredo, March 12, 1799, in ibid., 150.

[21] *Hofkriegsrat* decree, March 31, 1799, in Hüffer, ed., *Quellen, 1799*, 1:175.

peror told Suvorov only that his objective was to conquer Lombardy and Piedmont; he was not instructed to follow a detailed, prearranged strategy. Suvorov was merely to keep Vienna informed of plans and progress.[22] Only when the marshal began to take political as well as military matters into his own hands—notably by inviting the king of Sardinia to resume his throne in Turin—did Thugut set limits to the Russian's activities. Thugut insisted that Suvorov had no authority to issue such an invitation and admonished him to leave political decisions in Vienna's hands—words that raised Suvorov's ire and elicited from him long and loud complaints about Thugut's interference. It was the question of Piedmont, not Suvorov's military conduct, that sparked the foreign minister's concern.

Before Suvorov reached his headquarters in Italy, fighting had already begun both there and in Germany, and it had gone well for the Austrians. Two French armies, one under Jourdan and the other under Massena, had tried in early March to encircle Archduke Charles's forces in southern Germany, only to be defeated at the battles of Ostrach and Stokach and forced to retreat, Jourdan into Alsace and Massena to Zurich.[23] In Italy, the Austrians had assumed the offensive in March and had inflicted such losses on the French that, by the time Suvorov arrived, the Austrians were besieging Mantua and Peschiera and the French theater commander had been recalled.

Suvorov reached his headquarters at Verona on April 17, took command of a field army of 48,500 men (of whom 24,500 were Russians), and embarked on a campaign that would add more luster to his already impressive career.[24] The field mar-

---

[22] Hüffer, *Krieg des Jahres 1799*, 1:38, 282.

[23] Horsetzky argues that Archduke Charles was unable to score a crushing victory over the French because of orders from Thugut preventing him from doing so, but that seems far-fetched. General A. von Horsetzky, *A Short History of the Chief Campaigns in Europe since 1792* (London, 1909), 71. See also Rothenberg, *Napoleon's Great Adversaries*, 57; and Hertenberger and Wiltschek, *Erzherzog Karl*, 88.

[24] Duffy, *Russia's Military Way*, 217. See also Philip Longworth, *The Art*

shal immediately led his army westward, drove the French army and its new commander, Moreau, all the way back to Genoa, and thereby placed most of northern Italy in allied hands. Upon hearing of Suvorov's offensive, the commander of the French forces in southern Italy, Jacques-Étienne MacDonald, gathered all the soldiers he could muster and headed north to strike Suvorov's rear. The field marshal turned upon him and on June 18–19 inflicted a severe defeat upon him near the mouth of the Trebbia River, driving him and his battered force ultimately to Genoa. Under Suvorov's inspiration, Bellegarde's plan had worked brilliantly; Italy was again in the hands of the allies.

Perhaps inspired by Suvorov's success, Archduke Charles launched an offensive against the French positions around Zurich in late May and early June.[25] Earlier, he had been specifically ordered not to undertake this operation, because, to carry it out he had to employ troops the War Ministry had been holding in the Tyrol both as reserves for Italy and to protect the main route to Vienna.[26] Archduke Charles violated his orders and, because he was the emperor's brother, Thugut was in no position to prevent it. When he heard that the archduke was making his preparations to advance, Thugut wrote to Colloredo, "I will make no comment here because this matter has been argued about again and again, and it appears to be decided; all that remains is to see if we ourselves will cooperate gaily with the French in bringing about the total ruin of our own affairs."[27] Thugut was being unnecessarily gloomy; Archduke Charles captured Zurich and drove Massena's

---

of Victory: The Life and Achievements of Generalissimo Suvorov, 1729–1800 (London, 1965), 236–98.

[25] The archduke did not think much of Suvorov's skill as a commander. Upon hearing of the victory on the Trebbia, Charles remarked that it was a good thing "Bonaparte lingers in Egypt." Archduke Charles to Duke Albert, July 1, 1799, in Criste, Erzherzog Carl, 2:93.

[26] Francis to Archduke Charles, May 4, 1799, in Hüffer, ed., Quellen, 1799, 1:199.

[27] Thugut to Colloredo, May 20, 1799, in Vivenot, ed., Vertrauliche Briefe, 2:168.

forces into new entrenchments west of the city. Then the two armies settled down to observing each other for almost four months.

In the past, such military successes would have elicited from Thugut an outpouring of joy, but he commented little on these achievements, not because he was displeased, but because another problem had arisen to consume his time and attention. It involved the peace congress still in session at Rastadt. Despite the increasing likelihood of war, meetings had continued there throughout 1798 and into 1799 with ever-declining chances of achieving an agreement; yet neither side had wished to walk out and thus risk being labeled an enemy of peace. By early April 1799, however, the presence of hostile forces near Rastadt had made it dangerous for the delegates to remain in the city. On April 7 the elder Metternich announced that the Austrian delegation would set out for home.[28] Although some other German delegates left as well, others stayed, hoping to find some way even at this stage to avoid resumption of general war. The French envoys likewise remained, because they had specific orders from Talleyrand not only forbidding them to leave, but instructing them to protest if forced to depart.[29] On April 23, however, Colonel Barbaczy, commander of the Austrian reconnaissance cavalry in the area, announced to the delegates still there that he could no longer insure their safety and advised them to quit the city. Now seeing no alternative to ending the congress, they decided to go.

At 6:30 P.M. on April 28, as the three French envoys and their entourage were completing their arrangements, they received a message from an Austrian officer giving them twenty-four hours to depart the city for France. The formal explanation was that Austrian outposts would soon receive orders not to allow French citizens through their lines; after that the Frenchmen would be in danger if they were still in Aus-

---

[28] Hüffer, *Rastatter Congress*, 2:298.
[29] Sorel, *L'Europe*, 5:393.

trian-occupied territory. Upon hearing the warning, the envoys hastened their preparations, and between nine and ten that evening their carriage and small wagon train passed through the city's western gate on the way to the Rhine ferry that would take them to safety. The weather was stormy and, according to a witness, the sky "pitch-black."[30] A quarter of an hour later, a squad of horse soldiers fell upon the wagon train, pulled the three French officials from their carriages, sabered them, plundered their possessions, and fled. Within a few minutes a patrol of Austrian hussars came upon the scene, offered assistance, and escorted the survivors back to Rastadt. Of the three French officials, two were dead, but the third, although seriously wounded, had crawled off into the darkness and survived.

The murder of the French delegates caused a sensation, and another war of words erupted in the French and German popular press. French editors charged that Austrian troops had committed the crimes on orders from someone in authority who mistakenly assumed that the delegates carried secret papers of value to the Habsburg government. The Prussian press echoed these accusations, while newspapers elsewhere in Germany argued back and forth about the motives and identity of the assassins. One defender of Austria was Friedrich von Gentz, whose pamphlet "On the Murder of the French Delegates" won considerable favor at the chancellery and helped pave the way for his later association with the younger Metternich.[31]

Many contemporaries and later scholars blamed the deed on Thugut, mostly on the assumption that he wanted the documents the French were thought to have been carrying. But the evidence that he was involved is very slim. One widely circulated rumor in 1799 concerned a report from a Bavarian legation secretary, who at an inn supposedly heard Lehrbach tell a

[30] Albert Henche, "Der Rastätter Gesandtenmord im Lichte der politischen Korrespondenz des nassauischen Partikulargesandten Frhr. von Kruse," *Historisches Jahrbuch* 46 (1926): 558.

[31] Friedrich von Gentz, *Staatsschriften und Briefe* (Munich, 1921), 1:16–29.

fellow guest that Thugut had ordered Colonel Barbaczy to kill the Frenchmen and to steal their papers. The historian Hermann Hüffer examined the report in the archives in Munich and found that it said nothing of the kind; it simply recounted Lehrbach's surprise at the deed and his concern about its impact upon popular opinion in Germany.[32] Another source pointing to Thugut's involvement was a letter from Louis Cobenzl to Colloredo in 1804 reporting that officials compiling a history of the War of the Second Coalition had come across a document that seriously implicated Thugut in the murders, but which Cobenzl called "a calumnious invention of malevolence."[33] At the turn of our century, Oskar Criste, certainly no admirer of Thugut, published the sources Cobenzl was presumably referring to but could find nothing among them damaging to the foreign minister and did not contend that the incriminating evidence had been destroyed.[34]

Thugut was probably completely innocent of the murders. In fact, when he heard about them he was truly angry because he knew that they would damage the image of virtue and rectitude that Austria was trying to project. To Colloredo Thugut wrote, "What happened at Rastadt is a fatal event that will give to the Directory and to all the malevolents a good pretext to declaim against and to impute to us the most elaborate horrors." As Vienna's response to the murders, he recommended an inquiry "with publicity and in an honest manner." The archduke himself should assume responsibility for the investigation since it was committed in his theater of operations, and he should imprison immediately all those upon whom fell "the least suspicion of commission or negligence." Those suspected must be tried "with all the necessary publicity," and those found guilty "must be punished."[35] Prince Colloredo-

---

[32] Hüffer, *Rastatter Congress*, 2:345–46.

[33] Vivenot, ed., *Rastadter Congress*, 371.

[34] I used the French translation of Criste's work entitled *Rastatt: L'assassinat des ministres français* (Paris, 1900). See also Karl Th. von Heigel, "Zur Geschichte des Rastatter Gesandtenmordes von 28 Avril 1799," *Historische Vierteljahrschrift* 3 (1900): 478–99.

[35] Thugut to Colloredo, May 5, 1799, in Vivenot, ed., *Vertrauliche Briefe*,

Mansfeld even suggested that the French military commander send "a few upright men" to participate in the inquiry to verify its impartiality. Thugut found that excessive, but he did not object to allowing a representative from Prussia, Mainz, or Denmark to observe since their delegates to the peace congress were still nearby.[36] A speedy but thorough resolution of the whole matter was absolutely necessary to preserve Austria's reputation among the princes and public of the Holy Roman Empire.[37]

Regardless of Thugut's call, Archduke Charles had no intention of carrying out an impartial investigation of the murders. Although he never admitted it, the archduke apparently knew that Austrian hussars had committed the deed and had done so upon the orders or at least the strong suggestion of some high-ranking officers.[38] To pursue the affair, he established a military commission which, after a month of hearings, found all Austrian personnel innocent. The hussars who appeared as witnesses testified that they had come upon the scene just as the perpetrators were scattering into the darkness. As they rode up, they heard shouts in French and so assumed the murderers to be French émigrés dressed as Austrian cavalrymen to hide their identity. The commission accepted this testimony at face value, pronounced the deed an act carried out on Frenchmen by Frenchmen, and proclaimed all Austrian troops free of any wrongdoing.[39]

This report, issued at the beginning of June, convinced almost no one, especially in the Holy Roman Empire. On August 9 the Reichstag, while rejecting calls for beginning its own investigation, passed a resolution requesting the emperor

---

2:165; Thugut to Francis, May 13, 1799, in Vivenot, ed., *Rastadter Congress*, 119–21.

[36] Thugut to Francis, May 13, 1799, in Vivenot, ed., *Rastadter Congress*, 119–21.

[37] Public opinion in Germany by no means unanimously frowned upon the murders. According to Fichte, everyone in Weimar, including Schiller and Goethe, agreed that "those dogs must die." Quoted in ibid., cxxxiii.

[38] See the evidence in Heigel, "Gesandtenmord," 480–81.

[39] Criste's *Rastatt* contains the testimony and findings of the commission.

to look into the events further to see if the military commission had examined all of the evidence thoroughly.[40] Since he could not refuse, Francis again turned the matter over to Archduke Charles, under whose jurisdiction the initial inquiry had taken place. This time the archduke began no new probes but responded instead with a careful analysis of the situation, concluding with a recommendation as to the course that the monarchy should follow. "There are only two ways to have done with this business," the archduke began. Either the emperor must present the facts to the public as they happened—which would likely implicate the Austrian hussars—or he must try to prove that unknown assailants committed the crime. If he were to tell the public exactly what happened, then he must choose between either condoning the crime or punishing its perpetrators. If he were to condone it, he would become a violator of international order; if he were to punish the perpetrators, he would likely be condemning soldiers for following orders, and that would have serious repercussions within the army. If he were to hide the facts and attribute the crime to unknown persons, no one would believe him. Thus, the archduke concluded, the emperor should simply declare: (1) the Austrian government did not order the attack; (2) the commander in chief knew nothing about the event; and (3) it was an unfortunate accident. Then in time the incident would be forgotten. The archduke's recommendations appealed to Francis and especially to Thugut, and they were adopted.[41]

The report of the first commission enabled Thugut to turn

[40] Heigel, "Gesandtenmord," 481.

[41] Sorel, L'Europe, 5:400. Over time various sources named one or more of the following as instigators of the murders: William Pitt (or the British generally), Maria Carolina of Naples, the Directory itself, Bonaparte, and Lehrbach alone. Uhlirz, Handbuch, 1:446–47; Graf Hans von Schlitz, Denkwürdigkeiten des Grafen Hans von Schlitz (Hamburg, 1898), 66–68. Thugut speculated that, if any Austrian had arranged the murders, it was probably Matthias Fassbender, a civilian adviser to Archduke Charles, who, Thugut believed, was intentionally poisoning feelings of the archduke toward the foreign minister. Thugut to Colloredo, May 5, 1799, in Vivenot, ed., "Thugut und sein politisches System," 376–77.

most of his attention back to the war effort, which thus far had gone so well. With the allied armies apparently prevailing in Italy and Switzerland, one would expect to find enthusiasm not only in Thugut's writings but in those of the other allied principals as well. One would like to argue that Thugut's dream of cooperation, if not perfectly implemented, was becoming a reality in the wake of victory and that the old difficulties that had plagued the First Coalition, especially the failure of its common cause to transcend mutual suspicion and territorial competition, had given way at last to the idea of concert. In other words, it would be pleasant to contend that Thugut was establishing a model for Metternich's later effort to create allied cooperation on the basis of common principles and at least a degree of common trust. Unfortunately, such was not the case. Success had the opposite effect on the coalition. The correspondence of the allies at the moment of triumph was fuller than ever of mistrust, doubt, and skepticism, all of which boded ill for the future.

At the center of suspicion was Thugut. As mentioned earlier, both the Russians and the British nursed a fundamental distrust of Thugut and thought that his statements and deeds always concealed ulterior and probably perfidious motives. As the campaign progressed, these misgivings increased. For the British, the issue that deepened their suspicion of Thugut involved the Russian army of forty-five thousand men that they had purchased in December 1798. At the time of the arrangement, the allies still had hopes that Prussia would become part of the coalition; thus, this force was scheduled for a march across northern Germany to undertake operations with the Prussians on the Lower Rhine.[42] As it became clear that Prussia would neither join the allies nor allow the Russian army to enter its neutrality zone, another theater of operations had to be found. Since the army was in British pay, it was London, specifically Grenville, who decided where to send it, and his

---

[42] Thugut to L. Cobenzl, January 31, 1799, in Vivenot, ed., *Rastadter Congress*, 289–97.

choice was Switzerland.[43] He wanted it to replace the Austrian army operating there. Many observers besides Archduke Charles judged Switzerland the most important theater, both for its strategic location on the route to Vienna and for its usefulness as a base from which to invade France. Because of Switzerland's traditional neutrality, the Franco-Swiss border was not heavily fortified like the "iron frontier" facing Belgium and Germany and thus would be far easier for an invading force to penetrate. Moreover, the French provinces in the allies' path were known to be royalist in sympathy and thus, it was hoped, unlikely to resist an allied effort to restore the monarchy.

But Switzerland was in the Austrian military sphere. As Grenville made his plans for the Russian army in March 1799, Archduke Charles was already driving Massena back to Zurich, and it seemed likely that he would soon free Switzerland of French influence altogether. Military logic seemed to require that he be allowed to proceed. He commanded an army of one hundred thousand that was already advancing, so it only made sense to lend him support and encouragement in his effort. But Grenville wanted to replace the archduke's larger force with the smaller Russian one. The reason was that the British leader had no confidence in Austria's ability to carry out an offensive of the kind he envisioned. In his mind, Habsburg commanders were wedded to cordon warfare, defending or attacking a long line of strongpoints rather than concentrating upon one narrow, powerful thrust toward a single, vital objective, and he believed that this strategy had led to the Austrian defeats of the War of the First Coalition.[44] More

[43] The Russians agreed that an army goes where its paymaster chooses. "The country that pays for an army tells it where to go, and Great Britain wants it in Switzerland." Secretary of Foreign Affairs Fedor Rostopchin to Simon Vorontsov, May 21, 1799, in *Archiv kniazia Vorontsova* (Moscow, 1876–77), 8:213. London also did not wish to violate the Prussian neutrality zone because Hanover, a possession of the British ruling house, was protected by it. Thugut complained frequently about Hanover's not taking part in the war.

[44] Mackesy, *Statesmen at War*, 79–80.

importantly, Grenville had no faith in Austria's war aims. Still rankled by the refusal to ratify the loan agreement of 1797 and by the Treaty of Campo Formio, Grenville had become even more suspicious of Austria when, during minor Habsburg advances into eastern Switzerland in late 1798, Vienna had not restored the old local governments but established military rule instead. He immediately assumed that Thugut and his master had designs upon Swiss territory, either to trade to the French for something else or to annex to the monarchy. When Eden relayed Thugut's promise that Swiss independence would be restored and that Austrian provisional rule was only a temporary device to exploit Swiss resources better, Grenville was not convinced.[45] He feared that at any moment Vienna might bargain away its gains for some immediate, petty advantage; for that reason, he wanted his Russian army dispatched to Switzerland as quickly as possible.[46]

The Russians also suspected Thugut's motives. For them the issue was Austrian policy toward Piedmont, the principal possession of the king of Sardinia on the mainland. When Suvorov liberated Piedmont in late April and early May, he called upon the Piedmontese officials to resume their previous administrative posts and the Piedmontese soldiers to return to their old regiments, promising that soon their king would return.[47] Thugut, in the name of the emperor, immediately ordered Suvorov to rescind these appeals and his pledge to restore the king. Such matters were political, not military, Thugut insisted, and Vienna intended not to restore the for-

[45] Eden to Grenville, April 10, 1799, London, PRO, FO7, 55.

[46] Grenville's brother Thomas best summarized his worries: "The point I fear for in this project is that, if it does not too soon take place, the emperor may make again some wretched peace patched up with the old rags of Campo-Formio and sell them the republic of Swabia for a yard and a half of Bavaria or a little more elbow-room towards Ravenna." Thomas Grenville to Lord Grenville, March 18, 1799, in *Dropmore Papers*, 4:502.

[47] The king had abdicated at French insistence on December 9, 1798, and had taken up residence at Cagliari on the southern coast of the island of Sardinia. For the Russian position on Piedmont, see Ragsdale, "Russia, Prussia, and Europe," 88–89.

mer Piedmontese government right away but to place the country under military rule in order to exploit its resources to sustain the allied armies.[48] Moreover, there was no need to bring back a Sardinian king who had been singularly uncooperative toward the Austrians in the past, especially in matters of joint military operations. Why return Piedmont to a potentially recalcitrant prince, when, under Austrian administration, it would make a substantial contribution to the allied war effort in men, money, and materiel?[49]

Nothing could have aroused Russian suspicions more. Immediately Suvorov, Paul, and the Russian court assumed that the emperor intended to annex Piedmont. Upon reading Suvorov's report on the matter, Paul ordered the field marshal to disregard Vienna's orders and to invite the king to return to his capital as soon as the besieged citadel of Turin fell to the allies. Should the Austrians protest, Suvorov was to tell them that the whole purpose of the war against France was to restore traditional rulers and that he was only pursuing that purpose.[50]

The old bugbear of territorial compensation had appeared again to threaten relations among the allies, and, as it became more intrusive, Thugut needed to make the Austrian position concerning acquisitions absolutely clear. He obviously could not renounce territorial gain completely, for that would be tantamount to neglecting the monarchy's future strength and security, but for now he needed publicly to put the question of acquisitions aside until revolutionary France had been defeated. Only in that way was it possible to achieve the unity among the allies he believed so important for success. Thugut tried to make this point, but his manner in doing so only

[48] Francis to Suvorov, May 17, 1799, in Joseph Greppi, *Révélations diplomatiques sur les relations de la Sardaigne avec l'Autriche et la Russie pendant la première et la deuxième coalition* (Paris, 1859), 80–82.

[49] Thugut to L. Cobenzl, June 13, 1799, Vienna, HHSA, SK, *Russland*, 2:183.

[50] Paul to Suvorov, June 18, 1799, in G. Fuchs, ed., *Correspondenz über die Russisch-Österreichische Kampagne im Jahre 1799* (Glogau/Leipzig, 1835), 1:253.

heightened Russian and British doubts about his sincerity. He assured Eden of the emperor's policy to restore Swiss independence but then raised questions about that policy by complaining of the British-sponsored force in Switzerland "as a handle to interfere with, or endeavor to control, the operations of the emperor's armies."[51] On another occasion, he told Eden that it was time for the allies "to settle for what we are to fight," but when Eden proposed a few ideas, he sidestepped by saying that he would have to consult the Russians.[52] When assuring the Russians that the emperor did not intend to annex Piedmont or the other continental possessions of the king of Sardinia, Thugut ended by noting that Austria nevertheless deserved something for its monumental sacrifice to the common cause and that a portion of Piedmont might be a suitable reward.[53]

In these statements, Thugut was emphasizing Austria's intention to carry out its obligations as a loyal ally in the common struggle against revolutionary France; at the same time, he was voicing a legitimate concern to protect Austria's future. He did not realize that his comments about the monarchy's particular needs and worries actually increased the suspicion his allies harbored toward him. Not only were Grenville and Paul inclined to interpret Thugut's statements in the worst possible light, but they also shared their doubts with each other and with their subordinates. Such distrust only deepened as the campaign progressed.

In the summer of 1799 the major test of the allies' ability to cooperate centered on the British strategy in Switzerland. By early June Grenville had completed his plans for the Swiss theater, and they now called for a force considerably larger than the forty-five thousand Russians the British had paid for. Since Suvorov, in Grenville's view, had already defeated the French in Italy, the British statesman believed that the Austri-

---

[51] Eden to Grenville, April 10, 1799, London, PRO, FO7, 54.
[52] Eden to Grenville, April 13, 1799, ibid.
[53] Thugut to L. Cobenzl, June 13, 1799, Vienna, HHSA, SK, *Russland*, 2:183.

ans alone could contain the French remaining there so that Suvorov and the twenty thousand or so Russians in Italy could be transferred to Switzerland. Besides this substantial reinforcement, Grenville sent his favorite agent, William Wickham, to oversee the recruitment of twenty thousand truly patriotic Swiss to help the Russians expel the French from their homeland. All together, the main army in Switzerland would be enlarged to sixty-five thousand Russians and twenty thousand Swiss. And that was not all. When Prussia finally rejected the persistent British and Russian appeals to join the coalition, Grenville found a surplus of one million pounds in the war budget that the cabinet had set aside as a subsidy for Prussia. Since the money obviously could not go to Austria—"that country [having] disqualified herself by her attitude to the British loan"—Grenville decided to use it to finance a joint Russo-British amphibious invasion of Holland, which had fallen to the French in early 1795.[54] A landing in Holland would be a diversion, compelling the French to weaken their forces in the Swiss theater to prevent Holland's fall and a possible allied advance into Belgium. Although Grenville did not wish to depend on the unreliable Austrians any more than necessary, he knew that the offensive of the Swiss army could not succeed without supporting movements by the Austrian forces on both flanks. He planned for the Austrian army in Italy to invade Savoy while Archduke Charles led his troops against Alsace. Because Vienna's cooperation was essential in his plan, he ordered Eden to obtain Thugut's agreement.

When approached by Eden, Thugut did not accept Grenville's strategy unreservedly. Assigning a second large army to the same theater as the archduke's forces, he noted, would place a severe strain on the resources of Switzerland and southern Germany; providing logistical support from these relatively poor agricultural areas would pose serious, if not insurmountable problems.[55] To relieve the pressure on available

---

[54] Mackesy, *Statesmen at War*, 92.

[55] Shortages did hamper the Russians, but even more so the French, who by mid-August 1799 were complaining to the Directory that no more sup-

supplies, Thugut proposed moving the archduke's main army northward toward Mainz, while keeping a small force in Alsace and the Breisgau to maintain contact with the Russians in Switzerland. This step would also protect the Upper Rhine from a French counteroffensive and possibly allow the archduke to support the invasion force in Holland. In addition, Thugut doubted that the Austrian army in Italy could reconquer Savoy due to snow in the Alpine passes, and he thought that Wickham would find the Swiss "much less favorably disposed" toward joining an anti-French army than "they have been represented to be by their Emigrant countrymen."[56] Indeed, Thugut was not certain that the Swiss would welcome the Russian liberators. Alluding to the increasing number of reports of rapine and pillage in Italian areas freed by Russian soldiers, Thugut suggested that similar behavior in Switzerland could ignite serious anti-allied sentiment. He still preferred Austrian operations in Switzerland because, as he argued, culturally and linguistically "the Austrian troops can get along much more easily with the inhabitants of Switzerland than can the Russians and that could be very important to the allies."[57] In other words, Austrian soldiers would be less prone to plunder and to violate the local population.

Grenville received Thugut's objections as nothing but more evidence of his knavery. The suggestion that the Austrians should continue to operate in the Swiss theater seemed to him a veil to cover Austrian aggrandizement. Thugut's doubts about the invasion of Savoy and his proposal to move the archduke's army toward Mainz, Grenville was convinced, masked efforts to undermine British grand strategy so that Austria could conclude a favorable separate peace. Indeed, the proposal to attack Mainz looked like a plot to seize Belgium, which the British were by now thinking of turning over to a

---

plies could be extracted from the areas of Switzerland under French control. Miliutin, *Geschichte*, 3:75.

[56] Eden to Grenville, June 16, 1799, London, PRO, FO7, 55.

[57] Razumovsky to Paul, April 30, 1799, in Miliutin, *Geschichte*, 2:132.

Dutch Republic liberated from French domination. Grenville summarized his elaborate fears for his brother:

> I construe the whole thus, Thugut now thinking the Ital-
> ian acquisitions secure, and the Milanese reconquered,
> and the Novarese in his hands, looks back to the Low
> Countries as the next object of scramble. For the success
> of our forward move into France, and for the effects
> which that is to produce on the internal government of
> that country, the real root and origin of all its wickedness,
> he is not the least degree anxious; and considers it only as
> a diversion which will put Mayence, the Netherlands,
> and the left bank of the Rhine into the hands of Austria
> to cut and carve as she thinks proper.[58]

Thugut was in fact trying to cooperate. This is not to say that he subordinated all of his master's interests to the common cause; rather he was eager to comply with any reasonable wishes of his allies. On July 31 when Razumovsky and Eden presented the Grenville strategy as a joint Russo-British program, Thugut agreed to it, even though he and other Austrian officials seriously doubted that it was practical. Under the final plan, the Russian forces and the Swiss volunteers would first clear the French out of Switzerland and then advance on Paris through the province of Franche-Comté. Because of the difficulties in supplying two armies in Switzerland and southern Germany simultaneously, the two ambassadors accepted Thugut's suggestion that the archduke take sixty to sixty-five thousand Austrians northward, clear the right bank of the Rhine of French units, cross the Rhine at Philippsburg or Mannheim, and advance toward Mainz. Charles would then establish contact with the Russo-British forces in Holland and provide them what support he could without extending his own units into the former Austrian Netherlands. To cover the gap between the archduke and the Russo-Swiss army, the remaining

[58] Lord Grenville to Thomas Grenville, July 16, 1799, in *Dropmore Papers*, 5:147.

thirty to thirty-five thousand men in his command would support the invasion of Franche-Comté by marching into Alsace. Since this plan was accepted by the Austrian foreign minister and the two allied ambassadors in Vienna, orders were sent to the armies to begin their movements to comply with it.[59]

No plan in the wars of the First or Second Coalition has caused more controversy and speculation than this one. The debate usually ignores the question of whether the strategy was workable from the beginning. Instead, it centers upon the decision to move Archduke Charles's main army northward, an act that gave the French numerical superiority in the Swiss theater and placed the bulk of the Habsburg forces too far away to come to the Russians' aid. There is little doubt that the disposition of the archduke's army was Thugut's idea, which Eden and Razumovsky merely accepted. Accordingly, the blame for the ensuing debacle has fallen largely on Thugut, and the motive generally ascribed to him is that he lusted after territorial gain so intently that he would sacrifice anything, including victory over revolutionary France, to get it.[60]

To test this interpretation, one must understand why Thugut accepted Grenville's plan, what he imagined that the plan in its final form would achieve, and why he espoused the redeployment of the archduke's army. Regarding the first point, Thugut accepted Grenville's plan in large part to please his allies. As we have already seen, he had initially offered a number of objections to Grenville's strategy, but, when it became obvious that both London and St. Petersburg wanted it, he was willing to yield in the interests of allied cooperation. Indeed, when he sent the emperor's orders to Archduke Charles ex-

[59] Francis to Archduke Charles, July 31, 1795, in Hüffer, ed., *Quellen*, 1:1, 235–36; Eden to Grenville, August 3, 1799, London, PRO, FO7, 55; Razumovsky to Paul, July 31, 1799, in Fuchs, ed., *Correspondenz*, 2:122–30. For Thugut's explanation of the plan as he understood it, see Thugut to L. Cobenzl, August 6, 1799, Vienna, HHSA, SK, *Russland*, 2:183.

[60] For a summary of this position, see Steven T. Ross, *European Diplomatic History, 1789–1815: France against Europe* (Garden City, N.Y., 1969), 208–209.

plaining the plan, he had them delivered personally by Diet-richstein with instructions to tell the archduke that he must follow the plan, even though he would undoubtedly object, because the British and the Russians insisted. Some have interpreted this act as proof that Thugut knew the plan would fail and wanted to insure that the archduke and his subordinates would blame the failure on the British and the Russians. Yet, the documents provide little hint that Thugut clearly foresaw the coming defeat; the evidence that he truly wished to cooperate is far more abundant. It is true, however, that Charles objected strongly to the plan, not only because it would rob him of the opportunity to strike the decisive blow in Switzerland, but also because he anticipated accurately that its strategic weaknesses could lead to allied failure.[61]

But satisfying his allies was not Thugut's only motive for accepting Grenville's strategy. By the end of July he was eagerly seeking an excuse to remove Suvorov and his Russians from Italy. As pleased as he was with Suvorov's victories, Thugut was truly dismayed by the field marshal's independent policy regarding Piedmont, and he was deeply concerned about the growing animosity between Suvorov and the Habsburg generals. The Russian thundered more and more against the "yes-men" and "breadeaters" in the Austrian high command "whose service is directed toward the human commerce in titles, ambition, and egotism," while the Austrian generals complained about Suvorov's "eccentric plans and undertakings" and his utter ignorance of logistics and supply.[62] Thugut had become convinced that the ill will between the Russians and the Austrians in the high command could only be resolved by separating them completely. To Cobenzl Thugut wrote, "The innumerable inconveniences caused in Italy by the conduct of this general, acting according to foreign [Russian] or-

---

[61] Dietrichstein to Thugut, August 7, 1799, and Francis to Archduke Charles, August 9, 1799, in Hüffer, ed., *Quellen*, 1:1, 240–48, 255–58.

[62] Suvorov to Razumovsky, July 12, 1799, in Fuchs, ed., *Correspondenz*, 1:235–38; Tige to Melas, June 24 and July 11, 1799, in Hüffer, ed., *Quellen*, 1:1, 227, 230–34.

ders and obviously opposed to the interests of His Majesty, are of such a grave nature that His Majesty could easily do without his commanding an army [in Italy] if having him sent to Switzerland is happily followed." Besides, Italy now seemed safely in allied hands, and the inspiration of Suvorov as a field commander would no longer be needed there.[63]

Thugut also accepted the plan because he essentially hoped that it would achieve its goals. He believed that the united Russian army, while not as large as Grenville imagined (Thugut calculated the British-paid force at thirty-five thousand and Suvorov's army at fifteen thousand), would certainly be strong enough to secure Switzerland.[64] As to Archduke Charles's redeployment, Thugut perceived the mission of his army to be exactly what the plan envisioned: to prevent a shortage of supplies affecting the Russians in Switzerland, to cover the Upper Rhine in case of a French assault, and to establish contact with the Russo-British forces in Holland. When asked by Eden and Razumovsky whether the ultimate purpose of Archduke Charles's move was to reconquer Belgium, Thugut told them that the archduke would not extend his operations into the Netherlands and certainly not race into Belgium ahead of the Russo-British invasion force coming south from Holland. He was only to support allied operations in the region in any way that he could. In respect to Austria's aims regarding Belgium, Thugut informed them that, since the allies had not reached a final agreement about territory, the emperor still considered it a Habsburg possession and would not allow it to be disposed of without his consent.[65] Thugut also emphasized, however, that questions of indemnification and compensation should not be permitted to harm allied relations, especially at this time; for now the allies should only recognize that future compensation be equally beneficial to all.

[63] Thugut to L. Cobenzl, August 6, 1799, Vienna, HHSA, SK, *Russland*, 2:183. Suvorov would win his last great battle in Italy at Novi on August 15.

[64] Thugut to L. Cobenzl, August 22, 1799, ibid.

[65] Eden to Grenville, August 3, 1799, London, PRO, FO7, 55; Thugut to L. Cobenzl, August 9, 1799, in Hüffer, *Krieg des Jahres 1799*, 1:423.

To Grenville Eden wrote, "On the subject of indemnification, His [Thugut's] constant language has been, that the interests of Great Britain and Austria can never be at variance—that . . . His [Brittanic] Majesty appropriate to Himself, by way of compensation, whatever might appear to His Majesty to be most suitable for the strength and prosperity of His Dominions, and that His Imperial Majesty only asked for an observance of similar sentiments with respect to Himself."[66] Conciliatory words perhaps, but sufficiently vague to reinforce suspicion of Thugut in London.

Despite the distrust of his partners, Thugut, like them, wanted Grenville's plan to work as proposed.[67] But, again like them, Thugut did not perceive the weakness of the plan itself. None of the allied statesmen had a firm grasp of the military situation in the Swiss theater and how it was developing. The Russian army actually forming in Switzerland was far weaker than Thugut, Grenville, or Tsar Paul believed. The advanced units of the main force under the command of A. M. Rimsky-Korsakov did not reach Archduke Charles's headquarters near Zurich until August 12, and only then did Korsakov learn that he and his men would be the core of the force that was to liberate Switzerland and invade France. He protested at once. He did not have the forty-five thousand men imagined by Grenville or even the thirty-five thousand estimated by Thugut, but only twenty-eight thousand effectives, and they were short of pontoons, pack horses, and transport.[68] Moreover, the British call for Swiss volunteers had, as Thugut predicted, met with a meager response. Wickham had gathered only two thousand men by mid-August, substantially short of the twenty thousand envisioned, and various small

---

[66] Eden to Grenville, August 3, 1799, London, PRO, FO7, 55.

[67] Paul especially wanted no changes in the plan as agreed to on July 31, including Archduke Charles's assignment. "I find it so similar to my suggestions and ideas that I do not hesitate to send it straight back to you and to charge you to be especially observant that it engenders no change in Vienna." Paul to Razumovsky, August 15, 1799, in Miliutin, *Geschichte*, 3:348.

[68] Hüffer, *Geschichte des Jahres 1799*, 1:447; Criste, *Erzherzog Carl*, 2:106.

German contingents would arrive only a month or so later.[69] Suvorov and the Russian army from Italy were also supposed to join Korsakov, but that would take even longer. Only on August 17 (two days after Suvorov's victory at Novi, which shattered the remaining French field forces in Italy) did the emperor send orders to Suvorov to move to Switzerland, and they did not reach the field marshal until August 25. One wonders why, when the Swiss operation was agreed to on July 31, Suvorov's instructions were issued only two and one half weeks later. The most likely explanation is that Thugut wanted the emperor's directive to reach Suvorov at approximately the same time as a similar command from Tsar Paul (it arrived on August 27), because the foreign minister was certain that Suvorov would refuse to follow any orders from Vienna not endorsed by St. Petersburg. As late as they were, the emperor's instructions nevertheless appealed to the field marshal to reach Switzerland as quickly as possible.[70]

As a result of these miscalculations and delays, Switzerland gradually became not the staging area for the overwhelming allied invasion force that the plan of July 31 envisioned, but a weak point in the allied cordon from the Rhine to Italy. A number of persons told Thugut so. Archduke Charles was the first and most insistent, but the British had become alarmed as well. On August 24 the new British ambassador to Vienna, Lord Minto, accompanied by Razumovsky, formally appealed to Thugut not to allow the archduke to leave his positions in Switzerland until the Russian army was fully in place. Thugut assured them that the archduke had no intention of doing so, but, as a precaution, he promised to send orders "without delay" to the archduke to remain in Switzerland "until he could place it safely in the hands of the Russians."[71] The orders were sent but not "without delay"; they did not leave Vienna until

[69] Hüffer, *Geschichte des Jahres 1799*, 1:428.

[70] Francis to Suvorov, August 17, 1799, in Fuchs, ed., *Correspondenz*, 2:87–89.

[71] Minto to Wickham, August 24, 1799, in Wickham, *Correspondence*, 2:169–73.

August 31. It is doubtful that Thugut withheld the orders on purpose to handicap the allied plan. Given the archduke's own warnings, Thugut assumed that the Austrian forces would remain in Switzerland long enough to maintain the front. On August 22, two days before Minto and Razumovsky made their formal appeal, Thugut informed Louis Cobenzl that the archduke would hold his position in Switzerland for some time "even after the Russian army has been consolidated" there.[72] No orders needed to be sent quickly, because Thugut believed that the archduke would not be moving soon.

Thugut saw no reason for haste in redeploying the allied forces, essentially because he doubted that the great offensive could get underway in the autumn of 1799; he envisioned its occurring in the spring of 1800. As early as August 3 Eden reported that Thugut thought the plan of July 31 would be implemented only after the allies had cleared Italy and Switzerland of the French, "which, however, he repeatedly observed, would not, in his opinion, be effectuated this campaign."[73] A British officer attached to the archduke's headquarters, in warning against a premature Austrian advance toward Mainz, noted that Thugut actually intended the whole plan for the next year anyway.[74] Even in late September—as the Russian positions in Switzerland were collapsing but before the news reached Vienna—Thugut advised Archduke Charles that Vienna would let Suvorov and his fellow officers decide whether "to force the enemy to abandon Switzerland" immediately or to consolidate their lines, go into winter quarters and wait until spring.[75] In his recent study of the archduke, Gunther Rothenberg notes that at this time Charles himself was thinking of 1800 and that his advances northward

[72] Thugut to L. Cobenzl, August 22, 1799, Vienna, HHSA, SK, *Russland*, 2:183.

[73] Eden to Grenville, August 3, 1799, London, PRO, FO7, 55.

[74] Mulgrave to T. Grenville, August 18, 1799, in *Dropmore Papers*, 5:291–94.

[75] Francis to Archduke Charles, September 27, 1799, in Hüffer, ed., *Quellen, 1799*, 1:1, 377–79.

toward Mannheim and Mainz were only demonstrations, "while in reality he was to prepare going into winter quarters."[76] Thugut's belief that the allied armies in Switzerland and southern Germany would spend the winter in place might also explain his anxiety about adequate supplies being available in those regions.

Unfortunately, the leisurely pace at which the allies made preparations for their grand offensive allowed the enemy to seize the initiative. Under the watchful eye of Bernadotte, now the Directory's minister of war, the French army in Switzerland had grown to almost seventy thousand men supported by additional units gathered along the Upper Rhine. On August 13 the right wing of Massena's forces struck the Austrian left in the high mountains of the upper Rhône River and captured the Simplon and St. Gotthard passes, the principal avenues the allied forces in Italy would have to take to reach Zurich. Archduke Charles was able to halt the French advance, but he had not yet retaken the passes when he heard that other French forces were crossing the Rhine into southern Germany. Because that area was assigned to him under the agreement of July 31 and because he wanted to protect the allied right flank, the archduke decided to shift his main force northward to defend the Rhine. Since Suvorov was still in Italy, the archduke left a corps of twenty-one thousand Austrians under Lieutenant Field Marshal Conrad Hotze to reinforce Korsakov, whose forces were not yet firmly established in Switzerland.[77]

Following Archduke Charles's decision to march northward in late August, the allied campaign plunged toward disaster. Essentially, the movement of his army out of Switzerland before Suvorov's arrival meant that for approximately one month an allied force of less than fifty thousand men—Korsakov's twenty-eight thousand Russians and Hotze's twenty-one thousand Austrians—faced a French army of seventy thousand in the Swiss theater. And the French

[76] Rothenberg, *Napoleon's Great Adversaries*, 60.

[77] Archduke Charles to Korsakov, August 26, 1799, in Hüffer, ed., *Quellen, 1799*, 1:1, 312–13.

took advantage of that numerical superiority. On September 25 Massena launched an assault on the major Austro-Russian positions at Zurich and overran them. On the first day of the offensive Hotze was killed and Korsakov reduced to issuing meaningless orders while his troops beat a disorderly retreat. When Archduke Charles heard of the defeat, he rushed southward but arrived too late to stabilize the front near Zurich. Suvorov hastened his advance from Italy and in doing so conducted his famous march over the Alps, made especially heroic because of the unfamiliarity of the Russians with fighting in mountains. As the allies gathered their strength and their wits following the debacle, Archduke Charles appealed to Suvorov to join him in counterattacking the French.[78] The field marshal at first expressed interest in the project and suggested a few tentative plans, but by mid-October he gave it up. He informed the archduke and Vienna that he would take his army toward Augsburg and establish winter quarters there.

The great Swiss offensive had failed before it had really begun, and with its failure came the time to assign blame. Archduke Charles faulted the Russians, Korsakov in particular. Korsakov could have held Zurich, the archduke argued, but he was defeated because he had "no military sense." His troops were in chaos, he could not make decisions, and his supply system was woefully inadequate. As to the Russian officers, they "have no knowledge, know the topography not at all, and, what is worse, show no desire to learn about it."[79] The British liaison officers with the archduke—those who had vilified Thugut so much in the past—now heaped scorn upon Suvorov, Korsakov, and the Russians as well. Wrote Wickham, "It is impossible for anyone to be more thoroughly in the wrong than the Russians now are, and, if Mr. Thugut had hired them to play his game, they could not have done it better, or entered more thoroughly into the net, if he had spread it for them."[80]

[78] Hüffer, *Geschichte des Jahres 1799*, 2:95.
[79] Archduke Charles to Francis, October 10 and 20, 1799, in Hüffer, ed., *Quellen, 1799*, 1:1, 423–25, 454–55.
[80] Wickham to Grenville, October 19, 1799, in *Dropmore Papers*, 5:485.

Suvorov of course blamed the Austrians, with particularly harsh words for Thugut. "From his melancholy nest he got me out of Italy, from where my contacts went to Lyon and Paris. . . . Archduke Charles left Switzerland; he abandoned Lieutenant-General Korsakov and sacrificed me and the highly generous allies—he sacrificed in every instance the general welfare."[81] When the news of the defeat reached St. Petersburg, Paul's court had no doubt that Thugut was responsible. "All has broken loose against Thugut," Russian Secretary of Foreign Affairs Fedor Rostopchin informed Suvorov. "Everyone snatches at him, but it is not yet known if he will continue to rule."[82]

As for Thugut himself, the defeat was as much of a surprise to him as to anyone. As late as September 16 he told Cobenzl that all seemed to be going well and expressed some irritation at the various British alarms about the situation in Switzerland, which Thugut assumed Archduke Charles was adequately protecting.[83] When the news of Korsakov's rout reached Vienna, it was the archduke whom Thugut criticized first, because he believed that the commander had disobeyed the emperor's dispatch of August 31 ordering him specifically not to endanger the allied positions in Switzerland. To Colloredo Thugut wrote, "The vicious obstinacy against our carrying out an order of His Majesty since the beginning of the campaign has lost everything; eight or ten available battalions sent to Hotze only in the last few moments could have prevented all these misfortunes."[84] This initial response could not, of course, be the official one because no formal statement could openly fault Archduke Charles. The official explanation blamed the Russians, notably Suvorov's slowness in his march

[81] Suvorov to Razumovsky, October 20, 1799, in Fuchs, ed., *Correspondenz*, 2:251–52.

[82] Rostopchin to Suvorov, November 9, 1799, in ibid., 285.

[83] Thugut to L. Cobenzl, September 16, 1799, Vienna, HHSA, SK, *Russland*, 2:184.

[84] Thugut to Colloredo, October 1, 1799, in Vivenot, ed., *Vertrauliche Briefe*, 2:187–88.

to Zurich, Korsakov's loss of will and mind as the battle opened, and Suvorov's refusal to counterattack in October. Already anticipating what the allies (and later historians) would say about his own role, Thugut contended that the archduke had moved north at his own discretion to protect Philippsburg from a French assault and that the decision was the right one, conforming to the archduke's duty as commander in chief of the army assigned to protect Germany. It was, Thugut emphasized, "no sinister plot."[85]

The conclusion to these unfortunate events came from Tsar Paul, who was acutely angry not only about the defeat in Switzerland but about the concurrent rout of the Russo-British invasion force in Holland. He announced an end to his accord with Austria and called Suvorov and his troops home: "I have decided to give up completely the alliance with the Viennese cabinet," he wrote to his commander, "and to grant only one and the same answer to all its proposals because, as long as Thugut remains minister, I will believe nothing and consequently will do nothing."[86] Paul would change his mind twice before the final orders to return were sent to Suvorov, but in any case the Russians would not be at the Austrians' side in 1800.

The campaign of 1799 began as the realization of Thugut's six-year quest. At last Britain, Russia, Austria, and a number of lesser states had joined to fight against revolutionary France. In many ways it was a success: Italy was again essentially free of French influence; Germany was secure; and even at the end the British expressed their willingness to continue the struggle. But the loss in Switzerland overshadowed all of the benefits. If not a thorough strategic defeat, it was a devastating psychological blow because of the rancor and animosity it perpetuated in the coalition. There was (and still is) a compulsion to blame the defeat on someone or some event, but, given the vast distances affecting communications, the lack of

[85] Thugut to L. Cobenzl, November 2, 1799, Vienna, HHSA, SK, *Russland*, 2:184.

[86] Paul to Suvorov, November 9, 1799, in Fuchs, ed., *Correspondenz*, 2:308.

adequate information about enemy and even allied movements, the confusion that often plagued the headquarters of the armies, and the complications added by the mountains, it is no great surprise that the effort in Switzerland failed. One could even argue that a stroke of genius—or luck—on Massena's part was the real reason for the French victory or that the allied plan itself was utterly impractical to begin with. More than likely, however, the defeat was largely a result of the many handicaps characteristic of coalition warfare. Gordon Craig's digest of the difficulties encountered by the Grand Alliance in 1813–1814 could apply just as well to 1799: "To direct a widely separated group of armies toward a common goal and a decisive battle in an age in which there were no railways and few good roads, and no telephone or telegraph, was a formidable enough undertaking, even without the trouble caused by administrative duplication, international professional jealousies, and personal feuding within the separate commands."[87] Bonaparte himself perhaps summarized best the problems of coalition warfare when he asked an Austrian statesman, "How many allies do you have? Five? Ten? Twenty? The more you have, the better it is for me."[88]

[87] Gordon A. Craig, "Problems of Coalition Warfare: The Military Alliance against Napoleon, 1813–1814," in Gordon A. Craig, *War, Politics, and Diplomacy, Selected Essays* (New York, 1966), 31.

[88] Quoted in Criste, *Erzherzog Carl*, 2:4.

CHAPTER XII

FINAL DEFEAT,

1800

THE REVERSAL in Switzerland prompted Thugut to reassess the policy that he had followed toward his allies. In the wake of the recriminations exchanged following that defeat, Thugut realized that the cooperation he had sought in 1799 had foundered on the shoals of mutual mistrust and suspicion, some of it of his own making. He became aware that his stead-fast refusal to ratify the loan of May 1797, to reveal Austrian plans for Italy, and to discuss openly the advantages and disadvantages of military strategies had multiplied rather than diminished his allies' concerns about Habsburg intentions. In his assessment of Paul's decision to withdraw from the war, Louis Cobenzl had even listed as the primary reason not the tsar's mercurial personality but "our absolute refusal to explain ourselves."[1] Thugut reluctantly acknowledged this critique of his methods and in the late autumn of 1799 set out to establish a better understanding with his allies.

His new approach consisted basically of being straightforward and open, and he began with Austria's policy toward Italy. On November 19 he sent to London and St. Petersburg a

[1] L. Cobenzl to Colloredo, November 13, 1799, in Vivenot, ed., *Vertrauliche Briefe*, 2:197.

"friendly explication" of territorial adjustments the monarchy wished to make in that peninsula. The emperor did not covet all of Piedmont as his allies surmised, but only the Piedmontese land that had belonged to the Duchy of Milan prior to 1713. Aside from that, the emperor wanted the three Legations which would join Habsburg Italy to Tuscany and to the central lands of the Papacy, not only providing communication between Vienna and these regions but also creating an Austrian corridor across central Italy. The purpose of the changes, Thugut contended, was not only to compensate the emperor for his sacrifices but to enable him to protect the peninsula from France in the future "whether [France] be a monarchy or a republic." Having presented these points, Thugut expressed his hope that their revelation would at last end the speculation and rumors about Austria's aims in Italy.[2]

Just as Thugut was being more candid toward his allies, so too Grenville was extending more sympathy toward Austria. The immediate reason for his change of heart was a series of letters that he received from one of the few men he trusted, William Wickham, who was still with the Austrian and Russian armies in southern Germany. In mid-October Wickham had spent two weeks in the Russian camps near Lake Constance and, on the basis of his observations, composed scathingly critical reports of the Russian army and its commanders. He concluded that the Russians were of no further use in the war against France: the officers were brutes, the soldiers little more than animals, and the commanders, including Suvorov, ignorant and incompetent. "They cannot be called an army in any respect but the number of men."[3] If Grenville wished to continue the war, Wickham advised, then he must give up the Russians and trust the Austrians. "The question is fairly re-

---

[2] Thugut to L. Cobenzl, November 19, 1799, Vienna, HHSA, SK, *Russland*, 2:184. Thugut ordered this information revealed only to the British and to the Russians and not to any of the Italian envoys credited to their courts.

[3] Wickham to Grenville, October 17 and 19, 1799, in Wickham, *Correspondence*, 2:277–87.

duced to this: . . . are you prepared to throw yourselves into the arms of the House of Austria or no? If not, renounce at once every idea of a continental war against France; for you can neither carry it on without Austria, nor force her to carry it on in any other than her own way." And should Grenville decide to fight on—as Wickham knew he would—then he must reconcile with Thugut, for "the Russians have played their part so shockingly ill that they have fixed him on his throne for ever."[4] Grenville accepted Wickham's advice. As his first conciliatory gesture, he offered British approval for Austria to annex the whole of Piedmont.[5] Although it was actually more than Thugut asked for, Grenville believed that only such an offer would improve relations with the state that he now perceived as his single reliable ally.

Thugut responded to Grenville's concession with a friendly act of his own. On December 9 he informed Minto that the emperor would ratify the loan of May 16, 1797, although only on certain conditions: Vienna wanted to postpone paying interest on the loan for some time in order to maintain the monarchy's credit rating elsewhere; it insisted that the London government continue paying the interest on the advances received in late 1796 and early 1797 until the end of the war; and it requested an additional loan of £1,600,000. For Minto and Grenville these conditions did not matter; ratification alone had always been the primary issue. When he dispatched the news to London Minto was absolutely jubilant, for the stumbling block to an Austro-British alliance had at last been removed. Owing to an unusually cold winter that hampered river transportation, Minto's report did not arrive in London until early February, shortly before Vienna's formal ratification reached Starhemberg. As soon as all of the documents were in order, Grenville asked Parliament for financial advances for the monarchy, which were quickly approved. Bet-

---

[4] Wickham to Grenville, December 13, 1799, in *Dropmore Papers*, 6:73–74.

[5] Grenville to Minto, November 1, 1799, in ibid., 1.

ter relations between the two most persistent foes of revolutionary France seemed in store.[6]

The atmosphere of cooperation that Thugut had envisioned for the anti-French coalition seemed established at last, but at the same time the coalition itself was dwindling. Paul's initial fury at his army's defeat had tempered somewhat in December, and he had instructed Suvorov to halt his return home, a decision that inspired Minto and the Austrian general Bellegarde to journey to Prague to talk to Suvorov about staying for the campaign of 1800. But later news of a perceived insult to the Russian flag by Austrian troops at Ancona rekindled Paul's outrage, and in January 1800 he ordered Suvorov and his men home for the second and final time. By then Thugut was not unhappy to see them depart. During the short time that they had bivouacked in Bohemia, they had done so much damage that petitions for redress and relief from the local citizenry had come pouring into Vienna. Thugut noted that the waste, disorder, and excesses among the Russians were "unimaginable." "Thirty thousand Russians use in a day the same expanse of country that could support 60,000 other troops for a week."[7] Should the Russian army remain for the campaign of 1800, "famine in Germany would be unavoidable."[8] With the Russians gone, however, the coalition could rely only on the small German states for aid, and their contributions in the past had always been negligible; despite an announced British willingness to pay them for their contingents, there was no reason to expect much more help from them now.

In 1800 the coalition would consist basically of Austria, Britain, and some German states, which meant that Austria would do most of the fighting once again. Essentially Austria was back in the position that Thugut had previously struggled

<hr>

[6] Sherwig, *Guineas and Gunpowder*, 128–29; Helleiner, *The Imperial Loans*, 123–26; Mackesy, *War Without Victory*, 71.

[7] Thugut to L. Cobenzl, December 3, 1799, Vienna, HHSA, SK, *Russland*, 2:184.

[8] Thugut to L. Cobenzl, January 15, 1800, ibid.

so hard to avoid: it was matched practically alone on the continent against revolutionary France. In the circumstances, one might expect that Thugut would have revealed considerable anxiety about the prospects of such a confrontation. Instead, he expressed quite the opposite: confidence in the likelihood of Austrian victory. The allies may have suffered defeat in Switzerland, but it was by no means irrevocable, and he believed that it could be rectified in the next year's fighting. Besides, that defeat did not overshadow the stunning achievements in Italy. The victories of the spring and summer of 1799 had been followed by further successes in early November, which saw the remaining French troops split into two groups, one fleeing for Nice and the other barricading itself in Genoa.[9] In Germany Archduke Charles had secured the right bank of the Rhine, and the army was preparing to move back into Switzerland. As early as December 8 Thugut presented to Minto Vienna's general strategy for the coming campaign. Switzerland would be liberated not by a direct assault on the French positions near Lake Constance but by an advance behind French lines toward Basel. Once Switzerland was secure, the Austrians would launch a two-pronged invasion of France, one into Alsace similar to that planned in 1799 and the other through Nice and Savoy into Provence and Dauphiné.[10] Even if London desired a different strategy, Minto reported, "Thugut to-day [December 4] said of his own accord that I might be assured, England and Austria, if sincerely united, would at all times be an overmatch for France, even if Russia should withdraw entirely from the coalition."[11] Four months later Thugut had lost none of his confidence. Wickham reported, "Thugut to-day [mid-March 1800] is a very different man from the M. Thugut of the month of April, or even the month of July last, when the decided superiority of the Austrian armies was still problematical; and it is his opinion *now* that the

---

[9] Rothenberg, *Napoleon's Great Adversaries*, 62.
[10] Minto to Wickham, December 8, 1799, in Wickham, *Correspondence*, 2:351.
[11] Minto to Wickham, December 4, 1799, in ibid., 341.

chance of war may be risked without much danger, which was certainly not the case at either of the two periods I have last mentioned."[12] In the spring of 1800 Thugut believed the coalition poised to achieve victory.

The coalition was in fact on the verge of defeat, and not simply because Austria could scarcely stand against revolutionary France; Bonaparte had also returned from his ill-fated Egyptian expedition. On October 8, 1799, he had landed in France unannounced; after gathering about him a group of military and political supporters, he had staged the Coup of Brumaire (November 9) and established the Consulate, in effect a Bonapartist dictatorship. The news of yet another French revolutionary government—even when headed by Bonaparte—prompted a varied reaction among the Austrians. Archduke Charles foresaw no changes at all. Wickham reported his saying "that the late revolution at Paris ought to give no hopes whatever of peace; that every faction in succession has talked of peace, meaning nothing but war, . . . that the new rulers are to be as revolutionary, as ambitious, and as insolent as the last."[13] Thugut, however, was more circumspect. His first reaction to the news was to wait in order "to learn the origin and consequences" of these "extraordinary moves."[14] Bonaparte, after all, was the one Frenchman for whom Thugut had shown some respect in the past, and he wondered if the man warranted trust and confidence again. Thugut was uncertain about the full implication of Bonaparte's coup for the future, but he did offer the opinion that Bonaparte would likely be more favorable toward Austria than the members of the Directory had been.[15] For now, however, he would await developments.

[12] Wickham to Grenville, March 17, 1800, in *Dropmore Papers*, 6:166.

[13] Wickham to Grenville, December 13, 1799, in Wickham, *Correspondence*, 2:367.

[14] Thugut to L. Cobenzl, November 19, 1799, Vienna, HHSA, SK, *Russland*, 2:184.

[15] Keller to Berlin, November 30, 1799, in Heigel, *Deutsche Geschichte*, 2:358–59.

He did not have to wait for long. On Christmas day, 1799, Bonaparte sent the emperor and the king of England appeals for peace filled with elegant words but no concrete proposals. Grenville was quick to reply on behalf of his sovereign. The story of the French Revolution consisted wholly of French efforts to seize both friends and enemies by the ears, he wrote to Bonaparte, and inasmuch as the Christmas letter contained no terms or concessions, that story had not changed. Only a restoration of the Bourbon monarchy and a return to the borders of 1789 would bring peace, Grenville insisted; otherwise, the war would continue.[16]

Thugut's response was much less hasty and uncompromising. In a letter dated January 25 but not sent until February 10, Thugut put forth the appropriate encomium to peace, but he added that peace was not possible without a secure Europe, and that Europe could not be secure as long as France was in continuous turmoil and agitation.[17] This letter, much milder than that of Grenville, encouraged Bonaparte and Talleyrand to offer some specific terms in response.[18] Thus began a correspondence between the two foreign ministers that lasted until the great victory of Bonaparte over the Austrians at Marengo in June 1800.

Thugut's motives for carrying on a correspondence with Talleyrand at this time require examination. One possible explanation has already been suggested: he believed Bonaparte to be a man with whom Austria could negotiate, and he was probing for a sign that would indicate Bonaparte's willingness to talk seriously. Another is that he may have used the contacts to influence Britain. It is conceivable that Thugut delayed his initial response because he wished to see what the British would say; perhaps he also kept the exchanges going to worry his allies by hinting at a separate Austro-French peace. Most

[16] Grenville to Talleyrand, January 4, 1800, in Édouard Driault, *La politique extérieure du premier consul, 1800–1803* (Paris, 1910), 41.

[17] Thugut to Talleyrand, January 25, 1800, in Vivenot, ed., *Vertrauliche Briefe*, 2:441–42.

[18] Talleyrand to Thugut, February 28, 1799, in ibid., 442–43.

likely, however, he hoped to convince the French that Austria was seriously contemplating a settlement and preparing only half-heartedly for war. He certainly attributed this motive to the French. As early as January 10 he suggested that Bonaparte's talk of peace was only to mask an intensified French mobilization. To Colloredo he wrote, "All the newspapers from Paris confirm more and more the opinion that these French rascals are not losing a minute to complete their preparations in order to surprise us before we are ready." Therefore, Austria must also raise recruits and gather supplies as fast as possible. "In the name of God, we must realize the importance of it."[19] In the meantime, Thugut would gladly hide Austria's ongoing military buildup behind an exchange of elegant phrases and possible terms with his French counterpart. One must also acknowledge that, although Vienna and London both planned to continue the war, Austria's exposed position to French attack demanded that Thugut employ a certain amount of deviousness to mask Habsburg intentions. Britain, on the other hand, safe behind the Channel and its fleet, could be as insolent toward Bonaparte as Grenville wished it to be.

As both sides prepared for the campaign of 1800, Grenville's agent and confidant, Wickham, came to Vienna to discuss details of Britain's proposed agreements with the lesser German states. His mission was not particularly significant historically, but at its close he did send to Grenville a perceptive portrayal of the Habsburg foreign minister that provides considerable insight into Thugut's personality in the last year of his service.[20] At the first meeting, Wickham began, Thugut, as was his custom, tried to make his guest feel uncomfortable. "Nothing could have been more awkward than the first half hour," Wickham wrote. But some pointed remarks and "a few ill-natured things" from both men warmed Thugut to the discussion, "after which he left off squinting, and looked me full

---

[19] Thugut to Colloredo, January 10, 1800, in ibid., 205.
[20] Wickham to Grenville, March 17, 1800, in *Dropmore Papers*, 6:163–67.

in the face." Obviously enjoying the repartee, Thugut continued the first conversation for nearly two hours, and, when the
time came to end it, he encouraged Wickham "to return again
whenever I should find a moment of leisure."

Wickham went back a number of times and "had an opportunity of hearing him descant on almost every topic on
which I could have wished to have set him a-talking." The
Englishman found Thugut a spirited and passionate fellow, by
no means the cold, calculating, conspiratorial individual he
had imagined. Thugut spoke with enthusiasm about the issues
of the day and did not hide his feelings about either men or
events. Since he rather enjoyed Thugut's propensity to commit
indiscretions, Wickham would goad him into an intemperate
remark and then watch with amusement while Thugut tried
to cover it up. "I put him two or three times in a passion by
contradicting him, purposely to put him off his guard and
make him say ill-natured things, which nobody is more apt to
do than this good minister; and I regularly observed that he
took great pains to check himself, and to avoid saying anything that might give offense." Thugut's judgment could not,
however, curb his tongue—even if it were the tongue of a foreign minister—and he spoke his mind to the young man with
enthusiasm and vigor. He eagerly expressed his likes and dis-
likes, especially his scorn for certain persons, revealing, Wickham observed, that many of Thugut's judgments were based
on his assessments not of conditions and events but of the personalities of others and frequently of whether or not they
agreed with him. "He launched out against Russia, Marshal
Suvarow [*sic*], General Mack, Lord Nelson, and Sir Sidney
Smith . . . in a manner more marked by passion than discretion; and confirmed at once all the impressions that I had received of him, . . . that he was a man whose conduct was very
much governed, even in the most important occasions, by the
personal opinion he entertained of individuals with whom he
was called upon to act; and that his opinion was very often
formed on no other ground than the readiness or unwilling-
ness of these individuals to act according to his own wishes and

inclinations." Thugut detested many individuals. He spoke of the generals in charge of the next campaign as "though having a personal dislike to them all" and criticized Archduke Charles "whom M. Thugut hates most cordially."

Wickham detected flashes of considerable warmth in Thugut as well. As they discussed aspects of the Austro-British coalition, Wickham now and again evoked the memory of victories of the two states over France during the War of the Spanish Succession and especially during the War of the Austrian Succession, which saved the Habsburg throne for Maria Theresa. When Wickham mentioned the great empress and her trials, "I observed his eyes brighten up in a way that could not have been assumed for the purpose of deceiving me and he launched out immediately on the ambition of France under whatever form of government she existed, and the necessity of reducing her within proper bounds." This warmth was not limited to old memories, for Wickham reported that at the end of each conversation Thugut "was always unwilling to let us go [Minto was often with them]; and, when we parted, he gave me a kiss on each cheek which I shall long remember."

Wickham found Thugut an attractive character, "unquestionably a cunning, intriguing fellow," but far more than a mere schemer. Without doubt Thugut's age was beginning to show, for Wickham noted that he was generally "clear and able" when discussing affairs but was somewhat slow in comprehending a change of subject and rather bewildered when a matter came up that was both new to him and complex. In summarizing Thugut's personality, Wickham wrote, "His general character would be more correctly given if I were to call him an obstinate, self-willed old man, full of spleen and passion" and absolutely dedicated to combatting revolutionary France while protecting Austria's best interests in the process. And, Wickham advised Grenville, London should keep these personal qualities in mind when it dealt with him, for "many parts of his conduct which had hitherto appeared to me inexplicable, may all be cleared up by referring them to the above principle." Studying Thugut's character rather than interpreting Austria's policies in light of British needs, preconceptions, prejudices, and concerns would yield a greater understanding between the two powers.

As Wickham's evaluation of Thugut made its way to London, the armies began to move. The Austrian military plan for 1800 remained generally as Thugut had revealed it to Minto the previous December, but with one significant change.[21] No longer was Archduke Charles commander of the army in Germany, for the emperor had accepted his latest offer to resign. In his place Francis appointed Lieutenant Field Marshal Paul Kray, a specialist on fortifications who was out of his element when commanding a field army that needed to act quickly and effectively against the French. Kray was supposed to clear Switzerland first, while covering the approaches into the Tyrol, into southern Germany, and along the Danube, and then to invade France. But Kray was convinced that he did not have sufficient troops even to begin his assignment; rather than undertake any offensive at all, he waited with his main force at Donauschingen for the French to assume the initiative. In the last week in April, Moreau, again in command of the French forces in the German theater, crossed the Rhine from his bases in Alsace and western Switzerland and advanced slowly, ponderously, and straight ahead—as Moreau usually did—toward Kray's positions. Kray steadily withdrew before the French advance, with only a few minor, unsuccessful attempts to halt it, until he reached Ulm on the Danube where he finally dug in.

Somewhat to the Austrians' surprise and certainly not according to their plans, the lumbering movements of Kray and Moreau in southern Germany turned out to be only a side show in the campaign of 1800. Bonaparte was back on the continent, and his genius determined where the important battles would be fought. For a time no one was certain where that would be. Instead of going to the front in Germany, Switzer-

---

[21] Alfred Herrmann, *Der Aufstieg Napoleons: Krieg und Diplomatie vom Brumaire bis Lunéville* (Berlin, 1912), 128.

land, or Italy, Bonaparte gathered together what would become his famous reserve army at bases in eastern France from which it could deploy to any theater that he chose. Not until May did Bonaparte decide to invade Italy, where he spied the possibility of a decisive victory. In Italy the French held little more than the coast between Savona and Genoa, and their positions in the region were being threatened by an Austrian army under Melas. With the Austrians concentrating on the Riviera, Bonaparte moved his reserve army through the Great St. Bernard Pass, intent on drawing Melas into open battle on the northern Italian plain. Melas, fearful of Bonaparte's threat to his rear, moved the bulk of his forces northward to meet him.

On June 14 the two armies collided on the plains of Marengo near Alessandria in what would be the decisive battle for 1800, for the War of the Second Coalition, and, ultimately, for Thugut's career. The battle itself was not one of Bonaparte's best, and for much of the day it appeared that he might be defeated. The timely arrival of reinforcements turned the tide, however, and he emerged victorious as night fell.[22]

As important as the victory was, the armistice concluded by Melas and Bonaparte's chief of staff, Berthier, on the following day gave it even greater impact. The agreement required the Austrians to withdraw behind the Mincio River, thus allowing the French to occupy almost all of the land conquered by Suvorov in 1799. What made it doubly unfortunate was that the military situation did not demand such sacrifices. Despite the defeat at Marengo, Melas still possessed superior artillery and adequate supplies and ammunition, Austrian reinforcements were nearby and coming quickly, and the positions the Austrians occupied after the battle were practically unassailable.[23] But the seventy-year-old Melas, wounded twice at Marengo, was too tired and too demoralized to continue. An officer on

[22] For a good discussion of the strategy of this campaign, see Rodger, *War of the Second Coalition*, 236–45.

[23] Herrmann, *Aufstieg Napoleons*, 434; Ross, *European Diplomatic History*, 224; Heigel, *Deutsche Geschichte*, 2:364.

the scene attributed the truce solely to him, "this respectable old man whose morale was as shaky as his physique."[24]

At Vienna in mid-June Thugut and Minto, unaware of the events transpiring in Italy, were putting the finishing touches on the Austro-British treaty of alliance. Amidst the serious debate about compensation and payment, the provision that both sides accepted without reservation but that later would become a major issue was one calling for no separate negotiations and no separate peace by either party for the remainder of 1800. Minto and Thugut signed the agreement on June 23 but backdated it to June 20. The very next day the first courier arrived in the Habsburg capital with word of the defeat at Marengo and the signing of the armistice.

The news caused a sensation in Vienna. People in the coffee houses, wine cellars, beer halls, and salons proclaimed the state in peril, demanded the recall of Archduke Charles to save the country once again, condemned the Austro-British alliance as another vehicle to turn the wealth of the monarchy over to British usurers and war profiteers, and insisted upon immediate peace with France. The calls for peace became particularly strident on June 25 when a letter from Bonaparte to the emperor arrived offering a settlement with Austria alone—excluding Britain—based on the Treaty of Campo Formio.[25] The defeat at Marengo, the armistice, and Bonaparte's letter revived the peace party in Vienna, which had been somewhat subdued during the campaign of 1799. And the peace party, regardless of military bungling or ill luck, still held Thugut responsible for all of the misfortunes that had befallen the monarchy. In a comprehensive attack on the foreign minister, a new spokesman for the peace group, Count Heinrich Franz von Rottenhann, blamed him not only for the latest setback but for all those suffered by Austria since 1793. Thugut, Rottenhann insisted, had driven all good men "truly interested" in the welfare of the monarchy from the emperor's side and

[24] Quoted in Hüffer, *Die Schlacht von Marengo*, 120.

[25] Bonaparte to Francis, June 16, 1800, in Bonaparte, *Correspondance*, 6:365–68.

had sought to gather all affairs—military, diplomatic, and domestic—into his own hands, all the while keeping "his tortuous policies in the dark." The time had come, Rottenhann continued, for the emperor to find new advisers. "Since now peace is the general wish of all the people, since the uncertainty of political measures and of military operations has destroyed all hope of national honor, it is an essential step for the future to ask men for advice who view things differently than Baron Thugut." In fact, Rottenhann specifically recommended the men who would serve the emperor best from now on: Lacy, Kollowrat, and Prince Starhemberg—the core of the peace party. They should counsel Francis not only in an informal capacity but as a ministerial conference with designated powers, and their first and "most important measure" must be "the dismissal of Baron Thugut as the mainspring of all military and diplomatic measures."[26]

Stung by the defeat and disturbed by the public outcry, the emperor at last began to waver in his support for Thugut's war policy. He was not, however, necessarily eager to adopt an alternative to it. In fact, he was quite uncertain about the proper course to take. After relating Francis's desire to satisfy the public by appointing Archduke Charles to command the army, Colloredo confessed to Thugut that the young emperor was simply bewildered by the whole situation. He wanted to listen to everyone and do what was right, Colloredo remarked, "which often renders him confused, even apprehensive, and indecisive."[27]

Notwithstanding the alarm in the streets and courtyards, the outcry of the peace party, and the bewilderment of the emperor, Thugut had no doubt as to the rightness of his policy. In fact, the recent events made him determined to persevere. Again he summoned up the strength of will necessary to exert influence upon the young sovereign and to maintain control over Austrian decision making. The armistice concluded in It-

[26] Count von Rottenhann to Francis, June 27, 1800, in Vivenot, ed., *Vertrauliche Briefe*, 2:227–31.
[27] Colloredo to Thugut, July 3, 1800, in ibid., 236–37.

aly could not be undone and Bonaparte's letter need not be ignored, Thugut argued, and both could be turned to Vienna's
advantage. The emperor should not only accept the truce in
Italy but request one in Germany as well (where Kray was
doing poorly against Moreau), and he should offer at least to
talk with Bonaparte about concluding a general peace. These
conciliatory gestures would serve primarily to show the public
again that the emperor was a peace-loving man, eager to reach
a satisfactory settlement as quickly as possible; and they would
also give the army time to gather its resources and to collect its
wits in order to resume the fighting in a more efficient fashion.
As to Archduke Charles assuming command, Thugut advised
against it, "for the first thing that would happen would be [for
him] to demand 60,000 more infantrymen, and as 60,000 more
are not easy to find, to say that all is lost and to return the army
to Vienna crying peace, peace!"[28] The emperor accepted this
advice and put his name on a letter to Bonaparte endorsing an
armistice on all fronts and offering high-sounding but vague
phrases about "a just and durable peace."[29] Thugut entrusted
the message to General Joseph Guyard St. Julien, the same
Austrian officer who had brought Bonaparte's letter to the
emperor, and ordered him to take it to French headquarters
at Milan.

With St. Julien on his way, Thugut turned to the task of encouraging the Austrian generals to take advantage of the
pause in hostilities to consolidate their forces to make ready for
the war's renewal. Thugut warned Melas in Italy that Bonaparte's next offensive would likely be northward toward the
Tyrol to cut communications between the Austrian armies in
Germany and Italy and to establish communications between
the French armies in those same theaters. Melas therefore
should take the necessary precautions to retain control over the

---

[28] Thugut to Colloredo, July 2, 1800, in ibid., 234–35.

[29] Francis to Bonaparte, July 5, 1800, in A. du Casse, ed., *Histoire des négociations diplomatiques relatives aux traités de Mortfontaine, de Lunéville, et
d'Amiens* (Paris, 1857), 2:24–27.

threatened routes.[30] To Kray Thugut sent the same instructions, adding that he was also to hold the French west of Ulm and prepare to defend Bavaria and the crownlands against an enemy offensive. Thugut did not yet know that already Kray had withdrawn from Ulm and retreated a good distance down the Danube, allowing Moreau to occupy most of Bavaria, including Munich. On his own initiative Kray had concluded an armistice with Moreau at Parsdorf, essentially establishing the Inn River in eastern Bavaria as the boundary between French- and Austrian-occupied territory but leaving the fortresses of Ulm, Philippsburg, and Ingolstadt in Austrian hands. This armistice Thugut found as detrimental to Austria as the one in Italy. "Regarding the country [Germany], the armistice appears sufficiently bad and for the Tyrol detestable; . . . It is not only today that we are familiar with ignominy! We must now determine what position we will be in if we break this armistice."[31]

Despite the actions of the field commanders, for the remainder of July and into August Thugut continued to encourage, prod, and preach at the emperor, the generals, and the government to make changes and to gather the resources necessary to renew the fighting. Then, to his astonishment and chagrin, on August 5 St. Julien reappeared in Vienna, where he announced that he had concluded the preliminary peace treaty between Austria and France. The war, he proclaimed, was over at last. Thugut was dumbfounded. To Colloredo he wrote, "Count St. Julien has arrived this evening toward midnight. He has muddled things to a terrifying degree."[32]

St. Julien had muddled things indeed. Although it is not exactly clear what happened, when the count set off with the emperor's letter to Bonaparte he received—probably from Thugut—a set of instructions that he was ordered to keep

[30] Thugut to Melas, July 12, 1800, in Vivenot, ed., *Vertrauliche Briefe*, 2:45–47.

[31] Thugut to Colloredo, July 17, 1800, in ibid., 251.

[32] Thugut to Colloredo, August 5, 1800, in ibid., 253.

sealed until he met the French leader. Apparently, St. Julien assumed that the sealed instructions contained the authority for him to conclude the preliminaries that would lead to a general European peace. As he traveled through Italy and France in pursuit of Bonaparte, he became ever more convinced that his assumption was correct. When at last he arrived in Paris and made arrangements to meet with Bonaparte and Talleyrand, he opened the sealed instructions and found not a set of proposals for a treaty but only a brief paragraph ordering him specifically to do nothing except deliver the emperor's letter. Wrote a traveling companion, "I am convinced that it was his ambition, certainly excusable under the circumstances, that seduced Count St. Julien into thinking he was charged with a very important commission. One can imagine his surprise and embarrassment when he opened the letter and found not instructions and authorization for his mission, but only five or six lines warning him expressly to do nothing."[33] Having fantasized about his role as peacemaker, St. Julien was inclined to ignore his instructions and proceed as if he had full authority to make peace. This temptation was encouraged by Bonaparte and Talleyrand who, while acknowledging that perhaps St. Julien did not have expressed powers to negotiate, persuaded him to believe that he had implied powers to do so. Taken in by his own sense of self-worth and the smooth words of the Frenchmen, St. Julien opened talks on July 22 and six days later concluded the settlement that he would take to Vienna. Although based on Campo Formio, it altered some earlier provisions for territorial exchanges, but most important it specified that ratification take place by August 15, implying that, if the deadline were not met, the war would resume.[34]

On August 9 the emperor, Thugut, Lehrbach, and Colloredo met in an unusual formal session to decide on a response to St. Julien's action. All agreed that he had made a terrible

[33] Neipperg on St. Julien's instructions, July 21, 1800, in Hüffer, *Die Schlacht von Marengo*, 134–35.
[34] The agreement can be found in Vivenot, ed., *Vertrauliche Briefe*, 2:447–48.

error; the problem was to find a way out of the dilemma caused by it. If Vienna simply voided the treaty, the fighting would begin again, and that, the emperor himself emphasized, was unacceptable. The army was in a shambles; the men and officers were discouraged, food was growing scarce, and discipline was collapsing. Accordingly, the emperor declared, the agreement as concluded might be rejected, but his ministers must find a way to do so without risking a resumption of the war.

After discussing various means by which this end might be accomplished, the group finally adopted a solution offered, not surprisingly, by Thugut. He proposed to write a personal letter to Talleyrand informing him that St. Julien's treaty was unacceptable because he had no authority to conclude one. At the same time, however, Thugut would assure the Frenchman of the emperor's eagerness to continue the peace talks (but only with a British delegate present), and, as a mark of sincerity, he would suggest either Schlettstadt in Alsace or Lunéville in Lorraine as a possible site for future discussions.[35] Thugut's proposal smacked again of playing for time rather than searching for a resolution to the war, but the group accepted it and the appropriate letter went to Paris.

At this juncture, the French were also undecided as to what to do. Bonaparte was concerned about continuing unhappiness with the war at home and about shortages and indiscipline in the French army not unlike those afflicting the Austrians. Moreover, he wished for a period of quiet so that he could solidify his authority internally and devote time to the resolution of domestic problems. But he did not want to lose the advantages he had thus far won in the war. Talleyrand's answer to Thugut's message reflected these conflicting desires. It insisted that St. Julien had been fully empowered to conclude a peace and that, by rejecting it, Vienna had violated the honor among states, but it also welcomed the Austrian offer to open talks

[35] Minutes of the meeting of August 9, 1800, in Vienna, HHSA, *Kaiser Franz Akten*, 78b (81); Thugut to Talleyrand, August 11, 1800, in Vivenot, ed., *Vertrauliche Briefe*, 2:257–58.

and accepted Lunéville as the site for them; it contended that the British would sabotage a settlement, but it welcomed a British delegate at the forthcoming negotiations; and it expressed hope that hostilities would stop, but it insisted that the armistice must end and fighting recommence.[36]

While pondering all of the contradictory statements in Talleyrand's letter, Thugut had become convinced that, in any case, Austria had to make ready to resume the war.[37] Preparations included replacing the two defeated generals of 1800: Melas by Thugut's old friend Bellegarde and Kray by Archduke John, the emperor's eighteen-year-old brother. Archduke John was to serve as titular head of the army in Germany to inspire the troops through the pretense that he was a replica of Archduke Charles; actual decisions were entrusted to Franz von Lauer, a sixty-five-year-old engineering specialist who was as unqualified to face the French revolutionary generals as Kray had been. In addition to the changes in command, Thugut began to discuss efforts to raise the Hungarian *insurrectio*, a medieval calling to arms of the Magyar nobility, to announce a levée en masse in Bohemia, and to try yet again to put more order and regulation into financial affairs.[38] As part of the effort to increase the morale and fighting strength of the army, the emperor himself announced that he would visit the forces in Germany. He had not visited Habsburg troops in the field since his trip to Belgium in 1794, and he believed that a tour of the lines would inspire the army's confidence in his younger brother and his military staff and also strengthen their faith in themselves. In 1794 Thugut had objected to the emperor's visit to the camps because it took him too far from Vienna; now Thugut had no such objections. Austrian headquarters in Germany were at Altötting, two days' fast ride from the Habsburg capital.

Thugut should have been more concerned about the em-

---

[36] Talleyrand to Thugut, August 24, 1800, in Vivenot, ed., *Vertrauliche Briefe*, 2:260–61.
[37] Thugut to Colloredo, August 31, 1800, in ibid., 261–62.
[38] Thugut to Colloredo, September 7, 1800, in ibid., 270–71.

peror's being away this time than he had been in 1794. In reality, Francis dreaded resumption of the war. He had no faith in either his generals or his soldiers and was by no means convinced that a victory over the French would materially affect the ultimate outcome of the war. As he and the men about him at Austrian headquarters were mulling over the likelihood of renewed fighting and what it might bring, a messenger arrived from Moreau with a proposal for another armistice. Moreau explained that he had received orders from Paris to begin hostilities immediately but that the orders had also granted him the authority to offer the Austrians a forty-five-day truce if they agreed to turn over to the French a few "security places" as a sign of good will. Although not listed specifically in the note, the places, everyone involved knew, were Philippsburg, Ingolstadt, and Ulm, the fortresses behind French lines still in Austrian hands.[39]

The French offer of an armistice in exchange for the three fortresses was dispatched to Vienna, where Thugut dismissed it as an "insolent proposition" worthy only of the haughtiest rejection.[40] But Thugut was not in personal contact with his sovereign to press his opinions. Francis was now listening to the advice of other men. On September 19 the emperor called together Archduke John, Lauer, and Lehrbach, who was serving as the army's political officer, to discuss Moreau's offer. Lauer and Lehrbach, both eager to avoid any military showdown with the French, advised accepting it. Since the young archduke had no objections and since the arguments of the other two conformed to the emperor's own inclinations, he decided to follow that advice. He authorized Lehrbach and Lauer to negotiate an extension of the armistice at the cost of the three fortresses.[41] On September 20 at Hohenlinden near

[39] Herrmann, *Aufstieg Napoleons*, 495.

[40] Thugut to Colloredo, September 22, 1800, in Vivenot, ed., *Vertrauliche Briefe*, 2:285.

[41] Herrmann, *Aufstieg Napoleons*, 495–96. Minto wrote that the emperor "put himself at the head of his troops rather to countenance their weakness than to inspire them with new courage." Minto, ed., *Life and Letters*, 3:151–52.

Munich the two Austrians concluded terms with Moreau's delegate. The Austrians would remain behind the Inn River, the French behind the Isar, and the land between them would be neutral. The three fortresses would be delivered as "hostages" to the French, and the garrisons could depart from them with all of their weapons "except those belonging to the Empire."[42]

With the armistice settled, the emperor, Archduke John, and Lehrbach left Austrian headquarters for Vienna. The emperor believed that he had made the right decision, but he also knew that he must now face the wrath of Thugut. In explaining his decision to Colloredo on the day of the armistice's conclusion, Francis had written, "Let my brother read this letter [the brother was Ferdinand, Grand Duke of Tuscany, who was viceroy in Francis's absence]; otherwise I order you to tell no one—not even Thugut; arm yourself in all matters to bring him to reason if he explodes over Lehrbach's morning letter."[43] The following day he wrote, "God grant that we will finish in Vienna with Thugut without great turmoil, and that the instructions and powers for Lehrbach [to continue talks with the French] be drawn up quickly." Despite the hopeful words, the emperor knew that he would face an angry and stubborn Thugut and expressed the wish that his foreign minister could have been with him at Austrian headquarters and seen what he had seen. Then he would have realized that the armistice was vital to the preservation of the army. "I would be happier if Thugut and you [Colloredo] could somehow come here, because here one is covered with much colder blood than in the hysteria of Vienna."[44]

Thugut was not only angry at but profoundly shaken by what had happened. Minto wrote that, when Thugut informed him of the armistice and the price Austria had paid for it, "I never saw him, nor any other man, so much affected as

[42] Herrmann, *Aufstieg Napoleons*, 496.
[43] Francis to Colloredo, September 20, 1800, in Vivenot, ed., *Vertrauliche Briefe*, 2:281.
[44] Francis to Colloredo, September 21, 1800, in ibid., 282.

he was." Later, when discussing the matter again, "he burst into tears and literally wept."[45] The showdown came on Thursday, September 25, at a formal meeting in the chancellery attended by the emperor, the grand duke of Tuscany, Thugut, Lehrbach, and Colloredo. According to notes kept by Colloredo, Lehrbach opened the meeting by presenting his report on the truce and the future peace talks. When he finished and before Thugut could begin his assault on the report, the emperor personally interjected that Lehrbach was not responsible for what had occurred but had only followed the orders of his sovereign, who was now convinced that it was his duty to arrange an immediate and secure peace for his war-weary subjects. The army could fight no longer, and the country could sacrifice no more.

It was a moving plea, but it did not deter Thugut. Thugut proclaimed in terms reminiscent of 1797 that the armistice was unacceptable on two grounds, one diplomatic, one military. Diplomatically it violated the Austro-British agreement not to conclude a separate peace. Militarily it was unnecessary because the Austrians were by no means defeated. The army had one hundred thousand good men in the German theater alone, a force certainly equal to that of the French and much closer to its supply bases than the French were to theirs. As Bonaparte had found in Styria in 1797, the French had overextended themselves and would only grow weaker as the Austrians grew stronger. To these points Lehrbach attempted to respond, but he was verbally pushed aside by the emperor, who emphasized to Thugut that he had decided for peace precisely because he judged the military situation to be perilous. He had no wish to risk his throne and the welfare of his subjects on the chance of victory or defeat along the Inn River. Besides, Thugut had not seen the army and did not realize the poor condition it was in. The exchanges grew heated between Thugut and Francis, but there was no question who would

[45] Minto to Grenville, September 24, 1800, in Minto, ed., *Life and Letters*, 3:155.

prevail. The emperor finally pronounced the matter closed and asked Lehrbach for his report on the coming talks at Lunéville. At that moment Thugut offered to resign. The emperor accepted the offer and conferred the office of foreign minister on Lehrbach. Thugut congratulated the new minister, wished him luck, and departed the meeting.[46]

The confrontation between Thugut and the emperor on September 25 revealed far more than merely the issues that led to Thugut's resignation after seven and one half years as foreign minister of the Habsburg Monarchy. It also showed the awe with which Francis, Colloredo, and even Lehrbach viewed Thugut. To argue against Thugut's impassioned exposition of his own views, the emperor, regardless of his status as ruler, had to summon considerable courage and to fortify that of the men whose advice he now chose to follow. Effectively opposing Thugut's policies and the conviction behind them was not an easy task, not even for the sovereign himself. In the end, however, the decision had to be made by Francis, and if Thugut could not accept it, he had to step down. Of that there was no question and no argument.

Word of Thugut's fall quickly reached the streets and salons. Given the public antagonism toward Thugut, one might imagine that his resignation would elicit widespread rejoicing. But it did not, for, as much as the people disliked Thugut, they knew what kind of man he was and could predict what decisions he would make. With Thugut gone, uncertainty about the future caused considerable anxiety. Colloredo wrote that during the day following the meeting public places were full of talk of Thugut's resignation and troubled speculation about what would come next.[47] Although his view was colored by his own opposition to Lehrbach and support of Thugut, Minto noted Vienna's reaction to the latter's departure from office: "It is impossible to describe the universal dissatisfaction and terror which this change occasioned. The warmest partisans of

---

[46] Colloredo's notes dated September 26, 1800, Vienna, HHSA, *Kaiser Franz Akten*, 78b (81).

[47] Colloredo's notes of September 26, 1800, ibid.

peace began to call for an honourable war rather than igno-
minious concessions, and the most bitter enemies of Thugut
were lamenting his retreat and trembling at the loss of his advice and assistance in the present menacing crisis."[48]

But Thugut's resignation by no means ended his influence.
The British, formerly Thugut's detractors but now his supporters, demanded if not his outright return, at least the dismissal of Lehrbach and the resumption of Thugut's policies.
Lehrbach was totally unacceptable to the British as foreign
minister. In early September, having heard that Lehrbach was
with the army, Wickham had written, "He is full of trick, and
low cunning, and foolish affected mystery."[49] On September
29, without waiting for instructions from London, Minto formally protested Lehrbach's appointment in an audience with
the emperor himself. "I gave the Emperor fair notice of what
was sure to happen," he wrote later. "Viz: that England would
consider the elevation of M. de Lehrbach . . . as a declaration
that the Emperor renounced the Alliance, and I assured him
that His [Britannic] Majesty could place no confidence in Austria if her Government was administered by that gentleman;
& that the Emperor must choose between M. de Lehrbach &
England." Francis protested Minto's attacks on Lehrbach's
character and British interference in Austrian ministerial appointments "with more vigour than I [Minto] should have expected," but the strong objections of the British coming so
closely upon the nerve-rattling confrontation with Thugut seriously disrupted the emperor's resolve.[50]

On September 30 Francis called another meeting, this time
with Colloredo, Lehrbach, and Thugut, to discuss British objections to Lehrbach and the question of whether to pursue
peace without British participation. This second meeting provided Thugut with the opportunity to present his views again.

[48] Minto to Lord Carysfort, October 11, 1800, in Minto, ed., *Life and Letters*, 3:164–68.

[49] Wickham to Minto, September 7, 1800, in *Dropmore Papers*, 6:316.

[50] Minto to Paget, November 1, 1800, in Sir Arthur Paget, *The Paget Papers, 1794–1807* (London, 1896), 1:280–81.

If Austria sought a settlement without the British, he argued, then the British would void the alliance, and Austria would have to negotiate alone with the French. Since Austria did not have the resources to resist France by itself, Bonaparte could dictate any terms he wished, and the emperor would have no alternative but to accept them. Moreover, the terms agreed to might not be kept, for the French had hardly observed the conditions of any treaty that they had signed thus far. To conclude a separate treaty with the French, in other words, was to put Austria at their mercy. These were formidable words from the old foreign minister, but Lehrbach tried strenuously to refute them. By this time, however, the conviction of the emperor was no longer on his side. Cowed by Thugut's forceful presentation and by Minto's threat that Vienna must choose between Lehrbach and England, Francis decided to dismiss Lehrbach—a mere two days after he had received his formal appointment as foreign minister.[51]

It was now necessary to choose his replacement. Thugut refused to be a candidate. On September 28 he had informed Colloredo that "it is from now on totally impossible for me ever to resume [directorship] of the department of foreign affairs," and even after September 30 he insisted that he would not return to the post.[52] However, Thugut was willing to accept a new position among the emperor's policy advisers. Consequently, some shuffling of offices was needed that would satisfy the British, continue negotiations with the French, restore Thugut's influence in policy making, and not unduly humiliate Lehrbach. By October 5 the solution was found. The chancellery would be united with the cabinet; Colloredo would remain cabinet minister while Louis Cobenzl would formally take on the duties of director of foreign affairs with the titles of conference minister and vice-chancellor. The em-

---

[51] Colloredo's notes of the meeting of September 30, 1800, Vienna, HHSA, *Kaiser Franz Akten*, 78b (81). See also L. Cobenzl to Francis, October 8, 1800, ibid., *Vorträge*, 160.

[52] Thugut to Colloredo, September 28, 1800, in Vivenot, ed., *Vertrauliche Briefe*, 2:290–91.

peror would grant Lehrbach the honorific title of minister of
state, and Thugut would become director of "all that concerns
the government of my possessions in Italy, Dalmatia, Istria,
Albania, the marine, and any business involving these same
lands" but would remain in the chancellery in Vienna to counsel the emperor on any matters that arose.[53]

Among this group the only man who had not participated
in the debates of late September and early October was Cobenzl. After being expelled from St. Petersburg in May in the
wake of one of Paul's outbursts against Austria, Cobenzl had
returned to Vienna where he remained until July, when he
was dispatched to Karlsbad (Karlovy Vary) in Bohemia to
open talks with a delegate of the tsar concerning an Austro-
Russian reconciliation.[54] As part of the adjustments taking
place in the government after September 28, he was recalled
and arrived in Vienna to assume his new office and his new
title on October 5. The first task facing him—now that the
British were mollified—was to formulate a policy for the still
scheduled peace talks with the French at Lunéville and to appoint a plenipotentiary to conduct those talks on behalf of the
emperor. In the existing military and diplomatic situations,
the policy was fairly easy to adopt. It advanced two basic Austrian demands: a treaty similar to that of Campo Formio and
no treaty without British participation.[55] As to the man to conduct the negotiations, Cobenzl and the others discussed a few
names, but all knew that, in the end, the delegate would be
Cobenzl himself, the only man with the experience, skill, and
knowledge to do diplomatic battle with the likes of Bonaparte

---

[53] Colloredo's notes dated October 5, 1800, Vienna, HHSA, *Kaiser Franz
Akten*, 78b (81). Eleonore Liechtenstein wrote, "Cobenzl will not survive; he
is neither a Kaunitz nor a Thugut, much too weak and courteous, too much
the courtier of the old type for this hard, difficult time." Eleonore Liechtenstein to her daughter, December 6, 1800, in Wolf, *Fürstin Eleonore Liechtenstein*, 268.

[54] Thugut to L. Cobenzl, July 1, 1800, Vienna, HHSA, SK, *Russland*,
2:184.

[55] Instructions for L. Cobenzl, October 9, 1800, in Vivenot, ed., *Vertrauliche Briefe*, 2:466–73.

and Talleyrand.[56] As both foreign minister and chief plenipotentiary, Cobenzl set out for Lunéville on October 14 to talk peace once again with the French.

Cobenzl's departure meant that in Vienna Thugut was back in power. With Cobenzl en route to Lorraine, Lehrbach set aside, and Colloredo by no means willing to take on the routine of foreign affairs along with his other duties, Thugut came not only to advise the emperor but once more to compose much of the formal correspondence to his diplomats and generals. One might assume that Thugut would be smug about his achievement in effectively regaining his old job and in reestablishing his policy. Such was not entirely the case. In fact, when Colloredo asked Thugut to resume all of his former duties in Cobenzl's absence, he refused.[57] He did not want to appear ungrateful, he wrote in reply, but he simply no longer wished to assume day-to-day responsibility for the conduct of foreign affairs. He agreed, however, to counsel Colloredo and the emperor, and through that avenue he essentially resumed the regular tasks of his old office. Although without the title of foreign minister, he continued to be the leading policy maker in Austria's struggle against revolutionary France.

Thugut now focused attention on two matters: ongoing preparations for war should the armistice expire without a settlement and Cobenzl's mission to France. It became immediately apparent that he could exercise little direct control over the latter. When Cobenzl arrived in Lunéville on October 24, he did not find any French negotiators awaiting him; instead he was handed a letter from Bonaparte inviting him to come to Paris for discussions there. Cobenzl decided to accept because his past experiences at Udine-Passariano and at Selz had shown that the only man in France with whom one could negotiate seriously and with any likelihood of success was Bona-

---

[56] Thugut to Colloredo, October 6, 1800, in ibid., 297–98; Colloredo's notes of the meeting of October 7, 1800, Vienna, HHSA, *Kaiser Franz Akten* 78b (81).

[57] Colloredo to Thugut, n.d., 1800, in Vivenot, ed., *Vertrauliche Briefe*, 2:318.

parte. Talks with others were exercises in futility. Cobenzl knew, however, that when he informed Thugut of his decision, Thugut might conclude that he, like St. Julien, would be seduced by Bonaparte into concluding an ill-conceived separate peace. In his letter explaining his intentions, therefore, Cobenzl tried to assure Thugut that he had no misconceptions or unfounded hopes about what was in store for him in Paris. "I am not going more willingly than I have come here [Lunéville], or to Udine or to Rastadt. It is always with the same forced smile that you have seen me make . . . and it is always with the same resignation."[58]

Cobenzl's journey to Paris did upset Thugut but not necessarily because he feared that Cobenzl would repeat St. Julien's blunder; he also wondered if someone—particularly the emperor—had given Cobenzl special orders to go to Paris to reach a settlement without telling Thugut. If so, he informed Colloredo, then he would leave the service. Otherwise, Archduke John and Austrian headquarters should be placed on alert for some trick by the French, "who are so perfidious and infamous."[59] Thugut's worries were unfounded. Bonaparte's purpose in inviting Cobenzl to Paris was indeed to intimidate or to cajole the Austrian envoy into dropping the demand that the British take part in the Austro-French negotiations, but Cobenzl, experienced in such diplomatic devices, would have none of it. After a week in Paris, he returned to Lunéville, where he prepared to negotiate formally with Bonaparte's brother Joseph and a British representative. When he reached the city, he confirmed to Thugut that he had given nothing away while in Paris. "I understood all the circumspection our position demands; the necessity of remaining inseparable from England; and I assure Your Excellency that I am acting only according to this system."[60] To Colloredo he added wistfully that he had told Bonaparte and Talleyrand "that I wanted

[58] L. Cobenzl to Thugut, October 25, 1800, in ibid., 323.
[59] Thugut to Colloredo, October 31, 1800, in ibid., 324.
[60] L. Cobenzl to Thugut, November 15, 1800, in ibid., 334.

fewer cannon salutes, fewer escorts, fewer harangues, and one more province for His Majesty."[61]

Thugut's other concern in late October and November 1800 was Austrian military preparations. And in this matter he felt a renewed sense of urgency because the French were taking advantage of the current truce to gain certain advantages in ways that reminded him of their activities in Switzerland and Rome during the peace of early 1798. On October 23 word reached Vienna that the French had entered Tuscany, still formally a Habsburg secundogeniture and thus far largely unscathed by the war. For Thugut the French move showed once again that the revolutionaries did not keep either the letter or the spirit of the agreements they concluded. With an armistice in effect in Italy and a territorial arrangement still pending, neither side should have taken advantage of the cease-fire to make further military gains. Thugut cited the "perfidious act" as new evidence of French untrustworthiness and warned that it could lead to other French moves before the truce expired.[62] Given such a prospect, Thugut advised increased watchfulness on the part of the army and an acceleration of its preparations to resume hostilities.

Not at all to Thugut's dismay, a renewal of the war was becoming increasingly likely. Cobenzl's refusal to discuss a separate Austro-French peace with Bonaparte in Paris had persuaded the consul that only more fighting would convince Vienna to negotiate without the British. In fact, when Cobenzl left Paris for Lunéville, Bonaparte dispatched orders to Moreau to resume hostilities, because the forty-five-day-long armistice of Hohenlinden was about to expire. Thugut was not displeased. He had no confidence that the French would properly observe any agreement, and he now felt reasonably certain that the army was ready to take the field again. On his way to France, Cobenzl had stopped at the camps of the main Habsburg force on the Inn for a short inspection and had reported

---

[61] L. Cobenzl to Colloredo, November 10, 1800, in ibid., 328.
[62] Thugut to Colloredo, October 23, 1800, in ibid., 320.

the army to be in better condition than he had expected to find it. Morale was good and supplies, while short, were adequate. Officers had told him that, although a few contingents from the Holy Roman Empire (including that of Max Franz, elector of Cologne and the emperor's uncle) had left for home, the Austrians and remaining imperial forces were at least equal in numbers to the French.[63] On November 14 the armistice expired, and on the following day a courier arrived in Vienna from Archduke John's headquarters declaring that the French did not wish it renewed. Armed struggle was to begin again. To Colloredo Thugut wrote: "I cannot hide from Your Excellency that I could not be more calm about future events. . . . And since peace at this time is impossible, all thinking people agree that open hostilities are better than these unfortunate armistices that have been the veritable ruin of His Majesty's interests."[64]

Thugut might have expressed calm about the war's resumption, but few others did. The emperor and Colloredo were most upset. We must send orders to the armies, Colloredo complained to Thugut, but what orders do we send? We must appoint commanders, but whom do we appoint? We must respond to "the pleas, the jeremiads" of those who think peace absolutely necessary, but what do we say to them?[65] Nor did the army share Thugut's confidence. From headquarters Karl Schwarzenberg, the later commander of the allied armies in 1813 and 1814, wrote to his wife: "I still hope that we are not so utterly senseless as to start [fighting] again, especially with means in even worse condition than at the time we felt compelled to renew a less than honorable armistice."[66] The street also voiced its concern as Thugut encountered angry citizens shouting at him and pelting him with various objects when he traveled to and from the chancellery.

[63] L. Cobenzl to Colloredo, October 17 and 18, 1800, in ibid., 311–14.

[64] Thugut to Colloredo, November 14, 1800, in ibid., 329–30.

[65] Colloredo to Thugut, November 15, 1800, in ibid., 331–32.

[66] Schwarzenberg to his wife, October 23, 1800, in Feldmarschall Fürst Karl Schwarzenberg, *Briefe an seine Frau, 1799–1816* (Vienna, 1913), 66.

After the cease-fire expired, the two armies clashed almost immediately at Hohenlinden, the site of the signing of the second armistice. Following an initial success on their right wing, the Austrians broke under an assault on their center and were forced to retreat. Archduke John and his staff were able to keep the army together as they fell back to Salzburg, which they reached on December 12. The army had suffered badly. Of the forty-two thousand men committed to battle, fourteen thousand had become casualties.

News of the engagement reached Vienna on December 6. Upon hearing it, Thugut displayed the same stoicism with which he had received so much bad news in the past. The reports of the young archduke must be overly pessimistic, he told Colloredo, which was not unusual for someone of his youth. Now was not the time to panic, he continued, but to call upon the deepest resources the monarchy possessed, specifically the Hungarian *insurrectio*, which had gathered and was encamped in western Hungary ready to go into combat.[67]

Thugut's call for further sacrifice now fell on deaf ears. For some time all except him had wished to end the struggle, even if it required major sacrifices, but he had kept many supporting the war simply by the dint of his own will. The defeat at Hohenlinden was the final blow. To Thugut it meant once again pulling the monarchy up from disappointment and pushing it back into the fight; to the others—including the emperor—it meant that the war must cease. As the first step toward that goal, on December 9 Francis appointed Archduke Charles once again commander in chief of the army in Germany. When the archduke reached headquarters on December 17, he conducted a quick inspection and found the army incapable of further resistance. The troops were exhausted, desertion was rife, supplies were short, the enemy was vastly superior, discipline had collapsed, and both officers and men had declared openly and loudly that they would fight no

[67] Thugut to Colloredo, December 9, 1800, in Vivenot, ed., *Vertrauliche Briefe*, 2:343–44.

more.[68] Without waiting for orders from Vienna, Archduke Charles arranged an armistice with Moreau (concluded at Steyr in Upper Austria on December 25) and brought it personally to the capital on December 27.

Thugut and his policy now faced utter rejection. Before Archduke Charles even reached Vienna, the emperor charged Thugut to compose a set of instructions ordering Cobenzl at Lunéville to plead with the French for an extended armistice and to offer terms for a separate Austro-French peace.[69] Thugut complied, but he considered the message a death knell not merely for his own policies but for the Habsburg system. "I have written with trembling hands," he lamented to Colloredo, "the unfortunate instructions that I have the honor of submitting to Your Excellency and which I regard as the epitaph of the monarchy and of the glory of Austria; but His Majesty has ordered it absolutely, and one cannot contest his right to dispose of the heritage of his ancestors as he sees fit!"[70]

His policy now renounced, Thugut's dismissal followed shortly. When Archduke Charles arrived in Vienna, he received a savior's welcome, for all classes and groups regarded him as the only hope for a respectable peace and for a secure future. Even had he wished to do so, the emperor could no longer resist the public's demand that the archduke assume the principal authority in the government. On January 9, 1801, the emperor promoted his brother to the rank of field marshal, appointed him head of the War Ministry, and in effect placed policy making in his hands. One of the archduke's first steps in his new position was to remove Thugut. On January 10 the emperor and the archduke informed Thugut jointly that they would tolerate "no obstacles to peace" and were placing Thugut's duties in the hands of Trauttmannsdorff, a man "of fam-

[68] Archduke Charles to Francis, December 19, 1800, in Hüffer, ed., *Quellen, 1800*, 490–92.

[69] Francis to L. Cobenzl, December 23, 1800, in Vivenot, ed., *Vertrauliche Briefe*, 2:473–76.

[70] Thugut to Colloredo, December 23, 1800, in ibid., 349.

ily and fashion, remarkable for politeness and for those talents that distinguish a man of the world in society and conversation"—qualities certainly unlike Thugut's.[71]

Five days later, on Friday, January 16, Colloredo in the emperor's name asked for Thugut's formal resignation "as minister of foreign affairs . . . because the opinion of all classes is that Your Excellency has delayed and will delay always the conclusion of peace and that you will always raise difficulties."[72] In reply Thugut reminded Colloredo that he had resigned that office on September 25, that it was unnecessary to do so again, and that now he wished only to be treated without disgrace. Colloredo answered that Thugut's resignation in September was only for the sake of form and that now the emperor demanded "not only the form but all that deals with the subject."[73] On the same day the emperor in a kind, considerate note likewise asked for the resignation, and Thugut submitted it immediately.[74] To Cobenzl Colloredo wrote, "As so often happens to the majority of good and honest servants, their zeal inspires jealousy, envy, and even hatred; such is the case now of Baron Thugut. For a long time people have complained about this minister; one blames him for all our misfortunes and the state in which we currently find ourselves."[75] Remarked Thugut upon the cause of his dismissal, "The public has now spoken."[76] The public demanded that he go.

[71] Minto to Grenville, January 11, 1801, in Minto, ed., *Life and Letters*, 3:186–87.

[72] Colloredo to Thugut, January 16, 1801, in Vivenot, ed., *Vertrauliche Briefe*, 2:365–66.

[73] Thugut to Colloredo and Colloredo to Thugut, January 16, 1801, in ibid., 366–67.

[74] Francis to Thugut and Thugut to Francis, January 16, 1801, in ibid., 67–68.

[75] Colloredo to L. Cobenzl, January 19, 1801, in ibid., 373.

[76] Thugut to Colloredo, January 20, 1801, in ibid., 374.

CHAPTER XIII

RETIREMENT,

1801–1818

DESPITE Thugut's second dismissal, he still did not disappear from the policy-making scene. He retained his post as director of the Italian provinces and as such occupied a desk in the chancellery. Moreover, he remained Colloredo's close associate and continued to offer advice about foreign affairs. But for the new men in power and for the observant public, that situation was intolerable. Indeed, after his resignation on January 16, the demands for his removal from office turned into cries for his departure from Vienna altogether, and the emperor and Colloredo felt the pressure. In refusing a request from Thugut to have an audience with Francis, Colloredo wrote, "Each time one sees you come to court or to me it is an occasion to spread rumors that Your Excellency still directs foreign policy, that you have the same influence, that you possess all the confidence of your sovereign, that he acts according to the advice you give him. People are again complaining about Your Excellency, claiming that you are the one delaying the conclusion of peace and that, as long as you are in Vienna, you will have access to His Majesty and things will remain the same."[1]

---

[1] Colloredo to Thugut, February 3, 1801, Vienna, HHSA, SK, *Intercepte*, 2.

In response to the complaints about his continued influence, Thugut pleaded that he was merely doing his job, that he was offering advice only when asked and then only appropriately in his capacity as director of Italian affairs. He told Colloredo that he would soon leave for Italy and suggested that the government publicize his intention, so that knowledge of his imminent departure would quiet the clamorings for his ejection from the capital.[2] But Thugut also expressed his belief that now something more sinister lurked behind the popular calls for his exile. He warned Colloredo that the public uproar was directed at more than merely him; it was in fact "the first step toward revolution." Neither Colloredo nor the emperor should accede to pressure, he warned, because "Each concession, each mark of weakness encourages the insolence and pretentions of the conjurers, far from putting an end or quieting them, and it is as we have seen Louis XVI . . . destroying himself little by little in ceding without end all of his authority and finishing by being the deplorable victim of his pliancy." Thugut suspected the principal conspirators behind this coming revolution to be Prince de Ligne, Prince Starhemberg, and the "center of all being Trauttmannsdorff."[3]

The charges were obviously the rantings of a tired, exasperated old man. No sensible person could have accused men like the three he named of plotting to undermine the emperor's authority. The problem had become not them but Thugut himself, and by now even his own friends and supporters recognized that. Of Thugut's increasingly pathetic character Wickham wrote, "He should have retired like a man. . . . Instead of this he now keeps hanging about the throne, whispering in the ear of the Emperor . . . which clogs and embarrasses his antagonists . . . and renders the Emperor unhappy and discontented."[4] Even Colloredo realized that Thugut had to go,

[2] Thugut to Colloredo, February 6, 1801, in Vivenot, ed., *Vertrauliche Briefe*, 2: 392–93.
[3] Thugut to Colloredo, February 9, 1801, in ibid., 396–98.
[4] Wickham to Grenville, February 9, 1801, in *Dropmore Papers*, 6: 439.

and he tried to encourage him to do so under the cloak of his Italian duties. But, when Thugut understood that Colloredo wished first and foremost to send him away from Vienna rather than to employ him actively in some other function, he obstinately refused to leave without a direct order from the emperor.[5] Since Thugut had now become an acute embarrassment to all concerned, the order was given. In a memorandum drafted by Colloredo, the emperor offered Thugut a post in Italy but made it absolutely clear that the appointment was only a device to remove him from Vienna. "If this position is not convenient to you, I will give you the choice of retiring entirely; but I must insist that you leave the capital. I must and I want to put an end to all these outbursts and reports against you, since I can no longer resist them."[6]

Faced with exile either to a meaningless post in Italy or to retirement away from the capital, Thugut chose the latter, citing for the decision his old reason of ill health.[7] But he did not leave right away, because he needed money for his retirement. In an extensive and mildly sarcastic letter, Thugut declared to the emperor that throughout his career as foreign minister he had always received less in salary than he truly deserved. Since the death of Kaunitz in 1794, he had earned thirty thousand florins annually—ten thousand of which was "table money" for purposes of entertainment that he could not pocket if it was not spent—and that sum was substantially less than the sixty-two thousand florins paid annually to Kaunitz when he was in charge of the chancellery. Since Thugut now wanted "to be assured of a generous subsistance that I can enjoy a little after so many privations and disappointments," he asked for an annual pension of twenty-four to twenty-five thousand florins, which some ministers in the government who "know such matters" assured him was "not too much." He proposed that

---

[5] Thugut to Colloredo, February 9, 1801, in Vivenot, ed., *Vertrauliche Briefe*, 2: 398–99.
[6] Francis to Thugut, February 9, 1801, in ibid., 400.
[7] Thugut to Francis, February 12, 1801, in ibid., 404–405.

the sums come from estates in Galicia, which the emperor might cede to him for life.[8]

The emperor and Colloredo readily agreed that a pension as high as thirty thousand florins was customary and acceptable for a man of Thugut's position and years of service, but it took some time to work out the details, time which Thugut spent in Vienna.[9] And while he stayed, agitation and speculation about his status and predicted departure intensified. On February 25 Maria Carolina, now herself in the city, wrote, "We hear that Thugut leaves the first days of March"; on February 27 she noted, "All Vienna guesses at the departure and future residence of Thugut"; on March 3, "People here are eager to see him leave, . . . some say for Cracow, some for Dalmatia, some for England, and some say he will stay"; on March 19, "Rumors are that Thugut is really gone"; and on March 20, "Here it is said that Thugut will leave shortly."[10] The longer the departure was delayed, the greater the popular concern that it would not occur at all. Wrote Colloredo in mid-March, "It passes all imagination . . . how much [Thugut] is hated; he will part in a few days; it remains to be seen if the scandal-mongers cease to howl."[11]

By the fourth week in March Thugut's pension had been arranged. He would receive thirty thousand florins annually, ten thousand from the treasury of the Italian lands, ten thousand from the chancellery, and ten thousand in income from the former holdings of the Rátkay family in the county of Varaždin in Croatia. The Italian portion of the grant would not be in the form of direct payments; instead the emperor would allow Thugut to borrow two hundred thousand from the Italian treasury interest-free so that he could purchase additional

[8] Thugut to Colloredo, February 12, 1801, in ibid., 402–404.

[9] Ibid., 405–406; Colloredo to Thugut, February 13, 1801, Vienna, HHSA, SK, *Intercepte*, 2.

[10] Maria Carolina to Gallo, February 25, 26, March 3, 19, and 20, 1801, in Maria Carolina, *Correspondance inédite*, 2: 199, 202, 207, 220, 222.

[11] Colloredo to L. Cobenzl, March (17–20?), 1801, in Vivenot, ed., *Vertrauliche Briefe*, 2: 426.

property in Hungary. The annual allotment of ten thousand from the Italian fund would then serve to retire that loan. All of the property purchased would revert to the state upon Thugut's death.[12] The pension finally settled, on March 27, eight years to the day that he assumed the office of foreign minister, Thugut was received by the emperor in a farewell audience. The two exchanged the appropriate pleasantries, after which Thugut took his leave. On March 31 he left Vienna for exile in Pressburg (Bratislava), the Habsburg capital of Hungary. Wrote Maria Carolina, "Thugut departs this morning for sure, and I believe that it will be forever."[13]

When he left Vienna at the end of March 1801, Thugut was sixty-five years old; he had served the monarchy for forty-seven years, eight of them as foreign minister, and he would never again hold an office in the Habsburg government. But his life was far from over. He would live for another seventeen years, and, although allowed to return to Vienna after 1805, he would maintain his home in Pressburg until his death. Initially he planned to remain in Pressburg for only a short time. In his first note from the city he wrote, "Pressburg does not seem to be a particularly attractive place, but the air seems good and with my books and maps I should be able to pass a few weeks pleasantly enough until the acquisition that I hope to make in the country is finished."[14] Two days later he reported that he had found suitable lodgings; "in truth it would have been hard to find a better place even in Vienna."[15]

Thugut had every intention of assuming the life of a Hungarian country squire. In addition to the land granted to him

[12] Francis to Thugut, March 23, 1801, in ibid., 430–32.
[13] Maria Carolina to Gallo, March 30, 1801, in Maria Carolina, *Correspondance inédite*, 2: 228–29.
[14] Thugut to unnamed correspondent (Colloredo), April 5, 1801, Vienna, HHSA, SK, *Grosse Korrespondenz*, 447.
[15] Thugut to unnamed correspondent (Colloredo), April 7, 1801, ibid. Wrote Colloredo, "Pressburg is assuredly not a city to find amusements, even less so to find a society, but lacking both, you will always find the way to occupy yourself with the present, past, and even future." Colloredo to Thugut, May 6, 1801, ibid., *Intercepte*, 2.

by the emperor, he purchased property in the vicinity of Nagy-Tabor near Varaždin, which would serve as a permanent rural residence. But he discovered that both the land granted to him by the emperor and the estate he had purchased had various liens and ownership claims against them, and, in pursuing his rights to those properties, he ran headlong into the labyrinth of Hungarian customary and local laws and the accompanying lawsuits and legal actions. In mid-July 1801 he wrote to a friend in Vienna that "my land of Nagy-Tabor is worth nothing; it is nothing but a source of disagreements and disputes." He declared that all sorts of laws prevented or circumscribed this or that action and use of the land and that he was currently engaged in litigation with "twenty families" about various matters. He requested his friend to see on his behalf some persons in Vienna "who know the affairs of this country to the depths" and who could advise him about his problems.[16] By the spring of 1802 he had abandoned the idea of actually moving to his country property but intended to visit it to assess personally "my mélange of possessions that make my land a storehouse of perpetual legal obstacles."[17] In the ensuing summer he made the journey to Nagy-Tabor, and, if he still harbored any thoughts of living there, they were quickly dispelled by what he saw. "I will pass only two or three weeks at the most [on this land]," he wrote from Varaždin, "because of all the inconveniences; it is entirely isolated in the middle of the mountains, ten or twelve hours from Agram [Zagreb] by frightful roads, and without access to physician, surgeon, or pharmacist in case of illness or accident."[18]

One might think that this unpromising property would prompt Thugut to ask the emperor for another source of income on the grounds that possession of the Hungarian estate would cost too much money, effort, and time in litigation. But, as we have seen, Thugut was not one to quit when confronted

[16] Thugut to unnamed correspondent (Jenisch?), July 19, 1801, ibid., *Grosse Korrespondenz*, 447.

[17] Thugut to unnamed correspondent (Jenisch?), March 7, 1802, ibid.

[18] Thugut to unnamed correspondent (Jenisch?), June 22, 1802, ibid.

by a challenge. He forged ahead against Hungarian law and Hungarian lawyers with the same determination and persistence as he had struggled against revolutionary France. In late 1802 he wrote to Dietrichstein, "I have worked much to disentangle the chaos of my petty affairs. You wonder, I am sure, why I spend so much time on such mediocre business, but my dear count, not everyone is a rich grand seigneur like yourself."[19] Two years later he was no closer to resolving his legal problems but still as dogged (and perhaps angrier) about pursuing them as he had been before, willing by now to press his case even after his own death. "I never do anything halfway," he wrote to Colloredo. "I am resolved to surmount this disgusting mound of procedures, and I am not going to relax my pursuits against them until I breathe my last; and, if I should die before the complete resolution of this whole affair, I have decided to leave in my will the money necessary to continue the proceedings until these usurpers are forced to disgorge my possessions that they are holding against the clear and manifest tenor of the law."[20] Thugut had obviously lost none of the grit that had characterized him in the past.

Notwithstanding his legal battles and his seclusion from the excitement of Vienna, Thugut did not find retirement in Pressburg unusually burdensome. The first change that he noted in his new life was the opportunity that it afforded him to rest: "I have now returned to my old habit of sleeping nine hours a night of tranquil slumber."[21] He spent much time and some money adding to his collection of maps and books, mostly on subjects dealing with the Ottoman Empire and the French Revolution. He also enjoyed visitors. In contrast to the cold receptions that he had offered guests when serving as foreign minister, the welcomes in Pressburg were warm and enthusiastic and he tried to keep friends with him as long as possible. Describing a visit in mid-1802, Hammer wrote, "The reception by this minister in disgrace was far different from

[19] Thugut to Dietrichstein, September 14, 1802, ibid.
[20] Thugut to Colloredo, November 3, 1804, ibid.
[21] Thugut to Colloredo, April 5, 1801, ibid.

the one by the minister in office. . . . After dinner we walked for hours up and down in his room while he made me tell him about Constantinople, Egypt, and England. We ate around 1:00 P.M., then we walked and talked for six straight hours without a break until 9:00 P.M. I was astonished at the heartiness of this sixty-year-old; exhaustion overcame me, and I sank more dead than alive into the carriage."[22]

Thugut of course complained repeatedly of his weak constitution, but one fact noticed by all who visited him in the first years of his retirement was his apparent good health. In the autumn of 1801 Lord Minto, prior to his departure from Austria following his recall as British ambassador, went to Pressburg to bid Thugut farewell. To his wife he reported: "He came to me between nine and ten, and I never saw him so blooming and beautiful. Retirement certainly agrees with his health, and indeed with his spirits."[23] Two years later Johannes von Müller related, "I again visited Baron Thugut in Pressburg and was quite pleased with the fatherly reception, the touching farewell, and the repeated invitations [to come back to see him]. He lives alone, but has many visitors, is quite contented, looks healthy, and leaves to Providence what he cannot change."[24]

His social life consisted primarily of receiving guests from Vienna rather than making the rounds of the local aristocracy. Minto described Thugut's social surroundings as uninspiring. "His society consists of four emigrants. There are a few families in the country, but they live like rustics—dine at twelve, play at ombre with pipes in their mouths, and go to bed at eight o'clock."[25] The major social and political event in Pressburg was the meeting of the Hungarian Diet, the periodic gathering of the great noblemen and county representatives to

[22] Hammer, *Erinnerungen*, 132.

[23] Minto to Lady Minto, September 29, 1801, in Minto, ed., *Life and Letters*, 3: 222.

[24] Quoted in Hüffer, *Österreich und Preussen*, 289–90.

[25] Minto to Lady Minto, September 29, 1801, in Minto, ed., *Life and Letters*, 3: 223.

discuss issues with the emperor/king and his delegates. When the Diet met, local inhabitants had to provide housing for the members, either by turning their homes over to them completely or by lodging them within their own households for the duration of the session. Thugut was not exempt from this requirement. In 1802 he had to vacate his residence and seek shelter at the palace of the brilliant Esterhazy family, and in 1805 he had to take in some deputies as boarders. He hated not only the inconvenience but also the tumult caused by the presence of these fellows. "At first I resolved not to live in Pressburg during the Diet," he wrote to Colloredo in 1805, "aside from other reasons because I just cannot stand living in the middle of the brouhaha of all these gentlemen." He decided to stay at least for a time, however, not only as a sign of good will but also "in order to give one or two dinners for the Croatian deputies" in hopes that they might use a bit of influence on his behalf in his ongoing legal battles.[26] In general Thugut disliked Hungarians, their rowdy ways, their convoluted legal system, and their arrogant conservatism.

Despite Thugut's exile, contemporary political observers still wondered whether or not he continued to influence Austrian foreign policy. Many thought that he did. In the summer of 1801 a special Russian envoy from the new tsar, Alexander I, spoke of improving Austro-Russian relations but also expressed his sovereign's concern that Thugut was still a power behind the scene. "I cannot deny to you," he told Colloredo, "that I have been authorized, nay ordered to tell you that we fear Pressburg. . . . This may be only prejudice, but it exists and can do much damage."[27] In his instructions for the first French envoy to Vienna following the Treaty of Lunéville, Talleyrand ordered his representative to discover who in the government had influence. "We are assured from many quarters that Thugut, while appearing to be far from affairs, continues secretly to direct them and that, if all affections of the

[26] Thugut to Colloredo, September 9, 1805, Vienna, HHSA, SK, *Grosse Korrespondenz*, 447.
[27] Quoted in Criste, *Erzherzog Carl*, 2: 329.

country are directed toward Archduke Charles, the intimate confidence of the emperor always rests with this disgraced minister."[28] Bonaparte himself summarized the suspicions of many when, according to Eleonore Liechtenstein, he inquired of an Austrian officer how far Pressburg was from Vienna. When asked why he wished to know, Bonaparte replied simply, "Why, Monsieur Thugut lives there."[29]

The suspicions of both Austrian and foreign observers that Thugut still directed policy were based to some extent on a not-so-secret correspondence that Thugut and Colloredo continued after the former's retirement. Since Colloredo had been Thugut's patron earlier and continued to be the emperor's favorite despite the ascendancy of Archduke Charles, many assumed that Thugut was steering Habsburg foreign affairs through Colloredo. The correspondence itself reveals, however, that such suspicions were groundless. Colloredo's letters contain mostly gossip, news of business within the government, and complaints that Thugut's exile and the rise to power of his foes had resulted only in more indecision on the part of the emperor and in growing aimlessness in governmental affairs.[30] At times Colloredo asked for advice on personnel matters but rarely on actual decisions affecting Austrian policy. In fact, a common subject in Colloredo's letters was the rumor circulating that Thugut was still manipulating affairs. Not only was such talk rampant, he wrote on one occasion, but he even suspected the *cabal des malintentionnés*—Archduke Charles, Trauttmannsdorff, and others—of keeping such rumors before the public not only to disgrace Thugut's name but also to discredit Louis Cobenzl and Colloredo himself.[31]

Thugut on his part responded to Colloredo's letters mostly with encouragement to continue to do what he believed was right for the monarchy and with admonitions to rely for de-

[28] Talleyrand to Champagny, August 16, 1801, in ibid., 2: 503–504.
[29] Criste, *Erzherzog Carl*, 2: 230.
[30] Colloredo's letters can be found in Vienna, HHSA, SK, *Intercepte*, 2, and *Grosse Korrespondenz*, 447.
[31] Colloredo to Thugut, May 14, 1801, ibid., *Grosse Korrespondenz*, 447.

tailed advice on Thugut's old associates, Louis Cobenzl, Dietrichstein, and Louis Starhemberg. Thugut emphasized that he had no regret about the policies that he followed as foreign minister, but he made it equally clear that he would not return to any office even if his supporters regained the upper hand in Vienna.[32] "The disgust and discouragement inspired in me by all that I had seen and experienced and the gradual deterioration of my health have made me devoted to retirement, and I will never again participate in affairs in any way whatsoever."[33] He meant that in an official capacity; if asked, he was always willing to express his views on affairs and policy.

As long as the peace party dominated the government, Thugut could not have returned to office even if he wanted to, but in 1804 the peace party gave way as the actions of Bonaparte—after May 18, 1804, Napoleon I, emperor of the French—became increasingly threatening even to those who wished to avoid conflict. Between 1802 and 1804 the adjustments of possessions in Germany and Italy under Bonaparte's auspices not only had created new boundaries and new states but also had placed most of Europe at his mercy. Differences in policy and additional acts of French arrogance had caused a resumption of hostilities between France and Britain (Britain had concluded peace with France in March 1802), and the Russia of Alexander I was becoming increasingly concerned about future French aggression. In 1804 both Russia and Britain appealed to Austria to form yet another coalition against France.

With a new European struggle in the offing, Colloredo turned to Thugut and asked him specifically whether or not Austria should join the alliance. Given his previous policies, one would assume that Thugut would have favored it. After

---

[32] "I did nothing during my ministry without the personal conviction that it was good for the service, for the glory of His Majesty and his monarchy in order to defeat the evil that menaced us." Thugut to Colloredo, n.d., 1802, in Vivenot, ed., *Thugut, Clerfayt und Wurmser*, xxxvi.

[33] Thugut to Dietrichstein, March 1, 1802, Vienna, HHSA, SK, *Grosse Korrespondenz*, 447.

all, France was now clearly a greater threat than ever to the existence of the remaining independent states of Europe, including the Habsburg Monarchy. Moreover, Britain was again committed to war, and Russia soon would be, a Russia no longer ruled by the "completely demented" Paul but by Alexander, who, possessing "the genius and energy of the great Catherine," would probably battle the French with far more dedication than his father had done.[34] Austria thus could join the struggle confident of the support and aid of loyal and determined allies.

Nevertheless, in four long letters composed from November 1804 to April 1805, Thugut argued strongly against resuming hostilities with France. The reason for the turnabout in Thugut's thinking was his view that the European situation had changed markedly from earlier days when he was leading the Habsburg cause. It had changed because of the will of one man, Napoleon himself, called now by Thugut interchangeably the "new Charlemagne" or the "new Tamurlane." Napoleon, Thugut argued, had placed the resources of Europe at his disposal. "This immense mass, composed of the most essential countries of Europe in the hand of such an able man . . . provides this usurper with the means more than sufficient to rule the world." In achieving this feat, Thugut went on, Napoleon "has encircled the pope, the college of cardinals, the electors and princes of Germany, emptied the courts [Holy Roman Empire] of their proper chief in order to augment his following . . . and has forced the art, talent, and energy [of the continent] to make possible his personal elevation, to extend his dominion over other sovereigns, and to double or triple the power of France."[35]

In its present state, Austria could not resist such a man and such a force. Perhaps it would never be able to resist because, Thugut insisted, as France was an ascending power, so was Austria a declining one. "It is true that monarchies have their

[34] Thugut to unnamed correspondent (Dietrichstein), April 14, 1805, and Thugut to Colloredo, December 27, 1804, ibid.
[35] Thugut to Colloredo, December 26, 1804, and April 14, 1805, ibid.

youth and old age just as men do, and a man who has reached, or who at least I think has reached, ninety years old, has scarcely any other prospect than to vegetate quietly for a few months more." Pursuing this anthropomorphic analogy, Thugut continued, "When one man always goes forward reluctantly while another gallops, the distance between them must soon become insurmountable," and that was the case between Austria and France. In fact, Austria in his view was descending to the rank of powers "like Spain or Turkey." "I have always nourished the idea that Austria might become the first power of the world; it is difficult to contain my sorrow at seeing what we are and will become in the future."[36]

But Thugut did not advise the monarchy simply to resign itself to inevitable decay. Since the future was uncertain, he implored the government to prepare for whatever might come by instituting reforms, especially in the area of finances. Indeed, in these four letters Thugut was fairly obsessed with finances, in part no doubt because of the difficulties Austria had with them during his days in power but also because of the serious inflation that was gripping the monarchy by 1804. Despite the issue of large amounts of paper currency and the mounting deficits during the 1790s, the financial system of Austria   except for the run on the Viennese banks in 1797— had remained quite stable. The quantity of paper money poured into the economy had not caused the serious inflation that it should have, because during the war years merchants and vendors accepted the currency largely at face value.[37] The confidence in the currency along with good harvests kept prices of food and other products fairly stable throughout the period, which not only maintained the monarchy's financial

[36] Thugut to Colloredo, December 26, 1804, March 3 and April 14, 1805, ibid.

[37] Mayr, *Wien*, 44. In his recent study, John Komlos describes the years 1795–1800 as a boom period for the Austrian economy because the abundance of money and low inflation inspired many people to invest in business enterprises. John Komlos, *The Habsburg Monarchy as a Customs Union: Economic Development in Austria-Hungary in the Nineteenth Century* (Princeton, 1983), 188.

system but helped to preserve social and economic peace as well. By 1801, however, confidence in the money was eroding, and inflation was becoming serious. By 1803 prices in Vienna ranged from three to four times what they had been in 1790, and Thugut himself wrote, "For the three years I have been in Pressburg, all the prices have doubled and a few have even tripled."[38] True to form, Thugut acknowledged many factors in undermining the value of currency (none of which, however, he thought could be attributed to his policies during the war), but he placed most of the blame squarely on "the conduct of our officials in the Finance Ministry."[39] Remedying Austria's financial troubles he regarded as the first step in preparing for whatever the future held. He offered no specific suggestions to achieve monetary stability, but he did advise against raising taxes, which "will only cause discouragement, inflation, and not solve anything."[40]

Thugut may have been advocating peace and reform, but his former colleagues, especially Colloredo and Louis Cobenzl, were inclining toward war. It was not a decision to be taken lightly, however, and as part of their deliberations, in May 1805 they invited Thugut to visit not only Vienna but the chancellery and the emperor to offer his views in person. It was Thugut's first return to the capital since his exile four years earlier. The meeting with Colloredo was recorded by the cabinet minister himself, who noted that Thugut expressed his contentment to be "so far from affairs" but at the same time seemed "very well informed of all that was happening." Apparently Colloredo told Thugut of Austria's inclination toward war and of a preliminary alliance concluded with Russia in November 1804, because the interview focused not on whether to make war but on steps to be taken when war actually began. Thugut apparently did not openly advise against

---

[38] Mayr, *Wien*, 189; Thugut to Colloredo, November 3, 1804, Vienna, HHSA, SK, *Grosse Korrespondenz*, 447.

[39] Thugut to Colloredo, November 3, 1804, Vienna, HHSA, SK, *Grosse Korrespondenz*, 447.

[40] Ibid.

hostilities, as he had done in his earlier letters, but he did repeat his warnings to use care and circumspection in the approaching conflict. He offered one piece of specific advice: have Napoleon murdered. He was the only force holding France together, Thugut told Colloredo, and at his death the country would come apart internally. It was an interesting idea, but Colloredo dismissed it as eccentric. At the conclusion of his meeting with Colloredo, Thugut had an audience with the emperor. He told Colloredo that Francis was most gracious and had granted his request to be allowed to come often to the capital. "The emperor said that it would pose no difficulties and added laughingly that Bonaparte had told him that if he [Thugut] were ever employed in the ministry again, he would regard it as a declaration of war and would march to the walls of Vienna."[41]

Not long after, Louis Cobenzl and Colloredo, joined by the newly favored General Mack and Matthias Fassbender, convinced the emperor, over the objections of Archduke Charles, to declare war on France.[42] As the commitment was made and preparations begun, memories of old struggles and the prospect of a new one seemed to bring Thugut's blood up. "It is impossible to convince me that [the war] must be necessarily bad," he wrote in September 1805. "I am persuaded to the contrary that we possess the required means to render it advantageous, to restore the old splendor of Austria providing everyone in good faith resolves to keep foremost in his mind the salvation and interests of the monarch and abjure all other concerns." It was the Thugut of old. If everyone showed determination, courage, and sense of duty, all would come out well.[43] But Thugut had no illusions about the risks Vienna was running. If defeated on the battlefield, the monarchy could

[41] Colloredo's report of the interview with Thugut, c. May 18, 1805, Vienna, HHSA, *Kaiser Franz Akten*, 78b (81).

[42] Adolf Beer, *Zehn Jahre österreichischer Politik, 1801–1810* (Leipzig, 1877), 106.

[43] Thugut to Colloredo, September 1, 1805, Vienna, HHSA, SK, *Grosse Korrespondenz*, 447.

face severe retribution, perhaps even extinction. Even if victorious, Austria might only harm France momentarily and be subjected to a greater onslaught later on. "It seems that this war will be very difficult, that one can fear a complete defeat without hoping for a great victory or being able to do any damage to France." But the decision was made, and it was time to fight. "We have poured the wine; now we must drink it."[44]

The war was short and devastating for Austria. On November 12 French troops entered Vienna for the first time as they marched toward the main force of Austrians and Russians gathering in Moravia, where on December 2 they would win for Napoleon his most famous victory at Austerlitz near Brno (Brünn). Austria was finished. Colloredo and Cobenzl resigned, which solidified again the position of Archduke Charles. Johann Philipp Stadion, a man with no affinity for and little association with Thugut, became minister of foreign affairs.

After the war of 1805 the remaining correspondence of Thugut in the archives is thin indeed. In part, he had little motive to write because his old colleagues were no longer in power, but in addition, he was finding the physical act of writing increasingly arduous. On one occasion he complained that his hand "bothers me always more when it is hot, and it now requires the same amount of time for me to write a line as it formerly did to write a page."[45] He frequently complained about the unsteadiness of his hand and admitted that "my hand shakes to the point that, except for two or three hours a day, I cannot hold a pen."[46] Although his handwriting still appears strong in the first few years after his retirement, those letters remaining after 1805 clearly show a deterioration in its firmness.

Perhaps another reason for the decreasing volume of letters

[44] Thugut to Colloredo, September 23, 1805, ibid.
[45] Thugut to unnamed correspondent (Jenisch?), June 12, 1802, ibid.
[46] Thugut to unnamed correspondent (Jenisch?), July 31, 1802, ibid.

is that after 1805 Thugut was permitted to live in Vienna.[47] He maintained his residence in Pressburg but spent most of his time in the capital, where a small number of friends gathered regularly at his home to discuss affairs and culture. Hammer described Thugut's society in these years, noting that one regular guest, a Count Bentzel, was a known police agent invited by Thugut as a means to "quash unfounded rumors." As for himself, Hammer wrote, "Bentzel's presence inspired me to an even freer speech, and I talked of things I wanted the police to know." Thugut, he noted, "never discussed politics without a satirical smile."[48] Vehse described the aging Thugut and his friends in a more playful manner: "The discussion, at first very spirited, would slacken by degrees, until it died away altogether. Soon the company fell asleep, the master of the house last. About the hour when the theater in the Leopold Stadt [sic] began, the valet purposely slammed the door so as to awaken them; and then all went to be amused with the coarse ribaldry and the broad jokes of Casperl, the Vienna impersonation of Mr. Merryman."[49]

In 1809 Austria rose again against Napoleon, this time unexpectedly led by Archduke Charles and Stadion and without the support of allies. When hostilities began, Thugut expressed his wonder that the old critics of his war policy would now call for renewing the struggle, even if it meant fighting alone. "When I wanted war," he wrote at the outset, "we had allies and prospects of having more of them. Now one heads for the battlefield without allies, without hope of having any,

---

[47] Even after 1805 rumors persisted that Thugut was still a man of power. On January 11, 1806, Archduke Charles wrote from Pressburg, "I have found here people alarmed by the influence of [Anton] Baldacci. Since he is the natural son of Balassa, they expect Thugut returned to power." Archduke Charles to Duke Albert, January 11, 1806, in Criste, *Erzherzog Carl*, 2: 606–607. A French agent wrote in March 1806, "True power in the government rests not in the hands of the ministers but in those of Thugut, Colloredo, and Abbé Langenau." Quoted in Criste, *Erzherzog Carl*, 2: 415.

[48] Hammer, *Erinnerungen*, 174–75.

[49] Vehse, *Memoirs*, 2: 399–400.

and in the wake of a most unfortunate war. My Lord, that is a boldness that I was never capable of. These responsibilities would make me shudder, although I am certainly stiff-necked enough."[50] The result was the same as before: Austria suffered defeat and the French occupied Vienna once again.

This time Napoleon personally took up residence near Vienna, at the magnificent Habsburg summer palace at Schönbrunn, and it was here that he met his old antagonist Thugut for the first and only time.[51] Napoleon desired the meeting, but, given his status as arbiter of Europe, protocol dictated that Thugut request it. Despite encouragement from French officials, Thugut refused to submit the appropriate petition, declaring that he had simply nothing to say to the French emperor. Finally, on October 15, 1809, Napoleon's secretary of state, Hugues-Bernard Maret, called at Thugut's house and told him that Napoleon definitely wished to meet "the man with whom he had made war." Thugut responded that if the invitation was an order, he was prepared to obey, but otherwise he could see no point to the audience. " 'Good,' responded Maret, 'Let's go now. The emperor wants to speak to you before the opera, where he is going today since he has decided to leave tomorrow.' The baron objected that he was not dressed. The minister said, 'Get your wallet and your sword, and we can be at Schönbrunn just after 7:00.' "

Thugut arrived on time and was ushered immediately into the presence of the French emperor. The meeting lasted for approximately one hour, during which Napoleon discoursed on various subjects including the wars he had fought and his hopes now to live in peace with the Habsburgs, all the while "saying flattering things to the baron." As for Thugut's reaction, the secretary's account read that "Baron Thugut seemed to doubt these assertions and to wonder at the words and ramblings of the conversation, which became long and in which

[50] Quoted in Criste, *Erzherzog Carl*, 2: 457.

[51] The background and story of this interview are told by a secretary of Napoleon in a document dated October 16, 1809, Vienna, HHSA, *Kaiser Franz Akten* 78e (85).

the emperor spoke a lot and almost always by himself." Although there was some fanciful speculation that at this meeting Napoleon offered to entrust the Austrian government to Thugut, the secretary wrote that Napoleon's "purpose . . . was only a matter of curiosity, to make the baron's acquaintance, and to let him tell the actual ministers, if he wanted to, what the views and intentions of the French emperor were, that he was a friend and wanted to live in peace." The secretary also noted that Thugut "did not seem persuaded by all that he heard."[52]

The following day Thugut composed his own impression of the meeting, which he forwarded to Francis. Unfortunately it is a rather dry account, explaining the circumstances behind the audience and passing on Napoleon's expressions of peace and friendship. It contains no judgment of the expressions and no evaluation of Napoleon's appearance or personality.[53] As unrevealing as the account was, it impressed Francis and his advisers sufficiently to send a minister to Thugut to ask if he thought the monarchy should accept the terms of the Treaty of Schönbrunn, concluded between Austria and France on October 14. According to Gentz, "Thugut told him that the only surprising thing was that one would be able to waver an instant before accepting Bonaparte's conditions." If Napoleon suddenly retracted them and renewed the war, "The emperor would be left without a village."[54] The treaty was accepted.

Records for the last few years of Thugut's life are spotty. During the Congress of Vienna in 1814, he held a salon at his home about which police agents reported to their headquarters.[55] The reports reveal a gathering of cynical, older men who exercised their wit at the expense of the congress's dele-

[52] Hammer believed Napoleon had offered Thugut a ministry, and that he had refused it. Hammer, *Erinnerungen*, 404.

[53] Thugut to Francis, October 15, 1809, Vienna, HHSA, *Kaiser Franz Akten*, 78e (85).

[54] Friedrich von Gentz, *Tagebücher* (Leipzig, 1873), 1: 205.

[55] August Fournier, *Die Geheimpolizei auf dem Wiener Kongress* (Vienna/Leipzig, 1913), 77, 252.

gates and their deliberations. The emperor, however, still regarded Thugut as a worthy adviser and frequently sent one of his associates, Count Wilhelm Sickingen, to ask Thugut for counsel. In one matter that counsel may have been of considerable importance for the later history of the Habsburg Monarchy. In October 1814 several influential men—notably Stadion, Starhemberg, Schwarzenberg, and Colloredo—opposed Metternich's willingness to sacrifice part of Saxony to Prussia in exchange for Prussian support in restricting Russian aspirations in Poland. They also suggested that Metternich be asked to resign should he persist in that policy. The emperor asked Thugut for his judgment in the matter, and Thugut replied that Francis should endorse Metternich's stand largely because Metternich was the best man to guide Austrian foreign affairs. The only person qualified to replace Metternich was Stadion, and in Thugut's opinion he was "well below Metternich in talent." Francis accepted Thugut's advice, and Metternich remained in power.[56]

Thugut's endorsement of Metternich might have well reflected his satisfaction with Metternich's accomplishments, because they in fact vindicated Thugut's policies of the 1790s. Like Thugut, Metternich had learned that Napoleonic France was insatiable, that it would in the end accept nothing less than hegemony in Europe. Therefore, it had to be defeated, and that defeat had to be the joint effort of the traditional monarchies. Because a united effort alone would succeed, the Habsburg foreign minister had to concentrate his attention on reconciling the differences among the allies while being careful not to sacrifice the interests of the monarchy within the coalition. Moreover, Metternich understood the need to restore France to a position of respectability because, like Thugut, he understood that the future of Austria depended upon stability and mutual regard among the great powers. Metternich's policy reminded Thugut of his own, and, although he had failed

---

[56] Enno Kraehe, *Metternich's German Policy. Volume II: The Congress of Vienna, 1814–1815* (Princeton, 1983), 225.

Clemens Wenzel von Metternich-Winneburg
(Courtesy Bildarchiv, Austrian National Library)

in his effort, he must have taken considerable satisfaction in Metternich's success.

Following the Congress of Vienna, Thugut lived but three more years. He died on May 28, 1818, of unknown causes but probably of old age, being eighty-two at the time. He had no direct heirs, and it had been arranged earlier that his property would revert to the state upon his passing. Since most of his papers and personal property from his days as foreign minister were still in Pressburg, Metternich dispatched an official named Brettfeld to his home with orders to evaluate Thugut's possessions and to classify his materials.[57] Brettfeld found numerous old papers of little importance. He examined Thugut's library, "not large but containing many interesting historical, statistical, philological, and diplomatic books dealing especially with the Orient," and otherwise discovered of value only "three or four pieces of furniture that may be worth something" and "a considerable collection of silver [largely table services and lamps], most in an old-fashioned, massive style." The list certainly did not reflect the possessions of a rich or avaricious man, but those of a somewhat disorderly bachelor of an intellectual bent.

Thugut's old friend Dietrichstein took charge of his remains and arranged for their interment in his ancestral burial ground near Nikolsburg (Mikulov) in Moravia. He also wrote the obituary that appeared in the *Österreichischer Beobachter*, the official newspaper of the foreign ministry, on September 5, 1818. Dietrichstein admitted that Thugut never achieved two great dreams of those involved in politics, popularity and success, but that he was not without dedication and honor. The outstanding characteristic of Thugut, in Dietrichstein's view, had been the dogged pursuit of specific goals in foreign policy even in the face of disaster and to the exclusion of all personal considerations. After reciting a brief history of his life the obituary concluded:

[57] Metternich to Brettfeld, May 29, 1818, Vienna, HHSA, SK, *Grosse Korrespondenz*, 447.

Thugut's great qualities will be worthy of history. All who knew him, especially those who worked with him, witnessed an inexhaustible zealousness, the most vigorous application to the business of state entrusted to him as well as the various affairs connected to it, and a sense of duty that made him unsusceptible to any affairs not connected to his work that might promote his own interest. . . . Those who are called upon to explain the history of his times to the world to come will learn how to present truthfully and honorably the problems he had to solve, the difficulties with which he had to struggle, the goals that danced before him, and his perseverence when his efforts to achieve great and worthy results were not crowned with success.[58]

[58] *Österreichischer Beobachter*, September 5, 1818, p. 1306.

CONCLUSION

IN THE HISTORY of Habsburg foreign policy, Thugut pales in renown beside his illustrious predecessor Kaunitz and his equally notable successor Metternich. Reasons are easy to find. Thugut served as foreign minister for only eight years compared to Kaunitz's forty-one and Metternich's thirty-eight, and, unlike the other two, he did not symbolize an age. Moreover, Thugut introduced no great innovations in policy that historians would consider significant; he effected no diplomatic revolution as Kaunitz did and created no Concert of Europe as Metternich did. Most importantly, Thugut lacked the success achieved by the other two. His overriding goal was the defeat of revolutionary France, and that goal he failed to reach. Indeed, his years as foreign minister witnessed the victory of the very power he sought to defeat, and nothing could be more detrimental to a statesman's fame than that.

But Thugut cannot simply be scorned as a failure, nor can he be dismissed as merely the proponent of an outdated eighteenth-century diplomacy that the revolution had made obsolete. Thugut saw indeed that the new France was bringing social and political upheaval to Europe, and early on he realized that Europe's traditional powers had to resist it with armed force. He perceived that the threat to the well-being of the continent was not revolution as such—not the ideas, doctrines, or teachings revolutionary figures espoused—but the momentum that the revolution provided for the reemergence of France as the preponderant power in Europe.

It was the new France that he identified as the true danger, and he knew it to be a France that had somehow harnessed great new energy. By all previous measures, France should have been weak: the state was beset by economic, social, and political ills and led by governments that changed frequently and unpredictably in both structure and personnel. Yet this same France created armed forces of enormous size and brought forth commanders of remarkable ability, which together inflicted defeat after defeat upon the grand old European armies, especially that of the Habsburgs. What made the French especially frightening for Thugut was that there seemed no way to stop them. The army struggled year after year against the new French forces, but its victories were too few and its losses too great. And concluding peace was no more effective in stopping the French than prosecuting the war. As time went on and misfortunes mounted, a growing chorus insisted that peace alone would satisfy the French and preserve the monarchy from disaster, a chorus that Thugut resisted by arguing that the French would not honor a peace anyway. Events proved him right. After each solemn treaty, the French altered the terms, invaded new territories, and behaved generally in a way that showed that no lasting settlement was possible with them.

Thugut's duty, as he saw it, was to defend Austria and the remainder of monarchical Europe by military means, and he approached the duty by forging alliances with the other great powers, by soliciting the lesser powers to join in the effort, and by encouraging his own state to continue the struggle—the last a task he found as formidable as recruiting and maintaining allies. He encountered so much resistance in the Habsburg government to his policies that at times the war party in Vienna seemed to consist of Thugut and no one else. Moreover, in his struggle to muster support for his policies, he resorted to new techniques that he did not understand well, such as appealing to public opinion or calling for a levée en masse. Nevertheless, he persisted because he believed that the result he sought was worth any effort necessary.

He envisioned the end of the struggle in much the same way Metternich would later: the restoration of a moderate France within a European equilibrium. By that Thugut did not mean the restoration of the ancien régime. He knew that the French Revolution was no passing fancy and that conditions before 1789 could not be recreated. He did not advocate restoring the Bourbons since that would be tantamount to resurrecting the causes of the French Revolution. Thugut believed that a reasonable, moderate, and orderly France would emerge only when its government reflected the reasonable, moderate, and orderly elements in French society. But he had no clear idea of what those elements were, when they would emerge, or how to encourage them. He did know, however, that as long as France was beset by revolutionary enthusiasm and its accompanying expansionism, the war must go on.

Thugut in the end failed to curb revolutionary France and to restore the political balance in Europe. To a great extent the failure was not his fault. The key to his policy's success was the army, and the Habsburg army of the 1790s was not up to the role that Thugut had chosen for it. It faced young, aggressive enemy officers, commanding huge forces that were able to cross vast distances at remarkable speeds, to fight in any season, and to remain undiscouraged by defeat. Such radical innovations in military affairs the Habsburg forces—and all of the other traditional armies in the 1790s—were unable to adjust to quickly. Moreover, Austria's military leadership, especially its dominant commander Archduke Charles, openly opposed Thugut's policies much of the time. The very instrument upon which Thugut relied to achieve his goals frequently resisted both him and his efforts.

Just as the army failed to fulfill the mission Thugut assigned to it, so too the assiduously recruited allies proved unreliable. Whereas openly they espoused the need to curb revolutionary France, they were often so attuned to their own interests, advantages, prejudices, and sensibilities that they could not contribute effectively to the cause they self-righteously proclaimed. Ironically, the Prussians, Russians, and British frequently speculated that Austria was on the verge of reaching a separate agreement with France. All failed to notice not only that Austria was the linchpin of the alliance—and the state with the most to lose—but also that Austria steadfastly resisted an accommodation until the enemy armies were practically at its capital. After 1795 neither the British on their island nor the Russians in their remote vastness appreciated the risks that Austria was taking in the name of allied unity. Throughout Thugut's tenure, the allies were too petulant (Britain), too greedy (Prussia), too isolated (Russia), too faint-hearted (the German and Italian states), or too weak (Spain) to be of much help to the Austrians. Not until 1812–1814, after years of French domination and intimidation, would these same powers realize the need for the kind of cooperation that Thugut was trying to impress upon them earlier.

One cannot, however, place the blame for Thugut's lack of success on others. No statesman can escape responsibility altogether for the failure of his policies, and one can find much for which to fault Thugut. His expectations were too high. He expected of his country a heroic role in the struggle against revolutionary France that it could not then assume. He expected the Habsburg generals to succeed against the new and powerful French military forces, but he did not comprehend how difficult a task that would be. He expected the Austrian state to find the material resources to carry on the fight year after year, but he could not grasp that the structure and personnel of the government made such a challenge impossible to meet. And he expected the other leaders of traditional Europe to be as cognizant as he of the threat that they faced, but he did not appreciate how often they needed to be reminded of their common goal.

To a great extent, he harbored such high expectations of others not only because he thought the cause so important but also because he placed great demands on himself. The determination, stubbornness, and dedication that he displayed and that he believed others should display could be attributed to his most striking conviction: that men were responsible for their own destinies and for the destinies of the agencies they served. This belief may have been a legacy of his birth as a commoner and his subsequent rise by virtue of talent through the Habsburg foreign service. Although he did not express it in writing, the lifelong experience of his own advancement may have convinced him that men have it within themselves to surmount any obstacles in the path of the goals they wish to reach. Whatever the source of his belief, Thugut assumed that application, determination, and relentless work could overcome the worst adversities. Any reverse or hindrance—military defeat, financial failure, administrative delay—he usually blamed on the lack of will, incompetence, mistaken judgment, or treachery of individuals rather than on conditions beyond their control. In the face of misfortune, the solutions he recommended involved either more rigorous application by the persons responsible or their replacement by others. Indeed, that he kept Austria in the war for so long and through such sacrifices was a remarkable feat in itself.

As steadfast and willful as he was, perhaps his greatest failing was his own suspiciousness of others and the corresponding reluctance to reveal too much of himself. By withdrawing so completely into his work, he not only fed the widespread mistrust toward him but deprived himself of the opportunity to remove or at least to temper that mistrust. One might again attribute this withdrawal to an insecurity brought on by his origins. He was, after all, a commoner in an aristocratic world, a quality noted ever more pointedly by others as Austria's difficulties mounted. One might also attribute his retreat from society to his uncertainty about how to deal with an aroused public, whether in the salon or in the street. In either case, by closing himself to others, he encouraged the suspicion and doubt so detrimental to his efforts.

Thugut may not have been an entirely successful foreign minister, but one can admire him as a human being engaged in a great struggle. Indeed, in the long run his policy was the right one. He correctly assessed revolutionary France as an insatiable power that would not rest until it either dominated Europe or was soundly defeated. In that way Thugut anticipated Metternich, who likewise came to realize that Austria could not make lasting agreements with Napoleonic France.

Equally notable was Thugut's devotion to the Habsburg Monarchy, not just as a dynasty but as a state, and his laments were touching when he believed that the monarchy and its leadership were not living up to the high standards he had set for them. Thugut guided the foreign policy of the Habsburg Monarchy with dedication and vigor during a turbulent time in Europe's history. He was convinced not only of the rightness of his cause but of the necessity for pursuing it in the face of bitter odds. Such qualities in a statesman are not to be taken lightly.

BIBLIOGRAPHY

Manuscript Collections

Linz—Bischöfliches Ordinariat Linz
   Liber baptizatorum Parochiae Linciensis coeptus, 1731–1756
Paris—Archives du ministère des affaires étrangères
   Autriche, 368–69
   Turquie, 158
London—Public Record Office—Kew
   F07 (Austria), 32–55
Vienna—Haus- Hof- und Staatsarchiv, Staatskanzlei
   England, 130–35, 141–46
   Frankreich, 157, 178–82
   Friedensakten, 104
   Grosse Korrespondenz, 443–47
   Intercepte, 2
   Interiora, 55, 82
   Kaiser Franz Akten, 78b (81), 78c (82), 78ᵉ (85)
   Kriegsakten, 452–53
   Neapel, 14–15, 23
   Polen, 43–44, 57
   Regensburg
      Österreichische Gesandtschaft, 10
      Kurböhmische Gesandtschaft, 6–7
   Russland, 2: 79, 81, 88, 178–84, 216–17
   Sardinien, 25, 33
   Türkei, 2: 38–40, 55, 57–62
   Türkei, 5: 24
   Vertrauliche Akten, 38
   Vorträge, 153–60

PRINTED PRIMARY MATERIALS

Archiv kniazia Vorontsova. 40 vols. Moscow, 1870–1895.

Arneth, Alfred von. "Graf Philipp Cobenzl und seine Memoiren." *Archiv für österreichische Geschichte*, 67 (1885): 1–177.

————, ed. *Joseph II und Leopold von Toscana: Ihr Briefwechsel von 1781 bis 1790*. 2 vols. Vienna, 1872.

Auckland, William Eden, First Baron. *The Journal and Correspondence*. 4 vols. London, 1861–1862.

Bacourt, M. Ad. de, ed. *Correspondance entre le comte de Mirabeau et le comte de la Marck pendant les années 1789, 1790 et 1791*. 3 vols. Paris, 1851.

Bonaparte, Napoleon. *Correspondance*. 32 vols. Paris, 1858–1870.

Brunner, Sébastien, ed. *Correspondances intimes de l'empereur Joseph II avec son ami le comte de [Philipp] Cobenzl et son premier ministre le prince de Kaunitz*. Mainz/Paris/Brussels, 1871.

Casse, A. du, ed. *Historie des négociations diplomatiques relatives aux traités de Mortfontaine, de Lunéville, et d'Amiens*. 3 vols. Paris, 1857.

Chair, Somerset de, ed. *Napoleon's Memoirs*, New York, 1949.

Damas, Comte Roger de. *Memoirs of the Comte Roger de Damas (1787–1806)*. New York, 1913.

Frederick II, King of Prussia. *Politische Correspondenz*. 46 vols. Leipzig, 1879–1939.

Fuchs, G., ed. *Correspondenz über die Russisch-Österreichische Kampagne im Jahre 1799*. 2 vols. Glogau/Leipzig, 1835.

Gentz, Friedrich von. *Staatsschriften und Briefe*. 2 vols. Munich, 1921.

————. *Tagebücher*. 4 vols. Leipzig, 1873–1874.

Great Britain, Historical Manuscripts Commission. *The Manuscripts of J. B. Fortescue, Esq., preserved at Dropmore*. 10 vols. London, 1892–1927.

Hammer-Purgstall, Joseph von. *Erinnerungen aus meinem Leben, 1774–1852*. Vienna/Liepzig, 1940.

Herrmann, Ernst, ed. *Diplomatische Korrespondenzen aus der Revolutionszeit, 1791–1797.* Gotha, 1867.

Hof- und Staats-Schematismus. Vienna, 1740–1800.

Hormayr zu Hortenburg, Josef. *Lebensbilder aus dem Befreiungskriege.* 3 vols. Jena, 1841–1844.

Hüffer, Hermann, ed. *Quellen zur Geschichte des Krieges von 1799.* Leipzig, 1900.

————, ed. *Quellen zur Geschichte des Krieges von 1800.* Leipzig, 1901.

Hüffer, Hermann and Friedrich Luckwaldt, eds. *Der Frieden von Campoformio.* Innsbruck, 1907.

Keith, Sir Robert Murray. *Memoirs and Correspondence.* 2 vols. London, 1849.

Khevenhüller-Metsch, Johann Josef. *Aus der Zeit Maria Theresias.* 7 vols. Vienna, 1907–1925.

Ligne, Prince de. *Fragments de l'histoire de ma vie.* 2 vols. Paris, 1927–1928.

Mallet du Pan, Jacques. *Correspondance inédite de Mallet du Pan avec la cour de Vienne (1794–1798).* 2 vols. Paris, 1884.

Maresca, B., ed. "Memorie del Duca di Gallo." *Archivio storico per le Province Napoletane* 13 (1888): 205–441.

Maria Carolina, Queen of Naples and Sicily. *Correspondance inédite de Marie-Caroline avec le Marquis de Gallo.* 2 vols. Paris, 1911.

Mercy d'Argenteau, Florimund. *Le comte de Mercy-Argenteau et Blumendorf.* Brussels, 1919.

Metternich, Clemens von. *Memoirs.* 2 vols. New York, 1881.

Minto, Countess of, ed. *Life and Letters of Sir Gilbert Elliot, First Earl of Minto from 1751 to 1806.* 3 vols. London, 1874.

Montarlot, P. and L. Pingaud, eds. *Le congrès de Rastatt.* 3 vols. Paris, 1912–1913.

Morris, Gouverneur. *Diary and Letters.* 2 vols. New York, 1888.

Müller, Johannes von. *Sämmtliche Werke.* 40 vols. Stuttgart/Tübingen, 1831–1835.

Österreichischer Beobachter. 1818.

Ozanam, Didier and Michel Antoine, eds. *Correspondance secrète du Comte de Broglie avec Louis XV.* 2 vols. Paris, 1956–1961.

Paget, Sir Arthur. *The Paget Papers, 1794–1807.* 2 vols. London, 1896.

Pichler, Caroline. *Denkwürdigkeiten aus meinem Leben, 1769–1844.* 2 vols. Munich, 1914.

Richter, Joseph. *Briefe eines Eipeldauers über d'Wienstadt.* Munich, 1970.

Sayous, A., ed. *Memoirs and Correspondence of Mallet du Pan.* 2 vols. London, 1852.

Schlitter, Hanns, ed. *Kaunitz, Philipp Cobenzl und Spielmann: Briefwechsel (1779–1792).* Vienna, 1899.

Schlitz, Hans von. *Denkwürdigkeiten des Grafen Hans von Schlitz.* Hamburg, 1898.

Schwarzenberg, Feldmarschall Fürst Karl. *Briefe an seine Frau, 1799–1816.* Vienna, 1913.

Ségur, Louis Philippe. *Mémoires; ou souvenirs et anecdotes.* 3 vols. Paris, 1827.

Thürheim, A. Graf. *Briefe des Grafen Mercy-Argenteau an den Grafen Louis Starhemberg, 1791–1794.* Innsbruck, 1884.

Thürheim, Lulu. *Mein Leben: Erinnerungen aus Österreichs grosser Welt, 1788–1852.* 4 vols. Munich, 1913–1914.

Varnhagen von Ense, K. A. *Denkwürdigkeiten und vermischte Schriften.* 9 vols. Leipzig, 1837–1859.

Vehse, E. *Memoirs of the Court, Aristocracy, and Diplomacy of Austria.* 2 vols. London, 1856.

Vivenot, Alfred von, ed. *Zur Geschichte des Rastadter Congresses.* Vienna, 1871.

————, ed. *Thugut, Clerfayt und Wurmser.* Vienna, 1869.

————, ed. "Thugut und sein politisches System." *Archiv für österreichische Geschichte,* 42 (1870): 363–492; 43 (1870): 103–97.

————, ed. *Vertrauliche Briefe des Freiherrn von Thugut.* 2 vols. Vienna, 1872.

Vivenot, Alfred von and Heinrich von Zeissberg, eds. *Quellen zur Geschichte der deutschen Kaiser-politik Oesterreichs während der Französischen Revolutionskriege, 1790–1801.* 5 vols. Vienna, 1873–1890.

Wagner, Hans, ed. *Wien von Maria Theresia bis zur Franzosenzeit: Aus den Tagebüchern des Grafen Karl von Zinzendorf.* Vienna, 1972.

Walter, Friedrich, ed. *Die österreichische Zentralverwaltung.* 5 vols. Vienna, 1950–1964.

Wickham, William. *Correspondence.* 2 vols. London, 1870.

Wittichen, Friedrich Carl and E. Salzer, eds. *Briefe von und an Friedrich von Gentz.* 3 vols. Munich/Berlin/Oldenbourg, 1909–1913.

Wraxall, Nathaniel William. *Memoirs of the Courts of Berlin, Dresden, Warsaw, and Vienna, in the Years 1777, 1778, and 1779.* London, 1800.

SECONDARY SOURCES

Allgemeine Deutsche Biographie. 56 vols. Leipzig, 1875–1912.

Anderson, M. S. *The Eastern Question, 1774–1923.* London, 1966.

Aretin, Karl Otmar von. *Vom Deutschen Reich zum Deutschen Bund.* Göttingen, 1980.

―――. *Heiliges Römisches Reich, 1776–1806.* 2 vols. Wiesbaden, 1967.

Arneth, Alfred von. *Geschichte Maria Theresia's.* 10 vols. Vienna, 1863–1879.

Barton, H. Arnold. *Count Hans Axel von Fersen.* Boston, 1975.

Beer, Adolf. *Die erste Theilung Polens.* 3 vols. Vienna, 1873.

―――. *Die Finanzen Oesterreichs im XIX Jahrhundert.* Prague, 1877.

―――. "Die Sendung Thuguts in das preussische Hauptquartier und der Friede zu Teschen." *Historische Zeitschrift* 38 (1877): 403–76.

―――. *Zehn Jahre österreichischer Politik, 1801–1810.* Leipzig, 1877.

Bernard, Paul P. *Jesuits and Jacobins: Enlightenment and Enlightened Despotism in Austria*. Urbana, 1971.

―――. *Joseph II and Bavaria*. The Hague, 1965.

Bernier, Olivier. *Lafayette: Hero of Two Worlds*. New York, 1983.

Bibl, Viktor. *Erzherzog Karl: Der beharrliche Kämpfer für Deutschlands Ehre*. Vienna/Leipzig, 1942.

―――. *Kaiser Franz*. Leipzig/Vienna, 1938.

―――. *Der Zerfall Österreichs*. 2 vols. Vienna, 1922–1924.

Biro, Sydney Seymour. *The German Policy of Revolutionary France: A Study in French Diplomacy during the War of the First Coalition, 1792–1797*. 2 vols. Cambridge, Mass., 1957.

Blanning, T.C.W. *The French Revolution in Germany: Occupation and Resistance in the Rhineland, 1792–1802*. Oxford, 1983.

―――. *The Origins of the French Revolutionary Wars*. London/New York, 1986.

Bodi, Leslie. *Tauwetter in Wien: Zur Prosa der österreichischen Aufklärung, 1781–1795*. Frankfurt, 1977.

Braubach, Max. *Maria Theresias jüngster Sohn, Max Franz*. Vienna/Munich, 1961.

The Cambridge History of British Foreign Policy, 1783–1919. 3 vols. New York, 1922–1923.

Chandler, David G. *The Campaigns of Napoleon*. New York, 1966.

Craig, Gordon A. "Problems of Coalition Warfare: The Military Alliance against Napoleon, 1813–1814." In *War, Politics, and Diplomacy, Selected Essays*, pp. 22–45. New York, 1966.

Criste, Oskar. *Erzherzog Carl von Österreich*. 3 vols. Leipzig/Vienna, 1912.

―――. *Rastatt: L'assassinat des ministres français*. Paris, 1900.

―――. "Thugut und die Kriegführung, 1793–1801." *Streffleurs Militärische Zeitschrift* 49 (1908): 383–412.

Deutsch, Otto Erich. *Admiral Nelson und Joseph Haydn*. Vienna, 1982.

Driault, Édouard. *La politique extérieure du premier consul, 1800–1803*. Paris, 1910.

Drimmel, Heinrich. *Kaiser Franz: Ein Wiener übersteht Napoleon*. Vienna/Munich, 1981.

Duffy, Christopher. *Russia's Military Way to the West: Origins and Nature of Russian Military Power, 1700–1800*. London, 1981.

Ehrman, John. *The Younger Pitt. Volume I: The Years of Acclaim*. New York, 1969.

————. *The Younger Pitt. Volume II: The Reluctant Transition*. Stanford, 1983.

Ernstberger, Anton. *Österreich-Preussen von Basel bis Campoformio, 1795–1797*. Prague, 1932.

Feldbaek, Ole. "The Foreign Policy of Tsar Paul I, 1800–1801: An Interpretation." *Jahrbücher für Geschichte Osteuropas* 30 (1982): 16–36.

Ferrero, Guglielmo. *The Gamble: Bonaparte in Italy, 1796–1797*. 1939. Reprint ed. London, 1961.

Fournier, August. *Die Geheimpolizei auf dem Wiener Kongress*. Vienna/Leipzig, 1913.

————. *Gentz und Cobenzl: Geschichte der österreichischen Diplomatie in den Jahren 1801–1805*. Vienna, 1880.

————. "Die Mission des Grafen Saint-Julien im Jahre 1800." In *Historische Studien und Skizzen*, vol. 1, pp. 179–210. Prague/Leipzig, 1885.

Freudenberger, Hermann. "Kolbielski." *Neue Deutsche Biographie* 12 (1980): 455–56.

Gagliardo, John G. *Reich and Nation: The Holy Roman Empire as Idea and Reality, 1763–1806*. Bloomington, 1980.

Gebhardt, Bruno, ed. *Handbuch der deutschen Geschichte*. 4 vols. 8th ed. Stuttgart, 1954–1960.

Genelin, Placid. "Leopolds II äussere Politik." *Dreizehnter Jahresbericht über die deutsche Staats-Oberrealschule in Triest* (1882–1883): 1–46.

Giglioli, Constance H. D. *Naples in 1799: An Account of the Revolution of 1799 and the Rise and Fall of the Parthenopean Republic*. London, 1903.

Godechot, Jacques. *The Counter-Revolution: Doctrine and Action, 1789–1804.* New York, 1971.

Golda, Robert. "Der Friede von Sistov." Ph.D. dissertation, University of Vienna, 1941.

Görlich, Ernst Joseph and Felix Romanik. *Geschichte Österreichs.* Innsbruck, 1970.

Greppi, Le comte Joseph. *Révélations diplomatiques sur les relations de la Sardaigne avec l'Autriche et la Russie pendant la première et la deuxième coalition.* Paris, 1859.

Guyot, Raymond. *Le directoire et la paix de l'Europe des traités de Bâle à la deuxième coalition (1795–1799).* Paris, 1911.

Hafner, Karl. "Franz Josef Graf von Saurau." *Zeitschrift des historischen Vereins für Steiermark* 7 (1909): 24–94.

Hagen, William W. "The Partitions of Poland and the Crisis of the Old Regime in Prussia, 1772–1806." *Central European History* 9 (1976): 115–26.

Hammer-Purgstall, Joseph von. *Geschichte des Osmanischen Reiches.* 10 vols. Pest, 1827–1835.

Hantsch, Hugo. *Die Geschichte Österreichs.* 2 vols. 4th ed. Graz/Vienna/Cologne, 1959–1962.

Häusser, Ludwig. *Deutsche Geschichte vom Tode Friedrichs des Grossen bis zur Grundung des deutschen Bundes.* 4 vols. Berlin, 1861–1863.

Heigel, Karl Theodor. *Deutsche Geschichte vom Tode Friedrichs des Grossen bis zur Auflösung des alten Reiches.* 2 vols. Stuttgart/Berlin, 1899–1911.

―――. "Zur Geschichte des Rastatter Gesandtenmordes von 28 Avril 1799." *Historische Vierteljahrschrift* 3 (1900): 478–99.

Helfert, Joseph Alexander. *Der Rastadter Gesandtenmord.* Vienna, 1874.

Helleiner, Karl F. *The Imperial Loans: A Study in Financial and Diplomatic History.* Oxford, 1965.

Henche, Albert. "Der Rastätter Gesandtenmord im Lichte der politischen Korrespondenz des nassauischen Partikulargesandten Frhr. von Kruse." *Historisches Jahrbuch* 46 (1926): 550–62.

Herrmann, Alfred. *Der Aufstieg Napoleons: Krieg und Diplomatie vom Brumaire bis Lunéville*. Berlin, 1912.

Hertenberger, Helmut, and Franz Wiltschek. *Erzherzog Karl: Der Sieger von Aspern*. Graz/Vienna/Cologne, 1983.

Hock, Karl and Hermann Bidermann. *Der österreichische Staatsrat (1760–1848)*. Vienna, 1972.

Hollaender, A. "Zur Gesandtschaft Bernadottes in Wien 1798." *Monatsblatt des Vereines für Geschichte der Stadt Wien* 15 (1929–1933): 104–12, 141–49, 157–64.

Horsetzky, General A. von. *A Short History of the Chief Campaigns in Europe since 1792*. London, 1909.

Hüffer, Hermann. *Der Krieg des Jahres 1799 und die zweite Koalition*. 2 vols. Gotha, 1904–1905.

————. *Östreich und Preussen gegenüber der französischen Revolution bis zum Abschluss des Friedens von Campo Formio*. Bonn, 1868.

————. *Der rastatter Congress und die zweite Coalition*. 2 vols. Bonn, 1878–1879.

————. *Die Schlacht von Marengo und der italienische Feldzug des Jahres 1800*. Leipzig, 1900.

Ingram, Edward. *Commitment to Empire: Prophecies of the Great Game in Asia, 1797–1800*. Oxford, 1981.

Kissinger, Henry. *A World Restored: Europe after Napoleon*. New York, 1957.

Klingenstein, Grete. "Institutionelle Aspekte der österreichischen Aussenpolitik im 18. Jahrhundert." In Erich Zöllner, ed., *Diplomatie und Aussenpolitik Österreichs*, pp. 74–93. Vienna, 1977.

Komlos, John. *The Habsburg Monarchy as a Customs Union: Economic Development in Austria-Hungary in the Nineteenth Century*. Princeton, 1983.

Kralik, Richard. *Geschichte der Stadt Wien*. 2d ed. Vienna, 1926.

Kraehe, Enno. *Metternich's German Policy. Volume I: The Contest with Napoleon, 1799–1814*. Princeton, 1963.

————. *Metternich's German Policy. Volume II: The Congress of Vienna, 1814–1815*. Princeton, 1983.

Kunstler, Charles. *Fersen et son secret*. Paris, 1947.

Küntzel, Georg. *Fürst Kaunitz-Rittberg als Staatsmann*. Frankfurt, 1923.

Lacour-Gayet, Georges. *Talleyrand, 1754–1838*. 3 vols. Paris, 1930–1933.

Langsam, Walter C. "Emperor Francis and the Austrian 'Jakobins,' 1792–1796." *American Historical Review* 50 (1945): 471–90.

———. *Francis the Good: The Education of an Emperor, 1768–1792*. New York, 1949.

Longworth, Philip. *The Art of Victory: The Life and Achievements of Generalissimo Suvorov, 1729–1800*. London, 1965.

Lord, Robert Howard. *The Second Partition of Poland*. Cambridge, Mass., 1915.

———. "The Third Partition of Poland." *The Slavonic Review* 3 (1925): 481–98.

Lorenz, Reinhold. *Volksbewaffnung und Staatsidee in Österreich (1792–1797)*. Vienna/Liepzig, 1926.

McKay, Derek and H. M. Scott. *The Rise of the Great Powers, 1648–1815*. London, 1983.

Mackesy, Piers. *Statesmen at War: The Strategy of Overthrow, 1798–1799*. London, 1974.

———. *War Without Victory: The Downfall of Pitt, 1799–1802*. Oxford, 1984.

Madariaga, Isabel de. *Russia in the Age of Catherine the Great*. New Haven, 1981.

———. "The Secret Austro-Russian Treaty of 1781." *The Slavonic and East European Review* 38 (1959–1960): 114–45.

Magenschab, Hans. *Erzherzog Johann: Habsburgs grüner Rebell*. Graz/Vienna/Cologne, 1981.

Matsch, Erwin. *Geschichte des Auswaertigen Dienstes von Oesterreich-Ungarn, 1720–1920*. Vienna, 1980.

Mayr, Josef Karl. *Wien im Zeitalter Napoleons*. Vienna, 1940.

Mendelssohn-Bartholdy, Karl. "Die Conferenzen von Seltz." *Historische Zeitschrift* 23 (1870): 27–53.

Meynert, Hermann Günther. *Kaiser Franz I*. Vienna, 1872.

Miliutin, Dimitrius, and Alexander Mikhailovskii-Danilevsky. *Geschichte des Krieges Russlands mit Frankreich unter der Regierung Kaiser Paul's I im Jahr 1799.* 5 vols. Munich, 1856–1858.

Mitchell, Harvey. *The Underground War against Revolutionary France. The Missions of William Wickham, 1794–1800.* Oxford, 1965.

Morland, Paul. *Le prince de Ligne.* N.p., 1964.

Musulin, Stella. *Vienna in the Age of Metternich.* Boulder, 1975.

Nabonne, Bernard. *La diplomatie du Directoire et Bonaparte d'après les papiers inédits de Reubell.* Paris, 1951.

Otruba, Gustav. "Englands Finanzhilfe für Österreich in den Koalitionskriegen und im Kampf gegen Napoleon." *Österreich in Geschichte und Literatur* 9 (1965): 84–87.

Padover, Saul K. "Prince Kaunitz and the First Partition of Poland." Ph.D. dissertation, University of Chicago, 1932.

Pillwein, B. *Linz: Einst und Jetzt.* 2 vols. Linz, 1846.

Pimodan, Claude, Comte de. *Le comte F.-C. de Mercy-Argenteau.* Paris, 1911.

Pingaud, Léonce. *Un agent secret sous la révolution et l'empire: Le comte d'Antraigues.* Paris, 1894.

Ragsdale, Hugh. *Detente in the Napoleonic Era.* Lawrence, Kansas, 1980.

————, ed. *Paul I. A Reassessment of His Life and Reign.* Pittsburgh, 1979.

————. "Russia, Prussia, and Europe in the Policy of Paul I." *Jahrbücher für Geschichte Osteuropas* 31 (1983): 81–118.

Ranke, Leopold von. *Denkwürdigkeiten des Staatskanzlers Fürsten von Hardenberg bis zum Jahre 1806.* Leipzig, 1877.

Rauchensteiner, Manfried. *Kaiser Franz und Erzherzog Carl: Dynastie und Heerwesen in Österreich, 1796–1809.* Munich, 1972.

Real, Willy. *Von Potsdam nach Basel.* Basel/Stuttgart, 1958.

Reinalter, Helmut. *Aufgeklärter Absolutismus und Revolution: Zur Geschichte des Jakobinertums und der frühdemokratischen Bestrebungen in der Habsburger Monarchie.* Vienna/Cologne, 1980.

Reinalter, Helmut, ed. *Der Jakobinismus in Mitteleuropa*. Innsbruck, 1977.

Rodger, A. B. *The War of the Second Coalition, 1798–1801*. Oxford, 1964.

Roider, Karl A., Jr. *Austria's Eastern Question, 1700–1790*. Princeton, 1982.

————. "The Oriental Academy in the *Theresienzeit*." *Topic: A Journal of the Liberal Arts* 34 (1980): 19–28.

Ross, Steven T. *European Diplomatic History, 1789–1815. France against Europe*. Garden City, New York, 1969.

————. *Quest for Victory: French Military Strategy, 1792–1799*. South Brunswick and New York, 1973.

Rössler, Hellmuth. *Graf Johann Philipp Stadion: Napoleons deutscher Gegenspieler*. 2 vols. Vienna/Munich, 1966.

————. *Österreichs Kampf um Deutschlands Befreiung*. 2 vols. Hamburg, 1940.

Rothenberg, Gunther. *The Art of Warfare in the Age of Napoleon*. Bloomington, 1978.

————. *Napoleon's Great Adversaries: The Archduke Charles and the Austrian Army, 1792–1814*. Bloomington, 1982.

Sapper, Christian. "Josef Graf O'Donnell, Hofkammerpräsident, 1808–1810." *Mitteilungen des österreichischen Staatsarchivs* 33 (1980): 161–92.

Saul, Norman. *Russia and the Mediterranean, 1797–1807*. Chicago, 1970.

Sherwig, John M. *Guineas and Gunpower: British Foreign Aid in the Wars with France, 1793–1815*. Cambridge, Mass., 1969.

————. "Lord Grenville's Plan for a Concert of Europe, 1797–1799." *Journal of Modern History* 34 (1962): 284–93.

Silagi, Denis. *Jakobiner in der Habsburger-Monarchie*. Vienna, 1962.

Sorel, Albert. *The Eastern Question in the Eighteenth Century*. 1898. Reprint ed. New York, 1969.

————. *L'Europe et la révolution française*. 8 vols. Paris, 1885–1904.

————. "La mission de Poterat à Vienne." *Revue historique* 29 (1885): 280–315.

Sybel, Heinrich von. *Geschichte der Revolutionszeit von 1789 bis 1800.* 5 vols. Düsseldorf, 1865–1879.

Thompson, J. M. *The French Revolution.* Oxford, 1966.

Treitschke, Heinrich von. *Deutsche Geschichte im neunzehnten Jahrhundert.* 5 vols. Leipzig, 1879–1889.

Uhlirz, Karl and Mathilde. *Handbuch der Geschichte Österreichs und seiner Nachbarländer Böhmen und Ungarn.* 4 vols. Graz/Vienna/Leipzig, 1927–1944.

Vienna, Kriegsarchiv. *Krieg gegen die Französische Revolution.* 2 vols. Vienna, 1905.

Vivenot, Alfred von. *Herzog Albrecht von Sachsen-Teschen als Reichs-feld-marschall. Ein Beitrag zur Geschichte des Reichsverfalles und des Baseler Friedens.* 3 vols. Vienna, 1864–1866.

Wandruszka, Adam. *Leopold II.* 2 vols. Vienna/Munich, 1965.

Wangermann, Ernst. *The Austrian Achievement, 1700–1800.* London, 1973.

————. *From Joseph II to the Jacobin Trials.* 2d ed. Oxford, 1969.

Weckbecker, Wilhelm. *Die Weckbeckers: Karriere einer Familie.* Graz, 1966.

Wendland, Wilhelm. *Versuche einer allgemeine Volksbewaffnung in Süddeutschland während der Jahre 1791 bis 1794.* Berlin, 1901.

Wolf, Adam. *Fürstin Eleonore Liechtenstein, 1745–1812.* Vienna, 1875.

Wurzbach, Constantin von. *Biographisches Lexikon des Kaisertums Österreich.* 60 vols. Vienna, 1856–1891.

Zeller, Gaston. *Les temps modernes. De Louis XIV à 1789.* Paris, 1955.

Zimmermann, Jürg. *Militärverwaltung und Heeresaufbringung in Österreich bis 1806.* Frankfurt, 1965.

INDEX

Library of Congress Cataloging-in-Publication Data

Roider, Karl A.
Baron Thugut and Austria's response to the French Revolution.

Bibliography: p.   Includes index.
1. Austria—Foreign relations—France.
2. France—Foreign relations—Austria. 3. Thugut,
Franz Maria, Freiherr von, 1736–1818. 4. France—
History—Revolution, 1789–1799—Influence. 1. Title.
DB49.F8R64 1987   944.04   87–2240
ISBN 0–691–05135–6 (alk. paper)

KARL ROIDER is Professor of History at Louisiana State University. Among his works is *Austria's Eastern Question, 1700–1790* (Princeton).